Controlling East-West Trade
and Technology Transfer

Controlling East-West Trade and Technology Transfer

Power, Politics, and Policies

Edited by Gary K. Bertsch

The Center for East-West Trade Policy, University of Georgia

Duke University Press   *Durham and London*   *1988*

HF
4050
.C63
1988

copy 1

Contents

Preface

Gary K. Bertsch

This is a book about Western efforts—particularly those of the United States, Japan, and some of its West European allies—to control their strategic trade and technological relations with the communist economies of the East. Growing out of the cold war era, U.S. and allied efforts to control West-to-East commerce and technology transfer raise issues of considerable importance and controversy in the Western alliance today. To contribute to a fuller understanding of these issues this book examines contemporary U.S. and allied thinking and activity in the area of strategic trade with the East, including the competing interests, stakes, and distribution of power within the Western alliance in this policy area, and the politics and policies surrounding Western controls on trade with and technology transfer to the East.

Western efforts to control trade and technological relations with the communist East affect a multiplicity of powerful interests in both East and West. Currently, the Eastern countries are interested in expanding their commercial, technological, and scientific relations with the West. Many in the United States, Europe, and Japan are also interested in expanding these relations, while still controlling any trade and technology transfer that might make significant contributions to Warsaw Pact military capabilities.

Although there is general agreement in the Western alliance that export controls are necessary to restrict militarily significant contributions to the East, there is considerable controversy on the specifics, including the meaning of "militarily significant," how nations should administer both domestic and multilateral export controls, the extent to which export controls should be tied to East-West political relations, and a number of other important issues. Hardly a year passes without significant controversy in the United States and the Western alliance over such issues. In the 1980s we have witnessed major disputes over Western controls on trade with the USSR following its invasion of Afghanistan, over Western involvement in the Soviet natural gas pipeline project, and a variety of cases involving Western sales purported to have made significant contributions to Soviet military capabilities.

How nations balance the competing economic, foreign policy, and national security interests surrounding controls on exports, and how they organize an effective export control system is a matter of considerable challenge. The U.S. government addresses this challenge every few years when it reviews and renews the legislation authorizing U.S. export controls. In addition, a series of impressive studies and reports have addressed this challenge by examining the problems surrounding export controls and what can be done to resolve them. Despite these significant governmental and non-governmental efforts, little has changed over the years. Although the legislative reviews and studies on export controls resulted in important findings and proposed promising recommendations, the problems and controversies surrounding export controls continue.

A group of scholars at the University of Georgia believes that policy-relevant, scholarly inquiry can improve our understanding of, and better prepare us for, the problems and challenges that confront us. Accordingly, the University established the Center for East-West Trade Policy in 1987 to encourage research, teaching, and service programs that will examine important public policy questions such as those addressed in this book.

One of the goals of the Center for East-West Trade Policy is to bring together experts—scholars, practitioners, and policy-makers—who have much to contribute to a better understanding of the important policy issues surrounding East-West commercial, technological, and scientific relations. This book is the product of one of our efforts. The contributors have been meeting periodically over the last two years to examine and discuss the issues addressed in this book. Draft chapters were presented and critiqued at professional meetings and in private and, eventually, prepared for publication in this volume. Each of the contributors brings unique experiences, skills, and expertise to the project.

There are many who facilitated this project and many to thank. The first are the contributors to this volume, some of whom made special contributions beyond their specific assignments. William Root, for example, meticulously reviewed and provided extensive written critiques on every chapter in the book. Steven Elliott aided me in numerous ways throughout all stages of the enterprise. John Hardt, Martin Hillenbrand, and Henry Nau provided wise counsel, just as they have on numerous other projects relating to the work of the Center.

A number of people at the University of Georgia have also aided this work in important ways. Stephen McKelvey helped proofread the manuscript and Kevin Lasher prepared the index. My colleagues in the Department of Political Science and the University of Georgia in general have provided an environment for two decades now that continues to challenge, support, and stimulate. Members of the faculty, especially Martin Hillenbrand, Loch Johnson, Han Park, Dean Rusk, Louis Sohn, Thomas Schoenbaum, and Darl Snyder, as well as Harold Berman of Emory University and John McIntyre of the Georgia Institute of Technology, recognize the importance of our work and have provided valuable counsel at many stages. President Knapp, Vice Presidents Edes, Key, McBee, and Younts, and Deans Flatt, Niemi, and Payne have all supported and encouraged our efforts to establish a center to promote policy-oriented, scholarly inquiry on East-West trade issues.

A number of programs and institutions have contributed to my research in this area. The Dean Rusk Center at the University of Georgia involved me in research related to the 1979 renewal of the

Export Administration Act and kindled my original interest in U.S. export control policy. The Institute for the Study of World Politics, the North Atlantic Treaty Organization, the Air Command and Staff College of the U.S. Air Force, and the Fulbright Program all provided grants and fellowships that aided my work in numerous ways. The Politics Department at the University of Lancaster in England provided a comfortable environment to pursue some of my research on British export control policy. To these and many unnamed individuals and institutions I am grateful.

Athens, Georgia
November 1987

Foreword

Dean Rusk

Back in 1978 I was invited by Congress to give testimony pursuant to the renewal of the 1969 Export Administration Act (EAA)—the principal statutory instrument governing controls on East-West trade. At that time I suggested that the annual foreign trade deficit of $30 billion presented us with a situation that obliged us to review our foreign trade laws and practices. Although our laws and practices have changed precious little since that time, our problems have grown enormously. Our annual trade deficit now stands at over $150 billion, our technological base is being steadily eroded, our farmers and businessmen have lost important markets, our Western trading partners are reducing their dependence on U.S. technology, and the Western alliance has been severely strained by conflict over East-West trade policy. Thus, the debate is still very much alive, and with these problems and the EAA due for renewal in 1989, there is still a great need to examine our trade policies and practices, and some of our attitudes.

We should begin by rethinking our export control and licensing system. For example, our unilateral export controls that go beyond the COCOM controls put American exporters at a distinct disadvantage vis-à-vis their Western competitors; and the red tape involved in exporting high technology still represents a significant disincentive to doing business with communist countries. If we are to reduce our trade deficit, we should begin by minimizing such self-imposed obstacles. This requires a careful reevaluation of what controls are absolutely necessary to our national security and how they are implemented.

Minimizing these controls is not just a technical problem. Our export control system and practices are the way they are because of certain entrenched attitudes regarding the communist world and international trade. As William Long points out in this volume, America's export control system is largely a legacy of the Cold War and cold war thinking. The world is very different from what it was forty years ago but our attitudes, and thus our East-West trade practices, have been slow to change. Our allies (who are also, of course, our major trade competitors) have responded to changes in the international system and are therefore better placed to take advantage of opportunities that may arise in East-West trade. Our responses to changes have tended to be sporadic and piecemeal. Consequently, disincentives to trade still exist and America's export control system is still in need of careful examination and perhaps fundamental reform to best serve our national interests.

We must also reconsider our attitudes to international trade in general, for these may also be partly responsible for some of the economic and political problems that we face. Because of our massive domestic market and because of our strong trade position in the immediate postwar period, Americans have tended to neglect the importance of international trade and think of it as a "privilege," as icing on the cake. Our competitors, by contrast, see trade as a "right" that is of fundamental importance to their economic well-being, indeed to their national security. And herein lies a big difference between the United States and its allies and competitors. I would suggest that this is another outmoded attitude that we can no longer afford with our current trade deficit and alliance problems. It is an attitude that perpetuates our insensitivity to the costs of export controls. It means that we will fall farther behind in the competition for world markets and that future conflict within the Alliance over East-West trade is inevitable.

Minimizing these self-imposed obstacles to trade is further complicated by the fortunate fact that we live in a boisterous democracy where divergent views on East-West trade compete to influence policy. Some, mainly within the Pentagon, begin with the assumption that almost any Western export has military applications which will be exploited by the Soviets to increase their military capacity. Controls on East-West trade and technology transfer are therefore considered vital to Western security. Others believe that America's unilateral export controls are too restrictive and damage the country's long-term economic vitality. Still others, myself included, see the process of trade increasing our common interests with the Soviet Union and other communist countries, and reducing the range of issues on which violence might occur. If we can find points of agreement on matters large and small which broaden our bases of common interest, such efforts should be made. In examining and evaluating present policy, and tendering alternatives, we must be aware of these differing views, the actors who hold them, and the power resources that they can bring to bear in the policy-making process; in short, we must take into account the political realities of this policy area.

This important collection of essays addresses some of the issues I have raised here, taking into account the political realities within the United States and the Western alliance. Some of the essays are analytical in nature, some are prescriptive, but all increase our knowledge of this policy area and may thus assist us in recognizing or even, as members of a democracy, contributing to more enlightened policy.

This volume is an early product of the University of Georgia's Center for East-West Trade Policy. Drawing together scholars from the major research institutions of Georgia—Emory University, Georgia State University, the Georgia Institute of Technology, and the University of Georgia—and other scholars and practitioners in the United States and Western Europe, the Center's principal objective is to contribute to the making of more enlightened East-West trade policy that better serves our national interest. This is an important task because America's East-West trade policy impinges upon a number of other policy areas relevant to the national interest. America's international trade, technological competitiveness, Alliance relations and, of course, national security and broader East-West relations are all affected by its East-West trade policy. It is therefore imperative that we know as much as we possibly can about the various costs and benefits of different policy alternatives regarding our economic and technological relations with communist countries.

As one who has spent many years in public service in a variety of capacities, I believe that the work of the Center and academia in general has a valuable and essential role to play in policy making. Although much academic research is of limited help in solving public servants' day-to-day problems, it can contribute to the making of better policy in the long-term. Being outside the fray of executive-legislative struggles and bureaucratic turf battles, scholars can more objectively assess the merits and demerits of particular policies and practices. Free from standard operating procedures, they can also tackle problems in new ways, raising new ideas and asking new questions. This volume and other projects of the Center for East-West Trade Policy do just this, and can thus contribute to new, better, more enlightened policy.

Athens, Georgia
November 1987

Introduction

Gary K. Bertsch

Controls on East-West Trade

Americans have long been perplexed by the issues surrounding economic and technological relations with communist states. Should the United States and its Western allies sell their advanced technology to communist countries, and if so, under what conditions? There have always been some in the United States who oppose such trade and technology transfer on moral grounds, contending that one should never trade with adversaries or, as some have put it more bluntly, with "the devil." Others have opposed economic relations with the Communists for national security reasons and suggest that by engaging in such relations the United States and its Western allies are "selling the rope." Although there has always been considerable opposition to economic and technological relations with communist states, there has also been support for such relations. Some groups and individuals have been in favor of relations on foreign policy grounds, arguing that economic and technological relations can be powerful forces for changing communist behavior, improving East-West relations, and promoting international peace. Other supporters have called attention to the significant markets in the Soviet Union, China, and Eastern Europe and have argued that the potential economic benefits should impel the United States to loosen controls and expand its trade with the Communists.

This debate surrounding the control of East-West trade and technology transfer for reasons of national security sharpened in the late 1980s. Although there was little support for the extreme positions — that is, for economic warfare or, on the other hand, for selling the Soviet Union and its allies items of military relevance — serious debates have addressed a number of specific issues of considerable significance. For example, what precisely should be controlled for reasons of national security? Should the West control "dual-use" items such as computers, which have both civilian and military applications? Should the West share items that might reduce the risks of accidental war, or items such as SDI technology, which might render offensive ballistic missiles obsolete? The debate also sharpened over the economic costs and benefits of export controls. Given the decline of U.S. trade and technological competitiveness in the 1980s, more Americans began to ask whether the United States should continue its restrictive policies and whether it could afford to control trade more strictly than its allies. Many other questions were raised. For example, what impact do controls on West-East technology transfer have upon West-West trade and technological relations? And, with the growth of economic and technological relations on a global scale, what can really be controlled in the modern age? If the United States has great difficulty controlling the import of illegal drugs across its own borders, how successful can it be in controlling the export or re-export of high technology from other countries in today's complex global economy?

Finally, how should such controls be organized and administered? Before addressing these and related issues, and the power, politics, and policies surrounding them, we will begin with a historical overview of the evolution of U.S. export controls.

"Trading with the Enemy," or "Emergency" Controls

U.S. controls restricting economic and technological relations with communist countries have been authorized on a number of legal bases. First, under the legislative authority of the Trading with the Enemy Act of 1917 the president was authorized, "during the time of war or during any other period of national emergency declared by the President," to prohibit any type of economic activity—exports, imports, financial transactions, travel, investment, and so forth—with designated "enemy" countries or nationals of those countries. When Chinese forces entered the Korean War in 1950, for example, President Truman issued a Proclamation of a National Emergency which activated the provisions of the Trading with the Enemy Act. The proclamation and ban on economic relations with the People's Republic of China (PRC) remained in effect until Sino-American relations were finally normalized in the late 1970s.

Somewhat earlier, in 1974, President Ford reluctantly signed the National Emergencies Act, which was intended to terminate all states of national emergency and to eliminate numerous presidential powers depending on states of emergency. However, this did not mean that the United States government had decided to remove all restrictions on economic relations with perceived adversaries. Congress subsequently enacted additional legislation—the International Emergency Economic Powers Act (IEEPA)—with provisions similar to those provided under the Trading with the Enemy Act. Subsequently the IEEPA was used as the legal basis for sanctions against Iran during the hostage crisis of 1979–81 and against Nicaragua in 1985. Also, having failed to pass new legislation to extend the Export Administration Act in 1983, President Reagan used the IEEPA to invoke his authority to maintain U.S. export controls until the act was extended.

Credit and Tariff Controls

The United States also imposes credit and tariff controls on its economic relations with communist states. Although President Roosevelt created the Export-Import Bank (Eximbank) in 1934 with the acknowledged purpose of financing trade with the Soviet Union, it was thirty-nine years before this bank extended any credit to the USSR. The first obstacle to U.S. Eximbank credit to the USSR was based upon Soviet refusal to settle tsarist debts to U.S. citizens. Later, with the postwar deterioration in U.S.-Soviet relations and the growth of the Cold War, there was little support for government-sponsored financing of trade with the USSR and members of the Soviet bloc. With the exception of Yugoslavia, the Eximbank made no loans to communist states during the entire cold war period. The informal prohibition was formalized in 1964 when the Foreign Assistance and Related Agencies Appropriation Act prohibited the Eximbank from lending to any communist country except when the president determined that the granting of credit was in the national interest.

With the onset of détente in 1971, this prohibition was lifted for those countries not involved in armed conflict with the United States; and, once again, the president was empowered to provide credit to communist countries if the extension of such credit was judged to be in the national interest. President Nixon made such determinations and extensions for Romania in 1971 and Poland in 1972. Subsequently, President Nixon's trip to Moscow and the signing of the U.S.-Soviet trade agreement in 1972 paved the way for the USSR to receive its first Eximbank credits one year later.

However, in 1974 credits to the USSR became enmeshed in a larger U.S. political debate about the future of détente and relations with the USSR. An important aspect of this debate concerned the negative reaction of many in Congress to the issue of subsidized credit to the USSR. As a result, the U.S. Congress passed additional legislation putting new controls on financial relations with the USSR. The Stevenson amendment to the 1974 Export-Import Bank Act put a $300 million ceiling on new loans and investment guarantees to the Soviet Union. This limitation placed specific restrictions on energy-related projects, reflecting congressional concern with the advisability of assisting Soviet oil and gas development. The effect of this amendment was made moot, however, with the passage of the Jackson-Vanik amendment to the Trade Act of 1974. This amendment resulted in the scrapping of the U.S.-Soviet trade agreement and effectively terminated all credits to the USSR.

By linking trade benefits to communist countries to the free emigration of their citizens, the Jackson-Vanik amendment also raised the question of most favored nation status (MFN) and tariff controls. MFN guarantees nondiscriminatory U.S. tariff status to foreign exporters. The U.S. Trade Agreements Extension Act, passed in 1951 during the height of the Cold War, withdrew this MFN tariff status from all communist countries except Yugoslavia. Today, the major obstacle to granting MFN status to the USSR and those communist countries still not possessing it is the Jackson-Vanik amendment. This amendment proscribes the granting of MFN and the extension of government credits and/or investment guarantees to any communist country that denies its citizens the right or opportunity to emigrate. Two communist countries enjoyed MFN status before the passing of the amendment (Yugoslavia and Poland). The Reagan administration withdrew MFN status from Poland in 1981 but restored it in 1987, and the president has used his right of waiver to provide it to three more countries (Romania, Hungary, and China). Although there is some difference of opinion about the economic importance of MFN in controlling East-West trade today, there is no doubt that it is of considerable symbolic value in affecting the broader political relationship in which economic relations are conducted.

Export Controls

Under the legislative authority of the Export Control Act of 1949, the United States set up a system of peacetime export controls. This system of controls is far more significant than the "emergency," "trading with the enemy," credit, and tariff controls discussed above and will be the major topic of inquiry in this book. America's peacetime export control system relies on selective export licensing to protect national security and to foster foreign policy objectives. Export controls operate via a licensing system which controls the shipment of specific goods and technologies to countries with interests perceived to be adverse to those of the United States.

The Export Control Act was a consequence of the acrimonious East-West relations of the cold war era. The act was passed to ensure that nothing of military, strategic or, from 1962 to 1969, "economic" significance was exported to communist countries. To strengthen the embargo the United States worked with its allies to set up in 1949 the Coordinating Committee for Multilateral Export Controls (COCOM), consisting of the NATO states minus Iceland and plus Japan. To persuade its allies to participate in this voluntary body, the U.S. Congress passed the Mutual Defense Assistance Control Act of 1951 (the so-called Battle Act), which essentially called for the termination of military and economic aid to countries engaging in trade detrimental to the national security interests of the United States. By passing the Export Control Act of 1949 and setting up the multilateral COCOM control system, the United States and its allies expanded their capabilities to control East-West trade.

Although such expansion was significant, it was not easily preserved. West Europeans, in particular, were loathe to see a long-term continuation of the COCOM embargo restricting their traditional trading relationships with Eastern Europe. After the Korean armistice in 1953 some of the European allies demonstrated their opposition to the extensive and highly restrictive COCOM list. In order to ensure continued European participation in COCOM, the United States was forced to agree to certain relaxations, which were reflected in the 1954 and 1958 multilateral reviews of the COCOM embargo lists.

Although forced to liberalize the multilateral embargo, the United States continued to use the Export Control Act to pursue unilaterally a national export control policy that was far more restrictive than those of its COCOM allies. While European trade and economic relations with communist states began to expand in the late 1950s and throughout the 1960s, the United States remained largely committed to more restrictive peacetime controls.

However, as the political environment improved and the economic benefits of East-West economic relations became more apparent in the late 1960s, some Americans believed that it was time for the United States to loosen its restrictive policy. Senators like Walter Mondale, William Fulbright, and Edmund Muskie, and some leading American opinion-makers and economic interest groups, like the

New York Times and American grain growers, argued that it was time to reconsider the restrictive policies of the cold war era. This and related opinion and activity resulted in Congress replacing the economic warfare rhetoric of the Export Control Act of 1949 with the less restrictive policy statements in the 1969 Export Administration Act (EAA).

The Nixon administration was initially reluctant to encourage a loosening of U.S. export controls, preferring instead to link trade concessions to improvements in Soviet foreign policy. Apparently convinced that this was happening, with the conclusion of agreements on Berlin and accidental war, and the breakthrough on SALT by 1972, the Nixon administration became an avid supporter of expanded East-West economic relations, which necessarily meant a loosening of peacetime export controls. It was at this time that certain actors in Congress, notably Senator Henry "Scoop" Jackson, became concerned about the shrinking embargo and pursued a number of measures to slow and finally halt the expansion of U.S. economic relations with the Soviet Union and Eastern Europe. Therefore, while the peacetime export control system had been somewhat relaxed in the postwar era, it had certainly not faded away. American controls remained much more restrictive than those of its allies throughout the entire postwar era.

The differences in U.S. and European export controls, and the conflicts they generated, became increasingly apparent during the Carter and Reagan administrations. Under President Carter the U.S. government attempted to use export controls to place pressure on the Soviet Union on various occasions. Called "economic diplomacy" by some and "lightswitch diplomacy" by its critics, the Carter administration's policy was to deny some licenses and tighten and expand some areas of the controls in order to register American dissatisfaction with various elements of Soviet policy. In July 1978, for example, to protest the Soviet treatment of dissidents, the arrest of a U.S. businessman, and the harassment of two American reporters in Moscow, the Carter administration denied an export license for a Sperry Univac computer ordered by TASS for use at the 1980 Moscow Summer Olympics. In August 1978 the Carter administration imposed a validated license requirement for the export of oil and gas exploration and production equipment to the USSR. Then, in response to the Soviet invasion of Afghanistan, President Carter announced a number of economic sanctions, including a partial embargo on grain sales and a suspension of licensing of all high technology and products requiring validated export licenses. A few months later, following a review of U.S. export control policy, the U.S. Department of Commerce announced that more restrictive criteria would be applied to the licensing of exports to the Soviet Union. Even though Congress had just passed what was considered to be a less restrictive, trade-facilitating EAA in 1979, it was clear that American policy was becoming more restrictive and that it was being clearly linked to Soviet foreign and domestic policy. Both the restrictiveness and the linkage issues were highly contested in the United States and within the Western alliance. Many in the United States, most notably key congressmen and representatives of firms doing business with the USSR, opposed the more stringent controls and the administration's policy of linking the controls to Soviet foreign and domestic policy. Although pressed to join the restrictive American linkage policy, the European allies resisted and largely ignored American actions.

President Reagan and key members of his administration assumed power in 1981 with a deep concern about the military and strategic consequences of East-West trade and technological relations. The point men in raising these concerns, Secretary of Defense Caspar Weinberger and Assistant Secretary Richard Perle, warned of a massive, systematic Soviet effort to get advanced technology from the West. The purpose of this effort, they maintained, was to support the Soviet military buildup. Early in its first term the Reagan administration proposed a series of measures to curtail the eastward flow of military-related technology. The measures included efforts to strengthen U.S. and allied export controls, including restrictions on "militarily critical technologies," to strengthen safeguards against covert transfers, including foreign industrial espionage, and to persuade the scientific community to reduce Soviet access to the exchange of ideas and information in U.S. research programs.

Like the Carter administration before it, the Reagan initiatives generated considerable opposition in the United States and within the Western alliance. Domestically, a wide variety of actors both in the government and outside—particularly within the business and academic communities—registered their opposition to the restrictive Reagan initiatives. Nowhere was this opposition clearer than in the debate surrounding the renewal of the EAA between 1983 and 1985.

Members of the Reagan administration saw U.S. export control policy deficient on a number of counts. First, they saw national security export controls as excessively lax and allowing the transfer of strategic technologies which made significant contributions to Soviet military capabilities. Second, export controls applied for foreign policy reasons (e.g., in response to the Soviet invasion of Afghanistan) discriminated unfairly against some U.S. exporters (such as the grain producers). Third, the Reagan White House was critical of the lack of predictability in U.S. export controls; exporters were subject to unpredictable regulations and were not given clear signals about what could and could not be exported. Finally, the United States had inadequate control over exports and re-exports by subsidiaries, licensees, and affiliates in other Western countries.

These issues and the legislation required to update the EAA represented something of a dilemma for the Reagan administration. The administration was faced with reconciling its free-market orientation and its desire for unfettered free trade with its efforts to restrict the transfer of technology aiding the Soviet military buildup. It also had to be concerned about the adverse effect these controls were known to have on trade, technological, and scientific relations between the United States and other countries within the Western Alliance. There were also the difficulties and dilemmas surrounding the American Executive's traditional interest in using "foreign policy" controls. Although the administration believed that export controls should be linked to Soviet foreign policy behavior, they recognized that such a policy introduced the unpredictability that they sought to reduce; the administration was therefore loathe to spell out its exact policy on when foreign policy controls would be applied. The administration was also confronted by other difficult problems when it came to revising the EAA and U.S. export control policy: how to utilize and apply the "critical technologies approach" as required by the 1979 act; how to coordinate U.S. controls with those of the allies; whether to apply U.S. controls extraterritorially; whether to impose import controls on U.S. allies who did not comply with U.S. controls; how to apply controls differentially to various communist countries; and notably, how to relax export controls on the PRC while tightening them on the USSR.

Concerning the issue of foreign policy controls, the 1979 EAA retained the president's traditional authority to use export controls to achieve U.S. foreign policy goals—the United States remains the only member of the alliance with foreign policy controls—but mandated major revisions in the administration of such controls. The 1979 act stipulated the criteria the president must consider before using foreign policy export controls. The act also required the president to inform Congress when imposing, increasing, or extending foreign policy controls; to justify such controls to the public; and to extend the controls annually or let them expire. Despite these limitations on the presidential use of foreign policy controls the Carter and Reagan administrations subsequently initiated major foreign policy controls on exports to the Soviet Union and violated at least the spirit, if not the legal requirements, of the EAA.

Consequently, foreign policy controls emerged as one of the central issues in the review and extension of the EAA. In early 1983 President Reagan sent proposed legislation to Congress to amend and reauthorize the EAA of 1979. Responding to concerns and criticisms that America's use of foreign policy controls was making U.S. exporters unreliable suppliers, the administration's bill contained a provision concerning the sanctity of contracts in force when foreign policy controls were imposed. Some in Congress and the private sector, however, criticized the administration's proposal on contract sanctity, noting that it did not go far enough. They noted that the administration's proposal was limited to contracts requiring delivery of goods or technology within 270 days after the control is imposed; furthermore, the critics complained that the administration's proposal would still allow the president to prohibit exports for which contracts had already been signed if such contracts would prove detrimental to overriding U.S. national interests. The administration's bill did little to allay the concerns of the pro-trade coalitions.

In October 1983 the U.S. House of Representatives passed a bill to extend and amend the 1979 EAA, sponsored by Representative Don Bonker (D-Washington), that was much more to the liking of the pro-trade actors in Congress and the private sector. The House bill had an alternative provision on contract sanctity which would have prohibited the president from imposing foreign policy controls on exports for which contracts had already been signed; however, escape clauses permitting the president great latitude still concerned the pro-traders. Also, responding to U.S. and allied complaints about the extraterritorial application of foreign policy controls, the House bill would have prohibited the application of such controls to companies outside the United States.

Concerning the question of national security controls, the 1979 EAA provided for the control of exports which make a "significant contribution" to Soviet military potential. Defense-minded congressmen and members of the Reagan administration were concerned that the 1979 act was still allowing the sale and transfer of "dual-use" technologies that had at least indirect, if not direct, impact on the Soviet military buildup. They were also concerned that industrial acquisitions were allowing the Soviets to release resources to their military sector and allowing civilian-military interactions leading to the overall improvement of the technological level in the military sector.

The Reagan administration's proposed amendments in 1983 to the 1979 act were intended to address these national security concerns. Among other provisions the administration provided presidential authority to prohibit imports into the United States from foreign companies violating U.S. national security controls; authority for stronger enforcement measures and stiffer penalties for violators of export control laws; and other proposals for tightening national security controls. The more pro-trade House bill included some measures for improving enforcement of national security goals, but included many other provisions that were far less restrictive than the administration's proposals. The more security-oriented Senate bill also contained a number of provisions that might have led to more restrictive national security controls, including a provision allowing the president to impose import controls if a majority of the nations belonging to COCOM agreed that the foreign company was in violation of U.S. national security controls. The provisions and bills were changing continuously as the political infighting passed the September 30, 1983, legislative deadline and dragged on through 1984 and into 1985.

Finally, in June 1985 Congress passed a bill to extend the EAA to 1989. The 1985 Export Administration Amendments Act (EAAA) contained a number of changes, including what some observers considered relaxations of U.S. controls. These included the authorization of multiple export licenses to facilitate multiple shipments to non-controlled countries; the elimination of licensing requirements for exports of relatively low-technology items to other COCOM countries; the stipulation of additional requirements upon the president to consult with Congress prior to the imposition of new foreign policy export controls; the prohibition of foreign policy controls that would break contracts previously entered into except in cases where a "breach of the peace" poses a serious and direct threat to the strategic interest of the United States; and the termination of U.S. foreign policy export controls on items which are available from foreign sources, unless the president can negotiate with foreign governments to end foreign availability.

More concerns about the costs of restrictive U.S. export controls were raised in subsequent years. In January 1987 the National Academy of Sciences (NAS) issued a major study entitled *Balancing the National Interest: U.S. National Security Export Controls and Global Economic Competition*. Although affirming the necessity of export controls, the study argued that the existing system was cumbersome and insensitive to values promoting U.S. technological strength, economic vitality, and allied unity. In line with the NAS study's recommendations were a number of governmental initiatives in 1987, including both executive and congressional actions, to liberalize U.S. export control policy.

Some observers and analysts saw these and other developments as signs of a meaningful relaxation in U.S. export controls resulting from clashes and compromises between the more restriction-oriented Reagan administration and the more pro-trade, anti-control elements in Congress. Others considered the changes largely superficial and saw executive branch support for and dominance of a more restrictive U.S. policy as largely secure. Part I of this book delves into these questions. Who wants what? Who makes and implements U.S. export control policy? Is American policy the result of intense bargaining and compromise between different centers of power? Or is it a process that is dominated by the executive branch, with little input from congressional and interest group forces?

Political Science and the Study of Export Controls

Why Examine Export Controls?

Export controls represent an increasingly important and conflictual area of U.S. international economic policy. With a rather high level of consensus around the cold war policy of economic warfare in the immediate postwar period, there was relatively little domestic opposition to American controls. However, with the fading cold war consensus, the rise and fall of détente, and the highly politicized period of American foreign policy in which we currently live, a multiplicity of views are expressed.

There are some, for example, who are deeply concerned about the economic costs and benefits of U.S. export controls. At a time when U.S. trade and technological competitiveness and performance in the international economy are declining, there is growing concern about the heavy economic costs of American control policy. President Reagan's 1985 Commission on Industrial Competitiveness called attention, for example, to over $11 billion in lost sales each year due to extraordinary, unilateral American controls. A 1986 report by the Business–Higher Education Forum called American controls unproductive, counterproductive, and an overreaction to the perceived military threat of the Soviet Union. The 1987 NAS study found that attempts to keep high technology from Soviet bloc nations have cost the United States an estimated 188,000 jobs and $9 billion a year. These studies reflect a growing concern that export controls may be unnecessarily restrictive and increasingly costly to U.S. trade and technological competitiveness abroad.

Others feel that the economic costs are necessary and relatively insignificant when compared to the national security costs of relaxed controls. A study done for the U.S. Department of Defense (DOD) in 1985, for example, suggested that these costs are potentially very high, perhaps $20–$50 billion a year. Another DOD study in 1987 estimated that as a result of the Japanese (Toshiba Machine Company) and Norwegian (Kongsberg Vaapenfabrikk Company) diversion of machinery and computer software to improve Soviet submarine propellers, the United States would have to spend $8 billion over ten years to reestablish its technological edge. Such evidence is cited to argue that restrictive export controls are absolutely necessary in view of the Soviet Union's thirst for Western technology. And because many believe that the West's technology is being used to support the Soviet military buildup, many demand that the United States do everything within its power to control the eastward technological flow.

Still others view U.S. export control policy in terms of foreign policy rather than in economic and national security terms. The views are diverse, pro and con, just as they are concerning the economic and national security costs and benefits discussed above. Some feel, for example, that the United States can and should do more to use U.S. export controls to serve American foreign policy objectives. They argue that controls on advanced technology can be used as a powerful weapon to further American interests. By pursuing a policy of "economic diplomacy," for example, the United States may be able to encourage Soviet behavior that is more in line with U.S. and Western interests. Others refer disparagingly to such use of export control policy as "lightswitch diplomacy," and consider it damaging to American international relations with adversaries and allies alike. Lightswitch diplomacy antagonizes the Soviet Union and, because America generally expects its allies to join such a policy, also irritates the Western allies.

Three important points can be derived from the brief discussion of the issues raised above. First, U.S. export control policy is important and has considerable bearing upon American economic, security, and foreign policy interests. Second, the way that these interests are articulated and managed in the American political system may have considerable impact on policy. Third, these issues are also of considerable importance to America's allies, to communist countries in the East, and to the future of East-West relations. Obviously, these are important issues to those of us who engage in the study of politics, international economic policy, and East-West relations.

What to Examine?

To organize our studies in this book we will focus on the power, politics, and policies surrounding export controls. First, concerning *power*, we want to know more about the individuals, groups, and organizations who are interested in export control policy and about their sources of power. What are the different interests regarding export controls in the United States, Western Europe, and Japan? How are these interests organized and expressed? What are their sources of power? Political scientists are especially concerned with the sources of power, recognizing that they have much to do with the central question of politics: "Who gets what, when, and how?" There are, of course, different sources, including personality, property, and organization. For example, President Ronald Reagan and Assistant Secretary Richard Perle had a deep impact upon U.S. export control policy in the early 1980s for a number of reasons, including the power of their personalities. On the other hand, American high technology producers might be expected to have considerable power over U.S. export control policy making because of the influence that their wealth and property can provide. Finally, certain agencies of the U.S. government have considerable impact on U.S. export control policy because of their organizational source of power.

Political scientists are also keenly interested in the distribution of power within political systems, be they nation-states or an alliance. Is the power to make and implement U.S. export control policy centralized in the executive branch or is it dispersed among many competing centers of power? How is power organized within the executive branch and within Congress? And what about the distribution and organization of power within some West European democracies and Japan, or within the broader Western alliance? We are interested in power—its sources, distribution, and organization—because of its relationship to the other two central concepts in our study: politics and policy.

We are interested in the *politics* of export controls because it involves the exercise of power in the process determining "who gets what, when, and how." The politics of export control policy involves the struggle for alternative policy outcomes, outcomes that have considerable consequences for those who get involved in the political process. Is the process in the United States or Japan dominated by one group or agency of the government, determining that certain interests always get what they want, any time they want it? Or is the process one of conflict and compromise, where the interests of many are taken into account and considered in the policy-making process? There are also many important questions about interstate politics in the Western alliance. Is the political process dominated by a hegemonic power or is it one in which all states have relatively equal impact on alliance policy? The distribution and exercise of power in the politics of export control policy making is undoubtedly important in determining who gets what in terms of economic, security, and foreign policy costs and benefits surrounding U.S. and Western controls. This is not, of course, to deny the possible existence of other determinants of policy—some of which are also explored in this volume.

Finally, we are interested in *policy* because it represents the collection of outcomes (legislation, rules, and regulations) that governs U.S. and Western controls on East-West economic and technological relations. We are interested in knowing whether the controls are liberal or restrictive and how they impact on American and Western economic, security, and foreign policy interests. For example, how does U.S. policy impact on American interests and on those of its allies? How does broader alliance policy (e.g., that represented by COCOM rules and regulations) affect the interests of the member states and what are they doing to see that their interests are being served?

The Structure of the Book

The chapters prepared for part I of the book make major contributions to our understanding of the power, politics, and policy of U.S. export controls. In the first chapter William Long provides a broad and detailed analysis of the making and implementation of U.S. export controls. He suggests that the Executive and executive institutions have dominated export control lawmaking and policy-making processes. He sees the vital sources of American export control power as being contained within the organizations of the executive branch. This conclusion is contrary to both the pluralist understanding of policy making in a highly politicized "regulatory" arena and the prevailing theories of the role of the Executive and executive institutions vis-à-vis Congress in U.S. trade policy.

Specifically, Long argues that since 1969 the congressional majority and domestic business interests have focused their efforts on liberalizing U.S. export control laws as a means of pursuing a policy of expanding exports. During the lawmaking process the Executive and executive agencies, while not averse to expanding U.S. exports, have successfully fought for their prerogative to invoke controls selectively for national security and foreign policy reasons and have lobbied for procedural flexibility in the administration of export controls. In policy implementation the Executive has used its statutory authority and discretion to pursue its independent foreign policies and national security interests, while executive institutions have withstood many congressional attempts to liberalize export control policy by pursuing embedded institutional practices and self-defined bureaucratic interests.

The chapter by Steven Elliott complements Long's work by providing a theoretical and empirical analysis of the more specialized area of export controls on East-West energy trade. The chapter examines the role of the state in U.S. export control policy as applied to East-West energy trade since the early 1970s. The theoretical framework consists of three contrasting perspectives: statism, pluralism, and Marxism. Having described the major events in this policy area through the Nixon, Carter, and into the Reagan administrations, Elliott applies the theoretical perspectives to assess the state's autonomy and to appraise the utility of the theories. The results of the analysis are mixed. While all the theories have some validity, they also have certain difficulties. However, Elliott concludes that the contextual support for statism—which views the state as largely autonomous—is compelling. Although concessions are made to non-state actors, the broad national interest goals of the state remain largely uncompromised. Therefore, although Elliott finds signs of interest group and congressional involvement in the politics of U.S. export control policy, like Long he finds considerable evidence of executive dominance.

To complement the Long and Elliott chapters, John McIntyre's contribution focuses more explicitly and in a more applied fashion on the implementaton of U.S. export control policy. Describing export control policy as a "wicked problem"—that is, characterized by conflicting and ambiguous objectives, considerable uncertainty, a large number of actors with different priorities and conflicting values, and insufficient information—McIntyre sheds considerable light on the raging power struggles and bureaucratic politics surrounding the implementation of U.S. policy and the licensing of high-technology exports to the East. Although emphasizing that the power to implement U.S. export control policy resides largely in the executive branch, he indicates that this power is dispersed among a complex and often changing cast of characters.

The chapters in part II note, among other things, that East-West trade is important to America's European and Japanese allies. Although not a large part of these countries' global trade—their yearly trade turnover with Eastern Europe and the Soviet Union is generally under 5 percent of their total foreign trade—trade with the East is very important to certain sectors of the West European and Japanese economies, and to certain locales. And, although America's allies do not expect trade with the East to ensure peace and security, they do consider it an important currency for overcoming political and ideological barriers and contributing to improved East-West relations. Because of these and other reasons America's allies are loathe to place excessive controls upon their economic and technological relations with the East.

Yet, as part of their participation in the Western alliance, America's allies have agreed to control militarily relevant components of their trade with the East. The legal basis and institutional structure of these controls take somewhat different forms in the various states, but all involve the country's participation in the multilateral COCOM system and the administration of a national system of strategic trade controls. And although these national systems have certain similarities with the U.S. system, the chapters in part II of this book suggest that the features of power, politics, and policies surrounding the Japanese and West European systems can be quite different from their American counterparts. As the chapters indicate, there are many important reasons for these differences, not the least of which are contrasting historical experiences, geopolitical realities, economic situations, constitutional structures, and political cultures.

While part I of this book focuses on the questions of power, politics, and policy surrounding the making and implementation of U.S. export control policy, part II focuses on these and related questions in America's major COCOM allies—Japan, West Germany, France, and Great Britain. Among other things the chapters examine how East-West trade and the control of such trade are viewed in the various countries; the legal bases, structures, and processes involving the countries' efforts to control their militarily relevant trade with the East; the actors and institutions that become involved in the making and implementation of the policies; the impact that the United States has upon these policies; and the nature of the policies themselves.

The chapter by Gordon Smith notes that Japanese trade policy toward the Soviet Union and Eastern Europe, including controls on commercial and technological relations, is the result of a complex mix of factors. Smith calls attention to the decisive role played by industrial corporations and trading houses, the network of mixed and overlapping roles played by government offices and private business, and to the relatively low degree of institutionalization of economic policy making in Japan. All these factors are reflected in what Smith identifies as "the virtual absence of an institutional voice arguing for more stringent controls and more vigorous enforcement of existing export control regulations." One wonders if any of this will change in view of the 1987 scandal surrounding the Toshiba Machine Company's illegal export of machine tools that were thought to contribute to the improved grinding and therefore quieting of Soviet submarine propellers. In the absence of domestic pressure for tighter controls and enforcement in the past, the United States has always been the major actor placing pressure on the Japanese.

The chapter by Hanns-Dieter Jacobsen calls attention to the special role of the United States in German export control policy and to some of the resulting problems. Although emphasizing that the West German government shares the American conviction that the transfer of militarily critical goods and technology should not be allowed, he notes that there is considerable domestic opposition to expanding the controls beyond what is considered militarily critical. Unlike in the United States, there is a solid consensus in favor of trade with the East in West Germany and overwhelming resistance to those, including the United States, who might want to do more to control it.

Very little is known and very little has been written about French controls on East-West trade. Indeed, the French have been reluctant to admit publicly that COCOM exists. The chapter by Marie-Hélène

Labbé helps correct this situation by addressing the issue of French export controls. Having provided the historical setting of French East-West trade, Labbé describes the structures, processes, and actors involved in the making of French export control policy, and examines and accounts for some recent changes.

The final chapter in part II examines the experience of Great Britain. Gary Bertsch and Steven Elliott note that the British case differs in important ways from that of both its West European neighbors and the United States. Like other trading nations faced with pressing economic challenges, Britain is reluctant to restrict its international economic relations by placing excessive controls on East-West trade. It is even more opposed to having others try to control these trade relations for it, as the United States has occasionally attempted to do through the extraterritorial extension of U.S. controls. At the same time its "special relationship" with the United States and the conservative views of Margaret Thatcher have made Britain more responsive to American efforts to tighten export controls in the 1980s.

The chapters in part III examine the nature of and relationships among power, politics, and policies surrounding the Western alliance's control of East-West trade and technological relations. In the immediate postwar period, the United States—as a hegemonic power—was able to dominate the policy-making process and have a deep impact on alliance policies surrounding COCOM and other efforts to control economic, technological, and financial relations with the East. However, power relationships and political processes changed in the later postwar period and made it more difficult for the United States to impose its will and determine allied policy. More complex strategies for achieving unified alliance policies and stable policy coordination are now required.

Michael Mastanduno looks at these issues and attempts to document and explain the evolution of alliance cooperation surrounding COCOM in the post-1970 period. Mastanduno suggests that the postwar decline of American power may have made cooperation in COCOM both more difficult and more essential, although it is still attainable. Although American power may have declined in relative terms,

Mastanduno argues that the United States continues to possess sufficient power and prestige in absolute terms to achieve effective cooperation on Western export controls. According to Mastanduno, cooperation does not require the United States to possess an overwhelming preponderance of power, but to pursue a leadership role that provides appropriate incentives for multilateral participation. He concludes that alliance cooperation on strategic trade controls is possible without U.S. hegemony.

Beverly Crawford examines two perspectives for explaining Western policy coordination on East-West trade finance. The realist perspective suggests that power determines stable policy coordination. The institutional perspective suggests that a regime based on norms, rules, and procedures is more likely to achieve successful policy coordination. Tracing the interplay of U.S. power and the development of an East-West trade finance regime, Crawford suggests that U.S. power is not sufficient to achieve stable policy coordination. Rather, she argues that regime norms, rules, and procedures are of greater importance than the possession and exercise of power in achieving Western policy coordination on East-West trade finance.

Bruce Jentleson examines the role of American power and leverage in the West's control of East-West energy trade. Jentleson notes that although American capacity to use countersanctions and punitive measures against its allies remains formidable, there has been a clear decline of American hegemonic power and this has diminished the U.S. capacity to influence its allies' East-West energy trade policies. Taken together, the chapters in part III call attention to the decreasing significance of hegemonic power and the increasing need for cooperative strategies in achieving alliance policies for controlling East-West trade.

The four chapters in part IV, written by well-established experts with considerable professional experience in this policy area, examine the implications for U.S. and Western policy. Drawing upon their experience and the analyses and insights of the preceding chapters, the authors examine many of the fundamental issues confronting the West and offer some significant ideas for policy consideration.

John Hardt examines the powerful influence of the superpowers on East-West commercial relations in the postwar era. He calls our attention to some of the important economic developments that are taking place in the contemporary era and suggests that they may diminish the role of the superpowers in future years. He notes that powerful economic forces are at work in the Soviet Union, the United States, and the global system; that the forms of East-West economic exchange have broadened and deepened; and that we may see a trend toward economic normalization between East and West. As the role of these economic forces grows and the hegemonic role of the United States declines, the restrictive, unilateralist approach of past U.S. control policy may become increasingly untenable.

Martin Hillenbrand argues that the U.S. unilateralist approach has been a continuing and costly source of strain in the Western alliance. Examining some specifics that the United States might undertake to minimize these strains—including improving its diplomacy and appreciation of European interests—he suggests that the American role in contributing to more cooperative and stable policy is both important and possible. Although not sanguine about reducing all strains and developing an ideal system of export controls consistent with U.S. and allied interests, Hillenbrand argues that a better appreciation of today's realities is essential to addressing some of the differences that divide the Western alliance and making progress in the desired direction.

The chapter by Henry Nau notes that controls on East-West trade need not generate such strains and interfere with the free exchange of trade and technology within the Western alliance. Nau suggests that a Western "common market for export controls" would ensure a more effective multilateral system of export controls vis-à-vis the East and a liberalization of licensing controls among the cooperative countries of the West. This, Nau argues, can be accomplished within a strengthened COCOM but will require negotiations, bargaining, and on occasion the use of American leverage.

Taking a closer look at the multilateral COCOM mechanism, William Root argues that U.S. unilateralism has repeatedly undermined the cooperation needed for an effective control system. Root raises a number of provocative questions about East-West trade, technology transfer, and export controls. While noting that radical change in present control policy and systems is unlikely, Root calls attention to the urgent need to improve the administration of the control system, and by so doing reinvigorate multilateral cooperative spirits. Root suggests that important steps forward would include repeal of the Department of Defense "veto" in U.S. licensing policy, removal of U.S. extraterritorial controls on exports from cooperating Western countries, and opening up the COCOM process to greater participation from the non-governmental sector.

Taken together, the fourteen chapters in this book are intended to examine the "art of the possible" surrounding Western controls on East-West trade and technology transfer. Examining what is being done in the United States, the allied countries, and the Western alliance as a whole, these studies of power, politics, and policies are intended to present informed analysis to contribute to more enlightened policies in the years ahead.

I

Power, Politics, and Policies
of the United States

1

The Executive, Congress, and Interest Groups in U.S. Export Control Policy: The National Organization of Power

William J. Long

Introduction

This chapter explores the making and implementation of U.S. export control law and policy in the postwar period. The central proposition underlying this study is that the Executive and the relevant bureaucratic agencies (particularly the Departments of Commerce, Defense, and State)[1] influence and shape export control law and policy and are relatively more autonomous and important political actors vis-à-vis Congress and domestic interest groups than is appreciated by theories on the role of the American Executive and executive agencies in U.S. trade policy.

Moreover, Executive dominance persisted beyond the immediate cold war period when, arguably, the perception of a national security crisis and the relative unimportance of international trade to the American economy would suggest the possibility of congressional and interest group deference to the Executive. Since 1969, although the perceived threat to national security has receded, Congress has become more assertive in foreign policy, the presidency has been weakened by Vietnam and Watergate, and the business community's interest in export markets has vastly increased,[2] the Executive *still* dominates export control policy. Furthermore, during the post-1969 period the Executive has extended the original East-West national security thrust of export control policy to serve a variety of other foreign policy objectives, including human rights, anti-terrorism, and nuclear nonproliferation.

This chapter will examine U.S. export controls historically to discern a pattern of executive department dominance, to assess the capacity and instrumentalities of the Executive in defining and implementing policy, and to provide some insight into the content, impacts of, and motivations for the Executive's activities.

Theories of the Role of the Executive in U.S. Trade Policy

Liberalism and its leading modern variant, pluralism, have heavily influenced theoretical approaches to U.S. trade policy. Pluralism, which views the political process as dominated by interest group activities and suggests that the representative and leadership functions of democracy are the result of bargaining and competition among numerous voluntary, randomly arranged interest groups, tends to slight the role of the central state actors.

For example, in a recent work Gary Bertsch argues that, despite the high degree of centralization of authority within the Executive, the politics of East-West trade and technology transfer (roughly synonymous with the politics of export controls) are best understood through an appreciation of the "structural pluralism" of the American political system.[3] Bertsch aptly summarizes the reasons he believes pluralism should account for U.S. export control policy, especially in the past two decades:

> There are a number of reasons for this development . . . includ[ing] the weakening of presidential power in the post-Vietnam and Watergate eras; the increasing assertiveness of a Congress disposed to recapture its constitutional role in American foreign policy; . . . the increasing importance and power of U.S. commercial, and particularly agricultural, interests in a period of declining export performance, and U.S. reactions to Soviet foreign policy intrigues.[4]

As a consequence of these forces, Bertsch concludes, the cold war consensus on East-West trade and technology transfer has declined as the political process has become increasingly pluralistic, "marked by more political actors and centers of power with access to the making and implementation of U.S. foreign economic policy."[5]

Theoretical approaches to overall U.S. trade policy are consistent with the pluralist emphasis on particular interests focused on Congress.[6] Although often not explicitly defining trade policy as including export control policy, many studies of U.S. import policy imply that pluralism explains not only U.S. import policies, but U.S. export policies as well.[7] Consequently, many analyses of the role of the Executive in U.S. trade policy ignore or underestimate the Executive's importance and its strength and insularity from domestic interests.

Theories on general U.S. foreign policy, while accounting for Executive dominance during the early cold war period, do not adequately explain the *continuation* of Executive dominance of export control policy in the post-1969 period. Scholars have described the President as the primary force in foreign affairs in the second half of the twentieth century. Furthermore, the president's ascent to prominence in foreign affairs was thought to relegate Congress to a secondary role.[8] Congress's influence in foreign policy was viewed primarily as legitimating and amending policies initiated by the Executive.[9]

More recent discussions of U.S. foreign policy indicate that the depiction of extensive executive dominance is more accurate with respect to the 1945–65 period than it is to subsequent decades. By the mid-1970s Congress had reasserted itself in U.S. foreign policy making by repealing the Gulf of Tonkin "Resolution," overriding President Nixon's veto of the War Powers Act, terminating the president's authority to provide emergency military aid to South Vietnam, prohibiting continued CIA expenditures in support of anti-communist forces in Angola, and establishing a permanent intelligence oversight committee. In short, the anti-communist values that forged a bipartisan consensus on U.S. foreign policy in the 1950s and 1960s had eroded by the 1970s.

Thus, within the general foreign policy literature, my study seeks to explain why the Executive continues to dominate export control policy despite the growing importance of exports to domestic business interests, a far less accommodating Congress in matters of foreign policy, and the passing of cold war norms.

The Executive and U.S. Export Control Policy

This chapter will demonstrate that the above theories fail to capture fully the autonomy and importance of the Executive and its institutions and to explain their motivations and methods in shaping U.S. export control policy during the past forty years. This chapter maintains that the Executive has operated as an important and relatively autonomous political actor in U.S. post–World War II export control policy. The origins of the Executive's abilities stemmed from instrumentalities and capabilities fashioned to cope with wartime emergencies which continued in peacetime because of the international and domestic orientation of the United States.

The content of the Executive's policies is unique as well. Periodically since 1969 the Executive, to a greater degree than Congress or interest groups, has articulated and pursued export control policies that emphasize national security, foreign policy, and ideological goals (apart from wealth maximization through free trade) in opposition to the congressional majority and interest group emphasis on export expansion. The Executive has also fought to maintain its procedural flexibility and its prerogative to use export controls as it sees fit and has, over the years, developed a variety of policy instruments with which to exercise its authority. Once a degree of executive autonomy has been established, irrespective of the particular policy goal pursued, the Executive has often supported policies that reinforce its authority, flexibility, and control over society.

The second underlying theme of this chapter suggests that U.S. export control policy has also been shaped significantly by bureaucratic institutions. Institutions, it is argued, are "neither neutral reflections of exogenous environmental forces nor neutral arenas for the performances of individuals driven by exogenous preferences and expectation."[10] Emphasizing the Executive's role in U.S. export control policy further permits an assertion that policy outcomes are, in part, the result of institutional dynamics occurring within the Executive.

A corollary to this hypothesis is the assertion that, because policy is implemented through an active bureaucracy, Congress's enunciation or revision of a policy does not necessarily and automatically lead to a corresponding change in policy outcome. Unlike the clash of presidential and congressional interests that has provided focal points for assessing executive autonomy and capacity, institutional effects on policy are gradual, continuous, and rarely overtly political. Nonetheless, export control institutions shape policy by pursuing self-defined, discernible mandates. As a result, institutional practices can produce results different from those designed by Congress or hoped for by domestic interests.

The necessary second step in explaining the bureaucracy's role in contributing to the discontinuity between policy articulation and outcome involves defining *how* the bureaucracy shapes export control policy. A case study of U.S. export control policy implementation affords an opportunity to test several more specific hypotheses on institutional motivations and operations. In this regard this chapter suggests that the bureaucracy is motivated by a desire to fulfill established duties, obligations, and symbolic goals more than by a rational, instrumental pursuit of exogenously, i.e., congressionally, chosen goals embodied in export control legislation, or a representative pursuit of interest group demands. Despite societal changes established career officials, because they are insulated from immediate societal pressures, possess a greater ability to implement established policies resulting over time in relatively continuous policies. This chapter further hypothesizes that the origin of the export control bureaucracy's motivations lies in the ideological climate, the structure of the international system, and the alignment of domestic interests prevailing at the system's inception. Specifically, it is suggested that the U.S. export control institutions derived, and in large measure continue to derive their mandate from laws which were born and operated for two decades in a postwar period of cold war political rivalry, unparalleled American international economic hegemony, and domestic political consensus in the area of U.S. export control policy. In short, institutional history, as well as institutions, are important determinants of policy outcomes.

Because of the complexity of export control, inter- and intra-institutional processes, and the varying effects of institutional dynamics on export control policy, no single theory of institutional operation will be offered here.[11] As examples of bureaucratic influence over policy this chapter will set forth empirical examples of institutional practices that reflect rigidities and the pursuit of endogenous institutional goals.

Method and Organization

I approach the topic chronologically, beginning with a brief discussion of the inception and development of the American export control statutory and institutional framework. Specifically, I shall consider the history of the most important piece of domestic legislation that empowers the Executive to control exports and implement export sanctions in peacetime—the Export Control Act, later the Export Administration Act,[12]—and its bureaucracy. After a discussion of the origins of America's export control regime, I shall consider how subsequent export control laws and policies were shaped by the Executive and executive institutions, and how the Executive, after establishing a role in export control policy, became a relatively autonomous actor in the policy-making process.

Treating the Executive as a more autonomous actor requires a demonstration of two things: (1) that the Executive, although influenced by its domestic and international environment, defines and pursues interests distinct in some measure from any particular environmental interest or summation of interests; and (2) that the Executive has, to some extent, demonstrated an ability to accomplish its aims.[13] To illustrate the Executive's autonomous interests this chapter will compare and contrast the positions adopted by the Executive and executive institutions and those assumed by the congressional majority and domestic interest groups during the passage of export control legislation. I shall then consider actual policy outcomes in the issue areas that were central points of contention during the lawmaking process and assess the Executive's ability or inability to prevail in the areas where it has articulated an interest at odds with the congressional majority and domestic interest groups.

The Origin of U.S. Export Controls

Before considering the divergences between the Executive and Congress and interest groups in the 1970s and 1980s, it is necessary to consider briefly the configuration of executive-congressional relations, the perceived challenges, and the ideological currents prevailing at the origin of the U.S. export control regime.[14] It is suggested here that Executive capacity in export control policy making in the 1970s and 1980s, as well as the content of the Executive's policies and institutional procedures, can be traced in large measure to the forces and interests of this earlier period.

An examination of the origins of American export control institutions requires an investigation of the domestic and international environment that fostered them. In this respect the laws and agencies are treated originally as an endogenous variable. The creation of America's export control system can be explained in the following ways: as a product of existing ideological (anti-communist) forces, as a natural expression of the United States's hegemonic position within the structure of the post–World War II international political and economic system, and as a foreseeable outcome of bureaucratic and interest group relations.

Taken together, these explanations satisfactorily account for the origin of America's export control system. These approaches, however, while necessary, are not sufficient explanations for the subsequent operation and effects of this system. Once established, the legal and bureaucratic apparatus of the Executive influences policy making and policy outcomes as an important political actor.

At their origin, immediately after World War II, peacetime export control laws authorized the president to prohibit or curtail all commercial exports of any article, materials, or supplies (including technical data), except under such rules and regulations as he might prescribe for reasons of national security, foreign policy, or domestic short supply. Operating under this broad delegation of authority, the Executive established a relatively autonomous institution within the Department of Commerce—the Office of Export Control (OEC)—to issue export control regulations, grant or deny applications for export licenses, and investigate violations of the regulations of the Export Control Act itself. The Commerce Department, under statutory direction, acted with information and advice of several other executive departments and agencies.

Institutionally, the OEC continued in peacetime as an embargo policy of economic warfare against communist states. To implement this policy the OEC established procedures that would endure and profoundly affect future policy.

Foremost in this regard is the system of reviewing export license applications one at a time. Rather than identifying a priori the potential strategies of countries posing a threat to U.S. national security and foreign policy interests, and deducing which goods or technologies have a high utility in the service of those strategies, the OEC examined applications on a case-by-case basis, identifying which goods or technologies were intrinsically more strategic than others and determining if their export to a given destination should be permitted.

In addition to establishing a system based on incremental decision making and precedent, the control system handled difficult licensing and control list decisions through multi-agency reviews and clearances operating on the basis of unanimity. Despite the lengthy processing time resulting from this multi-agency and multi-layered decision-making apparatus, the Export Control Act did not establish any deadline for the processing of licenses. Further, the Export Control Act exempted the bureaucracy from judicial review for arbitrary and capricious actions.

At its inception in the immediate postwar period the U.S. export control system was generally consistent with the functional needs of society, the preferences of most political leaders both in the Executive and in Congress, and the country's basic political beliefs.[15] Throughout the 1950s and into the early 1960s America's export control system reflected this general congruence. This reference to congruence is not to suggest that differences of degree did not exist between the Executive and Congress over export control policy. Nonetheless, nascent American export control laws and institutions reflected, with little distortion, the collective sentiments of American society and the nation's position in the international system.[16] In addition, the bureaucracy's implementation of the Export Control Act accorded with the congressional design and there is little indication that the act, as written or applied, contradicted the wishes of the president.

Because in later years the Executive and its institutions would diverge to a greater degree from Congress and interest groups, an understanding of this earlier period is necessary to appreciate these departures. Moreover, the lasting imprint the events and ideologies of this early period left on institutional orientations and practices influenced the way executive institutions shaped U.S. export control policy in later periods.

There are times, however, when the Executive's interests conflict with those of Congress and interest groups. It is at these times that the Executive more clearly defines, as Krasner has phrased it, "the national interest"—the goals the state pursues.[17] By the late 1960s the confluence of forces that had given rise to America's export control system had changed and a variety of new forces placed strains on this once congruent system. Looking back over America's export control policy and its premises in the late 1960s, the U.S. Senate proclaimed that "virtually every circumstance which made the Export Control Act both advisable and feasible has changed."[18] In particular Congress expressed its awareness that the Soviet Union could either manufacture products that met its own needs or purchase what it needed from other nations. Moreover, Congress noted that tensions between the United States and the Soviet Union had lessened and that it was imperative that the United States improve its worsening balance of payments position.[19]

During the next phase in U.S. export control history Congress rewrote the Export Control Act to reflect these changes in the domestic and international environments. The Executive and executive institutions defined and pursued an alternative policy direction.

U.S. Export Control Policy in the 1970s

In 1969 Congress rejected the prior economic warfare objective of the Export Control Act and placed a new emphasis on expanding American exports and opening up trade to the Eastern bloc. The new Export Administration Act of 1969 provided that export licenses could be denied only if a product would contribute significantly to a potential enemy's military capability, and then only if a comparable product could not be obtained from a foreign supplier. In essence the 1969 act represented a change in the congressional focus of American export control policy from a strategic embargo seeking to limit East-West trade toward a policy of qualified free trade seeking to promote exports that did not endanger national security. Despite Congress's and the exporting community's interests in loosening export control restraints,[20] the Export Administration Act of 1969 did not quickly achieve many of its intended effects, and many were never realized.

The Executive initially opposed any relaxation in export control policies. Its attitude toward export controls did not change until three years later when, after securing certain concessions from the Soviet Union, and in the interests of détente, the Nixon administration expressed an interest in expanding East-West trade and loosening some export controls.

Congressional aims were unfulfilled, in part because of the Executive's opposition, but also because of the institutional implementation of the new Export Administration Act. Under the 1969 act the method of implementing export control policy continued to be left largely to the Executive's discretion. The president delegated primary authority to the Commerce Department to review the list of restricted items and technology, to make changes in accordance with U.S. policy, and to process license applications in consultation with other relevant agencies. Consequently, the executive departments that would administer the 1969 act were the same offices that for two decades administered its predecessor. Embedded institutional practices, delays in license processing, bureaucratic decisions regarding which commodities possessed "military significance," and "foreign availability" of controlled commodities made continued licensing impractical and led to greater burdens on U.S. exporters than they, or Congress, had anticipated.

Congress's major attempts at reform included efforts to: (1) limit the number of commodities subject to export controls for national security purposes; (2) instill a recognition within the Executive that the foreign availability of a controlled commodity should be an important factor weighed by the bureaucracy in granting licenses; (3) make the export licensing process more open and accountable to the business community; and, (4) harmonize the export practices of the United States with those of its allies through the multilateral coordinating committee known as COCOM.[21]

The Executive—the president and his appointees in the relevant departments—did not share the congressional enthusiasm for expanding East-West trade. In general the Executive placed greater emphasis than Congress on the national security and foreign policy purposes served by the existing export control system and fought to maintain the Executive's prerogative in the use and administration of export controls so that export control policy could be fashioned by the Executive without hindrance from legislative reforms.

At the time the 1969 act was passed the president had decreed that his appointees in the relevant departments should uniformly support a simple extension of the 1949 act then in effect[22] and should lobby for language in the new act that made many of the congressional reforms into recommendations rather than requirements. The Executive's actions were consistent with the foreign policy of the Nixon administration, particularly National Security Council Director Henry Kissinger's policy toward the Soviet Union at the time.[23]

Although the executive branch recognized, at least in part, the changing conditions that prompted the congressional attempt to relax export controls, it believed that a relaxation in export control laws would have little positive impact on East-West trade and that any trade liberalization should be closely linked to political relations. This greater willingness of the Executive to link exports to other political or general "national security" interests represented an important distinction in the Executive's perspective from that of the majority in Congress and the business community on the goals to be served by U.S. export control policy and the means by which to serve those goals. During the lawmaking process preceding enactment of the 1969 act, the Executive's efforts, in marked contrast to the congressional focus on export expansion, supported measures it believed would further the national security and traditional ideological purposes of the act and would allow the Executive the greatest policy flexibility. This orientation is reflected uniformly in the testimony of the heads of the relevant executive agencies before Congress during passage of the legislation.[24]

The Executive's overall approach to the new legislation was translated into specific opposition to the four major congressional reforms noted above. All three executive agencies (Commerce, Defense, and State) opposed any limitations on the president's authority to use trade controls for national security purposes.[25] The executive departments also made clear their opposition to the congressional recommendation that they give greater consideration to the foreign availability of controlled commodities as a factor in making licensing decisions[26] and claimed that existing agency policies and procedures were sufficiently responsive to business interests.[27] Furthermore, the State, Commerce, and Defense departments unanimously justified the need to regulate more commodities than were controlled by America's COCOM allies, who regulated only goods and technology of direct military significance.[28]

During the legislative process the Executive won important compromises from Congress on several points. Under the final version of the 1969 act agency and presidential decisions would not be subject to judicial review and the president would retain a good deal of flexibility in pursuing national security and foreign policy export controls.[29] The congressional approaches to liberalization through procedures more responsive to business, assessment of foreign availability, and licensing practices more in line with America's COCOM allies were reduced to essentially nonbinding recommendations.[30]

Although Congress had amended U.S. export control laws to serve the dual purposes of national security and free trade, the Executive reserved the authority to maintain a system of trade controls that could be used for national security and foreign policy purposes as the Executive chose to define them. Equally important, embedded institutional practices and procedures ensured the continuation of a burdensome export control policy more restrictive than that anticipated by congressional reformers. Furthermore, to the extent reforms occurred, they came late and at the behest of the president or executive appointees.

Several factors contributed to the Executive's ability to prevail during passage of the 1969 act. Foremost, perhaps, were the divisions within Congress on the desirability of export control reform. Although Congress was generally disposed to liberalize the act, the impetus for reform came primarily from the Senate, more particularly from Senate Democrats, and more particularly still from Senate Democrats on the Banking and Currency Committee. Thus, Congress was not uniformly interested in liberalizing the export control laws and a minority within Congress was opposed to liberalization. These divisions enhanced the Executive's maneuverability in dealing with Congress. Congress, as an institution, was far less able than the Executive to speak with one voice.

Moreover, institutional procedures within Congress made it difficult to sustain momentum for reform. James Sundquist has noted generally that "in the process of overcoming the countless legislative hurdles, policies may be compromised to the point of ineffectiveness."[31] This tendency to compromise is particularly pronounced where, as in 1969, the Executive takes a position in direct opposition to the congressional demands for change, marshals the loyalty of the relevant bureaucratic agencies in opposing the legislation, and exercises partisan influence over House members during passage of the legislation.

Two additional factors contributed to the Executive's legislative effectiveness. First, the Executive possessed the technical expertise required to construct or obstruct meaningful reform of the export control system. Moreover, congressional involvement in export controls is episodic and lacks the depth and continuity of the administrative agencies. This informational problem is compounded by the highly technical and scientific information that is part of the export control policy-making process. On a daily basis, the ability to make the technological assessments crucial to export control policy resides within the Executive.

Finally, because export control policy is a topic directly related to national security, a congressional challenge to executive prerogative and executive judgment cannot be made without peril. Congress is constrained in some measure by the threat that the Executive will brand efforts to liberalize the export control laws as reckless and a threat to national security waged for particular commercial interests.

The president's opposition to expanded East-West trade underwent a reappraisal in the early 1970s—a time in which President Nixon reopened relations (including trade relations) with the People's Republic of China and negotiated, in 1972, an unratified trade agreement with the USSR[32]—and the four major reforms sought by Congress in the 1969 act were slowly or incompletely realized. The reason congressional aims went unfulfilled lay initially in the Executive's ambivalence or redefinition of national security to include expanded, yet limited, East-West contacts. The Executive's failure to adopt a more liberal East-West trade policy until three years after passage of the 1969 act substantially affected its implementation. Additionally, the subsequent institutional implementation of the Export Admininstration Act would also profoundly influence policy outcomes. Under the 1969 act the method of implementing export controls remained essentially unaltered. The persistent nature of U.S. export controls procedures and institutions was summarized by Graham T. Allison in a government study conducted in 1975: "In the aftermath of World War II, in response to problems of the Cold War, security defined in military terms became the overriding purpose abroad—both in concept and in organizational form. Today, the concept has somewhat changed, but the organizational form mostly remains."[33] The effects of enduring "organizational form" on the four congressional initiatives will be the focus here.

Congress's first reform, the removal of controls on certain commodities and technologies controlled for national security reasons, was delayed for three years because of the Executive's independent timetable for East-West trade liberalization.[34] Additionally, institutional inertia contributed to the maintenance of national security controls on goods and technologies, despite their widespread availability or obsolescence throughout the 1970s. For example, despite the rapid technological advances and, hence, rapid technological obsolescence of computer technology, controls on computers remained unchanged from 1976 to 1985, and a similar situation existed with regard to circuit boards and other computer subassemblies.

Congress's second major reform effort, institutionalizing foreign availability assessment as a licensing criterion, was largely ignored by executive agencies, even though Congress called repeatedly for its institutionalization in the 1970s and 1980s.[35] While entries were made to and withdrawn from the Commodity Control List periodically throughout the 1970s, the Commerce Department consistently maintained the right to add or retain commodities under full security controls regardless of foreign availability.

During the 1970s the Commerce Department made little or no progress in establishing a capacity to monitor foreign availability.[36] As late as fiscal years 1980–85 no licenses were granted for reasons of foreign availability, and until 1985 only two Commerce Department employees were assigned to the assessment of foreign availability. In fact, the Commerce Department did not develop formal regulatory guidelines governing foreign availability assessment until 1985.[37]

The complexity of the export licensing system, institutional rigidity, and lack of accountability also resulted in licensing delays, unpredictability, and lack of responsiveness to American exporters,[38] notwithstanding Congress's expressed intent to the contrary. By the spring of 1972 Congress concluded that the Executive's consultation with business was limited because of insufficient agency procedures for consulting with domestic producers who knew the products, the foreign competition, and the "state of the art."[39]

In the Equal Export Opportunity Act of 1972 Congress sought to rectify this continuing lack of consultation by directing the secretary of commerce to appoint technical advisory committees (TACs) consisting of representatives of U.S. industry and government to review export control policy.[40] These committees were to be "consulted with respect to questions involving technical matters, worldwide availability and actual utilization of production and technology and licensing procedures which may affect the level of [unilateral U.S. and COCOM] export controls."[41]

In practice this additional congressional reform did little to respond to American exporters' needs. American business believes that the executive departments essentially ignored or rejected TAC recommendations without further consultation or notification of the technical advisory committee involved.[42] Administrators within the Defense, Commerce, and State departments during the period conceded that the effectiveness of the TACs in involving business in export control policy was, at best, limited. One former Defense Department official noted that his department was not averse to technical input from the business community before or after the creation of the TACs. He added, however, that business's advice on policy matters was never actively solicited by the Defense Department during the 1970s. Furthermore, the effectiveness of the TACs varied greatly. The semiconductor TAC was somewhat effective in funneling business advice and expertise into the system. The computer TAC, in contrast, was largely ineffective and other TACs deteriorated as a result of decisions by business that their needs were not being served through continued participation.

Part of the failure of the TACs to respond to business's need to participate in export control decision making and to receive feedback from the relevant agencies stemmed directly from the manner in which the bureaucracy implemented the congressional directive. The majority of TAC deliberations were classified, limiting access to much information that business needed to participate actively and effectively in the process. Second, business and industry representatives on the TACs were originally limited to a two-year term, whereas government members served indefinitely. Business and industry believed that this arrangement "caused disruption and allowed very little time for an individual to become familiar with the other members of the committee before they are required to step down."[43] Finally, the legislation enabling the TACs specified that the TACs would report to the secretary of commerce. The receipt of reports, however, was delegated within the Commerce Department to the Office of Export Administration, an overworked and understaffed processing office with a long history of not wanting or accepting industry input.

In implementing the congressional aim of aligning U.S. export licensing policy more closely with that of other COCOM members, the Executive's institutions continued to pursue a policy at odds with U.S. allies and the wishes of American business by regulating many commodities not directly related to military application and by subjecting American exporters to lengthy license processing.

Because of the differing viewpoints between the United States and its COCOM allies on export controls, and because by 1970 the United States was no longer the sole or even principal source of high technology, the COCOM consensus weakened and a greater commercial rivalry among members arose. Although a general agreement about the need to maintain a military embargo against the Soviet bloc for reasons of Western security remained intact, the COCOM allies did not share in a consensus for broader economic or industrial warfare against the Eastern bloc. Responding to this situation, Congress mandated in the 1969 act that U.S. licensing procedures become attuned with the changing economic and political balance between the United States and its COCOM allies. However, the Executive made clear its opposition to this recommendation in its testimony before the House and Senate.

Despite Congress's urgings the United States continued to pursue a more generally restrictive policy toward exports than its allies after passage of the 1969 act. The United States continued to control a large number of product categories not controlled by its COCOM allies. In 1972 the United States maintained unilateral controls on 461 classifications of goods and technology not under multilateral (COCOM) control.[44] The U.S. Commodity Control List of September 1978 still contained, by one estimate, 207 entries, of which 123 were COCOM controlled and 84 were unilaterally controlled by the United States.[45] By another government estimate the United States unilaterally controlled 38 unique industrial item categories in 1979.[46]

Throughout the 1970s the United States continued to pursue a more restrictive export control policy than the other COCOM nations. Gary Bertsch's recent study summarized the U.S. position during this period: "Although supporting much East-West trade liberalization, the United States reacted negatively to most efforts to loosen the strategic COCOM embargo in the 1970s. The United States continued, for example, to utilize its veto to avoid decontrols involving deletions from and exceptions to the embargo list."[47]

Although the United States and other COCOM countries mutually agreed to one set of lists of controlled products and technologies, disparities in outlook and policies manifested themselves through differing national interpretations of the list and enforcement policies[48] and the request for exceptions to controls within COCOM. For example, the United States continued to use its veto to avoid decontrolling or excepting from controls items on the embargo list.

The divergence between the United States and its COCOM allies with respect to commodity control practices was not solely the result of ideological or technological differences. Institutional export control processes also prevented U.S. licensing practices from aligning with those of COCOM. The process by which the United States arrived at its position for COCOM's list reviews in the 1970s continued to involve complex and time-consuming inter-agency coordination within the U.S. bureaucracy.

In addition to the Advisory Committee on Export Policy (ACEP), the interdepartmental committee which coordinates unilateral U.S. export control policy, a second interdepartmental group, the Economic Defense Advisory Committee (EDAC), chaired by the State Department, coordinates U.S. participation in multilateral export control policy through COCOM.[49] EDAC also decides whether COCOM exception requests to export controlled items should be approved. EDAC operates under a rule of unanimity as well. Its slowness in ruling on licensing and exception requests,[50] and business's lack of access to the administrative policy formulation process as it applies to COCOM have contributed to lengthy licensing practices.[51]

In sum, institutional arrangements, abilities, history, and policy orientation interacted to influence policy outcomes resulting in policies different from congressional directives or the desires of the American exporting community. Institutions were slow to change during the 1970s and, lacking sustained pressure from within the Executive to liberalize policy, pursued a restrictive and cumbersome export control policy more in keeping with that of the 1950s and 1960s.

Before considering the "autonomous" role played by the president and high policy-makers within the Executive in shaping U.S. export control policy, one final example of institutional influence on policy outcomes is noted. In response to chronic licensing delays in 1974, 1977, and 1979, Congress made significant amendments to the Export Administration Act in an effort to clarify, simplify, and thereby expedite the inter-agency export licensing process. Congress was responding to the business community's complaints of continuing delays and assertions that the commercial effect of delays is the same as a licensing denial—lost sales and sales opportunities and a damaged reputation for reliability. The heads of the executive institutions charged with processing licenses, however, lobbied against stricter licensing deadlines on the grounds that agency discretion and thoughtful review were required in licensing decisions to protect national security, that they were already sufficiently responsive and open to the export sector, and that they were making every effort to process license applications more efficiently.[52]

Although in 1974 Congress ultimately provided for ninety-day deadlines for most license applications unless delays were meaningfully explained to the applicant, inordinate licensing delays persisted. The number of license applications pending for more than ninety days in 1978 totaled almost 2,000 applications—nearly twice the 1977 figure.[53] In addition, private studies suggest that, with regard to many high-technology industries, delays actually worsened after the 1977 reforms.[54]

Rarely of direct concern to important executive actors, license-processing delays were in large measure attributable to the complex multi-agency license application review process. Occasionally licensing delays were purposeful. Executive institutions used delays to forestall either the approval or denial of a license application. Delays of this sort, however, were not the norm.

Institutional factors were more significant than purposeful actions in causing licensing delays. Especially in the area of high-technology exports, export licensing was an increasingly segmented process subject to the scrutiny of several agencies. In general the Department of Defense examined license applications from a broad-gauge national security standpoint. The Department of State, responsible for reviewing export controls imposed for foreign policy purposes and for chairing COCOM multilateral reviews, viewed export licensing from a diplomatic standpoint. The Commerce Department—as a result of the disparate views of the agencies it must consult and the ambivalent act that controls exports for national security, foreign policy, and short supply reasons while it simultaneously recognizes the need to stimulate American export performance—failed to adopt clear policy guidelines and frustrated many segments of the American business community because of its slow licensing procedures. Without exaggerating the importance of inter-agency disputes or presuming that inter-agency disputes were a consistent feature of U.S. export control policy that frustrated congressional reforms, evidence suggests that by the late 1970s differing agency viewpoints contributed to delay and hence a more restrictive export control policy.[55]

In addition to the number and varying orientations of agencies involved in export control licensing, the original decision-making process, based on precedent and the scrutiny of each item or technology to determine its military significance, remained fundamentally unchanged throughout the 1970s and contributed to the system's slowness and its resistance to reform. The ad hoc nature of the case-by-case method contributed to a lack of clear or uniform guidelines and to license-processing delays.

Export license processing was consistently at odds with congressional and interest group demands in the 1970s and 1980s. Executive institutions shaped policy to fit with institutionally defined goals and methods. They only occasionally deliberately opposed the will of Congress by purposeful delays. More often, institutions, in executing established duties and obligations, continued procedures certain to impede efforts to expedite license processing. Executive institutions with disparate but embedded mandates, insulated in some measure from societal pressures and only periodically the focus of congressional inquiry, proved to be highly resistant to reform.

Executive Autonomy in the Exercise of Foreign Policy Export Controls

The Executive at times has articulated and pursued successfully a discernibly different export control policy than that of Congress or domestic interest groups. I have mentioned briefly the influence and importance of the president and the inner circle of presidential advisers and cabinet heads within the Executive with regard to export liberalization during the early 1970s. The relative autonomy of the president and highly placed officials within the executive branch, however, is most clearly evident in the Executive's increasing use of export controls for foreign policy purposes beginning in the late 1970s.

The Executive's authority to undertake foreign policy export controls was virtually unbridled during the 1970s. Before 1979 the Executive's authority to use export controls for foreign policy purposes was broader and less well-defined than its national security authority. In the 1969 act Congress differentiated foreign policy controls from "national security controls," i.e., those controls intended to restrict exports that would make "a significant contribution to the military potential of any other nation or nations which would prove detrimental to the national security of the United States."[56] The president's national security control authority was limited by the 1969 act to regulating dual-use items, prohibiting in most instances their export directly or indirectly to communist countries. Unlike controls implemented for reasons of national security, the 1969 act did not limit the Executive's discretion to use export controls for foreign policy purposes. Export controls invoked for foreign policy purposes could be extended to all goods, strategic and non-strategic. Foreign policy controls, unlike national security controls, had no mechanism such as COCOM to coordinate their restrictions with the practices of U.S. allies. Because allied nations were less likely to agree and cooperate with export restraints not directly linked to their security interests, foreign policy controls also became a source of policy divergence between the United States and its allies.

Furthermore, while the Export Administration Act of 1969, as amended, stated that the Executive should consider the foreign availability of comparable products before applying national security controls, it was mute with regard to the Executive's necessary considerations before imposing foreign policy controls. In a situation where comparable goods were available outside the United States a purchaser could simply shift to a supplier of comparable products in another country, thereby subverting the effectiveness of unilateral U.S. foreign policy export controls. Finally, the 1969 act also required semiannual reports on foreign policy export controls, but these reports, by most estimations, did not adequately inform Congress or the public.[57]

In rewriting the Export Administration Act in 1979, Congress sought to limit the president's authority in using export controls for foreign policy purposes. Foreign policy export controls came under increasing attacks from the business community, academia, and America's allies in the late 1970s. The business community opposed these policies, believing that they abrogated existing contracts and foreclosed future ones, and damaged the reputation of U.S. exporters as reliable suppliers of goods and services without in any way serving national security interests. Analysts criticized foreign policy export controls as an ineffective means of achieving foreign policy objectives and concluded that these policies were costly and served little more than symbolic, signaling, or displacement functions. Furthermore, because no means existed for coordinating unilateral U.S. export controls promulgated for foreign policy purposes, foreign policy controls were a source of contention between the United States and its allies when they did not share foreign policy objectives or disagreed over the use of export controls as the best means to achieve shared goals.

As a result of these dissatisfactions, in the 1979 act Congress attempted to limit the situations where the president could use his foreign policy export control authority to those instances where the president had fully considered the likely effectiveness of the proposed controls, the compatibility of the proposed controls with overall U.S. foreign policy, the effect of the proposed controls on U.S. export performance, and the foreign availability of the goods or technology subject to the proposed controls.[58] Congress also attempted to instill greater accountability by the president to Congress and the business community through consultation and reporting requirements, including requiring the president to find that: (1) the controls will be likely to change behavior in the target state; (2) the controls will not cause undue hardship to the U.S. economy or employment; and (3) successful negotiations with foreign governments eliminating the foreign availability of the controlled products are likely to occur.[59]

The Executive adopted a very different outlook on the foreign policy provisions of the proposed legislation than that of the business community or Congress. While espousing the need to expand exports, the Executive opposed any changes in the foreign policy provisions of the 1979 act that would effectively limit the Executive's flexibility to impose controls for foreign policy purposes, even in circumstances where the controls would not be effective in denying the country the goods or technology in question. In particular the Executive opposed the imposition of strict criteria that must be considered before instituting controls for foreign policy purposes.[60] In addition, the Executive claimed that it already considered factors such as foreign availability in reaching its decisions,[61] but that it was executive practice to impose controls regardless of its findings should it desire to do so for moral or symbolic reasons.[62] The administration also opposed any provision that would permit Congress to veto the imposition of foreign policy controls and rejected a requirement that the Executive consult with affected industries or other governments *before* imposing foreign policy controls.[63] The Executive characterized these restrictions as either constitutional or practical encroachments on the president's ability to conduct foreign affairs.

During the lawmaking process the Executive won several important compromises from Congress. Congress wrote out of the new act the provision for a legislative veto of foreign policy export controls, instructing only that the president "shall consider" the criteria listed earlier before imposing foreign policy controls, provided that consultation with affected industries occur "as the Secretary [of Commerce] considers appropriate," and requiring that the president consult with and report findings to Congress prior to the imposition of controls "in every possible instance."[64]

In legislating these provisions Congress conceded their nonbinding nature. The committee report accompanying the legislation noted: "that the [foreign policy] provision as amended would not preclude the President from reacting promptly to extreme situations, nor prevent him from imposing or maintaining export controls regardless of his conclusion with respect to the factors listed, nor require a public report if the President decided a public report was not in the national interest."[65] The committee further noted that the new foreign policy provisions did not establish criteria to be met but rather set forth factors to be considered, and recognized that the president, having considered them, might find one or more of the factors irrelevant to a decision to impose controls.[66] Similarly, with respect to foreign availability determinations, the committee pointed out that "the provision will not preclude the use of export controls for foreign policy purposes despite foreign availability,"[67] and provided that the standard for assessing foreign availability in cases involving the imposition of foreign policy controls was not as strict as that required for national security controls.[68]

In sum, the foreign policy "restraints" on the Executive contained in the 1979 act were little more than procedural nuisances. The Executive remained free to interpret if and when adherence to the requirements of the 1979 act was required. Sustained effort by the Executive to retain authority and flexibility over foreign policy controls, divisions within Congress over the degree to which it was willing to limit executive authority, and congressional deference to the Executive's foreign affairs powers and prerogatives conspired to produce a tenuous and ambiguous act.

The Executive was a salient and generally undivided participant in the lawmaking process. Congress, although generally supportive of efforts to restrain the Executive's foreign policy authority, was often divided over the best means to achieve this end. Congress also deferred to the Executive's claimed need for flexibility in conducting foreign policy. Ultimately, the wording of the foreign policy provisions of the 1979 act reflects the ill-resolved compromise between the demands of the Executive branch for flexibility and autonomy in the use of foreign policy export controls and the congressional desire to limit, but not eliminate, their use.

In practice the foreign policy prerogatives of the president have predominated over congressional wishes that considerations of domestic economic costs and the effectiveness of the proposed controls be given greater weight. The new criteria written into the act and the consulting and reporting requirments did little to dissuade the president from extending existing controls and imposing new foreign policy controls in unprecedented numbers when that choice appeared expedient. New congressional guidelines did not curb executive efforts to limit exports to the Soviet Union following its invasion of Afghanistan.[69]

In that instance President Carter's foreign policy export control initiatives, implemented under the Export Administration Act of

1979, received a mixed reception from Congress. Some controls, such as the Kama River truck plant controls and the Olympic boycott, were made with congressional support. The centerpiece of the Carter administration's sanctions imposed against the Soviet Union following its invasion of Afghanistan—the grain boycott—met with significant congressional opposition, however. Despite substantial domestic opposition to the boycott, the Carter administration held firm and did not lift the embargo, thus demonstrating the Executive's endurance as well as initiative in the use of foreign policy export controls.

The Reagan administration has changed the direction of U.S. export control policy in some respects but it does not differ from the Carter administration in either its willingness to use export controls for foreign policy purposes or its belief that, despite the 1979 act, the use and administration of export controls is the Executive's prerogative. President Reagan has declined to impose controls on East-West grain sales but has been more willing to restrict both U.S. and foreign companies from engaging in the sale of certain equipment and technology to the Soviet Union and its allies. Furthermore, while deemphasizing the use of foreign policy export controls for human rights interests, the Reagan administration has linked American export trade to its opposition to international terrorism and has used export controls as a means of expressing its dissatisfaction with the policies of other nations. The presidential proclivity to use export controls for foreign policy purposes has proven to be a decidedly bipartisan one; changes in administration and the substance of foreign policy have not reduced the Executive's willingness to use foreign policy export controls despite the 1979 act.

President Reagan has issued foreign policy export controls over oil and gas equipment and related technical data to the Soviet Union. These controls were imposed in two parts. The first part, imposed December 30, 1981, expanded the existing requirement for validated export licenses for exploration-and-production-related goods to include those related to transmission and refinement. In addition, processing of all export licenses on goods destined for the Soviet

Union was temporarily suspended.[70] The second part of these controls, initiated in June 1982, expanded coverage of the oil and gas controls extraterritorially, i.e., beyond the territorial jurisdiction of the United States, to include exports of foreign-origin goods and technical data by U.S.-owned or controlled companies abroad and foreign-produced products of U.S. technical data not previously subject to controls. The pipeline controls were made at the urging of the National Security Council over significant domestic and international opposition.[71] President Reagan also expanded existing foreign policy controls against Libya and in 1984 made two additions to the foreign policy export control programs.[72]

In continuing its use of foreign policy controls, the Executive has largely ignored the guidelines set forth in the 1979 act. The Carter administration's reports to the Congress regarding foreign availability assessment reveal that the Executive was not dissuaded from imposing foreign policy export controls, despite the foreign availability of the controlled product, and did not feel compelled to explain to Congress its decision to impose the controls.[73] Similarly, the Reagan administration has been chastised by its staunchest supporters in Congress for its "disappointing" assessment of foreign availability in extending foreign policy controls and its failure to consider adequately the statutory criteria before imposing such controls.[74] The Reagan administration continued foreign policy export controls regardless of the foreign availability of the controlled commodities and technology and without demonstrating to Congress the efficacy of such controls.[75]

The Executive also repeatedly ignored the requirement of the 1979 act that Congress be notified before imposing export controls for foreign policy purposes. For example, although President Reagan imposed additional foreign policy controls on exports to Libya on March 12, 1982, the Commerce Department did not notify and report to Congress until more than two months later.[76] The Executive's disregard of the statutory requirements was even more apparent in the case of the expanded pipeline controls. On June 19, 1982, President Reagan directed that additional foreign policy controls be placed on exports of oil and gas exploration, production, transmission, and refining equipment, and technical data to the Soviet Union. Although these controls were *terminated* on November 13, 1982, following a severe rift between the United States and its allies over the extra-territorial application of these controls, Congress was not notified of their *imposition* until November 29, 1982—two weeks after their termination.[77]

In summing up the executive-congressional struggles over foreign policy export controls, one longtime insider to the process estimated that the Executive possesses greater latitude and power vis-à-vis Congress and interest groups in export control policy (especially in the use of export controls for foreign policy, rather than national security purposes) than in any other area of foreign economic policy. This estimation is presented—along with the considerable evidence of Executive autonomy offered in this chapter—to highlight the difference between the conventional wisdom suggesting that congressional dominance or equivalence best characterizes U.S. trade policy, or that Congress has become increasingly reassertive in foreign policy since the mid-1970s, and the real situation. Furthermore, those who would dismiss executive preeminence as simply an aberration because they believe that national security aspects of export control policy permit the Executive greater latitude in this policy arena, must also explain away the Executive's dominance in the use of *foreign policy* export controls discussed above.

Recent Developments in U.S. Export Control Law and Policy

Passage of the Export Administration Amendments Act of 1985 (the 1985 act) began in 1983. Although the House and Senate passed bills relatively early that year, conference negotiations to settle differences between the bills broke down after six months and a final bill was never put to a vote. The issue of export controls had become particularly fractious within Congress and within the Executive between pro-export forces and those committed to denying high technology to the Eastern bloc.

The Senate bill called for stricter limits on the use of export controls for foreign policy purposes, expanded authority for the Defense Department to review exports to COCOM and nonaligned Western nations, enhanced enforcement authority for the Customs Service, elimination of the president's authority to impose foreign policy controls on U.S. agricultural exports, and prevention of a presidential breach of existing contracts when imposing foreign policy controls. The House bill sought to liberalize licensing requirements for exports to COCOM, retain exclusive authority for review of West-West licensing in the Commerce Department, maintain primary enforcement responsibility in the Commerce Department, and require a congressional role in any presidential decision to extend foreign policy controls extraterritorially.

The administration generally opposed any restrictions on its authority to use export controls for foreign policy reasons. The primary battle within the administration was the jurisdictional dispute over West-West licensing between the Commerce and Defense departments. The White House did not favor the Senate bill—which reassigned a portion of West-West licensing review authority to the Defense Department—viewing resolution of the dispute as an Executive prerogative rather than a congressional one. The Commerce Department, led by Under Secretary of Commerce Lionel Olmer, and the Defense Department, led by Assistant Secretary of Defense Richard Perle, conflicted violently over this issue and over enforcement questions.[78]

The business community, in contrast to the administration and Congress, agreed on basic principles for revising the export control laws, including the need to recognize the sanctity of contracts, limit or prohibit the extraterritorial application of foreign policy controls, improve consultation between the Executive and Congress before imposition of foreign policy controls, and prohibit an increase in Defense Department authority in licensing exports.

Business leaders directed much of their efforts at reforming the foreign policy export control provisions. Business spokesmen particularly opposed unilateral U.S. foreign policy export controls on goods freely available from foreign suppliers, as well as the retroactive implementation of foreign policy export controls which in the past had permitted the president to break existing contracts.

In many respects the final version of the 1985 act reflected the concerns of the business community and those in Congress who sought to liberalize U.S. export controls. For example, the 1985 act contains a new provision prohibiting retroactive revocation of existing contracts by imposition of foreign policy export controls (the so-called "contract sanctity" provision). Furthermore, in situations where foreign availability of a controlled product exists, foreign policy export controls unilaterally imposed by the United States are now limited to six months' duration.

As in instances documented previously, these "successes" may be more nominal than actual. The contract sanctity provision, for example, allows the Executive to avoid its restrictions whenever the president determines and certifies that a breach of the peace poses a serious and direct threat to the strategic interests of the United States. This certification requirement, like other congressional requirements for executive reports, determinations, and findings before the imposition of foreign policy export controls, appears unlikely to deter the Executive from imposing foreign policy controls which could sever preexisting contracts.

Moreover, many of the changes in the foreign policy section of the 1985 act seem to be little more than semantic ones. For example, the prior requirement for "considerations" before imposition of foreign policy export controls has been changed to "determinations." Congress strengthened this provision because it believed the Executive had ignored the message contained in the 1979 act—that the Executive must carefully weigh the cost and consider alternatives before imposing foreign policy export controls. Again, Congress deferred to executive foreign affairs authority in not placing stricter limits on executive discretion, and thus it is highly unlikely that this new provision will impose any real restraint on executive authority.

In the area of national security export controls Congress eliminated U.S. licensing requirements for exports of relatively low-technology items and accelerated processing deadlines for exports of high-technology items to COCOM countries. In other particulars the national security provisions rewritten by Congress may prove less than reformers had hoped.

Despite Congress's efforts to eliminate unilateral U.S. national security export controls when the controlled good or technology is available from foreign sources, the 1985 act continues to provide a loophole for executive discretion. The 1985 act appears to add more stringent foreign availability assessment provisions to the national security section. Specifically, the 1985 act authorized the technical advisory committees to make initial determinations of foreign availability of specific commodities; these commodities must be decontrolled unless the Department of Commerce rebuts the evidence within ninety days. In addition, the legislation requires that the Commerce Department accept an applicant's representations regarding foreign availability if supported by "reasonable evidence" and grant an export license unless the department has "reliable" contrary evidence.

These efforts, however, are vitiated by the concurrent grant of authority to the president to maintain controls for up to eighteen months, despite a finding of foreign availability under the 1985 act. The Executive will thus maintain the ability to ignore foreign availability findings should it choose to do so.

Institutional barriers to decontrolling commodities because of foreign availability also remain formidable obstacles to reform. Although the Commerce Department's recently operationalized Office of Foreign Availability has begun foreign availability assessments and improved its data-gathering abilities, inter-agency (i.e., Commerce, Defense, and State) consensus on implementing the letter and spirit of the foreign availability provisions is clearly lacking. Consequently, to date, after two and one-half years of research and inter-agency review, the Commerce Department has made only one published positive finding of foreign availability. The finding applied to automatic wafering saws used to slice silicon for computer chips. The Commerce Department's finding removed unilateral U.S. controls on the West-West export of the wafering saws. Nevertheless, the Defense Department remains opposed to the decontrol and has stalled the West-East multilateral decontrol procedure in COCOM.

Finally, the 1985 act makes a number of changes intended to expedite the processing of applications for export licenses. The new timetable attempts to reduce most deadlines by one-third. While this effort may have some salutary effect on the efficiency of license processing, there are strong reasons to believe that delays will continue. The Department of Commerce recently released figures which reveal that as of January 17, 1986, 2,131 applications with a reported value of almost $1.9 billion were pending at the Commerce Department beyond their statutory deadline for action. The vast majority of the delayed cases, 1,920 applications, had been pending for over 120 days, despite the sixty-day processing deadline.[79]

The issues before Congress during the two and one-half years spent reauthorizing and amending the Export Administration Act should now ring familiar. Congress, at the urging of the business community, addressed provisions governing the assessment of foreign availability, the Executive's discretion in using foreign policy and national security export controls, the processing of licenses, and the act's jurisdictional scope.

Because of divisions within Congress over the preferred course of export control reform and congressional deference to the Executive's national security and foreign affairs authority, the legislative outcome also reflects a pattern whereby congressional efforts were embodied in several statutory reforms, but often in ways that are unlikely to prohibit ultimately the Executive's discretion in using either national security or foreign policy export controls.

It is still too early to determine whether the most recent congressional efforts will prove to be more effective than previous attempts to rein in executive discretion in the use and administration of export controls. The discussion of past congressional efforts presented in this study and the nature of many provisions of the 1985 act suggest, however, that in future instances where the Executive's interest in the use of export controls differs from that of Congress or the business community, the Executive is unlikely to be impeded by the 1985 act.

The Reagan administration undertook a variety of policies immediately before and after passage of the 1985 act that continue to demonstrate a great deal of executive autonomy and capacity in the use of export controls for foreign policy purposes. The most important policies were the embargoes against Nicaragua and Libya. The president implemented both of these policies under the International Emergency Economic Powers Act (IEEPA), rather than the Export Administration Act. The president invoked his authority under IEEPA in the case of Nicaragua because the Export Administration Act had expired and its provisions had been maintained through a presidential declaration of national emergency and the invocation of IEEPA. President Reagan imposed sanctions against Libya under IEEPA allegedly because the use of IEEPA may have been more appropriate than the 1985 act for implementing a total embargo, and the use of IEEPA allowed the president to avoid the contract sanctity provisions and the prohibition on the use of foreign policy export controls for agricultural products in the 1985 Act.[80]

Both the Libyan and Nicaraguan embargoes reflect the strength, initiative, and multiple instrumentalities of the Executive. The recent strengthening of controls against South Africa, however, presents a more atypical case in which Congress was the motivating force for foreign policy export controls and related sanctions.

In 1985 the president, who had opposed additional export controls against South Africa, when faced with the prospect that Congress would pass a sanctions bill effectively fashioned a program of limited export controls and other punitive measures, thereby heading off congressional demands for stronger measures. In essence the president's export control authority was used in a preemptive way to fashion a second-best policy.

The president's South African policy ran aground the following year. In perhaps the most important foreign policy defeat of the Reagan presidency, Congress enacted a law imposing economic sanctions against South Africa. President Reagan had vetoed the bill on September 26, 1986, but both houses voted to override the veto, the

House on September 29 and the Senate on October 2. Although the bill did not expand the export restraints imposed by President Reagan in 1985, it imposed several additional economic sanctions and represented a clear rebuke of the Executive's policy. The South African sanctions are, by their exceptional and unprecedented nature, an exception that proves the rule that export sanctions are policy instruments primarily under control of the Executive.

Conclusion

Theories of U.S. foreign policy and U.S. trade policy do not fully explain U.S. export control policy. An understanding and appreciation of the role of the Executive and executive institutions is also necessary. The Executive is more than merely one player among many shaping export control policy. Moreover, executive institutions exert an enduring influence over the making and implementation of policy.

What role do the Executive and its institutions play in U.S. export control policy? Looking back over forty years of U.S. export controls, certain patterns emerge. First, the lawmaking process often reveals a divergence of executive and congressional interests. Although differences existed between agencies and within Congress on export control policy, the Executive generally presented a unified front in expressing statutory preferences distinct from the congressional majority. Contrary to the congressional emphasis on making the export control system more efficient, more accountable, and less burdensome to exporters, and its use as a tool of general foreign policy exceptional, the Executive has stressed the need to use export controls as a means of furthering its national security and foreign policy goals. Moreover, during the lawmaking process the Executive repeatedly was capable of prevailing on Congress to modify legislation such that Executive authority and flexibility would not be altered.

The sources of executive strength and influence over Congress during the legislative process are numerous. In addition to a greater singularity of purpose, the Executive possesses a host of other means by which it can shape export control legislation, including: (1) partisan influence in Congress; (2) a historic and constitutional role in protecting U.S. national security and furthering U.S. foreign policy interests; and (3) superior technical expertise and experience in export control administration.

In the implementation of export control policy the Executive often used export controls to serve self-defined goals, despite the domestic opposition that attended many of its policies. The Executive's increasing use of foreign policy export controls beginning in the late 1970s is a vivid example of the high level of Executive autonomy.

Furthermore, executive institutions have pursued distinctive goals and realized them in varying degrees. In contrast to the post-1969 congressional emphasis on export expansion, executive institutions throughout the 1970s and 1980s have consistently limited exports that they believed could endanger national security. Institutional practices reflected less concern than Congress with the competitive detriment that export licensing posed for American exporters. This institutional orientation was formed during more than twenty years of implementing an export embargo against communist countries and is illustrated by the manner in which the export control institutions resisted the reforms mandated by Congress in the 1969 act and the amendments of the 1970s.

The origins of the executive authority, institutional and otherwise, can be traced to its wartime emergency powers, retained and expanded during two decades of U.S. hegemony, cold war rivalry, and executive-congressional–interest group congruence on the purpose to be served by U.S. export controls. The Executive has used its original delegation of authority to establish an elaborate and insulated export control apparatus.

The nature of the Executive's export control apparatus has enabled it to preserve its autonomy and resist societal demands for change. Export controls are a policy area particularly susceptible to institutional control and highly resistant to outside pressure for reform. Export controls monitor all exported civilian goods and technology. The resources needed to administer this inclusive system are necessarily vast and complex. Numerous bureaucracies are involved in making thousands of individual, highly technical rulings on the export of particular goods or technology to particular destinations. Moreover, the institutions making these decisions are generally unaccountable either electorally, through oversight, or in the courts.

Executive institutions have been slow to change. In part this fact is attributable to the difficulty of translating legal, statutory directives into meaningful institutional change when institutional practices are well entrenched and the institutions are largely unaccountable to those mandating their change. Moreover, the mandates themselves —the statutes—harbor many ambiguities and ill-resolved compromises, perhaps none greater than the dual purpose of the act—to expand U.S. exports while protecting national security.

Furthermore, institutional structures and practices preclude the possibility of certain internal reforms. For example, export license processing may be "system limited" because numerous institutions with varying mandates and vested interests in the existing system, coupled with the case-by-case method of licensing, prohibit more expeditious processing of licenses. Absent a fundamental change in one or more of these institutional features, significant reform is unlikely, if not impossible.

In sum, the Executive has defined relatively autonomous interests in the domestic lawmaking process, and its policies reveal a significant capacity to prevail over domestic preferences in the implementation of policy. This chapter has endeavored to demonstrate not only the Executive's autonomy and capacity, but also to provide some insight into the sources of the Executive's authority and the content of its policies and procedures in an important, but often overlooked aspect of U.S. foreign economic policy.

2

The Distribution of Power and the
U.S. Politics of East-West
Energy Trade Controls

Steven Elliott

Introduction

The formulation and implementation of export control policy has
tended to be a conflictual affair in American politics. It has often
pitted volatile coalitions involving the Executive, Congress, business, and U.S. allies against one another. The nub of the controversy
lies in the tension between "national" and commercial interests.
Pro-control forces perceive these interests to be mutually exclusive
or hold the latter hostage to the former. Anti-control, pro-trade forces
contend that commercial interests frequently enhance national interests. The interaction of these forces, the coalitions they form, and the
events that influence them constitute a complex political process
—one, indeed, that has often been characterized as pluralistic in
nature. Yet the preceding chapter by William Long suggests that
despite the hullabaloo over U.S. export controls, this policy area has
been dominated by the Executive throughout the postwar period.
Long clearly demonstrates that the Executive has a near monopoly of
control over the institutional policy instruments.

This chapter has three related purposes. Like Long's, it explores
the nature of U.S. export control policy making. Here we focus on the
particularly conflictual energy equipment sector of East-West trade
and technology transfer, where extremely powerful corporate inter-

ests have often opposed the national security and, especially, the foreign policy interests of the state. The chapter also takes a closer look at Long's basic conclusion of Executive dominance by systematically considering theoretical alternatives for understanding and explaining export control policy. Finally, in doing this the chapter makes some assessment of the utility of these theoretical alternatives.

U.S. East-West trade policy has been one of starts and stops, especially in the energy sector. As cold war attitudes softened in the early 1970s the Nixon administration began to liberalize U.S.-Soviet trade. Long-term joint energy projects were particularly important in the Nixon-Kissinger "structure of peace" and so, when the Soviets proposed the North Star and Yakutsk natural gas pipeline projects, the administration gave American business consortia the green light to investigate the proposals. However, an unusual coalition of Congress, some State Department officials, organized labor, and other groups managed to raise the political and economic costs of trade too high for the Soviets and, in 1975, they took their business to Western Europe and Japan.

A few years later, in July 1978, President Carter's human rights foreign policy led him to suspend licensing for oil and gas equipment and technology. However, shortly thereafter a variety of events led to a resumption of trade, and 1979 heralded a new start for energy equipment exports to the Soviet Union. Indeed, there was even some hope in the business sector that the North Star project might be resurrected. But such hope was quashed with the Soviet invasion of Afghanistan and Carter's revival of the high-technology embargo, including even tighter controls on oil- and gas-related equipment.

Later, in an effort to disrupt the Urengoi gas pipeline to Western Europe, President Reagan first expanded the scope of the Carter controls in 1981, and then extended them extraterritorially to American subsidiaries and licensees in Western Europe. This unprecedented move caused outrage in Europe, increased the opposition of Congress, business, and the American public, and prompted the resignation of Secretary of State Alexander Haig. Under pressure from inside and outside the administration, President Reagan and the hard-liners capitulated and the controls were lifted in November 1982.

A close analysis of American policy in this area would raise and explicate some potentially interesting questions. These may be shaped by the particular policy area but have broader applicability to U.S. export control policy in general, and perhaps even to U.S. foreign economic policy. Some of the most pertinent questions revolve around the role and, particularly, the autonomy of the state—an entity similar to, but not synonymous with, Long's "Executive." Is the state an independent actor, an implement of societal preferences, a guardian of capitalist class or system interests, some combination of these, or something else? A confused or varying role for the state might well have significant implications for policy per se.

Theoretical Framework

A useful way of examining U.S. East-West energy trade policy, with these questions in mind, is to analyze it from the contrasting perspectives of three theories of the state and policy making: statism, liberal pluralism, and Marxism. The approach has been employed fruitfully in the past by Stephen Krasner, who elaborated and defended a statist paradigm against liberalism and Marxism in the area of international raw material investments.[1] More recently Jacobsen and Hofhansel have appraised the theoretical utility of statism and structural Marxism by examining the regulation of civilian nuclear trade.[2] Similarly, David Lake has juxtaposed statism and pluralism, looking at American tariff policies at the turn of the century.[3] Indeed, although not explicit about it, the preceding chapter has posited a statist position against a pluralist one in the area of export control policy.

The present piece is complementary to these studies in that it examines the explanatory capabilities of the three theories in the area of U.S.-Soviet energy trade policy. Notwithstanding Lowi's caveat, the study represents an application of some broad political science concepts to public policy.[4] While it is recognized that meaningful generalizations cannot be based upon just one policy-area study, it is assumed that some valid middle-range generalizations about the state and foreign economic policy can be drawn from present, past, and future studies. This and Long's chapter represent part of this process.

The theoretical perspectives of statism, liberal pluralism, and Marxism are analytically useful because they emphasize different distributions of power and different interests within the polity. They also ascribe different roles to the state and are, consequently, particularly valuable in examining the state's role in policy formulation and implementation.

Statism

The statist perspective views the state as an autonomous and dynamic entity.[5] As such, the state is thought to pursue a set of independently conceived goals in the name of the national interest. These policy goals have a number of distinctive features: they are the preferences of central decision-makers; they are general societal goals that do not consistently favor certain groups over others; they are rank ordered to determine priority and facilitate choice when there is conflict among them; they persist over time; they may include ideological as well as material objectives; and, although they are in the interests of society as a whole, they cannot "be understood as a reflection of societal characteristics or preferences."[6]

Through the use of its inherent, institutional power and shrewd leadership, the state is thought to be able to resist or deflect societal pressures which act against its conception of the national interest. Eric Nordlinger asserts that the democratic state is "markedly autonomous . . . even when its preferences diverge from the demands of the most powerful groups in civil society."[7] Indeed, the state may use its "autonomy-enhancing capacities and opportunities" to manufacture a "shift in societal preferences and/or the alignment of societal resources in order to make for non-divergent preferences," and translate its "preferences into authoritative actions."[8]

For each policy area there should be a list of central policy-makers' preferences for pursuing the national interest. An important task here will be to identify the national interest objectives of U.S. export control policy, especially how they relate to energy trade. If it can be demonstrated that the state formulated these goals independently, it will be necessary to judge how successful it has been in implementing them. This judgment can be made only if there is a "policy crisis," where the objectives of the state diverge from those of other public or private interests. U.S. energy equipment trade offers considerable promise in this respect, being situated at the crossroads between the strategic interests of the state and the economic interests of big business.

For Nordlinger the state consists of "those individuals who are endowed with society-wide decisionmaking authority."[9] For Krasner it is "a set of roles and institutions having peculiar drives, compulsions, and aims of their own that are separate and distinct from the interests of any particular societal group."[10] Both authors make a Hegelian state-society distinction which, though simplistic, is analytically imperative if the relative policy-making capabilities of the state and society are to be weighed.

Krasner's more limited, and flexible, distinction is the more useful starting point. In foreign economic policy, and foreign affairs generally, he holds the president and secretary of state to be the most important state actors by virtue of their "high degree of insulation from specific societal pressures" and their duties to further "the nation's general interests."[11] Other components of what we usually consider the state—for example, Congress and the Commerce and Defense departments—are more susceptible to societal pressures and are therefore excluded from, or at least denied a pivotal position in a statist conception of the state.

In identifying national interest objectives and determining the state's ability to implement them, it is therefore necessary to consider what an appropriate conception of the state is as far as export control policy is concerned.

Pluralism

Since political science moved away from formal-legalism in the 1940s, the pluralist perspective has dominated the study of American government and, as Long points out, has especially influenced theoretical approaches to trade policy. In contrast to statists, most pluralists look outside the state for the loci of policy-making power. For them politics consists of competition among societal interest groups, and public policy is the outcome of that competition. The role of the state is largely passive. It is confined to ensuring fair play and implementing the preferences of the strongest societal actors. It has no role in policy formulation and is frequently constrained by and dependent on private interests in implementing others' policy. It is in foreign economic policy that decisions have a specific impact on highly interested and powerful private actors and, consequently, this is where policy might be most influenced by private preferences. Certainly with export controls the economic costs fall disproportionately on particular business sectors, be they energy equipment or agriculture.

Neopluralist revisions view the state as one of the many competing groups, but even here it is denied an autonomous role. For example, the state is not thought to conceive of policy independently in terms of a national or public interest that transcends an aggregate of private interests. For pluralists national interest, if it exists at all, is not formulated independently by an autonomous state but rather is merely a reflection of general societal preferences.[12]

The state is also denied an autonomous role because it has "no cohesive center of decision-making." Whether defined as a collection of formal institutions or individuals occupying particular positions, pluralists see the locus of power shifting within the state "depending on the interests and power resources associated with particular issues."[13] If a case were to be made for statism in foreign economic policy, it would have to be shown that the locus of power was seated firmly within a limited conception or part of the state rather than passing between a variety of public bureaucracies and private groups depending on the issue in question. To make a statist argument in export control policy, therefore, one would have to show that that part of the state responsible for policy demonstrated a consistently high degree of autonomy. Theoretically, one has to choose between a limited conception of the state or, as suggested earlier, a limited part of the state.

Marxism

Marxism cannot be neglected as a tool of analysis because of the size and resources of the business interests involved in energy trade. Marxist perspectives on the state may be divided into the instrumental and structural. Like pluralists, instrumental Marxists hold that public policy is a direct response to societal pressure. Unlike pluralists, however, who believe that no societal group is "able to achieve a decisive and permanent advantage in the process of competition,"[14] instrumental Marxists contend that a cohesive capitalist class exerts a monopoly of control over the state through an old-boy network, and through a process of assimilation into the ruling, capitalist class. They would cite as evidence the high turnover of personnel between the highest echelons of government and big business. Kautsky summed up this position concisely with his observation that "[t]he capitalist class reigns but does not govern. It is satisfied, however, to rule the government."[15] This is not to say that other societal groups cannot influence the state, but if their preferences are incompatible with those of capitalism they will likely go unheeded.

Structural Marxists view the state from a somewhat broader perspective. Rather than seeing the state defending particular capitalist preferences as a result of common class ties, structuralists assign the state the slightly more autonomous role of ensuring the continued viability of the capitalist system by managing its inherent contradictions. Policy may therefore be seen as the state's attempt to cope with these contradictions. Marxists from Lenin on have concluded that because of declining rates of profit, underconsumption, and other "contradictions," the state is compelled to pursue an expansionary, imperialist foreign economic policy. Thus, while the state may be autonomous of direct pressure from the capitalist class, it must, nevertheless, formulate and implement policy according to the imperatives of the capitalist system as a whole. Occasionally this may put it in conflict with the myopic preferences of segments of the capitalist class, perhaps even the whole business sector. One might wonder whether U.S. export control policy and the restrictions placed on energy equipment and technology could be justified in terms of the long-term viability of the capitalist system despite their apparently anti-expansionary impact.

It follows from this that, like pluralists, Marxists are skeptical of the notion of an autonomously conceived national interest. The state pursues policies that are in the interests of elements of the capitalist class or the capitalist system in toto.[16] Moreover, given the legacy of historical materialism and economic determinism, state policies are ultimately related to economic goals; "other objectives are instrumental not consummatory."[17] From this perspective, therefore, one has to look behind strategic and ideological justifications of policy.

Export Control Policy and U.S.-Soviet Energy Trade[18]

The Nixon Administration

Although the Nixon administration is usually characterized as pro-trade, it was highly reluctant to ease East-West trade restrictions when it came into office in 1969. It was Democratic senators who initiated pro-trade legislation. Most importantly, Senators Muskie (D.-Maine) and Mondale (D.-Minnesota) introduced the 1969 Export Expansion and Regulation Bill to liberalize American-Soviet trade. They argued that the prohibitive Export Control Act (ECA) was no longer reflective of the international climate and that low industrial productivity and sluggish export growth necessitated a change from cold war policies.

Nixon and Kissinger opposed the Muskie-Mondale bill; they contended that a liberalization of trade without linkage to the political aspects of East-West relations made no strategic sense, especially since the Soviets would derive most of the economic benefit from such a move. Despite public opinion and business interests that favored a less restrictive stance, the Nixon administration resisted and worked to gain the support of the more conservative House to force compromises on the Senate bill.

The legislative outcome was the 1969 Export Administration Act (EAA).[19] Although the new act was less restrictive than the ECA, the Senate version had been diluted considerably. The president retained much of his discretionary power in implementing export control policy and had to report his actions to Congress only to the extent that national security interests were not jeopardized by doing so; and, of course, this extent was itself subject to presidential discretion. Pro-trade measures were on the books, but the president remained the ultimate arbiter of when, where, and how much to liberalize East-West trade. Bruce Jentleson makes the point that in successfully mobilizing House support against the Senate bill, the Nixon administration demonstrated that a majority could still be mustered "against calling off the Cold War . . . and for deferring to the President (even one of the opposite party) in the sensitive area of foreign affairs."[20]

Yet just two and a half years later the same administration was engineering a major turnabout in East-West trade policy. Although some large-scale energy projects had been discussed earlier, the diplomatic foundations of the new policy were laid with the Nixon-Brezhnev summit in May 1972 when SALT I was signed. Of commercial significance was one of the Basic Principles of Relations between the superpowers, which held that: "The USA and the USSR regard commercial and economic ties as an important and necessary element in the strengthening of their bilateral relations and thus will actively promote such ties. They will facilitate cooperation between the relevant organizations and enterprises of the two countries and the conclusion of appropriate agreements and contracts, including long-term ones."[21]

Certainly the Nixon administration took its pledge seriously. It organized a number of governmental and quasi-governmental agencies as well as commercial agreements to facilitate a liberalization of East-West trade. At home the administration enlisted the support of its old liberal adversaries in the Senate to pass the Equal Export Opportunity Act, which gave the president discretionary power to, inter alia, drastically reduce the Commodity Control List (CCL) of restricted export items over a two-year period.[22] In July 1972 a three-year grain deal was signed with the Soviet Union that provided $750 million worth of credit through the Commodity Credit Corporation.[23] This set the stage for the comprehensive U.S.-Soviet Trade Agreement in October that sought to expand trade between the superpowers and provide most favored nation (MFN) status for Soviet exports in exchange for a settlement of the Soviet Lend-Lease debt. In addition, President Nixon opened up Eximbank financing of exports to the Soviet Union by declaring American-Soviet trade to be in the *national interest*.[24] However, with major financing required for some long-term projects under consideration, including $4 billion in credits and guarantees for the North Star and Yakutsk natural gas projects, Nixon requested an increase in Eximbank's loan authorization from $20 billion to $30 billion. Both this and MFN status required congressional approval, which was to prove elusive.

There were, of course, important economic reasons for the Nixon administration's dramatic policy change. Prominent and influential businessmen such as Armand Hammer, Donald Kendall, and David Packard had long criticized cold war trade policies and had vigorously espoused the economic benefits that new markets and investment opportunities in the East would bring, such as profits, jobs, and much-needed raw materials (especially energy). Certainly, in the throes of economic crisis, reflected in two years without industrial growth and a merchandise trade deficit, the administration was appreciative of these arguments, and with the 1973 OPEC crisis the particular economic benefits of East-West energy trade were brought sharply into focus. However, the primary motive for the new direction in policy was political; not so much the translation of a healthier economy into votes, but rather the more grandiose political benefits derived from economic interdependence with the Soviet Union that was the cornerstone of the Nixon-Kissinger "structure of peace."[25] The administration's purpose, as explained by Secretary of Commerce Peterson, was "to build in both countries a vested economic interest in the maintenance of a harmonious and enduring relationship. . . . If we can create a situation in which the use of military force would jeopardize a mutually profitable relationship, I think it can be argued that security will have been enhanced."[26]

Even more than agriculture, energy-related trade was of special importance in creating such a long-term "vested economic interest." The principal architect of the new strategy, Henry Kissinger, firmly believed that this sort of trade and investment would "leaven the autarkic tendencies of the Soviet system, invite gradual association of the Soviet economy with the world economy, and foster a degree of interdependence that adds an element of stability to the political equation."[27] This was largely because the Soviets were beginning to deplete their sources of easily exploitable oil and gas in the Urals and were seeking to develop massive but less accessible reserves in Siberia. Because Western equipment, technology, and credit were critical for the Soviets to do this, energy trade was considered particularly well suited to the economic inducement strategy. Consequently, the administration gave particular encouragement to energy-related projects. Indeed, at the June 1973 summit Nixon specifically urged "American firms to work out concrete proposals on these projects" that involved "the delivery of Siberian natural gas to the United States."[28] Although business required some governmental assistance in creating a conducive political environment for trade, liberalizing export control regulations, and providing some financial support, it needed little encouragement. The Soviet Union represented a massive, untapped source of profit as well as energy, and "[v]isions of billion-dollar deals danced like sugarplums in the heads of some American businessmen."[29]

In the aftermath of the 1972 Moscow summit and throughout 1973 numerous export contracts, technical and economic cooperation agreements, and major long-term projects were signed by American companies with the Soviet Union in the energy sector: General Electric had orders for $250 million of gas turbine compressors, Dresser Industries for $27.5 million, International Harvester for $26 million, and Caterpillar Tractor had an export order for $68 million of pipe-laying equipment; moreover, companies such as Occidental Petro-leum and Cooper Industries had agreed to find and exploit oil and gas reserves in return for some of the production. However, the jewels in the crown were the North Star and Yakutsk natural gas projects, for which the estimated export earnings were tremendous: $6.7 billion and $2.3 billion, respectively. In short, business's economic interest and the administration's political interest were great and coincidental.

However, there was no time to develop a sufficient degree of inter-dependence before East-West trade was effectively scuttled in Wash-ington. Vietnam, Watergate, and the White House's general lack of consultation with Congress combined to create a mistrust of the Exec-utive. Feelings on Capitol Hill were harnessed by presidential aspi-rant Senator Henry Jackson (D.-Washington), and used to pass con-vincingly an amendment to the 1974 Trade Act that made MFN status for Soviet exports contingent upon increased Jewish emigration from the Soviet Union.[30] This and the Stevenson-Church amendment, which similarly shackled Eximbank credits, were opposed to no avail by both the administration and business.[31] The amendments made both the economic and political costs of trade too high for the Soviets and, in 1975, they renounced the trade agreement and took their business to Europe and Japan—a move that was to cause numerous strategic, political, and economic problems for subsequent U.S. administrations.

The Carter Administration

The East-West trade and export control policies of the Carter admin-istration were unclear when it came into office. It wanted to expand trade but was concerned with the strategic costs involved and, to add another dimension of complexity, the president was personally com-mitted to promoting human rights as part of his foreign policy agenda. In August 1977, however, a policy was articulated in Presidential

Directive 18. This was largely inspired by Samuel Huntington, who had been brought into the White House by NSC adviser Zbigniew Brzezinski. Huntington wove his and Brzezinski's concerns about Soviet intervention in the Third World and Carter's human rights concerns into a policy of economic diplomacy that advocated the use of trade as a tool to reward or punish, and thereby influence Soviet behavior. Although a more explicit and tougher variant of Nixon's economic inducement, it was again a strategy formulated within and to be implemented from the White House.

Energy trade was again considered especially susceptible to linkage. The beliefs that had influenced the Nixon administration had been reaffirmed in Carter's with the release in April 1977 of a CIA report that forecast grave problems for the Soviet oil industry.[32] Another CIA report released in July confirmed for many the dependence of the Soviets on Western equipment and technology, and their consequent vulnerability in this sector.[33] America's technological superiority in petroleum equipment (as evidenced by its 26 percent share of the Soviet market in 1977)[34] was thought to provide a particularly useful policy tool with which to influence Soviet behavior.

In July 1978 the trials of Soviet dissidents Ginsburg and Shcharansky, two American reporters, and an American businessman obliged the administration to implement the "stick" component of economic diplomacy. President Carter demonstrated his displeasure and tightened export controls by placing oil and gas equipment on the CCL and by freezing the review of Dresser Industries's license application for a turnkey rock-drill-bit factory. The effect of placing energy items on the CCL was not to create an embargo as such, but to subject export license applications to a case-by-case examination by the NSC and, ultimately, to presidential approval.[35] Huntington later explained that such institutional changes were necessary to "provide the president with the means to engage in creative and flexible economic diplomacy with the Soviets."[36] Part of this flexibility involved having no publicly announced guidelines for licensing. The Carter administration apparently saw an inverse relationship between *public* policy and flexibility: the less policy, the more flexibility.

The administration's actions in July and August seemed to yield results as September 1978 saw an improvement in American-Soviet relations: on September 5 the American businessman was convicted and expelled from the Soviet Union, and the next day the Dresser license was approved. Progress was also made on the SALT II negotiations and, furthermore, a number of dissidents were permitted to emigrate.

The administration's decision to resume energy trade was also related to the growing awareness of the problems associated with the trade deficit. In September President Carter presented a set of initiatives for a "New Export Policy." Among these were measures to "reduce the domestic barriers to exports" in which the president instructed executive departments to take the export consequences and foreign availability into account when "considering the use of export controls for foreign policy purposes."[37] Such an initiative had obvious application to East-West energy trade and, while the highly controlled licensing process was still tiresome for exporters, no license applications were turned down for the next fifteen months. As a result, many pre-1978 orders were filled and, with new orders, oil and gas equipment exports increased by almost 100 percent to $164 million in 1979. The United States became one of the Soviet Union's most important suppliers, with up to 45 percent of the market at one time.[38] Moreover, despite the barriers posed by amendments to the 1974 Trade Act, even the ill-fated North Star project was "reactivated" with the help of West European financial support.[39]

The security-economic tension in East-West trade was evident in the divisions outside and within the admininstration when the EAA came up for renewal in 1979. While some congressmen and Defense officials wanted more restrictive legislation, others in Congress, along with State, Commerce, and Treasury officials, business interests, and the president, were more export conscious and favored a further liberalization of trade.

The time and money that energy equipment and other trade associations had invested in their lobbying effort seemed well spent in that the final act was indeed more pro-trade. Some business representatives even contended that the act put "significant constraints on the presidential use of controls for foreign policy reasons."[40] However, the "constraints" amounted only to directions to consult with Congress, to negotiate with other governments (to eliminate foreign availability), and to exercise restraint in imposing export controls. What is more, a proposal for a congressional veto of foreign policy export controls was rejected by Senate-House conferees and replaced by the requirement of prior consultation with Congress.[41] Indeed, although Carter's effectiveness in influencing the legislative process had been hampered by disagreement within the Executive, the final act was largely as he had wished.

The degree to which the new EAA was only nominally pro-trade, and to which the president's discretionary powers remained intact, became evident in the aftermath of the Soviet invasion of Afghanistan. President Carter declared that no nation "committed to world peace and stability can continue to do business as usual with the Soviet Union."[42] In addition to the much-publicized grain embargo, a ban on phosphate exports, and a prohibition on exports connected with the 1980 Moscow Summer Olympics, Carter expanded energy equipment controls and suspended all existing validated licenses for high-technology exports to the Soviet Union (including that for Dresser's $144 million deal) pending a review of U.S. export-licensing procedures. When that review was completed in March 1980 a case-by-case reevaluation of outstanding validated licenses and pending applications was conducted, applying new, stricter criteria and subjecting oil and gas technology to a "presumption of denial." Of 476 current licenses reevaluated by the Department of Commerce, 115 were revoked, 54 were canceled, and (as of September 1981) 26 remained suspended.[43] The effect on American-Soviet energy trade was devastating: oil and gas equipment exports fell 67 percent to $51 million for 1980, and an estimated $1 billion in sales was lost when four energy-related projects were shelved.[44] Although the White House, and society at large, was divided over the question of sanctions, the president's will prevailed.

The Reagan Administration

Even before he reached the White House Ronald Reagan's position on East-West technology transfer was unambivalent. Capitalizing on the widespread anti-Soviet sentiment during his election campaign, he asked: "Why shouldn't the Western world quarantine the Soviet Union until they decide to behave like a civilized nation?"[45] He opposed East-West trade on moral, economic, and strategic grounds; and with the appointment of like-minded men to key executive positions, such objections pervaded his administration.

State policy developed out of an NSC paper that outlined a "prudent approach" to East-West trade. It emphasized the strategic objections to such trade and technology transfer, reflecting the deep concern in the administration about the direct and indirect contribution of Western equipment and technology to Soviet military capability. Early in its term the administration conducted a review of export control policy and concluded that it was necessary to tighten both U.S. and multilateral controls to prevent the "leakage" of items that could contribute to the Soviet defense industry.

Of course, energy trade was especially affected by the tighter regulations. However, exceptions were made, and a number of validated licenses were issued in 1981 for energy-related exports. In July, for example, a license was granted to Caterpillar to export one hundred pipe-layers worth $40 million; and early in December President Reagan approved a license for the company to export a further two hundred pipe-layers worth $90 million.[46] Caterpillar's success was partly due to its bargaining with the president (and its agreement that at least the first hundred pipe-layers should not be used on the Soviet–West European Urengoi pipeline), and certainly not unrelated to the support of its senator, Senate Foreign Relations Committee Chairman Charles Percy, and its congressman, House Republican leader Robert Michel.

Despite its useful connections, however, Caterpillar was one of many energy equipment companies to suffer when the Reagan administration reacted to Soviet complicity in the December 1981 imposition of martial law in Poland. Sanctions against the Soviet Union included the suspension of issuance or renewal of validated export licenses, an expansion of the list of oil and gas items requiring validated licenses, and non-renewal of certain energy and technical cooperation agreements. General Electric alone stood to lose $170 million in sales of rotor blades to its European manufacturing associates.[47] Nevertheless, because American high-technology exports accounted for only 4 percent of the Western total, the impact of the sanctions was extremely limited. They did nothing to change the situation in Poland and, more important perhaps, failed to affect progress on the Urengoi pipeline, which was the main target of the sanctions and which the administration had been opposed to from the outset.

Impelled by its own strategic concerns and harangued by congressional hawks like Henry Jackson for not doing enough, the administration extended the sanctions to U.S. subsidiaries and licensees abroad in June 1982. The extraterritorial extension was widely condemned. The allies were furious, calling the action an unacceptable interference in their sovereign affairs and "repugnant to international law."[48] At home the new controls prompted the resignation of Secretary of State Haig and, inevitably, produced a strong reaction from business. The U.S. Chamber of Commerce expressed its concern about the direction of U.S. international economic policy and contended that with exporters standing to lose an estimated $1.2 billion directly, the sanctions were "not in the best interests of the country." The president of the National Association of Manufacturers decried the action as "confusing, contradictory, and counterproductive."[49] Congress was also alarmed by the turn of events, especially the apparent ease with which the president had ridden roughshod over the spirit of the EAA. Rejecting administration protests that the president's "flexibility and authority" to deal with major crises would be crippled, the House Foreign Affairs Committee initiated legislation to repeal the oil and gas controls.[50] Without strong support from the public, and under pressure from Secretary of State Shultz, the administration was unable to resist the powerful coalition of the allies, business, and Congress and was forced to lift the sanctions in November 1982. Despite their classification as transmission equipment, however, pipe-layers remained on the CCL—with exploration and production equipment—until the Senior Interagency Group on International Economic Policy recommended decontrol in August 1983.[51]

Although the administration lost the pipeline battle, the war was not over. During the lengthy renewal of the 1979 EAA the hard-liners continued to push for tighter U.S. and multilateral controls of high technology. The EAA debate was to prove highly contentious. While the president wanted to safeguard and even extend his authority in this policy area, many in Congress felt that he, and President Carter before him, had violated the spirit, if not the letter of the EAA.

In April 1983 President Reagan sent his security-oriented bill to Congress. It proposed an expanded role for Defense in licensing in order to guard against the transfer of dual-use technology and contained a provision to ban imports from overseas companies that violated U.S. national security controls. The bill sought to pacify business with a clause protecting contract sanctity against foreign policy export controls. However, pro-traders dismissed this for not doing enough because, for one thing, it was limited to contracts requiring the delivery of goods within 270 days. This was inadequate for energy-related contracts, which were typically longer term. In addition, the president could still apply controls retroactively if the contracts would adversely affect overriding U.S. national interests. Consequently, the "administration's bill did little to allay the concerns of the pro-trade coalitions."[52]

In an effort to protect and promote export interests a House bill sought to prohibit the extraterritorial extension of foreign policy export controls, deny the president an import ban, liberalize West-West licensing procedures, require the president to seek specific congressional approval for extraterritorial national security controls, and generally reduce the president's discretionary powers.

An amended EAA finally emerged from Congress in June 1985. Although some concessions were made to the pro-trade lobby, the combined security consciousness of the Executive and the Senate was quite evident. For trade, some low-technology items to COCOM countries were decontrolled, licensing was eased if comparable goods were widely available, and retroactive foreign policy controls were prohibited "except in the most extreme circumstances" where U.S. strategic interests were threatened.[53] The president was required to specify the nature of the national security threat and the necessity of retroactive controls to Congress. Such consultation provisions were to be "strictly honored." For control, the act increased the Pentagon's role by establishing a national security control office under a Defense under secretary, included provisions to strengthen COCOM, continued the NSC's overseer function, and incorporated the import ban provision—a new arrow to the president's export control quiver. Although Reagan was unhappy with the reporting requirements, he was generally pleased that the act maintained "adequate presidential authority to respond to those instances where the country's strategic interests are at risk."[54]

Like the 1979 EAA, the amended act requires that all foreign policy controls be renewed and justified by the administration on an annual basis. Despite business opposition, controls on energy equipment and technology were renewed in 1986. The administration did, however, change the licensing policy from general denial to one of case-by-case review with the presumption of approval.[55] Throughout 1986 numerous government and private institutions reported that the foreign policy controls on oil and gas equipment were ineffective and, indeed damaging to the ailing U.S. energy equipment industry. Consequently, in January 1987 Commerce Secretary Baldrige concluded "that it is no longer in our national interest to keep these unilateral foreign policy controls on exports of oil and gas equipment and technology to the Soviet Union," and allowed them to lapse.[56]

Analysis

Having presented the raw data, as such, the task is now to apply each of the three theoretical perspectives. In doing this it is hoped that more will be learned about the nature of export control policy making, the validity of Long's conclusion, and the utility of the theories. The analysis proceeds by theory rather than administration, outlining some of the major issues, tasks, or problems associated with each theory and then considering their contextual support in relation to the points outlined.

Statism

In determining the applicability of statism to this policy area, one is faced with a number of tasks: defining the state, identifying the goals pursued for the national interest, determining whether the state formulates these goals independently, and assessing the state's success in implementing them.

It is apparent from the preceding description of events that there was rarely any policy consensus within what we might consider the state. Disagreements between and within the executive and legislative branches of government were frequent. Statism requires a conception of the state as an actor within which there is considerable consensus on what policy should look like and how it should be implemented.[57] The White House provides us with the most cohesive actor on export control and energy trade policy within each of the three administrations discussed. Although the evidence suggests that the president was the single most important individual, it is also apparent that certain NSC officials were instrumental in policy making in this area. One has only to reflect on the influence of Kissinger and Brzezinski in this regard.[58] Of course, a conception of the state that includes the NSC extends it beyond the physical location of the White House because of the positions of the State and Defense secretaries on the council. I shall use the White House label here, though, because it not only emphasizes the roles and interests of State and Defense NSC members as "White House men," rather than outside bureaucrats, but also allows for the inclusion of other "outsiders" who shape and facilitate the president's designs.[59] I am particularly mindful here of Reagan appointees Perle and Brady who were in Defense and Commerce, respectively.[60] My conception of the state therefore extends beyond the president and key White House staff to include other government officials who help formulate and implement policy. Although it may appear arbitrary to manipulate the state thus, it is necessary to bear in mind that the state is not a tangible entity; rather it is a useful fiction to be fashioned into an appropriate analytical tool.

Having conceptualized the state, we must identify those objectives that constitute the national interest in this policy area. Since the EAA is and has been the basic export control statute since 1969, it is instructive to look at its declared objectives. Despite disclaimers that it is U.S. policy to minimize uncertainties in export control policy and to encourage trade, each EAA has posited three rationales for imposing restrictions on U.S. exports: to preserve national security, to promote U.S. foreign policy, and to guard against short supply of important commodities in the domestic economy. These fundamental objectives are concerned with broad national interests and have persisted through each of the three acts. Given their breadth and the latitude of the state to make policy within them, it is not surprising that each administration has understood them to be in the national interest.

What evidence is there to suggest that the state autonomously formulated and implemented export control and energy trade policy in this period? To begin, the Nixon-Kissinger state resisted congressional and societal pressure to liberalize East-West trade. It succeeded in defeating a more pro-trade Senate bill, passing instead the 1969 EAA, which established its national interest objectives and retained the president's discretionary or "autonomy-enhancing" powers in this area. Only after Nixon and Kissinger had formulated the policy of détente, and only when the time was politically ripe, was business encouraged to do the state's will by creating a "vested economic interest" for a "harmonious and enduring" superpower relationship;[61] as Long points out, this was almost three years *after* the EAA was passed.[62] By channeling business's interests, the state demonstrated a capacity to implement a policy that it had autonomously conceived and that it believed was in the national interest by enhancing national security. Moreover, Congress was rarely consulted and was constantly bypassed in the diplomatic and economic negotiations with the Soviets. Nixon's and Kissinger's preference for "quiet diplomacy" and "back channel" meetings was well known, as was Kissinger's belief that "Congress was to be seen and not heard in the *affairs of state.*"[63] However, the White House was to discover the limits on what it could do without Congress, and ultimately Kissinger's penchant for centralized decision-making power was to prove disastrous. Arguably, it was the state's general alienation of Congress from the foreign policy-making process that led to its decline—especially with the passage of the Jackson-Vanik amendment (to be discussed later). From an analytical perspective, however, the Nixon admininstration provides an insufficiently critical test of statism because of the "happy convergence" that existed between state and business interests in this policy area. This rarely existed in the Carter and Reagan admininstrations.

Carter's commitment to human rights and his advisers' concerns with Soviet–Third World relations formed the bases for the formulation of a new approach to export control and energy trade. Although his policy was different from the Nixon administration's, its formulation and implementation were still very much centralized within the White House. Both Kissinger and the architects of Carter's policy believed that this centralization was crucial to provide maximum flexibility for the president in policy making. This became apparent in July 1978, when a policy crisis developed between the state and American high-technology exporters after the Soviets arrested three Americans in Moscow. Had President Carter not been particularly sensitive to human rights issues the arrests may well have gone unpunished by the United States in any material sense. However, the president chose to override the business interests at stake and tighten export controls. This was a clear illustration of the state's ability to implement an autonomously conceived policy against the wishes of a very powerful societal actor. Moreover, by placing certain energy items on the CCL, thereby subjecting them to NSC review and presidential approval, the state increased its "autonomy-enhancing capacities and opportunities" for the future. Indeed, when superpower relations improved the state began to ease controls and issue licenses for controlled energy technology. Of course, this rare convergence between the state and business interests again makes it analytically difficult to determine whether statism, pluralism, or some hybrid was at work. Was the improvement in U.S.-Soviet relations the sole determinant, was it business pressure, or was it some combination? In the real world, which theories rarely replicate, I suspect it was the latter possibility.

Nevertheless, even with a supposedly pro-trade EAA, the state could use these capacities to condemn the Soviets for their invasion of Afghanistan at the expense of American business. Again, during a policy crisis between national and commercial interests, the state's conception of the national interest prevailed. Obviously the state was not alone in wishing to take action against the Soviets, but it is significant that it could do so in the face of considerable opposition from business, with its vast resources and influence in Congress.

The Reagan administration faced a similar policy crisis during the pipeline dispute, when the state's objectives came into conflict with business's multi-million-dollar interest. The dispute is interesting, from a statist perspective, in that the state was able to exploit the Polish situation to manufacture some congressional and societal support for sanctions against the Urengoi pipeline—a project that few outside the state saw as a security threat. This was done by framing the national interest primarily in terms of the need to react to Soviet complicity in Polish martial law, rather than the need to prevent West European dependence on Soviet natural gas. Although the support that the state acquired through this tactic was not needed, it increased the state's capacity to act or, in statist terms, enhanced its autonomy.

The pipeline case is also interesting because it is arguable that, in restricting foreign use of energy equipment previously exported from the United States, the Reagan administration violated international law and because Congress did not intend the EAA to override international law, the state implemented policy beyond that legislation's permissible bounds.[64] This implies that even if the state is denied the necessary institutional means to achieve its goals in the formulation of policy as legislation, a statist case might still be made by examining the way legislation is actually used (or abused). This goes beyond Long's basic conclusion and raises an important question about the accountability of the state to Congress and to the American public. The pipeline example seems to reveal a gap between legislative intent and policy implementation that allowed the state to act to the disadvantage of business.

Pluralism

At first glance the complexity of actors, interests, and perceptions seem to make pluralism the most useful way of making sense of this policy area. However, there are problems. For one thing the evidence for statism is fairly compelling, and one would have to demonstrate here that the locus of power shifted among a variety of competing public and private actors, rather than being located within the state —albeit a limited conception thereof. Moreover, it is important not to mistake the mere existence of different interests and disagreement with pluralism in action. To make a case for pluralism one would have to show that competition and disagreement actually resulted in different outcomes—outcomes that did not consistently favor any one particular group, be it the state or business.

The evidence immediately demands that pure pluralism, or any variant that views the state as a passive receptacle of societal interests, be rejected in this instance. The state *is* an independent actor; the question is whether it has a monopoly of policy-making power or whether power is distributed among it and other actors interested in export control and U.S.-Soviet energy trade policy.

The Jackson-Vanik and Stevenson-Church amendments sharply constrained the state's capacity to pursue détente independently by denying it the necessary economic "carrots." The amendments undercut state policy and, in effect, formulated a more demanding policy of explicit linkage. This new policy was undoubtedly a result of pluralistic pressures. A coalition of labor, consumer, academic, and influential Jewish organizations joined forces with a newly assertive

Congress to pass the damaging legislation.[65] This was done against both the economic interests of business and what the state perceived to be the national interest.

Additional evidence of pluralism in action is sketchier. One could, for example, regard Carter's human rights concerns not as an autonomously formulated element of his foreign policy but rather as a response to a need of the American people, perhaps a societal need to recapture the moral high ground in the post-Vietnam and Watergate period. Unfortunately, it is analytically difficult to assess the relative merits of pluralism and statism here because of the convergence between state and societal preferences. Of course, one might argue that Carter's concerns were *part of* the societal need. This would pose a serious problem for statism regarding the degree to which the state can be insulated from society.

The EAA renewal debate in 1979 (and similarly in 1983–85) is often viewed from a pluralist perspective.[66] The plethora of actors, the inter- and intra-governmental divisions, and the opposition of economic and security interests set the stage for a classic pluralistic struggle. The final act is thought to reflect the considerable time and money invested by high-tech and other trade associations and the ineffective role of an Executive crippled by internal dissention. Yet just three months later, despite the pro-trade EAA, the dissolution of cold war attitudes, increased export needs, and a "weakened presidency," Carter emerged as the "key player" who "acted decisively" in the face of "considerable resistance," to punish the Soviets for their incursion into Afghanistan.[67] Most of the economic sanctions remained in effect for the remainder of Carter's presidency. Arguably, the very lack of consensus in favor of the sanctions attests to the capacity of the state to act independently in what it perceives to be the national interest. Moreover, the rare "success" of the export lobby in renewing the EAA becomes questionable. The state's continued ability to act decisively in this admittedly small policy area throughout the fragmented and supposedly vacillatory Carter tenure casts doubt upon a pluralistic interpretation of events. Whatever its merits or demerits, the state's policy of economic diplomacy (or "light-switch diplomacy")[68] was by its very nature erratic and therefore *apparently* irresolute and subject to pluralistic pressures.

The pipeline embargo has already been analyzed from a statist perspective but the final outcome of the imbroglio was neglected —that is, that the state was finally obliged to rescind the controls. Bearing this in mind, the whole episode may also be usefully viewed from a pluralist perspective. Up to the imposition of sanctions, the granting and denial of licenses for Caterpillar (and perhaps Dresser before that) could be interpreted as a pluralistic struggle between the company and its congressional supporters on one hand, and the state and other security-conscious actors on the other. Interestingly, the same argument applied in the statist analysis about the increased autonomy of the state to act because of the Polish crisis may be used in a pluralist interpretation of events; that is, it was a change in the international context that gave the state additional resources (i.e., public support and even moral justification) in its competition with business. From the pluralist perspective the extraterritorial extension of controls is also significant because it expanded the pluralist arena to include a whole new set of important and influential actors who sided with American business in its struggle against the state —the European allies. With the benefit of hindsight we can see that the overseas application of controls was a strategic error in terms of state autonomy; the international pressure that the allies brought to bear tipped the balance of power against the U.S. state. Remember, however, that the state was *able* to impose extraterritorial controls even though they were to prove unenforceable and, ultimately, counterproductive. It is also worth remembering at this point that the analysis only applies to the effect of export controls on energy trade. A stronger pluralist argument might be made if we were looking at agricultural trade, for example, which President-elect Reagan had promised immunity from controls.[69]

Like the 1969 EAA renewal, the 1983–85 debate is often seen as a pluralistic struggle. Indeed, the very length of the renewal of the 1979 act is taken to be indicative of pluralism. I would suggest though, bearing in mind the interests of the actors, that the actual outcome of the debate is more important than its nature. Even more so than the 1979 EAA, the 1985 amendments protected the capacity of the state to act and to control East-West trade. A problem arises, however, if one engages in "what if?" speculation. For example, what if the state did not have to contend with congressional or business concerns? What if the state had a completely free hand? If so, the 1985 Export Administration Amendments Act might well have been as restrictive as the cold war Export Control Act. Unfortunately, while this speculation raises valid questions, it can never be resolved categorically.

Finally, the lifting of export controls on non-strategic energy equipment in January 1987 could be explained as a result of pluralistic pressures. There were certainly many business groups, such as the National Association of Manufacturers and the Petroleum Equipment Suppliers Association, who lobbied hard for decontrol. And, given their involvement, it would be difficult to argue that the state decided independently to lift the controls. There were also some conservative congressmen and Jewish groups who opposed decontrol. However, it would be simplistic to attribute the decontrol of energy equipment to successful lobbying alone; there were most likely a multiplicity of reasons behind the decision, some unrelated to business's lobbying efforts. Obviously the reasons cited by the administration and business were important: some claimed that the original objectives of the 1978 controls had been achieved and so they were no longer necessary; others identified the existence of over six hundred foreign suppliers of comparable equipment;[70] and, finally, everybody recognized the debilitating effect that the controls had on the already depressed energy equipment industry and the loss of tens of thousands of U.S. jobs. There was also the broader concern about the trade deficit in Washington at this time. President Reagan had pledged himself to improve the trade deficit and U.S. global "competitiveness," and the fact that the Soviet 1986–90 Five-Year Plan earmarked 20 percent of all industrial investment for the oil industry made decontrol of energy equipment a useful way of helping to tackle these problems.[71] Then there was the possibility that decontrol had more to do with politics than economics: namely the hope within the administration that helping the Soviets develop their domestic energy resources would discourage Soviet involvement in the oil-rich Gulf region.[72] In short, it would appear that during the second Reagan administration a "happy convergence" of interests developed between the state and business. Foreign availability, a depressed energy equipment sector, the trade deficit, and possible foreign policy benefits made for an unusual consensus between the state and business on the advantages of decontrolling oil and gas equipment. Again, it becomes difficult or even inappropriate to interpret the events in terms of either statism, pluralism or, indeed, Marxism. Nevertheless, while the theoretical perspectives may not offer any definitive explanation of events, they are still useful to the analyst in identifying different possible explanations. Using only a pluralist perspective, for example, one would automatically attribute the decontrol solely to a successful lobbying effort by business without any consideration of other, broader factors.

Marxism

The most important task for a Marxist interpretation of events in this area is to explain policy crises; that is, to explain why the interests of the state and business apparently diverge so often. Related to this is the problem of how export controls can be reconciled with the interests of exporters and/or the state's expansionist function. When controls on energy equipment cost exporters millions of dollars in lost sales, and billions more in lost market share, it is impossible to make a defensible case for instrumental Marxism. If there are socioeconomic ties between business and governmental elites, and if key administration officials hold corporate positions, the losses of Caterpillar and others suggest that such connections do not translate into political power over the policy-making process. Certainly Long's discussion of technical advisory committees demonstrates that business has very little institutionalized power over export control policy.[73]

Nevertheless, one might find an instrumental Marxist approach more fruitful when there is a happy convergence of state and business interests. Applying the approach to the period of détente, it is important to identify the direction of influence between the state and business, and to establish whether policy consistently favored business interests. The statist evidence about the formulation and carefully timed implementation of détente suggests, however, that the state was firmly in control of policy, and it was purely fortuitous for business that its interests happened to be in the national interest: what was good for America was good for General Electric!

Perhaps most damaging to an instrumental interpretation, however, is the fact that when administrations changed, policies changed —sometimes to the detriment of that sector of the capitalist class interested in energy technology exports. If the capitalist class did exert significant influence in this area, we would expect policy to consistently favor it *across* administrations. This is quite obviously not the case.

A more defensible case can be made for structural Marxism. Most important, policy crises may be explained by arguing that foreign policy efforts to curb Soviet expansionism are in the long-term interests of the capitalist system. This is because they attempt to safeguard overseas investment opportunities, markets, and raw materials. Brzezinski's and Huntington's concerns about Soviet activities in the Third World, for example, might be seen from this perspective; and Carter's sanctions against the Soviet Union could be interpreted not as a punishment for invading Afghanistan but rather as a warning that more serious measures would follow any Soviet attempts to jeopardize "the world's [read America's] oil supplies" in the Persian Gulf.[74] This warning was later made explicit in the "Carter Doctrine."[75] In this sense, as a means of protecting overseas economic interests, export controls represent a passive or negative variant of Lenin's imperialist arguments.

Similarly, policy crises may be explained by making a national security argument that "selling them the rope" is not in the long-term interests of the capitalist system. That is, while the short- to medium-term profit opportunities of high-tech exporters may be restricted, their long-term interests are safeguarded by denying the

Soviet Union any strategic value derived from dual-use or "resource-freeing" energy technology. Export control policy could, therefore, be seen as the state's way of coping with an inherent, but ultimately self-destructive tendency within the capitalist system to export regardless of the security costs. Paradoxically, this is precisely the argument used by many security-conscious conservatives;[76] it is also an odd denial of the business maxim "export or die!" The national security and foreign policy arguments are also interesting given the express goals of the EAA.

This structuralist rationalization of export controls, however, is not entirely satisfactory. For example, it is difficult to balance the security and foreign policy benefits of extraterritorial controls and strict West-West licensing with the economic costs. The resultant tendency of Western allies to reduce their dependence on American technology, for fear of future controls applied retroactively, can hardly be reconciled with the long-term interests of American exporters. Furthermore, this structuralist argument raises the problem of differentiating between the capitalist interest and the national interest. Krasner, for example, points out that "[o]ne man's foreign policy goal is another's long-term preservation of capitalism."[77] I shall return to this problem in the remaining section.

Conclusion

The analysis quite obviously presents a mixed picture. No one theoretical perspective adequately explains export control and East-West energy trade policy throughout this period. However, while each appears to have some validity and provides us with an interesting perspective on policy, I would contend that statism has considerable explanatory potential, and would therefore concur with Long's conclusion regarding the dominant power of the Executive in this policy area. Over three admininstrations the state adopted unique and distinctive policies, all formulated within the White House. While it would be naive to think that state actors can be entirely insulated from societal experiences and pressures, the policies formulated were not mere reflections of societal preferences. Although there was outside influence, it was not so much that of contemporary actors but rather that of certain geostrategic constants and the passive influence of the past—that is, the perceived need to improve on past policy in order to better serve the national interest. Having formulated policy, such as Carter's economic diplomacy, the state was able to implement it—sometimes in the face of tremendous opposition and intraexecutive conflict. In short, using its considerable resources, the state has been quite successful in pursuing its policy—up to a point.

It is important to bear in mind that although the state occasionally made concessions to other actors (e.g., pro-trade EAA language and licenses to Caterpillar and others), it rarely compromised its basic objectives in the pursuit of the national interest. The constant theme throughout the period, just as it was during the Cold War, was the state's concern with national security and foreign policy vis-à-vis the Soviet Union. This was reflected in the basic objectives of the EAA and in policy implementation. We can even see the pro-trade policy of détente as an attempt "to accomplish the same fundamental aim that animated the entire tradition of post-war American foreign policy: the containment of Soviet power."[78] Concessions can be made and East-West trade can still exist without the state's overall objectives being compromised because the state and other actors are not competing in a zero-sum game. The inclusion of an import ban in the amended EAA does not mean the end of East-West trade, nor does an export license for Caterpillar mean the complete erosion of national security.

Whereas the important work of Bertsch and Jentleson has emphasized the opposition and difficulties the state has faced in pursuing its policies, I have tended to emphasize the degree to which it has overcome constraints by considering policy outcomes—legislation and action—and how they compare with the state's preferences. Unlike Bertsch and Jentleson, I would conclude that although battles are lost and concessions made from time to time, the state has achieved a large measure of success over the years that is even more impressive *because of* the constraints and overall lack of consensus in this policy area. Again, it should be remembered that state power can only be assessed adequately when there is opposition and conflict—thus it would be inappropriate to test statism in the consensual cold war period. One should not assume that the mere existence of competition necessarily undermines the power of the state. Curiously, this suggests that the conditions for pluralism must be present to make a good case for statism.

The most conspicuous problem for the statist interpretation, however, is the Jackson-Vanik amendment, which curtailed the state's ability to pursue U.S.-Soviet trade as it had intended. While not denying the pluralistic nature of this, I would argue that the episode was exceptional. A variety of factors unrelated to export controls and energy trade conspired by chance to disrupt state policy: the state's indifference to Congress, Vietnam, Watergate, Senator Jackson's presidential aspirations, and a young, activist Congress ready to reassert its role in foreign policy making. These represented what Paula Stern calls the "idiosyncratic qualities of this period."[79] Most damaging to the capacity of the state to function effectively was, of course, Watergate. The scandal and possible impeachment so distracted and weakened Nixon that, according to Kissinger, he barely governed during his last eighteen months in office. Stern concludes that the Jackson-Vanik amendment "shows under what circumstances a congressman can effectively compete with the executive branch on foreign policy issues."[80] It is evident that such circumstances are highly unusual and that this episode represents a unique problem for a statist interpretation of events, rather than an undermining of the general applicability of the theory.[81]

Theda Skocpol suggests that "one of the most important facts about the power of a state may be its *unevenness* across policy areas."[82] This may offer a different, but related, explanation of the "defeats" of the state. Different policy areas are not isolated from one another, and there is often overlap between them. We might ask, therefore, what happens when a policy area in which the state is dominant overlaps with one where it is not? If the overlap is sufficiently great perhaps the state will lose power where it once prevailed. It is most likely the case that the state does not dominate all policy areas. Given this, the broader an issue becomes, the more policy areas it affects and the more the state's autonomy and power are dissipated. Perhaps instances of pluralism in export control and energy trade policy could be explained by this phenomenon, which I call the "policy overlap" thesis. The evidence suggests that the state has a high degree of autonomy in this policy area, but there are times when other actors enter the arena to challenge the state, perhaps when there is overlap with policy areas in which the state is not dominant. Certainly the Jackson-Vanik amendment was not just about export controls or energy trade. As I mentioned earlier, a wide range of issues was involved. Most broadly, in this respect, was perhaps the alienation of Congress from foreign policy, a problem that, in the aftermath of Vietnam, Congress sought to redress. Lacking sufficient power in the wider foreign policy arena, the state's East-West trade policy fell victim to this assault. Similarly, the pluralist finale of the pipeline fiasco could be explained in terms of an overlap of policy areas. Arguably, the overlap of American export control policy with West European trade policy and, more broadly, its interference with the allies' sovereignty resulted in the state's loss of autonomy in the smaller policy area it previously had dominated. Again, this is not to deny the pluralist interpretation of events but rather to explain them as aberrations from the "normal" statist pattern in this policy area.

I have suggested that no one theoretical perspective adequately explains the events described in this policy area. While I have favored the statist perspective, it is not without problems. I am led to believe that there is some convergence among all of the theories at certain points. Statism may be useful in explaining some policy areas (e.g., U.S.-Soviet energy trade), while pluralism may account for other areas and the broader picture (e.g., U.S. foreign policy or East-West trade in general). There is therefore a convergence of the two theories at the border between policy areas. Rejecting the policy-overlap thesis makes it even more difficult to distinguish between statism and pluralism when the state is *usually* dominant. That is, at what point do state "defeats" discredit statism? How many times does the state have to be defeated in a policy area before the pluralist model becomes applicable? The same problem exists in differentiating between pluralism and Marxism. How many times does the capitalist class or system have to lose out on an issue before pluralism becomes more appropriate? Of course there is no magic number, and it may even be inappropriate to talk about "defeats" given the non-zero-sum nature of competition. This lack of clear winners and losers on an issue makes it even more difficult to distinguish among the theories at times. These are intriguing problems but, unfortunately, they are beyond the scope of this chapter. Of course, the big problem regarding convergence is distinguishing between statism and structural Marxism: "What is good for society as a whole will be good for its leading economic institutions."[83] Krasner suggests that state actions that violate the fundamental tenets of capitalism do not square with a structuralist interpretation.[84] However, the national security and foreign policy arguments I posited earlier are fairly compelling. When policy crises arise between national security or foreign policy goals and capitalist principles, the latter are sacrificed. Export controls per se are antithetical to free-market principles, but this does not necessarily undermine the structuralist argument if national security and foreign policy objectives defend capitalism from the anti-capitalist designs of the Soviet Union.

To sum up, a good case can be made for statism in the area of export control and energy trade policy. Proceeding along a slightly different route and in a different fashion, this chapter supports the findings of the preceding one. Undoubtedly, pluralist episodes exist, but they can be explained either as unique aberrations or by reference to the policy-overlap thesis. However, while the evidence offers instrumental Marxism little support, structural Marxism poses a major theoretical difficulty. This represents a pressing research problem, one that needs to be resolved if we wish to assess the distribution of political power by applying these theoretical perspectives to other areas of East-West trade and foreign economic policy in general.

3

The Distribution of Power and the Inter-agency Politics of Licensing East-West High-Technology Trade

John R. McIntyre

Introduction: A Perennial Problem

This chapter focuses on the bureaucratic implementation[1] of U.S. national security export control policy[2] in the East-West context and, by logical extension, in the West-West context for dual-use commodities.[3] In the past ten years or so a growing body of literature on U.S.-Western export policy specifically, and technology transfer more generally, has emerged.[4] To a large extent this evolving body of writing has focused on the legal, economic, and commercial dimensions of technology transfer regulations.[5] Since 1981 the strategic dimension has also been the focus of much government attention and research.[6] In the same period the politics of the Western alliance and COCOM on matters of technology trade have also received much attention.[7] The institutionalization, codification, and operation of the U.S. national security export control regime has, however, received scant scholarly treatment, though congressional committees have devoted extensive oversight hearings to the topic.[8] A systematic review of the literature reveals substantial gaps in treatments of the export administration machinery and the politics of the implementation of the Export Administration Act.[9] This lacuna is due in part to the genuine problem of data access to a somewhat hermetic bureaucracy, and the marked preference of scholars for the policy-formation phase, to the detriment of internal and inter-agency considerations.

One of the first scholars to research the export control process stated in a landmark study in 1974 that the fundamental policy problem confronting export control was "to structure and manage the trade-off between [U.S.] benefits from trade and the adverse implications of them: a problem briefly stated, yet difficult to specify."[10] Former Congressman J. Bingham, a longtime actor in the export administration reform process, posed the problem differently in 1979: "How can we fashion an export control system that protects the national interest, without overburdening the bureaucracy that would implement the controls with either impossible judgments or unmanageable paperwork? How can we impose export controls without unnecessarily frustrating U.S. exports and losing business to other countries, including some of our closest allies?"[11] Writing some seven years later, after the 1979 and 1985 revisions to the Export Administration Act, Congressman Don Bonker (D-Washington), Bingham's successor as chairman of the House Foreign Affairs Subcommittee on International Economic Policy and Trade, noted that the Reagan administration "has been unsuccessful in implementing an export control policy that balances the equally critical goals of protecting national security and promoting U.S. exports."[12]

Devising an implementation mechanism that can minimize both strategic risks in transferring dual-use technologies and the uncertainty for exporters in regulating trade flows is by no means a novel problem. Cipolla has noted that the problem of regulating the exportation of new metals and metal-working techniques or sail-making techniques generated much controversy in Elizabethan England. In Cipolla's words the natural result was a "succession of petitions, proposals, arguments and counter-arguments, acts of Parliament and regulations of licenses on a scale sufficient to delight the heart of any Dr. Parkinson of those days."[13] This description is not altogether inapplicable to the present-day peacetime dual-use controls.

The character of export control problems is strikingly similar in the postwar era, no matter what administration occupies the White House. The central premise of this chapter is that current export licensing performance is not satisfactory, however measured and from whatever perspective, due to both the actual policies and their implementation. It may in fact be impossible to say whether the policies misfire because they are based on bad theory or overly complex legislation, or because they are sound ideas poorly executed by the bureaucracy.

The chapter first reviews the statutory embodiment of export control policy—the Export Administration Act—in terms of the mandate it specifies for the executive branch to implement. Second, the dynamics of export control implementation are reviewed in the light of well-known inelasiticities of process in implementing international economic policy in the United States. Third, we address the organizational and political controversies surrounding the question of where in the executive branch to locate the export control function. Fourth, a statutory analysis of the distribution of power among the licensing actors is presented. Fifth, a functional analysis of the export control actors is presented in terms of the listing, licensing, and enforcement functions. Sixth, a brief assessment of the national security export control system's performance is presented, and last, conclusions are offered in the form of recommendations.

Incompatible and Ambivalent Legislative Goals: The Search for Mandate Specificity

Within the overall framework of constitutional distribution of powers, legislative acts and executive orders define the general mandate and tasks for implementing agencies. If agencies are staffed with personnel who have values and worldviews at odds with the legislative mandate, the tendency will be to modify the legislative mandate during the implementation phase. Moreover, if the legislative language is ambiguous or vague—as is often the case in foreign economic or national security legislation—the executive agencies will have even freer latitude in interpreting the statute through regulatory and operational practices.

Since no legislative act can anticipate all administrative actions that may arise, it becomes difficult for the legislator to ensure congruency of congressional intent and bureaucratic action. The problem is further compounded when several agencies with opposite worldviews must implement the same legislative mandate.

How can legislators ensure that bureaucratic organizations implement the mandate in a way responsive to their expressed wishes? There are a number of traditional means to accomplish this, including oversight hearings, court review, clear lines of authority and responsibility, and so on. These techniques, when applied to export control policy, are problem ridden for a variety of reasons: (1) the well-accepted doctrine of executive branch dominance over the legislature in matters of national security and foreign affairs limits congressional oversight;[14] (2) the general exemption from the Administrative Procedures Act granted to export controls largely insulates the export process from the long arm of judicial review; and (3) the multi-agency nature of shared responsibility and authority blurs clear lines of accountability.

Since these techniques are of limited use, the basic conundrum for legislators binds the bureaucracy. This is often termed the "tight-loose" law dilemma. The more stringent and clear a statute's language, the less discretion for the implementing bureaucracy; the less stringent (i.e., the more general and vague) the statutory language, the more discretion is placed in the hands of implementors.

The Export Administration Act of 1979, as amended in 1985, offers a classic case of a statute positing incompatible and vague congressional goals. At the heart of the national security export control regime, and enshrined in the policy declarations section of the most recent avatar of the act, is a fundamental policy dilemma. The government is required simultaneously to promote one type of trade and control another type. These twin aspects of trade policy are exquisitely difficult to trade off against each other as they become politicized, yet they permeate all aspects of export control policy implementation. Section 3(1) of the act states, on the one hand, that it is the policy of the United States "to minimize uncertainties in export control policy and to encourage trade with all countries with which the United States has diplomatic or trading relations . . ." while, on the other hand, it is also U.S. policy "to restrict the export of goods and technology which would make a significant contribution to the military potential of any other country or combination of countries which would prove detrimental to the national security of the United States."[15]

This ambivalence of purposes can be traced back all the way to the original 1949 Export Control Act. The policy findings section of the act seeks to overcome this situation by providing further guidance for the act's administrators. But, in fact, it further highlights the profound contradictory nature of congressional intent in seeking simultaneously to optimize trade expansion and national security.

The history of export control legislation since 1949, and particularly since 1969, can be broadly characterized as a twofold attempt at reconciling these fundamentally, and often mutually exclusive policy goals, and at rationalizing export control procedures by binding the bureaucracy's discretion.[16]

The necessary underlying domestic political consensus that may have existed in the early days of the Cold War and American economic hegemony has eroded, leaving in its wake much ambiguity of purpose. Congress has produced increasingly more ambiguous mandates in seeking to please increasingly polarized interest groups and bureaucracies. This situation foreordains implementation problems.

Export Control as a Microcosm of the Implementation Inelasticities of International Economic Policy

Governmental regulation of international trade usually reflects a complex balance of contending values, which find their embodiment in statutory policies. What is of concern here is not so much the legislative policy itself but the policy's intended and unintended by-products as it is translated into action by multiple government agencies. A concern with implementation shifts the focus onto the organizational dynamics of the bureaucracy. It also entails an analytical shift from legislative and electoral (or grand) politics to bureaucratic politics.

Such a perspective is all the more relevant when the mandate is vague, contradictory, or highly complex, thereby enhancing the role of government machinery. While it is true that "good organizations do not ensure successful policy," as the Murphy Commission pointed out in the 1970s, organization does in fact "affect more than efficiency of government; it affects the outcomes of decisions."[17] A competing, though complementary view is that the priority issue is not so much mechanisms, or the allocation of powers and responsibilities to certain agencies, but people. Former Secretary of State Dean Rusk best expressed this view when he stated that the "real organization of the government [for the conduct of foreign affairs] is . . . how confidence flows from the President."[18]

Allison and Szanton, as well as Destler, have combined both emphases in their studies of foreign economic policy making, defining organizations as inclusive of structures (i.e., goals authority), process (how issues are identified, assessed, and decided), and people (i.e., influence, skills, attitudes).[19]

Running like a thread throughout the postwar efforts at reorganizing foreign affairs bureaucracies is the central problem of coordination and fragmentation. Harold Malmgren, a keen observer of the international economic policy area, succinctly diagnosed the problem as follows: "Widespread confusion exists as to who is responsible for what. Both policy and daily decision seem to be aimed in several directions simultaneously."[20]

While the appropriateness of organizational arrangements must be judged on a policy-by-policy basis, the export control regime offers a veritable laboratory to study the politics and organizational inelasticities of implementation evident in many areas of international economic policy.

Cohen, in a landmark study, boiled down to nine the major deficiencies of organizational process by which international economic policy is formulated and implemented in the U.S.[21]

— First, there is no optimal way of constructing a "grand design" to provide basic policy guidelines, consistency, and a sense of overall mission between the numerous sectors of international economic policy.

- Second, authority tends to be seized by the most power-oriented bureaucrats rather than being assigned on a rational basis.
- Third, at the upper echelons, organizational arrangements tend to be short-lived without the benefit of long tenures by high-level civil servants.
- Fourth, personalities often tend to dominate policy.
- Fifth, organizations often downplay the unique integrating perspective that might be provided by the White House; moreover, lacking presidential leadership and sustained involvement, no integrated vision exists.
- Sixth, there is no internal incentive to resolve inter-agency differences, barring the involvement of the president or a close surrogate.
- Seventh, coordination is exquisitely complex and often leads to inconsistency, duplication, and a haphazard treatment of issues.
- Eighth, actions are usually balanced and do not benefit from cost-benefit analysis. Political factors often prevail.
- Ninth, governmental institutions and business are separated by a wide semantic chasm and often the relationship is adversarial.

All these characteristics, to one degree or another, are evidenced in the export control process.

Where to Locate the Export Control Function and Why

The best guarantor of legislative mandate specificity, beyond specific and clear language itself, is the statutory specification of an implementation structure. The mere appointment of a lead agency and the legislative command to coordinate is not sufficient. The first organizational decision is in fact crucial to determining the fate of the policy. The course of institutional development is often irrevocably set by the choice of administrative agency. Seidman rightly notes that a policy is affected as much by *how* it is administered as by *where* it is administered.[22]

The original Export Control Act (ECA) of 1949 did not "indicate what Department of the Executive branch would administer the controls."[23] It merely authorized the president to delegate the authority conferred upon him to such departments or officials as he deemed appropriate. The ECA, however, did lay the groundwork for a multi-agency process when it specified that information and advice "shall be sought from the several executive departments and independent agencies concerned with our domestic and foreign policies and operations having an important bearing on export controls."[24]

On September 27, 1945, export control was transferred from the State Department's Office of Exports to the jurisdiction of the secretary of commerce, where it has since resided in a succession of bureaus and offices, under an assistant or deputy assistant secretary responsible for overall management.[25] Since then, a succession of executive orders has consistently reinvested the secretary of commerce with the necessary authority delegated from the president.

Whatever the motivation may have been to choose the Department of Commerce—aside from the obvious fact that export control did not readily fit anywhere else—it probably had a lot to do with the return of a peace economy and the nature of the Department of Commerce, which resembles an "interlocking directorate," covering a great many unrelated functions. The choice remains somewhat paradoxical if one considers that the main thrust of Commerce is to promote and develop trade. Berman and Garson have noted that this locational strategy was bound to result in the control office "feeling a certain lack of congeniality in its surroundings."[26] This may have been an understatement. Klitgaard has called the choice an "organizational accident" that may be at the root of the performance difficulties experienced by the system throughout the postwar period.[27]

In any event, subsequent legislative enactments have confirmed the initial choice. Thus, despite basic changes in policy over the past forty-two years, the "apparatus that grew to administer these controls has survived nearly intact to the present."[28]

During the 1961 oversight hearings, then Secretary of State Dean Rusk stated, on the issue of the proper location of export controls, that "as advised by the Department of Defense, broadly from the security point of view and from State largely on the foreign policy and security side, I would say this is located in the right place."[29] This sentiment does not seem to have changed, although the operational role of Defense has been considerably enlarged and a proposal originally dated April 24, 1980, by Senator Jake Garn (R-Utah) would have statutorily removed controls from Commerce and created a new Office of Strategic Trade under the Executive Office of the President. This proposal was renewed in 1983 during the renewal of the 1979 act. A Senate bill, S. 979, which would have required submission of a plan for the creation of an Office of Strategic Trade, was approved by the Senate but not by the House.

While the primary authority is vested in the Department of Commerce as lead agency in the export licensing process, other agencies have specific statutory authorities, advisory duties, and rights of review on licensing, listing, and enforcement functions of export administration. No matter which department may act as lead agency, the essential inter-agency character of the decision process will prevail because the technology transfer problem is intractable and cuts across agencies' jurisdictional lines.

The Actors: The Distribution of Statutory Powers and Budgetary Resources

A statutory analysis of the most recent national security provisions of the EAA, presidential executive orders, and internal administrative agency directives discloses the current basis for different agencies' involvement in the process. This brief analysis will be complemented in the next section by a functional overview of export control tasks undertaken by each major actor, separately and jointly.

In general it can be said that the complexity of the mandate has yielded a high degree of jurisdictional and functional differentiation for export controls. The statutory provisions endowing agencies with specific powers reflect political compromises over the years. The statute is relatively silent on a precise hierarchy of agencies within the system it establishes, beyond the designation of a "lead" agency. This concept usually means coordination responsibility without commensurate hierarchical authority.

Former Secretary of State Dean Rusk, reflecting on his years in office, has often remarked that the "bureaucracy does not defer horizontally,"[30] or across agencies. Even though two agencies are part of the federal government, their closest common authority position may be in the White House—far too removed to be of assistance in daily coordination of decisions and resolution of conflicts. The incentives for cooperation among agencies may in fact be lacking even though inter-agency mechanisms may be in place to achieve precisely this.

The Department of Commerce: Lead Agency

The EAA repeatedly refers to the secretary who is defined as "the Secretary of Commerce, unless otherwise specified."[31] The secretary is endowed with the following powers to implement the policies and objectives of the act:

— section 4 (a) and (b): to establish and maintain a control list and licensing requirements;
— section 5 (a) (1): to prohibit or curtail the export of any goods or technology or person subject to the jurisdiction of the United States;
— section 5 (1) (2): to make necessary revisions to the control list with respect to goods or countries of destination;
— section 5 (b) (c) and section 4 (b): to establish and maintain a control list specifically for national security export control purposes;
— section 5 (f): to make foreign availability determinations "in consultation with the secretary of defense and other appropriate government agencies";
— section (5) (g): to remove obsolete technology from the control list through an "indexing" procedure "unless any other department . . . objects to such removal";

— section 10 (a) gives primary "responsibility" to Commerce to issue and deny licenses. The section states that it is congressional intent that "to the greatest possible extent" Commerce shall process licenses "without referral of such applications to any other department." However, this provision is tempered by a command to Commerce that "to the extent necessary" it "shall seek information and recommendation" from other government agencies whose "policies and operations" have "an important bearing on exports." The act, therefore, does make Commerce the point of entry and exit into the licensing process but it does not make Commerce a true primus inter pares by any stretch of statutory imagination.

The Department of Defense: A Unique Status

While Defense is not primarily charged with implementation of the act, it has for a variety of technical and political reasons come to play a paramount role in the export control process. The statute reflects its unique position among the configuration of actors involved in export administration. The specific grants of power to Defense reflect long-standing compromises between the agencies, the president, and Congress:

— section 5 (a) vests in the secretary of defense joint authority with Commerce for implementing national security export controls;
— section 5 (c) (2) gives the secretary of defense and "other appropriate departments" the power to "identify goods and technology for inclusion" on the control list. It further requires Commerce and Defense to concur on what items shall comprise the list and if "unable to concur . . . the matter shall be referred to the President for resolution." In practice, "the President" means the National Security Council and a specialized group within the NSC.
— section 5 (d) gives the secretary of defense prime responsibility for "developing a list of military critical technologies" (MCTL) with a view to "integrat[ing]" items on the MCTL into the official control list (the Commodity Control List, or CCL). It provides that dis-

agreements regarding integration "shall be resolved by the President." (See functional analysis section on this issue);

— section 5 (f) gives Defense a consultative right with Commerce on foreign availability determinations as a prior condition of decontrol of CCL entries;

— section 10 (g) is a broad grant of power to the secretary of defense "to review any proposed export of any goods or technology to any country to which exports are controlled for national security purposes." It gives Defense direct access to the president to recommend the disapproval of any export "detrimental to the national security." It also includes a highly controversial provision, never used to this day, to the effect that the president "shall promptly report to the Congress" if he "modifies or overrules" a Defense recommendation. William Root, former director of the State Department Office of East-West Trade, believes that this subsection is highly unusual and that "it indicates that the Commander-in-Chief is not master in his own house."[32] Root further notes that as a result of this provision, Defense officials "consider the views of other agencies and of other governments to be irrelevant."[33]

The reach of this provision is the subject of much controversy. It has never been clear in the definition of those "countries" to which exports are controlled for national security purposes. Defense prevailed in its understanding of the provision to include Free World cases and, by presidential decision of January 1985, it has been allowed to examine export licenses to certain non-proscribed destinations (i.e., West-West, largely non-COCOM). This presidential decision obviated the need for amending section 10 (g), which to this day probably remains broad enough to allow the president to stretch the reach of Defense's review beyond what the original drafters of the section envisaged. It is interesting to note, in this regard, that Defense's right of mandatory review on East-West licenses goes back to an earlier law passed by the Ninety-third Congress and enacted August 5, 1974. This provision came to be known as the so-called Jackson amendments, after the late Senator Henry "Scoop" Jackson, whose legislative assistant was Richard Perle;

- section 15 (b) was amended in 1985 to provide for mandatory review by Defense of any proposed changes in the Export Administration Regulations (EAR) having any bearing on national security controls.

The Department of State: A Special Status

State's role is less salient in national security than in foreign policy controls. These two types of controls were clearly differentiated in the 1979 revision of the act. Most national security controls, however, have immediate foreign policy ramifications that require State's input. Moreover, State's role is paramount in COCOM list review negotiations with COCOM member countries, a role which in recent years has been contested by the Department of Defense.

For these reasons section 4 (e) (presidential delegation to departments) and section 5 (a) (Commerce's responsibility to consult with appropriate agencies) apply with particular relevance to the Department of State. Section 5 (i) also designates the president to "enter into negotiations with the governments participating in COCOM." This function has naturally been delegated by executive order and tradition to State. Section 5 (k) specifically entrusts to State the "coordination" of "negotiations" with non-COCOM countries regarding the export of goods and technology. While the act does not involve State in as intimate a manner in national security export controls as it does Defense, it nonetheless makes it a full-fledged participant in the process.

The National Security Council: The Invisible Hand

This body is often viewed as an instrument of interdepartmental coordination in matters broadly relating to defense and foreign policy. However, the secretary of commerce is not a member. Especially since the Kissinger years, the NSC staff has come to be a decision-making force, sometimes competing with line agencies for the ear of the president.

Its statutory role in national security export controls is, however, left undefined in the EAA, save for section 4 (e), which specifies that "no authority under this Act may be delegated to, or exercised by any official of any department or agency the head of which is not appointed by the President, by and with the advice and consent of the Senate." It is clear that the intent of Congress was to check and limit what has been perceived by line agencies as NSC encroachment in day-to-day licensing and listing decisions. Thus, this exclusionary clause does more to the operational aspects of implementation than it does to broad policy guidance.

It must be noted, however, that during the Reagan years the NSC created a new structure for export control policy at the behest of the State Department Political Military Bureau. From 1981 to mid-1982 the Senior Inter-agency Group on Foreign Policy (SIG-FP) sought to coordinate the implementation of policy on some unilateral and multilateral dual-use high-technology export controls. The group, under the aegis of NSC, was chaired by the State Department. In June 1982, in the wake of the Siberian pipeline affair, NSC established a new Senior Inter-agency Group on International Economic Policy (SIG-IEP), whose main purpose was to focus NSC's attention on high-technology export issues. Since 1983 a lower-level working group has been handling this issue. It is now primarily focused on expediting U.S. decision making relating to the COCOM list review process. It is chaired by the under secretary of state for security assistance, science, and technology, with full participation by all agencies having input in export control matters. This relatively informal body seems to have evolved into an ad hoc, policy-making, high-level inter-agency structure. It has, however, been unable to forestall inter-agency conflicts between Commerce and Defense and probably has steered clear of such line agencies' disputes, focusing more on broader policy guidance.

The Department of the Treasury-Customs: The Enforcer

In 1982–83, with the Reagan administration tightening controls, the issue of enforcement and criminal investigation and prosecution for violations under the act came into focus as more stories of Soviet illegal transfers surfaced. Senator Sam Nunn (D-Georgia) introduced legislation to transfer criminal enforcement from Commerce to Customs. A bitter turf battle ensued between these two agencies, whose outcome was a dual capability to enforce controls. Commerce created a separate and enhanced Office of Export Enforcement, and Customs retained its traditional investigatory and inspectional authority.[34] The statutory authority for Customs is wide and well established in numerous statutes.

The Minor Actors: Sideline Participants

The Department of Energy has over the past twenty years become a significant actor in the licensing process, though the EAA is not overly precise in vesting it with specific powers. Energy has a unique technical expertise for nuclear and energy-related exports which justifies its ad hoc involvement. The Nuclear Non-Proliferation Act of 1979, as amended, has established Energy's joint responsibility with Commerce for the control of nuclear exports. Under this act Energy is also the principal agency that provides technical reviews for such licensing cases as may be referred to it by Commerce.

There are many other participants. On occasion export control cases go far afield from the privileged domains of the major actors and require the participation of specialized line agencies. The act generally leaves the president and the secretary of commerce full discretion to involve the full range of agencies as appropriate. This has moved Congressman Bonker (D-Washington), current chairman of the House Subcommittee on International Economic Policy and Trade, to charge that the executive branch has "exceeded its authority" by including so many agencies that "everybody except HUD is involved in licensing."[35] Agencies with an occasional role include the Departments of Justice, the Treasury, and Transportation, NASA, ACDA, the intelligence agencies, and the Nuclear Regulatory Commission.

Resources and Reorganization: An Enhanced Control Capability

To implement the act's objectives Congress has substantially increased the resources available to both the Commerce and Defense departments since 1981. These departments have also engaged in substantial internal reorganizations of their export control operations.

Commerce in fiscal year 1980 had 170 positions for both export administration and enforcement, with a total appropriation of $6.2 million. By fiscal year 1985 Commerce had 309 positions (221 for export administration, 88 for export enforcement), and a total budget of $17.3 million. This represents increases of 82 percent in staff resources and 179 percent in funding, reflecting a significant congressional commitment to enhancing export administration and enforcement as a regulatory function of government.

Commerce also reorganized its export control operation, clearly dividing export administration from export enforcement and placing each under the separate authority of two deputy assistant secretaries reporting to an assistant secretary for trade administration.[36] The 1985 amendments to the act also require the appointment of an under secretary of commerce for export administration (section 15 [a]), thus upgrading the export administration function within the Department of Commerce and within the councils of government. The Reagan administration has expressed reservations about this provision. The congressional oversight committees—the Senate Committee on Banking, Housing, and Urban Affairs and the House Foreign Affairs Committee—do not seem disposed, however, to rescind this statutory provision, which mandates a form of reorganization. (Indeed, the Export Administration office was established on October 1, 1987, headed by Dr. Paul Freedenberg.) This is a prime example of "tight" law at work, binding the bureaucracy beyond what is generally seen in export control policy.

On January 17, 1984, Secretary of Defense Weinberger approved a directive which reorganized and institutionalized the technology control program within Defense.[37] By early May 1985 Defense had completely reorganized itself and created the Defense Technology Security Administration (DTSA) to administer Defense's technology security program (which includes not only dual-use export administration but also arms export controls, whose jurisdiction it shares with State).[38] DTSA's director reports to the under secretary of defense for policy and also serves as a deputy under secretary of defense for trade security policy.[39]

Representative Bonker pointed out the dramatic increases in budgetary and staff resources for the Defense Department's technology security program, "going from 4 to 77 people in a year."[40] For fiscal year 1987 Defense has analyzed its resource requirements for export controls as follows: 135 personnel (84 civilians, 51 military) with a total budget of some $9,050,000.[41] Defense has also provided some funds for Customs's export enforcement efforts and has led the way in automating various aspects of export administration.

Clearly, both actors have significantly enhanced capabilities to implement the export administration mandate. While the export control system had resource difficulties in the 1970s, in the 1980s it seems fully funded and staffed. Whether these large resource outlays will eventually result in more effective and efficient administration remains an open question in the minds of many of the business clients of the process and of many somewhat more dispassionate observers.

Core Functions of Export Administration:
Listing, Licensing, and Enforcement

Three central and interrelated functions of export administration must be analyzed to understand how power, as reflected in statutory provisions, is distributed in practice among the major actors. The export control system has three main functions: (1) to identify technologies and products that need to be controlled to certain destinations; (2) to review and evaluate individual export license applications; and (3) to enforce export controls both preventively and criminally. From an administrative law viewpoint the first function is the classic function of rule making, while the second is that of adjudication. Each of these functions is a focal point of turf battles among the licensing agencies. These functions are analyzed below in terms of power, politics, and policies.

The U.S. Commodity Control List (CCL)

The CCL specifies the particular goods, technologies, and technical data for which an individual validated license (IVL) is required.[42] Other goods can be shipped on a general license, which permits exports without submission of an application to the Department of Commerce.

The current CCL is 128 pages long and contains 240 entries divided into 10 basic commodity categories. Controlled destinations are divided into eight country groupings.[43] Several types of items are included in the CCL: "A" items, which appear on both the U.S. CCL and the International COCOM List, and U.S. unilateral entries.[44] For reasons of national security the United States controls about 27 categories of dual-use products unilaterally. In fact, of all the COCOM members the United States (and to some extent Canada and Germany) has the largest number of unilateral national controls beyond the COCOM levels.[45]

From an exporter's viewpoint the CCL has been described by William Howard, a vice president at Motorola, as "one of the most impenetrable documents" in a world of "highly obfuscated governmental rules and regulations."[46] Bodhan Denysyk, a Department of Commerce official, echoed this assessment when he described the CCL as "a random walk" through open-ended corridors of regulations.[47]

In a real sense the CCL gives meaning and substance to congressional intent. It is the flesh on the legislative skeleton. Its evolution is a constant series of deletions, additions, and amendments. A predictable tug of war occurs between Commerce and Defense on the contents of the national security control list. Since Defense has a pronounced military security preference and would rather err on the proverbial side of caution in transferring technology, it usually seeks to add new items to the list and is generally not inclined to decontrol. Commerce, on the other hand, has a mild pro-trade bias and might be more willing to give industry the benefit of the doubt when the strategic and military uses or implications of a transfer are not demonstrable. Commerce is therefore somewhat more inclined to favor list changes that mirror moving technological frontiers in the United States, the West, and the Soviet bloc.

Each actor has its own notion of which dual-use technology can be labeled "strategic," "militarily relevant," or "critical," and is therefore includable on the list.[48] Since 1981 the momentum has been to increase list coverage, given the Reagan administration's sense of priorities. Overly extensive coverage may well decrease business's voluntary compliance and, ultimately, sap the very legitimacy of the system.

The 1979 act proposed the creation by the Department of Defense of a parallel, though not regulatorily binding, military critical technologies list (MCTL). The MCTL is an eight-hundred-page, classified compilation of militarily useful technologies and manufacturing equipment. It is a well-intentioned attempt at incorporating the 1976 report of the task force of the Defense Science Board chaired by J. Fred Bucy. This report, known as the Bucy Report, argued that know-how rather than end products should be controlled.[49] The report was intended to reduce coverage rather than increase it. Defense has repeatedly tried to make the MCTL the basis for CCL changes. Gustafson, in a Rand study, observes that if this were the case, "the entire Department of Commerce would not have been large enough to administer the export control program."[50] Section 5 (d) of the 1985 amendments calls for efforts at integration of the two lists, with Commerce-Defense disputes to be resolved at the presidential level. No one outside of Defense thinks this provision of the act will ever be meaningfully implemented.

Defense's efforts at using the MCTL as a basis for COCOM list reviews would have met with outright refusal by the allied COCOM members had it been tried. In general the U.S. COCOM delegation tends to favor extension of the International List, while most of the other COCOM members tend to oppose extending coverage.[51]

Defense must concur before the contents of the U.S. control list can be changed. Lacking such concurrence, the president becomes the ultimate arbiter. However, thus far the president has never had to make such a determination. Rather, what tends to occur is that Commerce will be sympathetic to proposed deletions while Defense will often "study them to death" or veto them. Alternatively, Defense may propose an addition to the list and Commerce will often procrastinate.

The EAA provides for some private sector participation in the preparation of list review proposals in the form of nine technical advisory committees (TACs) consisting of representatives from U.S. industry and the major licensing departments. The TACs advise the secretary of commerce on technical matters (e.g., foreign availability, levels and parameters of control, etc.). It should be noted that a separate technical advisory procedure exists for making proposals to amend the COCOM list under the aegis of the Department of State.

The length of the CCL is in fact one of the major inter-agency bones of contention. Its length can be viewed as a surrogate measure for Congress and private interest groups to determine administrative responsiveness to changes mandated by Congress. The 1987 National Academy of Sciences export control study concluded that there is "no effective mechanism for weeding out from the Control List those products and technologies that have ceased to be strategic or that have become so widely available that control for all practical purposes is impossible."[52]

This observation holds in spite of two 1979 statutory provisions (indexing and foreign availability) precisely designed to encourage and rationalize decontrolling. The act requires Commerce to decontrol an item once a determination is made that it is available abroad from a non-COCOM source, if this foreign availability cannot be stemmed within eighteen months. Commerce and its Office of Foreign Availability had made only three positive availability findings out of some twenty assessments completed through 1986. Since the 1985 act specifies no deadline to complete assessments, the process is generally quite lengthy. Major disagreements between Defense and Commerce about the existence of foreign availability and the standards used to make such determinations have all but thwarted congressional intent so far.[53]

A prime example of the difficulties encountered in foreign availability is the decontrol of wafering saws for Western destinations. The process started in 1984. Defense disagreed from the first with Commerce's technical analysis. Although Commerce was not required to do so under the act, it took the case to the NSC, and received their backing. In late 1986 Defense was still trying to reopen the decontrol decision and to reverse the NSC's position.[54]

Indexing is another decontrol technique that allows Commerce to "provide for annual increases in the performance levels of goods and technology subject to licensing" and to decontrol items which no longer meet the new performance levels. Any other department, however, may object to such removal, thus making this procedure subject to predictable turf battles and paralyzing inter-agency conflicts.

There is, in sum, a direct relationship between inter-agency politics, the length and coverage of the control list, the licensing workload placed on the system, and the stringency of requirements placed on exporters.

Licensing: The Complexity of Joint Action

This section will not delve into the actual organizational processing of licenses. Rather, it examines licensing as one of the central foci where the conflicting forces at play in the system converge. The licensing function also illustrates vividly the inherent complexities of joint action in a multi-agency, multi-goal decision process. It is at this level of routinized decision making that security risks and economic benefits are ultimately reconciled in achieving the national interest.

Four basic types of national security export licensing can be distinguished conceptually and organizationally: first, Warsaw Pact licensing, where the criteria are oriented to delay Soviet acquisition and to preserve existing technological gaps; second, Free World/non-COCOM licensing, where the primary concern is diversion to the Soviet bloc or unauthorized end use; third, Free World/COCOM licensing, where the emphasis is on re-export controls; and last, People's Republic of China licensing.

The 1987 National Academy of Sciences study estimated that for the year 1985 the United States exported some $62 billion of dual-use goods under the two most frequently used licenses (i.e., IVL and the distribution license). The same study estimated that U.S.-controlled exports amounted to about 40 percent of total exports of manufactures while it was "almost equivalent to the value of all high technology exports."[55] The vast bulk of U.S.-controlled trade is with Western countries, and roughly one-half of it goes to the COCOM allies.

Between fiscal year 1981 and fiscal year 1985 the number of validated, licensed applications increased by more than 70 percent (from some 71,400 to 121,000 applications). This increase, which has exceeded the rate of increases of U.S. high-technology exports, is due to the boosted manpower and budgetary resources mentioned earlier, to a heightened public awareness of the export control program, and to a more rigorous enforcement effort. Data do in fact indicate that for Free-World licensing very few if any licenses are denied (about 1 percent) while some 10 percent are denied for Soviet bloc destinations. This low rate of denial prompted Congressman Lagomarsino, in the 1979 export administration hearings, to make a telling point. He observed that it is "pretty obvious that there are problems with a system that requires review of 65,000 [as of 1978] applications in order to catch less than 1 percent of those that should not be granted."[56]

The job of processing an individual license is first and foremost an analytical one, in which technique and policy are often barely distinguishable. In the current system decisions tend to be made on an inductive, or case-by-case, basis. With personnel turnover and shifts in policy, institutional memory is easily eroded and the development of a reliable export-licensing case law is stunted. There have been attempts, particularly at Defense, to computerize case processing and build up a data base containing references to case decisions. The project to develop a case precedent system at Defense as a decision aid is far from complete. It was thought that the MCTL might offer a more systematic and deductive way to make licensing decisions. Many were disappointed, however, and viewed the MCTL as a stratagem of Defense to assert its operational dominance over both listing and licensing decisions.

The case-by-case approach suffers from two shortcomings. First, each time a complicated case comes up the debate as to congressional intent is rekindled within the bureaucracy to justify a particular decision. Second, it multiplies the number of agencies' opportunities to disagree by the number of controversial cases processed and the number of decision criteria to be considered, causing untold delays.

Ten national security licensing criteria, in the form of operative questions, have evolved with the system. These questions must be answered by participating agencies—given their expertise—on the basis of existing policy determinations, licensing precedents (to the extent they are codified), and technical analysis. Information for answering these questions is usually quite imperfect and therefore decisions must be made on the basis of best judgment. The ten licensing criteria are as follows:[57]

1. Is the proposed export designed for military purposes? Is the intrinsic nature of the commodity or data such as to make it significant for military use? Is it currently used by the military establishments in the West and in the country of destination?

2. Is there a risk of diversion to end uses other than stated or to different end users (either inside or outside the country of destination)?

3. Does the item incorporate advanced or unique technology of strategic significance that can be extracted or "reverse engineered"?

4. Are comparable commodities or data available to the country of destination in sufficient quantities and quality? If the item is controlled by COCOM, are there sources outside the COCOM system?

5. Would significant economic-commercial benefits flow to the United States from consummating the transaction?

6. Is the quantity proposed for export compatible with intended

end use? Is there a shortage of the item in the area of destination that affects military potential?

7. What is the nature of the intended end use? Is it commercial or military?

8. Are there special foreign policy considerations with domestic ramifications to take into account?

9. What will be the likely impact of the proposed export on the recipient country? Will it be easily assimilated, diffused, duplicated? Will it change production frontiers drastically?

10. To what extent is the case under review similar to previously decided cases?

Even with the best and most reliable sources of information to answer the above questions there are bound to be disagreements on each factor and its relative weight. The dual-use nature of most technology exports makes a balanced application of the strategic and economic criteria doubly complex for the agencies involved.[58] The configuration of inter-agency disagreements will naturally vary from case to case. Agencies inclined to deny issuance of a license but lacking the information to justify a decision may simply equivocate and become punctilious. Placing the burden of proof on an agency wishing to issue the license may doom the license, given an information base that is less than complete. Moreover, some agencies may be inclined to view their information or technical expertise as inherently superior and therefore refuse to move from an original position on a particular license in the face of rebutting evidence. Technical expertise is a fount of power in bureaucratic politics.

Who the bureaucratic players are in a particular licensing case depends, in large measure, on what policy and technical questions need to be answered. The more complex the case, the more players "come on board the licensing train." The license application is therefore referred by the Department of Commerce on an ad hoc basis. Granger has rightly noted that the "way the U.S. government organizes itself to deal with the [licensing of] export of advanced technology depends largely on the case questions."[59]

The major areas of inter-agency disagreements have been studied in depth.[60] A survey of all bureaucratic participants indicated that foreign availability was the number one ground for inter-agency disagreement, followed by the possibility of internal diversion of the exported item. This study indicated that the potential benefits to the U.S. economy derived from consummation of a sale were the least likely ground to generate inter-agency disagreements. This underlines the low weight generally accorded to this criterion in licensing deliberations.

The deliberations are often endowed with the character of a ritualized dance. Often the actor's positions on informational, technical, and policy issues are eminently predictable. An authoritative government study in 1975 characterized actors' positions during the period of détente:

> The positions taken by each of the agencies appear almost a caricature: Defense officials vetoing any item they can get a handle on, if only to delay for a couple of years Communist acquisition of the technology; State . . . prepared to make an exception for almost any item, as long as it appears to contribute to détente; Commerce, making American firms' case that since technology is going to be sold in any case, the U.S. should at least reap the benefit of making the sale. In addition, CIA, the sole source of official judgment on "foreign availability". . . continues to interpret "availability" and "equivalence" in the narrowest terms, preferring to delay trade whenever possible.[61]

By the mid-1980s, taking into account a drastically different East-West climate, these positions had preserved much of their original empirical validity. As recently as February 1987, in connection with the proposed sale of a supercomputer to India, the secretary of defense stated that "every sale creates a national security problem," underlining Defense's fundamentally unchanging attitude.[62] While the licensing process is unpredictable from the standpoint of exporters, it has a high degree of predictability internally as to actors' positions.

As to levels of disagreements and outcomes of these disagreements, we can glean some information from the experience of the 1960s, 1970s, and 1980s. In 1961 then Secretary of Commerce Hodges noted that licensing disagreements between Defense and Commerce "have run 40 or 50 percent on everything discussed for a long time."[63] Former Congressman Bingham observed in 1979 that in no case has Defense "been overruled by the Commerce Department or by any other agency of the government . . . for the export to the Soviet Union of an item."[64] This, however, cannot be said of Defense in regard to West-West licensing cases. A 1986 General Accounting Office study found in a sample of sixty West-West applications where Defense had recommended denial that "Commerce generally disagreed with Defense's recommendations and approved 39, or 65 percent, of the 60" recommended denials.[65]

Undoubtedly inter-agency rivalries between Commerce and Defense have reached a peak of intensity during the Reagan years, as is made broadly evident by press reports. In part, the lack of clear guidance from the White House and the division within the administration on the issue of technology transfer policy has allowed a kind of inter-agency "law of the jungle" to become an accepted mode of interaction. Fueling the disputes have been the personalities of some of the key participants, who have oftentimes used their center-stage positions to score debating points.

The accepted wisdom for coping with inter-agency inelasticities is to resort to the so-called "three C's" of coordination: clearances, committees, and compromises. In theory the need for operational, day-to-day coordination is not as widespread as might be thought for the simple reason that, even though all applications for a validated license could be submitted to a full-fledged inter-agency review, the bulk of them are handled unilaterally by the Department of Commerce with the tacit consent of other agencies. Cases that do undergo inter-agency review are, however, critical because they not only test the system's effectiveness in dealing with conflict and complexity but also set precedents for future similar cases.

Inter-agency clearances, in the form of policy determinations (i.e., standards as to when certain actions or review are required), provide guidance to Commerce as to when and to which agencies referrals of a license should occur. In the early years clearances were informal. As the process has become more politicized, particularly after 1981, agencies sign memoranda of understanding (MOU), which are akin to inter-agency "treaties" to guard or even enhance their prerogatives. In the case of West-West licensing review, the president had to issue a presidential directive to add to Defense's preexisting review of exports to the Soviet bloc and China all applications for eight product categories exported to fifteen Free World destinations.[66] The dispute was one of the most divisive ever experienced in the history of the licensing system. Commerce felt that Defense was abusing its power, while Defense considered this review essential to discharge its newly expanded licensing role under the act.

A four-tiered committee structure has developed over the years. At the top of the pyramid is the Export Administration Review Board (EARB), which is a cabinet-level mechanism. Next is the Advisory Committee on Export Policy (ACEP), which is at the assistant secretary level. A sub-ACEP exists at the deputy assistant secretary level. Finally, at the senior staff level is the Operating Committee (OC).[67] The EARB is, in a sense, the court of last bureaucratic resort. It is chaired by Commerce, and membership includes State, Defense, and any other agency head the board wishes to invite. It has been used only rarely as a conflict-resolution mechanism. The tendency is for Commerce and Defense, in particular, to bypass the EARB by going to the NSC or the White House staff. The ACEP has not been used much either, and has failed to provide useful policy guidance. The sub-ACEP has met more often than the upper bodies. It can be said, however, that truly important licensing disagreements are handled outside the inter-agency appeals committee structure.

The Operating Committee, for its part, has seen a lot of action. While not a decision-making body, the OC is a useful forum both for handling controversial cases and for CCL list review proposals within the government. It also reviews delegations of authority among participating agencies. The OC functions on the basis of the rule of unanimity and seeks to build consensus. This may on occasion lead to impasses. In past years the OC has handled as many as six hundred controversial cases a year. In recent years its efficacy has somewhat declined, largely because Defense decided not to participate.

The functioning of the structure of clearances and committees is not automatic. Effective functioning is based on the actors' willingness to compromise. When differences cannot be resolved the result is paralyzing conflict. Conflict is also often heightened by the personalities of key players. In this respect Representatives Bonker and Mineta (D-California), in a February 1987 press conference announcing a new round of proposed legislative reforms, took to task departing Assistant Defense Secretary Richard Perle, under whose leadership Defense had come to dominate the licensing process.[68]

Enforcement: The Necessary Adjunct to Export Administration

Enforcement is the essential complement to an effective and equitable export control regime.[69] The 1980s have seen a sharp rise in export enforcement resources and activities. The exporting community generally feels that export administration has become more of a "policing" activity than a regulatory one. While effective enforcement will generally promote greater corporate compliance and deter criminal violations of the act, overzealous enforcement may create a climate of paralyzing uncertainty for exporters. To meet this concern Commerce has tried to move at the same time on both the education and enforcement fronts.

Since 1982 enforcement has been endowed with a separate organization. This change was prompted by pressures emanating from Defense and Treasury-Customs, which felt that the enforcement function had been neglected by Commerce. A turf battle of unusual ferocity unfolded in 1983–84 in which attempts were made to remove the enforcement function from the Department of Commerce and to place it entirely in the Customs Service. Notorious diversion cases, like the VAX computer case, turned this turf battle into a public matter. Eventually it was resolved in a fashion characteristic of the fragmented export control process. Traditional Department of Commerce jurisdiction would be shared with Customs for enforcement in the United States and overseas.

Commerce has pursued a policy of preventive enforcement with both pre-license and post-shipment checks. It has also sought to foster a relationship of trust with the private sector by encouraging business community cooperation in stemming illegal export transactions.[70] However, developing inter-agency cooperation for enforcement among Customs, Defense, State's overseas facilities, and the intelligence community has replicated some of the turf battles evidenced in listing and licensing decisions.

Assessing the Performance of the System

Asking how well or how poorly the export control machinery functions requires specification of which particular goal priorities should be pursued. Deciding how well the mechanism controls or facilitates the transfer of technology, moreover, requires one to know the relative weight to be attributed to strategic risks, economic benefits, and political costs of a given licensing or listing decision. Since the EAA does not clearly provide us with a ranking of goals, but rather leaves ample discretion to the bureaucratic actors, it is hard to have fixed and well-defined benchmarks against which to measure the system's performance.

The issue of system performance is a complex and multidimensional one that revolves around three basic questions: (1) are national security controls effective in denying or delaying Soviet acquisition of Western dual-use technology? (2) what economic, commercial, and technological innovation effects do the controls have on the United States and more generally on the Western economies? and (3) are controls efficiently administered? Answers to the first two questions have proven elusive. They require an in-depth assessment not only of the U.S. control system, but also of the broader multilateral control system, something not within the ambit of this chapter.

Reviewing briefly, by way of background, the available evidence on the first two questions illustrates the difficulties. The benefit of controls may be measured by the degree to which Soviet military advances are forestalled or delayed and the degree to which NATO countries realize defense budget savings. A Department of Defense study attempted to do precisely this.[71] The study reached the conclusion that $6.6–$13.3 billion was saved over a thirteen-year period in the seventy-nine instances where license requests were rejected. It further claimed that an additional $7.3–$14.6 billion would have been required to compensate such gains had the licenses been approved. The 1987 National Academy of Sciences Panel on the Impact of National Security Controls on International Technology Transfer challenged the Department of Defense's expert judgments as to "their criteria and assumptions" and "question[ed] how much weight these estimates should be accorded."[72]

Evaluating the economic costs flowing from the export control system is almost as difficult as evaluating its benefits. The 1987 National Academy of Sciences panel study sheds some light on this. The panel surveyed a sample of 170 U.S.-based high-technology companies for the year 1985, focusing mostly on their experiences in applying for individual validated licenses.[73] Fifty-two percent of the respondent firms reported direct lost sales as a result of U.S. export controls; 38 percent had existing customers expressing a preference to shift to non-U.S. sources of supply specifically to bypass U.S. controls; 26 percent reported deals turned down by Free World customers (in more than 212 ascertained instances) due to controls.[74] Smaller companies in most cases were more severely impacted. Another National Academy of Sciences–commissioned study estimated that the short-run direct costs of U.S. national security controls to the U.S. economy might be about $9 billion annually.[75] The breakdown for these 1985 estimated losses is as follows: lost West-West sales, $5 billion; lost East-West sales, $1.4 billion; administrative costs incurred to apply for an export license, $.5 billion; other losses, $1.5 billion. The same study estimated that this economic loss translated to some 188,000 U.S. jobs lost, not taking the multiplier effect into account.

The U.S. Department of Defense, speaking through (then retiring)

Assistant Secretary Richard Perle, found the National Academy of Sciences panel studies "rich in assertion, poor in evidence," terming the overall findings "complete rubbish." Secretary Perle concluded that the study was fundamentally and irretrievably biased since it was produced by panel members who were themselves "involved in the business of exporting technology."[76]

These two studies amply illustrate not only the analytical complexities and the insufficiency of data but also the politically charged nature of policy evaluation, given the high stakes of the bureaucratic actors and business interests involved.

Dealing with the issue of administrative efficiency is somewhat easier and can be done on the basis of an internal criterion. It does not require evaluation of the validity of the policy itself but rather of the manner in which it is implemented. The immediate problem is therefore to decide on which internal measures of efficiency to use to conduct such an assessment and to identify a data base that can be compared across several time periods.

A standard that can be measured with relative ease is the time it takes to process a license application from entry into the licensing system to issuance or denial. Time delays are always a problem in regulatory matters. In the issuance of a license to export, delay takes on a critical dimension with contracts, jobs, and reputation at stake.

Until the early 1970s Congress had chosen to ignore the timing aspects of export licensing. The outcry of the business community eventually led in 1974 to the legislation of specific time deadlines. The bureaucracy in general has much preferred administrative to statutory deadlines because of the additional flexibility. In 1974 Congress set a ninety-day statutory limit to deny or approve a validated license. In 1979 Congress kept this deadline at ninety days, but it was reduced to sixty days in the 1985 amendments to the act. This was justified by the substantial budgetary increases appropriated for export administration, thus presumably making faster processing possible. If a license is referred to an outside agency, however, the 1985 amendments provide a number of suspense points which can run up to an additional forty days, for a grand total of one hundred days.

Commerce also benefits from an additional sixty days for delibera-
tion after receipt of the other departments' recommendations.[77]

The statutorily imposed processing deadlines respond in large measure to the recommendation of a General Accounting Office study
which called for Congress to "involve itself more in defining the kind
of administration or decision making structure it believes will make
the policy ends of export control possible."[78]

Data based on Department of Commerce figures indicate that the
average processing time for various types of cases and destinations
for the first quarter of 1986 was twenty-seven days. A word of caution
needs to be said about this figure. The distribution of the processing
time curve tends to be rather skewed—i.e., 74 percent of all cases are
completed within twenty-five days but some 5 percent go beyond one
hundred days, "with an extended tail stretching as long as several
months and in a few instances even years."[79] The National Academy
of Sciences panel study contrasts the twenty-seven-day average figure
reported by Commerce with its own survey-derived figure of fifty-four
days of average processing time.[80]

A comparative standard of export administration efficiency may
also be useful. The 1985 President's Commission on Industrial Competitiveness Report compared mean licensing delays to Eastern bloc
and Western destinations for the United States and its main COCOM
partners.[81] Delays to non-COCOM destinations averaged sixteen weeks
in the United States, eight in France and the United Kingdom, and
four in Canada and Japan. Delays to COCOM destinations were four
weeks in the United States and one week in France, Canada, the
United Kingdom, and Japan.

Another measure of the system's efficiency is voluntary compliance. Judging by the sheer increase in the number of applications
processed, compliance must have improved. Looking at the number
of cases prosecuted, administrative penalties imposed (i.e., export
privilege denials, civil fines, etc.), and pre- and post-licensing
checks, all the figures are up and rising. What is not known is
whether the enforcement effort has indeed reduced violations and
diversions.

Four simple tests of internal efficiency for multi-agency decision making can be posited:[82]

1. Does disagreement among bureaucratic players get resolved in a reasonable length of time?
2. Is the resolution effected with a reasonable expenditure of effort and processing time?
3. Is the resolution reasonably satisfactory to the disputants and decisive enough to be lasting?
4. Are the negative effects on the clients of the process minimal?

How does export licensing meet these four tests? It would appear that the level of inter-agency conflict and the time required to resolve it have not improved significantly over those of the 1970s, notwithstanding governmental claims to the contrary and frequent promises of improvement. Given sharply increased resources and heightened conflict, it appears that ease of conflict resolution is inversely proportional to resources placed in the hands of the bureaucratic actors. While the bureaucratic actors are loathe to talk about it, the resolution of differences has not been satisfactory and has caused deep acrimony. The effects on the clients of the process are fairly well documented and substantially deleterious.

Conclusions

Analysis of the inter-agency export licensing process has shown that the distribution of power is a function of a variety of factors. Institutional and statutory authorities provide the broad implementation framework and reflect congressional compromise. These factors are not sufficient, however, to grasp how actual decision-making power flows. The personalities of key policy-makers are often a governing factor that will magnify the statutory and regulatory powers granted an agency and its overall role in the process. Key policy-makers' access to the White House and the consonance of their views with that of presidential policy-makers should not be underestimated in assessing how power flows from the White House to the actual bureaucratic players.

Technical and intelligence information is also a strong pillar on which an agency can base its power in listing and licensing decisions. Clearly, certain agencies will possess more authoritative information sources on such issues as foreign availability, military significance of a particular dual-use technology, and so on. Defense and intelligence agencies have often asserted their preeminence on the basis of informational superiority. Closely related to information gathering is policy and technical expertise. In recent years the Department of Defense has built up its expertise by relying on increased budgetary outlays for more personnel and computer systems.

Nor should the ability of an agency to capitalize on international developments and its uses of political symbols in achieving its licensing policy objectives be underestimated. Defense tends to use the symbols and trappings of national security and technological military superiority in pleading for its views both in the councils of government and before Congress and public opinion. Commerce treads a finer line, seeking at once to achieve international competitiveness and national security in the broad sense of the word.

Bearing in mind the diversity of factors that affect the policy process and policy outcomes, some broad trends may be derived from the statutory, organizational, and functional analysis of the politics of East-West high-technology export administration. First, there is an abiding permanence to the policy and political problems of export controls. The tensions between the competing priorities of the right to export and national security tend to be as durable and predictable as the system to which they have given rise. Graham Allison underlined this feature in 1975 when he stated that "the concept [of controls] has somewhat changed . . . the organization form mostly remains."[83] Export control is naturally a more visible issue now than in the 1960s. But in a highly interdependent and competitive world this cannot come as a surprise.

Second, the power shift initiated with the Jackson amendments to the act has proceeded apace in the 1980s. The bureaucratic balance of power has evidently shifted to the Department of Defense. This is made manifest by Defense's cumulation of statutory powers over the years, enhanced operational capabilities, increased administrative right of licensing review and, more often than not, control of the policy agenda.

Third, Commerce has been placed in the largely reactive, not to say defensive, position of fighting a trench warfare with agencies such as Defense and Customs, which have a significant advantage because of the clarity and singularity of purpose of their organizational mandates. Theodore Thau, one of the most knowledgeable individuals in the field of export administration, has described Commerce's dilemma as the "Willy Loman" syndrome—too much of a "salesman" (trade promoter) to be a dedicated controller.[84] The 1985 amendments to the act, which remove export administration from the Department of Commerce's International Trade Administration and make it stand on its own, reporting directly to the secretary of commerce, does not obviate this fact. Perhaps Klitgaard was correct when he proclaimed the choice of Commerce as the locus for the export control function to be an organizational accident.

Fourth, in the 1980s the policy thrust has been to turn the export control system into a dam rather than a sieve. The policy of strategic and selective controls seems to have turned into a far more encompassing policy. This means placing more emphasis on security, on adding rather than paring down the control lists, on extending control to West-West technology flows, and on intelligence and law enforcement. The effect has been, paradoxically enough, to segregate export control even further from the broader issues of technology transfer and economic competitiveness of which, of necessity, it should be a part in crafting a coherent national policy.[85]

Fifth, the export control system is highly permeable to its broader environment. It has never been clearer that shifts in the policy pendulum and in the bureaucratic balance of power are hostage to East-West relations and presidential politics.

Sixth, the system is curiously resistant to externally mandated change. The EAA of 1979 was a significant watershed in the history of export control policy, mandating major procedural and substantive changes such as foreign availability assessment, indexing, improvements in average processing times, greater "due process," and so on. Years after the passage of the act the bureaucracy is still announcing plans to implement them and very little, if any, substantive progress has been achieved on the all-important issues of foreign availability and unilateral controls.

Seventh, the system is suffused with a risk avoidance predisposition—decision factors favor "erring on the side of caution." As a corollary, inertia rather than innovation prevails in individual licensing or listing decisions. While it is true that enhanced resources, reorganizations, and computerization of licensing (e.g., the ELISA and LARS systems) have improved license processing at the margin, it might perhaps be more accurate to say that they have made it possible to cope with greater licensing loads—due to the renewed stringency of controls—rather than to deal with these loads more efficiently.

What can be done to bring about change in the system and improve its performance? It is clear that proposed solutions to the inelasticities of export administration must go beyond a mere reordering of organizational arrangements, without falling prey to the temptation of a grand design for it all in the form of an export control tsar. Three organizational models of change have been considered: first, the creation of a single export control agency, as proposed in the Garn bill; second, establishing an export license management group to oversee and direct processing at each of the participating agencies; and third, splitting policy-making and licensing activities, consolidating each at an existing agency but keeping the corps of technicians at each of the existing agencies. None of these organizational reforms addresses the fundamental policy problems. Reorganization cannot be a substitute for coherence of policy, nor does it do justice to the complexity of export administration. A "big fix," or structural approach to reform does not appear to be in the offing.

Rather, what may be called a "small fix," or an incrementalist approach, is a more promising, though frustrating, course of action. Such an approach is predicated on retaining the current system of diffused export administrative responsibility while seeking to increase decision-making efficiency, rationality, and predictability.

Foreign availability assessment should be fully implemented (the organizational capacity is now in place); unilateral list entries should be brought into conformity with COCOM levels, or vice versa. The lists are far too inclusive and need to be more selective and better targeted, as noted in a 1982 General Accounting Office study.[86] The private sector needs greater involvement in list reviews than is actually the case.

These reforms need to be pursued aggressively and systematically. Commerce should lead the way, as behooves a lead agency. At the same time some internal action-forcing mechanism should be created to act when the system is paralyzed. The inter-agency, multitiered committee structure already in place should be revived to the fullest extent. Section 10 (g), which gives Defense a special status, should be reviewed in the light of the experience of the past few years. Increasingly, the competitiveness question will drive the arguments for and against reforming controls. Care should be taken not to overreact to sloganizing and let the pendulum swing back too far in the direction of unhindered free trade.

II

Power, Politics, and Policies
of the Allies

4

Controlling East-West Trade in Japan

Gordon B. Smith

Japanese trade policy toward the Soviet Union and Eastern Europe is the result of a complex mix of governmental and non-governmental actors. In Japan, more than in most other COCOM member nations, industrial corporations and trading houses play a decisive role in shaping governmental policies. The central role played by Japanese businessmen in export control and trade policy decisions is due in part to the relatively low degree of institutionalization of economic policy making in Japan and to the extensive network of mixed and overlapping roles played by both government officials and private businessmen there.

In addition, Japanese export control policy since World War II has been formulated carefully in response to U.S. trade policies. While the government of Japan does not simply mimic U.S. policies, American policies and pressures are keenly felt and present Japanese leaders with real constraints in formulating their trade policies toward the USSR and Eastern Europe. This chapter examines these complex relations, assessing their impact on Japanese trade policy as well as on Japanese reactions to COCOM.

Japanese-Soviet Trade and Japanese Politics

Trade and commercial cooperation between the Soviet Union and Japan proceeded on a very modest level from 1917 until the mid-1950s. In 1956 the Japanese Cooperative Trade Corporation was established to foster barter exchanges of Soviet timber for Japanese textile goods. However, trade remained at very low levels—less than 1 percent of total Japanese trade turnover. Japanese cooperative trade with the USSR was conducted primarily through small and medium-sized firms. Large Japanese trading corporations (*sogo-shosha*), which relied heavily on trade with the United States, created dummy firms for handling their trade relations with the USSR, rather than trading directly, in order to prevent antagonizing the U.S. government.

In the 1960s the Japanese steel industry, needing to expand its sources of coking coal, began to lobby for more extensive trade relations with the USSR. A delegation of Japanese steel industry officials headed by Shigeo Nagano, chairman of New Japan Steel, visited Moscow in June 1965 and exchanged memoranda for the creation of the Japanese-Soviet Economic Committee. Improved economic relations were also being actively supported by Keidanren, the powerful Federation of Economic Organizations. Originally it had been the intent of the Japanese government to establish a joint Japanese-Soviet chamber of commerce under government auspices. However, after the success of the steel industry delegation's negotiations with Soviet officials, the government deferred to the plans for a privately organized joint economic committee.

Most of the early developments in Japanese-Soviet commercial relations resulted from economic missions such as Nagano's—that is, missions headed by highly respected Japanese business leaders. These were reciprocated by visits to Japan by key Soviet political figures. Among the most significant visits during the early 1960s were:

August 1961:   Visit to Japan by Anastas Mikoyan, first deputy chairman, USSR Council of Ministers

August 1962:   Japanese economic mission to the USSR led by
                    Yoshinari Kawai, president of Komatsu Manufac-
                    turing Company

September 1962:   Japanese civil engineering delegation led by Yomo-
                    matsu Matuhara, chairman of Hitachi Engineer-
                    ing and Shipbuilding; Kaneo Niwa, chairman of
                    Mitsubishi Shipbuilding and Engineering; and
                    Toshio Doko, chairman of Harima Heavy Indus-
                    tries Company

September 1962:   Japanese petrochemical delegation

October 1962:   Japanese chemical textile industrial delegation
                    led by Shinza Oyo, president of Teikoku Rayon
                    Company

May 1963:   Japanese machine tool delegation

June 1963:   Japanese trade mission to the USSR led by Toku-
                    taro Kitamura, chairman of the Japan-Soviet and
                    Eastern European Trade Association

May 1964:   Soviet parliamentary delegation led by Anastas
                    Mikoyan, first deputy chairman, USSR Council of
                    Ministers

June 1965:   Japanese steel mission led by Shigeo Nagano, chair-
                    man of New Japan Steel

August 1965:   Japanese economic missions led by Kogoro Uemura,
                    chairman of Keidanren

Of these missions the Kawai, Nagano, and Uemura delegations
were particularly noteworthy because they were headed by highly
influential Japanese businessmen and they resulted in substantive
talks with top-level Soviet leaders including First Secretary Khrushchev, Premier Kosygin, and Foreign Minister Gromyko.

The Japanese-Soviet Economic Committee was established in 1965
in order to promote trade between the two countries. The committee
is a nongovernmental body but it cooperates closely with the Japanese government. In contrast to its counterpart committees in other
Western nations, it is not headed by a governmental official. Various

subcommittees have been formed within the Japanese-Soviet Economic Committee to oversee the planning and implementation of large-scale cooperative projects. Given the scale of these projects and their reliance on government credits through the Japanese Export-Import Bank, government officials from the Ministries of Foreign Affairs, Finance, and International Trade and Industry (MITI) participate in subcommittee sessions as advisers. In 1972 a policy committee was formed within the Japanese-Soviet Economic Committee, comprising all subcommittee chairmen and high-ranking officials from these three ministries. The efforts of the committee have resulted in seven large-scale, long-term joint projects, spanning the years 1968 to 1975:

1. Soviet–Far East Forest Resources Development Project (1968)
2. Wrangel Port Construction Project (1970)
3. Chip and Pulp Development Project (1971)
4. South Yakutian Coking Coal Development Project (1974)
5. Soviet–Far East Forest Resources Development Project—Phase II (1974)
6. Yakutian Natural Gas Project (1974)
7. Sakhalin Continental Shelf Oil and Gas Project (1975)

It was not by accident that three of the projects centered around energy development. All three energy projects were undertaken during the period 1974–75, soon after the oil price shocks to the Japanese economy. In addition, all of the joint projects were signed at a time when there was ample investment capital available in Japan and the political climate was favorable for improving relations with the USSR.

During the early 1970s the Nixon administration actively pursued expanded commercial relations with the USSR that included not only bilateral relations between the United States and the Soviet Union, but also economic ties between the allies and the Eastern bloc. The Japanese followed the American lead and trade expanded rapidly, growing at an average rate of 20 percent per year during the 1970s. As U.S.-Soviet détente began to falter in the late 1970s,

Japanese-Soviet trade continued to expand, albeit at a slower rate. The most noticeable result of the changed political climate was that no additional joint projects were undertaken, despite repeated expressions of interest from the Soviet side. By the late 1970s the Japanese had diversified their sources of raw materials (especially energy) and thus were less interested in large-scale Siberian development projects. Furthermore, the Japanese economy had become increasingly geared toward high-tech and service industries, reducing demand for oil, gas, timber, and other raw materials from the USSR. Finally, investment capital that had financed the joint development projects was being drawn off into other technology-intensive areas.

The hardening Japanese position on long-term joint projects with the USSR reflected not only changed economic conditions but also a changed political climate in Japan. In the late 1970s the Soviets deployed SS-20s in Asia and openly acknowledged targeting sites in Japan. Soviet aircraft and ships routinely violated Japanese airspace and territorial waters and the Soviet position on the disposition of the Northern Territories grew increasingly intransigent. Few of the anticipated economic and political benefits of expanded Japanese-Soviet trade materialized.

After a decade of rapid trade expansion Japanese trade with the USSR grew by only 4.8 percent in 1980. The slowdown in trade that year can be attributed in part to Japanese support for the U.S.-led embargo in reaction to the Soviet Union's invasion of Afghanistan. In contrast, in 1980 French and German trade with the USSR increased by 23 and 20 percent, respectively.[1] These increases in trade resulted in large part from French and German firms replacing contracts voided by the president's actions. For example, Japan bowed to U.S. pressure and canceled a deal between Armco and Nippon Steel to build a steel mill at Novolipetsk. The Novolipetsk contract was picked up by Creusot-Loire, much to the annoyance of both the United States and Japan. In responding to U.S. protests, France noted that the French contract did not include automation technology equivalent to what Armco and Nippon Steel would have supplied. In responding to the Japanese complaints, France noted that whereas it had agreed not to undermine U.S. sanctions, it had made no similar representations to Japan. Cases such as this convinced the Japanese government that the embargo was fruitless as long as other COCOM members were not honoring it. Consequently, in mid-1981 the Japanese government resumed a cautious policy of trade promotion with the Soviet Union.

In one notable area, namely pipe-layers, the Japanese undermined U.S. restraint. Export sanctions and processing delays experienced by Caterpillar led to a major shift in the Soviet pipe-layer market to favor Komatsu of Japan. In 1979 approximately 85 percent of all earth-moving and pipe-laying equipment imported into the Soviet Union was manufactured by Caterpillar. By 1981 only 15 percent was purchased from Caterpillar and 85 percent from Komatsu.[2] Japan also successfully pressed the United States to continue to license exports needed to support the Japanese-Soviet Sakhalin natural gas project throughout the embargo.

Japanese-Soviet trade increased by 12.3 percent in 1981 and by 1982 soared to a record 3.6 billion rubles, an increase of more than 21 percent over the previous year. Given the necessary lead time for commercial deals to be reflected in these export figures, it is likely that many of the sales in 1981 and 1982 were negotiated during the height of the U.S. embargo, further bringing into question the extent to which Japan complied with the American trade sanctions.

In the period from 1983 to 1985 Japanese-Soviet trade decreased by more than 21 percent. The cause of this decline is clearly attributable to a precipitous decline in Soviet imports of Japanese manufactures and high technology. From 1982 to 1984 Japan fell from being the second leading trading partner of the USSR (behind West Germany) to sixth (behind Germany, Finland, Italy, France, and Britain). Although a slight rebound was reported in 1985, total trade turnover for that year only recovered to the 1981 level.[3]

Since the Soviet invasion of Afghanistan the Japanese have been unwilling to provide credits at preferential interest rates to the USSR, thus depressing the ability of the USSR to import machinery and equipment from Japan. In February 1980, under pressure from the U.S. government, Japan canceled $1.4 billion in credits to the Soviet

Union. The Japanese Export-Import Bank resumed lending to the USSR in 1982; however, the terms of loans have been much less favorable. For example, in 1985 Japanese Export-Import Bank interest rates offered to the USSR ranged from 8 to 8.5 percent, compared to 6 percent for preferred clients.[4]

Given the difficulty the Soviets face in obtaining cheap credits, they have turned to demanding export financing by trading houses and private companies, as well as increased countertrade measures. Currently the Soviet Commercial negotiators have been demanding corporate financing for approximately 7 percent of all purchases, while countertrade (buy-back) demands are made for 50–100 percent of sales to the USSR.[5] Furthermore, the Soviets want counterpurchases to come in the form of manufactured goods rather than in raw materials. These demands, for the most part, have been unacceptable to Japanese firms since Soviet products are simply not marketable in Japan's sophisticated consumer market. The resale of Soviet manufactured goods in third countries is cumbersome and also has the potential for eroding Japanese markets in those same countries.

Economic sanctions and stiffer COCOM controls have also restricted the volume of Soviet technology imports from Japan and other Western nations. The Japanese followed the lead of the United States at least initially in imposing a partial embargo on exports to the USSR in retaliation for their invasion of Afghanistan in late 1979. Japanese official trade policy toward the USSR remains cautious and conservative, reflecting both the inherent conservatism of the Nakasone government toward the USSR and a reluctance to deviate too radically from the trade posture of the United States.

The Japanese government has also been pressured by its major trading partners—the United States, Canada, and Australia—to buy more raw materials and forestry products from them in order to alleviate their growing trade imbalances. In 1985 the Reagan administration targeted timber and forestry products for discussions with Prime Minister Nakasone in an effort to increase Japanese purchases from the United States. Similarly, the Canadians have been urging the Japanese to purchase timber from them. In 1986 Congress lifted a restriction on the sale of North Slope Alaskan oil to the Japanese in an effort to reduce the trade imbalance. Faced with an estimated $48 billion trade surplus with the United States in 1985, and confronting an angry and protectionist Congress, the Japanese apparently cut back on imports from the USSR and expanded their imports from their major trading partners in North America and Australia.

The development of Japanese-Soviet trade has been dramatically shaped by both Japanese private organizations and corporations and American trade policies toward the USSR. The crosscutting pressures these two influences exert on Japanese trade policy toward the USSR are especially evident in the area of export control, as we shall see below.

Japanese Trade Policy toward the USSR and Export Control

The legislation governing Japanese export control policy dates to December 1, 1949, with the passage of the Foreign Exchange and Foreign Trade Control Law.[6] This legislation was drafted when Japan was still under U.S. military occupation and the law itself was promulgated to bring Japan into line with the U.S. Export Control Act of the same year. Given the underdeveloped nature of the Japanese economy during this period, and U.S. military occupation, the question of Japanese-Soviet technology transfer was minor. The Japanese policy on trade with the USSR and Eastern Europe at this time was wholly consistent with that of the United States government, including supporting the U.S.-led embargo on trade with the Eastern bloc. In one of its first acts after the end of U.S. military occupation in 1952 the government of Japan joined COCOM and has participated in its activities since.

The Foreign Exchange and Foreign Trade Control Law has been amended numerous times since 1949, but most of its original provisions stand. Among the most significant revisions was a 1980 amendment clarifying the competence of MITI and the Ministry of Finance in setting, administering, and enforcing Japanese export control policies.[7]

The Foreign Exchange and Foreign Trade Control Law currently in force adopts a decidedly pro-trade orientation and makes no specific mention of controls for strategic or political reasons. Article 47 states: "Export of goods shall be permitted with a minimum of restrictions insofar as it is consistent with the objectives of this Law."[8]

Article 48 assigns power to the Ministry of International Trade and Industry to approve export licenses. Article 51 empowers MITI to impose embargoes for up to one month when it deems such action to be urgently necessary. Article 53 empowers MITI to impose sanctions (including prohibition on export activity for a period of up to one year) on companies for violations of the Japanese export control regime.

In addition to the trade sanctions imposed in article 53, article 70 of the law specifies criminal penalties for violations of articles 48, 51, and 53. Criminal sentences up to three years and/or fines of one million yen are established. Criminal penalties of six months' imprisonment or a fine not exceeding 200,000 yen are specified in article 72 for failure to provide sufficient and accurate attestation as to the nature or destination of goods exported.

More specific provisions affecting Japanese export control policy are contained in the Export Trade Control Order (Cabinet Order No. 378) of December 1, 1949.[9] This document, which has been frequently amended since 1949, incorporates an attachment listing all items and destinations requiring licenses from MITI. It is significant that no specific mention of the USSR is made in the attachment, meaning that no special exclusions or prohibitions apply. Most of the prohibitions are ostensibly for political reasons, as in the prohibition on exporting various items to South Africa, Iran, or Iraq. Other prohibitions or exclusions have been instituted in retaliation against EEC or U.S. import quotas or reflect mutually negotiated trade levels for given products. Since no exclusions are stated, virtually all items being exported to the USSR and the East European countries require a license from MITI.

All licenses issued by MITI are single licenses, issued on a case-by-case review.[10] No multiple or project licenses are issued. The average processing time for an export license is only two weeks, indicating that the scope of scrutiny is not very elaborate or extensive. MITI evaluates export license requests using its own list of strategic technologies, which is similar to the COCOM list with a few notable exceptions. The Japanese list includes a few classes of items that are not included on the COCOM list, for example, chemicals that could be used in the manufacture of chemical warfare weapons.[11] On the other hand, the Japanese list aggregates various classes of technologies into large, relatively undifferentiated categories that make review more difficult. Thus, until 1985 the Japanese control list entry for computers was simply "electronic computer (excluding those for office business)."[12] The COCOM agreement on computers included many conditions for excluding office computers. The 1985 amendment to the Japanese list incorporated more detail but still omitted much of the revised COCOM texts.[13]

Japanese export controls extend to both tangible and intangible technology (i.e., technical data), but in practice controls on technical data appear to be enforced only when related to a specific existing product.

MITI frequently requests international import certificates (IICs) and end-use certificates in order to ensure that Japanese technology does not transfer to controlled countries in violation of Japanese and COCOM export laws. Officials acknowledge, however, that the only practical follow-up to ensure the enforcement of re-export and end-use provisions is provided by Japanese businessmen, who might have a vested interest in not reporting violations. More active government enforcement of re-export and end-use provisions is widely seen as extraterritorial intrusion, against which the government of Japan has taken a strong stand in the past.[14]

As we indicated at the outset of this chapter, Japanese trade policy toward the USSR is the result of a process heavily influenced (if not virtually monopolized) by large private firms. The blurring of governmental and private distinctions is evident in the central roles played by MITI and Keidanren in trade policy and export control decisions. It is standard practice for retired bureaucrats in Japan to take senior management positions in private enterprises. This practice, known as *amakudari* (descent from heaven), provides important links between the government and the business community.

The principal government agency responsible for formulating Japanese trade policy toward the USSR and Eastern Europe is the Ministry of International Trade and Industry. MITI was created in 1949 to centralize the administration of production and trade. MITI is a major economic policy-making and implementing arm of the Japanese government, yet when compared to the other large and influential components of what the Japanese public calls the "economic bureaucracy" (Finance, Agriculture and Forestry, Transportation, Construction, and the Economic Planning Agency), MITI is not the most powerful. None of the government agencies is as powerful in influencing trade policy as the private trading houses and trade associations. In fact, MITI commands the smallest budget of the six government agencies and has the fewest retired officials who have assumed seats in the Diet or have served as prime minister.[15] Certainly in the critical area of timber trade with the USSR, the Ministry of Agriculture and Forestry jealously guards its jurisdictional authority (*nawabari*). Sectionalism, which has characterized Japanese policy-making and administration since the Meiji era, places a premium on establishing consensus—not only among governmental bodies but also between the government and the private sector.

MITI was reorganized in 1973 into nine bureaus and two agencies. The two subdivisions most actively involved in trade with the USSR are the International Trade Policy Bureau, which formulates and advises the government on overall trade policies, and the International Trade Administration Bureau, which (among other things) is responsible for issuing export licenses.

MITI works closely with (and not infrequently finds itself in conflict with) two other powerful ministries—Finance and Foreign Affairs. During recent years as much as 80 percent of all financing of Japanese-Soviet trade has come from the Japanese government, primarily through the Export-Import Bank.[16] Thus, without the cooperation of the Ministry of Finance, joint ventures with the USSR are simply impossible.

The Ministry of Foreign Affairs provides liaison between the government of Japan and the international community on issues of East-West trade. Consequently it is responsible for representing the Japanese government and the interests of Japanese companies with COCOM. However, it is common for the Foreign Ministry official to be accompanied by an industry representative at COCOM deliberations. Of the major ministries in Japan, the Ministry of Foreign Affairs takes the most cautious approach toward trading with the USSR. Japan has yet to conclude a peace treaty with the Soviet Union, and the continued Soviet occupation of the Northern Territories, in the eyes of many in the Ministry of Foreign Affairs, precludes the possibility of greatly enhanced economic cooperation. The ministry has repeatedly and successfully opposed efforts to conclude a long-term trade treaty with the Soviet Union, arguing that to do so would remove a major bargaining chip that could be used in securing the return of the four islands. In 1983 an official of the Ministry of Foreign Affairs stated: "The amount of military outlay required to overcome intensified military strength attained by the USSR through procurement of Western technology was far greater than the profit which was made by the West through lawful export of the equipment and technology to the Soviet Union."[17]

Notable for its absence in Japanese export control policy is the military. By and large the Japanese Defense Agency (JDA) does not see Japanese-Soviet trade as a threat to Japanese security and has not demanded a larger role in export control decisions.[18] Even if it desired an expanded role, the JDA currently lacks the necessary personnel and expertise to assess the military potential of dual-use technologies.

Overall trade policy toward the USSR appears to be made largely on economic or commercial grounds by the government, working in close cooperation with the private sector. Export control licensing is the sole prerogative of MITI, which has a pronounced pro-trade orientation. License applications approved by MITI are transferred to the Ministry of Foreign Affairs if they require action by COCOM. However, the action of the Ministry of Foreign Affairs is largely formal; it

provides no independent assessment of the license on either technical or national security grounds.

The Federation of Economic Organizations (Keidanren), which represents the bulk of Japan's industrial firms, maintains an intimate
relationship with all the aforementioned ministries. Of the five presidents of Keidanren from 1945 to the late 1970s, three were former
ministers in one of these ministries. In addition, MITI routinely posts
young officials to Keidanren headquarters to foster improved hori-
zontal communications.

Since its founding in 1965 the Japanese-Soviet Economic Committee has in practice fallen under the organizational umbrella of
Keidanren. As we noted earlier, the committee's influence has been
felt most dramatically in the promotion of large-scale joint development projects in Siberia and the Far East.

Another organization designed to promote trade with the USSR is
SOTOBO, the Japanese Association for Trade with the Soviet Union
and Eastern Europe. SOTOBO was established in 1967 and is a quasi-
governmental organization representing roughly two hundred corporations, industrial firms, trading houses, banks, insurance companies, industrial associations, transportation and shipping companies,
and local governments.[19] Unlike Keidanren, which is financed independently but influences governmental policies in significant ways,
SOTOBO is financed in part by MITI but wields only limited influence
over Japanese trade policy toward the USSR and Eastern Europe. The
primary purpose of SOTOBO is trade promotion. It does not act as a
trading house and it does not undertake specific joint projects. Instead,
SOTOBO is responsible for: (a) collecting and analyzing data related to
foreign trade and industries in the USSR and distributing reports
among member companies of SOTOBO and the government of Japan;
(b) organizing participation of Japanese companies in trade fairs and
exhibitions to be held in the USSR; (c) cooperating with the USSR in
their marketing activities in Japan, including market research, public
relations, symposia, factory visits, etc.; (d) coordinating and assisting parties concerned in solving problems regarding trade between
Japan and the USSR; and (e) drafting ideas and proposals in connec-

tion with trade promotion and submitting them to the government of Japan and to member companies.[20]

The current president of SOTOBO is Koji Kobayashi, chairman of NEC, and he is assisted by a secretariat that includes business leaders from several other major industrial firms.

While overall Japanese trade policy toward the USSR is the result of compromises struck among these private and public interests, in the area of export control fluctuations in policies appear to have occurred more in response to pressures from the U.S. government than from inside the Japanese government or business community. In the face of strong U.S. pressure in 1980 and 1981 the Japanese tightened their licensing standards, attempting to bring them closer into line with the more stringent policies of the Reagan administration.[21] A few celebrated cases of violations of COCOM standards and illegal sales of some Japanese technologies to the East have also prompted tighter enforcement efforts since 1980. For example, from 1983 to 1985 Kokusai Koeki Company of Tokyo exported to the USSR and Eastern Europe several automatic programming devices for numerically controlled metal-molding machines. The sales violated COCOM and Japanese export control standards. The violation was brought to the attention of the government of Japan by the United States. In September 1985 the Ministry of International Trade and Industry ordered Kokusai Koeki to suspend its export business for one month as punishment.[22] No case has had as great an impact on Japanese export control policy, however, as the highly publicized episode involving the Toshiba Machine Company.

The Toshiba Case and Its Aftermath

A recent scandal involving two high-ranking officials of Toshiba Machine Company has drawn worldwide attention to inadequacies of Japanese export controls and has resulted in substantial revisions in Japan's export control legislation and policy. The two are charged with illegally exporting four machine tools to the USSR in 1982 and 1983. The machines were used to grind submarine propellers to specifications the Soviets could not achieve using indigenous technology. Two of the machines were installed in the Baltic Shipyard in Leningrad, which produces only surface vessels. However, Kazuo Kumagai, the former Moscow chief of Wako Koeki, the trading firm that arranged the sale, believes that the other two machines were installed by the Soviets in the nearby United Admiralty Shipyard, where Sierra- and older Victor-class submarines have been built.[23] The propellers run with significantly less noise, making them more difficult to detect.

The deal originated as a request from Igor Alexandrovich Osipov, nominally vice president of Technology Machine Import Corporation (TMI), but in fact a KGB agent. According to Kumagai, Osipov approached him in the fall of 1980 seeking automated machinery for the production of propellers for large ships.[24] Wako Koeki turned to Toshiba Machine, whose technology most closely approximated that specified by the Soviets. The numerical controls were purchased from Kongsberg Vaapenfabrikk, a Norwegian defense company, and the deal was carried out by the C. Itoh Trading Company.

A secret assessment of the impact of the sale by the Defense Intelligence Agency and Naval Intelligence, released in 1986, says that the Soviets gained seven to ten years in propeller development as a result of the transfer. They calculate that the United States will need to spend $25 to $30 billion on antisubmarine warfare in the next fifteen to twenty years to counteract the gains the Soviet made with the Toshiba equipment.[25] Japanese and American experts challenge this assessment, however. Hideo Aoki, a prominent Japanese defense analyst, points out that the Soviets began deploying quieter submarines as early as 1980, whereas the Toshiba equipment was installed only in late 1984.[26] Norman Polmar, a naval analyst, argues that it is "highly unlikely that they [the propellers] had effect on the quieting of the latest class of Soviet submarines"—the Sierra- and Akula-class attack submarines.[27]

Facts of the Toshiba case were first made known to Japanese authorities in December 1985 when Kumagai wrote a letter to COCOM, detailing the illegal transfer as well as the names of other Japanese firms that he believed had engaged in similar illegal acts. In early 1986 officials of MITI, the police, and the Foreign Ministry met to discuss Kumagai's letter, which had been brought to their attention by COCOM officials in Paris. Officials of Toshiba Machine, C. Itoh, and Wako Koeki were all questioned about the sale and all asserted the accuracy of the falsified documents for the sale. Kumagai himself was not questioned until April 1986 because the government did not consider him "reliable."[28] Kumagai's complaint was dismissed as that of a disgruntled former employee. Only when officials in the United States brought evidence of the security implications of the machine transfer did MITI finally take Kumagai's complaint seriously, according to Kiroyuki Fukano, a senior MITI official.[29] Kumagai's letter, combined with U.S. intelligence information, persuaded Japanese authorities to act. Criminal charges were lodged against the two Toshiba officials two days after U.S. officials traveling with Defense Secretary Caspar Weinberger in Europe claimed the technology transfer had a "very serious" impact on U.S. antisubmarine warfare capabilities.[30] But a Japanese spokesman denied reports that Washington pressured Tokyo into the move.

Criminal sanctions could not be imposed in this case because a three-year statute of limitations had expired, but the government of Japan did prohibit Toshiba Machine from selling anything to fourteen communist nations for one year, beginning May 22, 1987. Toshiba faces the potential loss of $35 million in sales; however, in similar cases in the past Japanese conglomerates such as Toshiba have bailed out their troubled subsidiaries.[31] C. Itoh, the trading house which executed the deal, was prohibited from selling machine tools to the same nations for a period of three months. Wako Koeki was given a "serious warning." In addition, MITI issued warnings to some 150 trade and industry associations in Japan against such exports to the communist bloc in the future.

The Toshiba case ignited already inflamed American opinion about Japanese trade policies. On July 1, 1987, the Senate voted to ban Toshiba and Kongsberg Vaapenfabrikk from selling products in the United States for at least two years and possibly as many as five years.

Senator Jake Garn led a small group of disgruntled congressmen who smashed a Toshiba radio with sledge hammers on the front lawn of the Capitol to symbolize their pique with Japanese export control policies and lax enforcement of those policies.

The point of the Senate's action, however, was as much to force the Japanese and other COCOM member states to tighten their export control legislation as it was to punish Toshiba. Representative Don Bonker, chairman of the Foreign Affairs Subcommittee on International Economic Policy and Trade, urged that the sanctions against Toshiba be delayed in order to give the Reagan administration time to persuade U.S. allies to adopt tougher penalties for illegal export of vital technology to Soviet bloc nations. Such a strategy would provide "a kicker so that if the countries did not enact tougher legislation, there would be a penalty," Bonker said.[32]

Within a few weeks of the Senate's action U.S. Commerce Secretary Malcolm Baldrige, meeting with Japanese Trade Minister Hajime Tamura, urged the Japanese to increase their financial support for COCOM. In addition, Baldrige proposed an exchange of teams of experts to improve Japanese monitoring of its own companies. Baldrige described Japan as "one of the weak links" in COCOM, noting that Japan had only two export control inspectors, compared to 500–600 in the United States.[33] MITI claims to have twenty-five full-time export control inspectors, but acknowledges that they are overworked, handling more than 10,000 export license applications every year.[34] As a consequence, they have not made serious attempts to verify the accuracy of information provided to them by applicants. Shoichi Shaba, the former chairman of Toshiba Corporation who resigned in the wake of the scandal, conceded that there has been a "rather loose attitude" toward the observance of export licensing laws within Japanese corporations.[35]

While in Washington Tamura proposed a series of changes to Japan's export control legislation and enforcement policies, designed to lessen U.S. criticism. Acting with unusual urgency, a special committee of the ruling Liberal Democratic party prepared the new legislation, which was approved by the cabinet July 31, 1987. The changes link export control explicitly to maintaining international security and mandate consultation with the Ministry of Foreign Affairs. In addition, MITI will be required to hold talks with the Defense Agency on efforts to check on possible violations of COCOM restrictions. The government also plans to establish committees to review potentially sensitive exports, to expand the export control staffs of several ministries, and to increase Japanese support for COCOM.

The new legislation extends the maximum criminal penalty for violations from three to five years and similarly lengthens the statute of limitations from three to five years. Administrative penalties—including the prohibition on export of goods and services by a violating company—were extended from one to three years. A notable addition is the broadening of such export exclusion on both goods and services, whereas the previous law restricted only the sale of goods. Finally, the maximum fine for illegally exporting items to Soviet bloc countries was increased from $6,700 to $13,500. In addition, MITI has ordered Japanese companies to establish in-company monitoring and security systems to ensure compliance with the new export control legislation.

In the course of investigating the Toshiba case it was disclosed that Toshiba Machine Company began selling advanced ship-propeller milling tools to the Soviet Union as long ago as 1974 and that those sales may have helped the USSR with its program begun in 1979 to make their submarines quieter. Toshiba claims that the earlier sale of two large machining tools did not constitute a violation of COCOM restrictions. According to company representatives, the equipment had been modified to ensure that it fell within the restrictions, which prohibit the export of any tools that allow the simultaneous use of more than two axes. Pentagon officials claim that the modifications were temporary and easily reversible. A recently declassified U.S. Defense Department report asserts that "by 1981 the Soviets had acquired modern computer-controlled drafting equipment and a five-axes, numerically controlled propeller milling machine, which used Kongsberg numerical controls."[36] Another, more serious violation occurred in 1981, when Toshiba sold the Soviets several 11-m milling machines with nine grinding axes.

In addition, two other Toshiba officials have been implicated in the 1986 sale to Soviet embassy personnel of documents pertaining to the advanced F-16 fighter, including information concerning its on-board computer and weapons systems. The spy case gave added impetus to the Nakasone government's proposed anti-spy bill, which was before the Diet. Japan currently has no law governing espionage and the new legislation is intended "to contribute to the security of Japan by preventing acts of espionage [and] punishing such acts as monitoring and collection of defense secrets."[37] Persons convicted under the proposed legislation could face fines or jail sentences of two years to life in prison.

The additional security measures permitted by the proposed anti-spy legislation have been praised by U.S. officials, who are concerned over security leaks in Japan's increasingly sophisticated high-tech industries. American concerns were raised in 1979 when Stanislav Levchenko, a KGB defector, described Japan as a "spy's paradise" and claimed that fifty to sixty spies were operating in Japan at the time.[38]

These highly publicized scandals have caused widespread reconsideration of Japanese participation in research associated with President Reagan's SDI program. After nine months of negotiation, in July 1987 Japan became the fifth country to sign a formal accord permitting Japanese companies to compete for SDI contracts. However, in the wake of the scandals Toshiba suspended negotiations with LTV Corporation of the United States on one such contact. Other Japanese firms are afraid that the U.S. Department of Defense, with its narrow definition of strategic technologies, might regard all technological developments to be SDI-related and demand that they be kept confidential.[39] It is clear that the enforcement of stringent export controls from Japan will remain a continuing source of tension between the United States and Japan.

Conclusions

As in all COCOM member states, opinions on export controls on trade with the Eastern bloc vary. In the case of Japan, however, the range of

variance between policies favoring trade, on one hand, and restricting trade, on the other hand, is perhaps less than in other COCOM
member states. Japanese trading companies and manufacturers have
a strong pro-trade bias and they generally argue that export controls
are too restrictive and ultimately ineffective or even counterproductive. In light of the USSR's proximity to Japan and the size of the
Soviet economy, Japanese businessmen feel that trade with the Soviet
Union should exceed the current level of only 2 percent of total
trade. They also view the Toshiba case in a fundamentally different
way than do U.S. policy-makers. Rather than seeing Toshiba's actions
as a serious breach of Western security, they tend to regard it as
another chapter in the ongoing trade war between the United States
and Japan.[40]

Given the strong institutional representation of the business community within MITI and Keidanren, and its central role in COCOM
deliberations, it is not surprising that a pro-trade orientation
influences Japanese policy to a profound degree. Coupled with this
is the virtual absence of an institutional voice arguing for more stringent controls and more vigorous enforcement of existing export control regulations. In part, the atrophied role of the Japanese Defense
Agency in the export control process is the result of U.S. policy since
World War II to demilitarize Japan. It is unlikely that the Ministry of
Foreign Affairs has enough expertise or bureaucratic self-interest to
present an effective counterweight to the pro-trade policies favored
by MITI and the business community.

The atrophied role of defense analysts in the Japanese export control process is particularly significant in the assessment of dual-use
technologies. A relatively high proportion of Japanese high-technology
exports to the world have dual-use capabilities (e.g., computers, electronic components, measuring devices, automated production technology, etc.). Japanese firms export relatively fewer technologies
clearly falling under COCOM's absolute prohibitions—nuclear technology, armaments, aircraft, etc. The United States has been pressuring the government of Japan to scrutinize more carefully the dual-use
potentialities of its high-tech exports rather than to rely on the United

States for assessment and enforcement of COCOM regulations. Given the absence of a highly developed defense industry in Japan, however, the Japanese may not have adequate expertise to assess the potential of these technologies for damaging the national security interests of the Wetern alliance. In the end the United States will inevitably play a prominent role in assessing Japanese exports of dual-use items through the COCOM exceptions procedures.

The primary force pressuring the Japanese to tighten their export policies is the United States. For the past seven years the Reagan administration has taken a hard line on technology transfers to the USSR and Eastern Europe. The policy stance of the United States has been unprecedented in both intensity and duration. Never before has an administration devoted so much attention to the problem, and the fact that the pressure has been sustained for more than seven years merely increases its overall impact.

The Japanese cannot avoid being sensitive to American pressures for a variety of reasons. The Japanese are dependent upon the United States for the bulk of their security. Similarly, the Japanese are dependent upon the American market. Finally, the Japanese are to a considerable extent dependent on American technology. Many Japanese manufacturing plants operate on licenses from U.S. firms. Japan's objective in cooperating in U.S. and COCOM export controls is in part explained by their desire to enjoy continued access to American technology. An official with the Ministry of Foreign Affairs expressed the concern in 1983: "When there is no fear of re-export to communist countries, we may be able relatively easily to receive high technology from free nations."[41] Reports of delays in the issuance of distribution licenses by the United States in February 1984 that detrimentally affected several Japanese manufacturers were reported with alarm in Japan.[42]

Given this heavy and multi-faceted dependence on the United States, Japan is not willing to risk adversely affecting its access to the U.S. economy in order to expand its relatively minor economic ties with the USSR. But neither does American pressure translate into overly stringent restrictions on exports. Instead, the Japanese appear to be placating the United States by tightening controls and stepping up enforcement, but at the same time they have tried to remain competitive with Germany, France, and Italy in the Soviet market. Japanese export control policy is thus the result of an intricate balancing process that seeks to accommodate various conflicting groups and interests, not only within Japan, but also in its external relations.

5

East-West Trade and Export Controls: The West German Perspective

Hanns-Dieter Jacobsen

Introduction

There is a basic consensus in the Federal Republic of Germany (FRG) on the desirability of non-strategic trade with the East. This consensus includes the business and banking communities, the labor unions, and all of the major political parties. There is virtually no opposition to improving economic ties with the East. Indeed, there has been no domestic public debate about the necessity or desirability of export control vis-à-vis the East for decades.

This chapter will discuss the reasons for this free trade approach and the main goals and interests which are behind the economic policies of the FRG vis-à-vis the East, putting particular emphasis on its economic relations with the second German state, the German Democratic Republic (GDR). Then the West German export control system will be discussed with particular reference to the security implications of intra-German economic relations. The third section of the chapter analyzes the major areas of conflict which have arisen with allied countries, particularly the United States. The last section includes some speculation about the future of West Germany's trade with Eastern Europe and the Soviet Union as well as the consequences of this for its relationship with the United States.

West Germany's Trade with the East:
Goals and Interests

In economic dealings with the communist countries several political goals, theoretically speaking, can be identified.[1]

General Isolation of the Soviet System

This approach is based on the assumption that the Soviet Union is fundamentally opposed to all other states in the international system and should therefore be isolated. The West could (and according to some, should) conduct a general, comprehensive, and permanent economic policy of denial, refusing to grant any benefits which could be derived from the exchange of goods, technology, and services. This declaration of economic warfare characterized the Western alliance's East-West trade policy during the Cold War—including that of the FRG.[2] However, it turned out that this approach was not feasible over the long-term, and most of the allies ceased to comply as they gained their economic independence from the United States.

Containment of Soviet Expansionism

This approach holds that the control of trade could deter the USSR from forcing its system upon other countries or ensnaring them in its sphere of influence. Trade controls could limit the Soviet Union's ability to exploit social movements or destabilize Western or Third World countries. This containment of Soviet expansionism has been the basis for a variety of economic sanctions.[3]

Destabilization or Change of the Soviet System

By exploiting weaknesses in the Soviet economic system through trade denial, the economic problems which characterize the inefficient and inflexible planned economies of the East could be aggravated, political and human contacts with the outside world increased and, finally, party and state forced to transform the communist system of planning and society. At the same time the leadership could be forced to divert resources from the military to the civilian sector, thus causing a reduction of the military buildup and a diminution of the Soviet threat. These motives played a decisive role during the 1950s, and reemerged at the end of the 1970s when President Carter linked his human rights demands to the availability of Western technology.

Whatever combination of these approaches influenced Western economic policies vis-à-vis the Soviet Union in the past, West Germans believed that they greatly underestimated the economic potential of the Soviet Union, its societal rigidity, and particularly the priority structure of Soviet foreign policy. Furthermore, the use of economic leverage overestimated its effectiveness and ignored potential counterproductive effects.

However, during the period of détente and the improvement of East-West relations, trade was not used as either a weapon or an instrument of isolation, containment, or destabilization to cause high costs and create pressure. There were some initiatives to influence Soviet behavior and to induce changes or modifications of domestic or foreign policies by employing "positive" sanctions and by providing incentives to develop and increase economic relations with the East.[4]

Linkage of Economic and Political Issues

The United States hoped that by linking economic benefits to political or humanitarian demands, the Soviet Union and other Eastern countries could be induced to curtail aggressive actions, to accept a certain openness in their systems, and to reduce repression against their own citizens. Such ideas have characterized the intra-German relationship for several decades, and under Nixon and Kissinger they became the basis for a global linkage concept. Linkage remains the conceptual basis of the Final Act of the Conference on Security and Cooperation, which posits an insoluble connection between the different "baskets." There is one more way of using economic means in East-West relations.

Entanglement and the Creation of Mutual Responsibilities

By developing a web of bi- and multilateral economic relations with the Soviet Union and other communist countries, mutual dependencies could be created which increase the interests of both—particularly the Eastern—sides to maintain and even improve their political relationship.[5] The Federal Republic followed this functionalist concept from at least the early 1970s, when the government tried, by improving the economic relationship, to stabilize the overall East-West relationship.

"Inducement" or "entanglement" strategies always contain some political risk because better economic relations alone will not guarantee the desired behavior of the other side. Moreover, when one side does not act in the desired fashion, the withdrawal of economic concessions, once granted, can lead to serious political problems. On the other hand, the reduction of economic benefits could increase aggressive behavior because then there are no remaining incentives to encourage moderation. In fact, the existing asymmetric interdependence of East-West economic relations (trade being much more important to the East than to the West) reduces the risk to the West of political blackmail or pressure.

Three general conclusions can be drawn from the preceding discussion of the goals concerning economic relations with communist-governed countries. First, the FRG has employed combinations of all the approaches mentioned above. Second, the composition of these approaches has varied over time. Third, since the late 1950s, and especially since the early 1970s, West Germany's East-West trade policy has been of a creative and cooperative nature. With the exception of the Nixon-Kissinger and the early Carter periods, U.S. East-West trade policy has been the opposite—destructive and antagonistic.

The political dimension of West Germany's trade with the East is based on the conviction that this trade builds up confidence between the blocs and helps to stabilize East-West relations in general. The two-track strategy of NATO's *Harmel Report* of 1967 still guides West Germany's East-West trade, which is seen as strengthening East-West cooperation via détente, dialogue, entanglement of interests, and the creation of partial interdependencies.[6] West German representatives from the government and the business community have been eager to point out that they do not expect an automatic "change through rapprochement" (a slogan coined by Egon Bahr as early as 1963).[7] Nevertheless, they point out that trade with the East has proved to be a necessary, though insufficient, precondition for a policy of preserving peace and trying to restrain the Soviet arms buildup. Economic cooperation might reduce conflicts. However, it is unlikely that they will be totally removed. At best, economic cooperation and the movement of technicians, business and banking representatives, and politicians can strengthen the readiness of the East to solve conflicts peacefully, thus gradually creating mutual confidence.

The Structure and Management of the Export Control System in West Germany

A major problem of East-West economic and technological relations involves the transfer of militarily relevant goods and technology to the East which might adversely affect Western security interests. These security concerns have been voiced most vociferously by the United States and have led to both domestic and multilateral control initiatives. The West German government shares the conviction that the transfer of these militarily critical goods and technologies should not be allowed. Therefore the FRG participates in COCOM and is part of the COCOM consensus that the classification of goods and technologies on the control lists should depend on their relevance to the military potential of proscribed countries and their effect on the security of the Western alliance.

The criterion of significant military relevance is of particular importance to the FRG for several reasons. For one thing it improves the practicability and efficiency of the control system; and, for another, it enhances the cooperation of neutral countries such as Austria, Finland, Sweden, and Switzerland, and of newly industrialized countries such as Brazil, India, Korea, Taiwan, and Singapore. From a

West German perspective the COCOM lists are not considered to be a general embargo instrument for controlling advanced technology. As far as dual-use goods and technologies are concerned, the West Germans have always pointed out that there should be a reasonable balance of the foreign policy, security, and economic aspects of the controls.

West Germany's legal basis for the control or denial of exports is the foreign economic law (*Aussenwirtschaftsgesetz*) of 1961 (which has been amended several times since), together with the foreign economic decree (*Aussenwirtschaftsverordnung*. Section 1 of the law declares the movement of goods, services, capital, and finance to and from West Germany to be generally unrestricted. However, section 7 provides certain qualifications. These include the guarantee of the security of the Federal Republic, prevention of the interference with the peaceful coexistence of nations, and noninterference with the external relations of the FRG. For this purpose part of section 7 emphasizes certain commodity groups which are noted in an appendix of the *Aussenwirtschaftsverordnung*, the export list (*Ausfuhrliste*).[8] The export of the listed commodities is subject to a licensing procedure. The *Ausfuhrliste* consists of three sublists: a munitions list, a nuclear energy list, and a list of "other commodities of strategic relevance." Thus it approximates the basic coverage of the COCOM lists, but it omits many COCOM notes.

The transfer of knowledge used to produce restricted goods and of technical data which are not publicly available is also regulated by the *Aussenwirtschaftsverordnung*. However, the provisions here allow a broad interpretation. The application of something like the "critical technologies" approach of the United States by West Germany has proven to be very difficult legally because regulations about fines and penalties are subject to the principle of determination; that is, they require exactly defined factual findings, which is difficult when the provisions are vague.

If a company in the FRG (including West Berlin) wants to export a listed product to an Eastern country, it applies to the *Bundesamt für Wirtschaft* (BAW), the federal agency for commercial transactions.[9]

This agency, which is subordinate to the *Wirtschaftsministerium* (Ministry of Economics), is responsible for granting licenses if it considers that they are not covered by COCOM or one of the few additional domestic restrictions. A company requesting an export license must deliver signed end-use statements and the promise that the products will only be used for the stated purposes. Furthermore, the company has to provide a statement to ensure that the products under consideration will remain in the country of destination. If the BAW is not able to issue a license on its own it sends the application to the higher-level Ministry of Economics for further consideration. This ministry consults other government agencies, especially the *Auswärtiges Amt* (Ministry of Foreign Affairs) and the *Verteidigungsministerium* (Ministry of Defense), on whether COCOM rules apply, and therefore whether to take the case to COCOM. All the agencies involved apply criteria such as end use, possible strategic relevance, the character of the product or technology, and foreign availability. The technical expertise for making these decisions is basically "in-house," (although list review questions involve consultation with business associations and larger companies). If the ministries agree that a license application has to be taken to COCOM, the Economics Ministry prepares the case and the Foreign Ministry passes it to the West German delegate at COCOM.

All in all the licensing procedure is one of consultation and consensus building. Although the Ministries of Foreign Affairs and Defense have vetoes on individual licensing decisions, these have not been used for many years. Also, the *Bundessicherheitsrat* (Federal Council for Security), consisting of representatives from the Chancellor's Office and the Ministries of Foreign Affairs, Interior, Economics, and Defense, exists to handle any inter-governmental disputes. However, since any disagreements that do arise tend to be resolved informally at the lower levels of the bureaucracy, few officials can remember when the council was last used; indeed, some were even unaware of its existence! There is also a notable absence of dissent between the government and business. The major reason for this is the early and extensive involvement of business in the list review process that gives business a full role in establishing and early notice of the "rules of the game." The criticisms that are heard tend to concern U.S. actions, such as its reluctance to accept exception applications and grant re-export licenses. The close cooperation that characterizes inter-governmental and business-government relations in the FRG in this policy area is, of course, in sharp contrast to the acrimony that surrounds export control policy making in the United States.

The economic interaction between the Germanys poses a particular problem.[10] The legal basis of intra-German trade is fundamentally different from those regulations which govern West German trade with the rest of the world because West Germany, for legal and political reasons, does not consider intra-German trade to be foreign trade. In contrast to the provisions of the *Aussenwirtschaftgesetz*, intra-German trade is still subject to allied legislation enacted before the FRG was founded. As such, these regulations are much more in accordance with American law, which declares foreign trade a privilege, not a right. According to law no. 53 of 1949, on the "Control of Foreign Exchange and the Movement of Property,"[11] *all* West German deliveries to the GDR are subject to a licensing procedure. There exists a list of goods which are under general license.[12] All other goods—including controlled goods and technical data about patents, inventions, production methods, and experiences with respect to the production of controlled goods which are not publicly available and which are not part of that list—are subject to validated licensing procedures. These licenses are issued by the proper economic administration of the state (*Bundesland*) where the company is located and have to be confirmed by the BAW. This procedure not only guarantees that COCOM regulations are applied to intra-German trade, but goes even further by controlling virtually all exports to the GDR not covered by a general license. Violation of these regulations may lead to severe penalties.[13] Thus for a long time intra-German trade has been the most controlled and administered economic interaction with another state by the Federal Republic.

Criticism has been voiced in the United States about the effectiveness of the West German export control system and particularly its enforcement mechanisms. For example, there have been reports that West German firms "continue to be the main instrument of Soviet-bloc diversionary efforts."[14] Certainly the possibility for such diversionary efforts exists; for example, by taking advantage of the transit routes between West Germany and West Berlin or of the transfer points in Berlin which are not subject to Western customs controls.

Dealing with these loopholes, the real effects of which are unknown, remains a complicated matter because political, legal, and security considerations have to be balanced. This is particularly true for Berlin. After all, it was East Germany, not the West, which built the wall and made the access of East Germans to West Berlin a matter of death or life. Therefore, it has been the policy of the Western powers not to further impede traffic between the sectors of Berlin, but to maintain the claim that Berlin is still one city. It would ultimately play into the hands of the East Germans and the Soviets if the Western allies or the West Berlin authorities were to put up customs controls for people trying to enter East Berlin. Such measures would appear to confirm the Eastern standpoint that there is a border between East and West Berlin and that East Berlin is an integral part of East Germany.

It is true that these illegal channels make it somewhat easier for the East Germans and other communist countries to occasionally satisfy specific high-technology or other pressing needs by going shopping at West Berlin stores or picking up deliveries which have been sent to West Berlin from West Germany or other Western countries. With only a few exceptions, however, there have been no indications that these channels have been used extensively by the GDR or other Eastern countries. According to well-informed official sources in both West Germany and the United States, there is no documented evidence that such leakage has been an ongoing problem. This is due to the fact that the authorities in charge of fighting diversion are well aware of these loopholes. By increasing the control of advanced technology entering West Berlin, Eastern efforts—and particularly those of the GDR—to get hold of sophisticated technology are not likely to take place via West Berlin.

The existence of such a balanced control system, which has obviously been accepted by the United States, could lead to the conclusion that there have only been minor problems involved with the formulation and implementation of export controls by the West Germans. However, this is by no means true.

U.S. Power, Politics, and Policies in American-German Controversies on East-West Trade[15]

As was already pointed out, there has been astonishingly little public debate about the rationale, goals, and implications of East-West trade and export controls in West Germany. This is particularly true since the left-of-center coalition between the Social and the Free Democrats started Ostpolitik in 1969, which involved improving economic ties with the East as a means of stabilizing the overall East-West relationship. Although the conservative opposition rejected the political consequences of the West German government's détente policy, they did not question the economic consequences of better trade relations with the East. After all, improved trade and cooperation had been a goal of industry and the banking community since the 1950s. For example, in 1952 a CDU government initiative led to the creation of a Committee on East-West Trade, and in 1958 the conservative government of Chancellor Adenauer concluded a trade agreement with the USSR. Due to the traditional economic relations with Eastern Europe before the war, industry and its conservative political representatives always had a strong interest in maintaining these traditional markets and sources of raw materials. Consequently, West German business and the conservative parties went along with the trade opportunities brought about by Ostpolitik. This became particularly clear when the SPD/FDP coalition of Schmidt and Genscher was succeeded by a CDU/CSU/FDP coalition under Kohl and Genscher in 1982, and the new government followed the policies of its predecessors. It even turned out that the Kohl government was no more prepared to support the restrictive U.S. policies than was the Schmidt government. This does not mean that there was no opposition at all against improving economic relations with the communist countries of Eastern Europe. But the few groups within and outside the CDU and CSU which rejected such economic ties hid behind the initiatives of their most influential ally, the United States. Thus, the controversies between the West German and the United States governments in the Western alliance served as a kind of substitute for domestic conflicts concerning East-West economic relations.

The Early Years and the Pipeline Embargo of 1962–63

This FRG-U.S. conflict, however, was not evident during the peak of the Cold War. Because of the unequivocal dominance of the United States over West Germany, many of the present structural and political differences were not apparent.

The United States was then largely successful in manipulating the allies, particularly West Germany's East-West trade relations. In the event of noncompliance with export controls there was the big stick, provided by the 1951 "Battle Act," of withholding Marshall Plan aid. Prohibited export goods were on a published Battle Act list, which was identical to the COCOM list. COCOM members, eventually including West Germany, had to stop exporting goods to communist countries that were under the U.S. embargo in order to continue receiving U.S. aid. Although they initially complied, the West Europeans stressed that there had been economic ties between Western and Eastern Europe for centuries—namely, in the form of a division of labor between the more industrialized West and the more agricultural East. The trade-denial policy of the United States, designed to maintain the West's technological hegemony, was met with skepticism. Preventing the Eastern countries from acquiring goods they were determined to get seemed almost impossible. The dependence of the Eastern countries, and especially the resource-rich and self-sufficient Soviet Union was and still is far less than the United States had hoped for; dependence was certainly not so great that it could bring about major political concessions. West Germans and the other allies had reservations about the way in which the United States might use its hegemony within the alliance to bring about a political situation that could be detrimental to their interests. They feared that such a hard-line stance would only force the East Europeans closer to the Soviet Union and prevent the reconstruction of a united Europe and the reunification of Germany.

At the beginning of the 1950s West Germany did not join British and French criticism of U.S. policies. Instead, West Germany chose to pursue a political course which gave priority to regeneration and growth over reunification with East Germany, and it subordinated its East-West trade policies to those of the United States. West German foreign policy steps, such as the development of diplomatic relations with the Soviet Union in 1955 and the conclusion of a trade agreement in 1958, resulted only after close consultations with its allies. West Germany had, after all, profited more than other West European countries from the Marshall Plan, which had made the rapid reconstruction of its economy and its political rehabilitation possible. In 1953, however, the Marshall Plan ended, and the economic lever with which the United States could punish the West European countries for expanding trade with the East practically vanished. When Western Europe pressed for a reduction of the strategic controls, the United States was, for the time being, willing to accept only a minor revision of the COCOM lists. In 1954, after the end of the Korean War, and again in 1958 the U.S. government agreed to a considerable shortening of the embargo lists. They did this mainly to prevent a severe rift within the alliance.

During the late 1950s and early 1960s West Germany expanded its trade with the East while the United States continued to attempt to restrict it. American efforts even resulted in preventing the delivery of German large-diameter pipes for a Soviet oil pipeline in 1962 and 1963.[16] A subsequent NATO resolution obliged the West German government to force West German companies to break delivery contracts already closed with the Soviet Union, causing a temporary worsening of West German–Soviet relations. While West Germany complied with U.S. wishes in NATO, Britain, Italy, and non-NATO Japan ignored the resolution and delivered their pipes to the Soviets. This evoked great bitterness on the part of the West Germans and demonstrated for the first time the major difficulties that confronted the alliance in establishing a united economic policy on sanctions and export controls. Moreover, it became obvious that the United States and Western Europe differed in their interpretations of political objectives and individual economic interests. West Germany, despite great internal resistance, followed American policy directions and suffered economic and political damage. Yet, due to other West European countries and Japan, the Soviets were still able to complete their "Friendship" pipeline without substantial delays. The pipeline incident increased West German resolve to resist future U.S. demands, contributing to mistrust and an erosion of NATO.

The Détente Period

A new American approach, drafted as early as 1965 in the Miller Report, sought to influence socialist countries politically by intensifying trade relations instead of limiting them as had been done in the past.[17] The new objective was an attempt to contribute to the erosion of Eastern unity. The United States hoped to detach certain countries from the Eastern bloc or at least to strengthen their tendencies toward autonomy. In the early 1970s the Nixon administration sought to expand East-West trade and emphasized a "linkage" concept, by which it would become possible to make the extent of economic relations with the Soviet Union dependent on its conduct in other parts of the world. A principal motive in encouraging non-strategic trade with the USSR was to increase the potential for future Western leverage in the form of a threatened or actual cutoff of such trade by the West to further Western political objectives. This policy could entangle the Soviet Union in a far-reaching web of relations from which it would be unable to detach itself without considerable economic loss. As the United States promoted East-West trade in the early 1970s, the difficulties which had arisen with the West Europeans, and in particular with the West Germans, in previous years diminished. In fact, the Nixon-Kissinger policies moved the United States closer to those of the West Europeans.

In the United States there have always been critics of economic relations with communist countries. In the early to mid-1970s these critics became more concerned with the political, military, and humanitarian implications of economic exchanges with the East. The most publicized reason for U.S. public opinion turning against détente was Soviet restrictions on Jewish emigration, which prompted the Jackson-Vanik amendment to the 1974 Trade Act. Public opinion in the United States continued to be against détente as the Soviet Union became more active in areas such as Angola and the Horn of Africa. Fears arose that the Soviet Union, having been able to attain relative stability in its relationship with Western Europe, would reactivate its support of revolutionary movements in order to change the worldwide balance of power in its favor.

These developments led to different lines of reasoning in the United States and in West Germany. While the United States attempted to limit its economic relations with the East and link them to Soviet policies, the West Germans strove to protect the fruits of détente. In the late 1970s the West Germans and other West Europeans feared that President Carter's campaign to promote human rights would endanger East-West political and economic relations. They also feared that the United States would pressure its allies in Europe to carry out its policy objectives. American and West German perceptions of the Soviet Union began to diverge. Accordingly, the West Germans attended more to their own economic and political interests in East-West relations, reiterating their belief that improved economic relations would tend to stabilize long-term relations with the East as a whole.

Afghanistan and the Urengoi Pipeline Deal

Given these differing perceptions of East-West relations, it came as no surprise that differences again arose between the United States and most West European countries on the issue of the Soviet invasion of Afghanistan in December 1979. While President Carter ordered a series of sanctions against the Soviet Union, such as a partial grain embargo, the West Europeans reacted more hesitantly. Although all West European countries condemned the Soviet aggression, only West Germany participated in the U.S.-led boycott of the Moscow Olympics in the summer of 1980.

The deterioration of détente led to increasing intra-alliance controversies over the political implications of East-West trade and technology transfer in the early 1980s. Differences came to a head after President Reagan took office in 1981. The new administration was deeply concerned about the economic and military gains the Eastern countries had been able to obtain through trade and technology transfer, which had contributed to a relative reduction of Western security and cost the West billions of dollars.

The most publicized U.S. action was directed against the Urengoi natural gas pipeline deal of several West European countries, especially West Germany, with the Soviet Union. The Americans opposed that deal for two reasons: one, they feared that the Soviets would gain huge amounts of hard currency; and two, they feared that Western Europe would become dependent upon Soviet gas deliveries. On the other side, the West Germans were convinced that oil and gas imports from the Soviet Union would spread their general dependence on foreign energy. After all, full-capacity deliveries of gas from the Soviet Union would not exceed 5 percent of their total energy imports. Furthermore, the Europeans pointed out that they had contingency plans in effect that would adequately respond to a disruption of Soviet deliveries. Finally, the Europeans pointed out (with some sarcasm) that the Soviet Union needed the hard currency that would be gained from the deal in order to continue to buy Western non-strategic goods, such as U.S. grain.

After the decree of martial law in Poland at the end of 1981, President Reagan imposed economic sanctions that forbade U.S. firms from exporting parts for the construction of the pipeline. The United States, in its attempts to prevent pipeline construction, placed itself in clear opposition to the West Germans. Aside from export credits, which will not be discussed here,[18] this was particularly true for the issue of export controls.

Foreign Policy Export Controls

A basic difference exists between the United States and West Germany regarding the use of economic sanctions. This became particularly clear when President Reagan extended the pipeline sanctions to American subsidiaries in third countries and foreign companies which used American technologies under license in June 1982. The West Europeans strongly objected to the extraterritorial application of American legislation to previously concluded delivery contracts of West European companies. Such measures, they argued, undermined their sovereignty.[19] The Americans imposed sanctions against French, British, Italian, and West German firms after they had begun to deliver equipment with American components to the Soviet Union. When those firms continued to deliver the United States blacklisted them and prohibited them from importing U.S. energy equipment.

At this point it is useful to elaborate a little on the differences of opinion and the different approaches that have been voiced in the United States and in West Germany with regard to economic sanctions. Whereas the Americans use them to send political signals, the West Germans doubt the economic effectiveness of such measures vis-à-vis the East. Certainly, they argue, there are cases where punitive economic sanctions such as embargoes and boycotts may be effective. However, these require at a minimum the strong dependence (i.e., vulnerability) of the target country, the universal application of the embargo imposed, and the acceptance by the imposing countries of the costs on their own economy. Assuming that these preconditions are met, the sanctions may be effective in the purely economic sense that they will increase the adjustment cost of the target country. However, in practice these ideal preconditions rarely exist in the Western relationship with the Eastern bloc. As I mentioned earlier, the USSR in particular has an overwhelming capacity for autarky and economic independence, and it has a strong political interest in preserving the status of its allies in Eastern Europe, even to the extent of subsidizing them if necessary. Furthermore, the case of the U.S. embargo of 1981–82 (as well as the grain embargo of 1980) proved that it is nearly impossible to form a united front in support of the sanctions. Even if the preconditions mentioned are fulfilled and the sanctions have their desired economic effect, there remains the important question of whether the attendant political effects will be those which the sanctions-imposing countries had intended. For the targeted country questions of national prestige are likely to gain in importance and, therefore, make the desired compliance unlikely. Further, sanctions may produce a "rally 'round the flag" effect in the target country. They may even inadvertently increase popular support for an otherwise unpopular or unwanted government to the point that economic disturbances are accepted with an outpouring of patriotism. Finally, as has been experienced by the West Germans during the 1950s vis-à-vis East Germany, sanctions which do not succeed tend to backfire on the government of the imposing country, giving the impression of weakness. This is particularly true when the sanctions have been imposed primarily to impress the domestic constituency. Therefore West Germany has been reluctant to impose economic sanctions on its own, and it goes along with Western measures with some misgivings. The FRG prefers "carrots" to "sticks" when using economic levers for political goals—"positive" rather than "negative" sanctions. West German experience has shown that economic incentives can lead to a favorable reaction of the target country, but only when expectations are not overly ambitious. For instance, the first West German–Soviet gas pipeline deal of 1970 created an important positive predisposition, rather than a precondition, for the conclusion of the Moscow treaty between both countries, and it paved the way for subsequent treaties with Poland, Czechoslovakia, and the GDR. The other major West German agreements with the USSR, including the 1978 framework agreement on long-term cooperation in the economic and industrial fields and the gas pipeline deals of the early 1980s, contributed to a stabilization and normalization of political relations between the countries, which in turn enabled hundreds of thousands of ethnic Germans to emigrate to West Germany, secured the status of Berlin, and ultimately made an improvement of intra-German relations possible.[20]

The noncompliance of West European countries with the American sanctions in 1982 caused severe conflict within the alliance. The U.S. administration could not help but acknowledge that the developing American–West European conflict was becoming so intense that it could seriously damage the alliance. Efforts were once again made to find a settlement. After a series of hectic meetings in late 1982, President Reagan announced that all sanctions directed against the Urengoi pipeline project would be lifted.[21] In his speech he emphasized that the Western industrialized nations had agreed on a common plan of action for future East-West trade policy. However, the preparedness of the West Europeans to participate in a series of studies of the economic, political, and security implications of the trade with the East could not obscure the fact that the United States had suffered a major diplomatic defeat. After all, the White House had not been able to stop or even delay the construction of the pipeline and, as a close examination shows, the agreement with the West Europeans did not contain any significant concessions by the allies.

Security-related Export Controls

The "compromise" of November 1982 included the provision that the COCOM rules should be subject to further study. This turned out to be a complicated matter because the United States pressed for additional curbs on high-technology exports to the East.

Neither the United States nor the West Europeans ever maintained that goods or technologies with direct military significance should be exported to the Soviet Union or other communist countries. However, when the COCOM lists in which these products are described were established, it was apparent that it was not possible to agree upon exactly which products could significantly contribute to Soviet military potential, and disagreement arose concerning proposals to revise those lists. The United States considered the West European allies "suspiciously naive," and believed that alliance members interpreted the controls too loosely.[22] For their part, the West Europeans believed that the Americans were too restrictive; after all, a number of controlled items were already produced by Eastern countries or available in non-COCOM countries by legal or illegal means. They argued that, aside from narrow security considerations, the basic aim should be the promotion and not the limitation of economic exchanges with Eastern countries.

During the various high-level meetings which, after a long interval, were taken up again in January 1982, the United States called for an updating of the list of security-sensitive technologies which had been in force since the mid-1970s, improved policy coordination efforts and enforcement measures domestically and multilaterally and, finally, reenforcement of the COCOM machinery through structural improvements and greater financial contributions by the member countries. The West European countries, and particularly West Germany, were prepared to streamline the COCOM rules and to cover not only sensitive goods but also certain high technologies which were of military relevance. However, they were afraid that stricter rules could adversely affect their economic interests and limit their political leverage potential vis-à-vis the East. Whereas the United States advocated increased enforcement measures and a longer list, the West Germans called for "high fences around a clearly arranged area" (that is, a list as short as necessary and enforcement measures as strict as possible). The allies believed that each member country should be responsible for the enforcement of its own control regulations; the administrative efforts should be reduced (particularly with regard to the additional burden some companies had to accept); and the COCOM lists should be reduced at the lower level up to 50 percent. Goods should be eliminated which do not represent the highest international standards and which are available on the world market in equivalent quantity and quality. The considerably shortened list which has been in effect with respect to China could serve as a guideline.

Of particular concern has been the possibly unintended, but nevertheless existing effect of the U.S. controls on West-West cooperation. During recent years the U.S. administration has stressed time and again that there exists an insoluble connection between the global technological leadership of the United States and its military role in the international system. As other advanced industrial countries succeeded in gaining technological competitiveness, the United States began to make efforts to minimize its dependence on high-tech imports. This is seen as a problem with international as well as domestic implications. After all, the United States perceives its role in the international arena "both as the principal guarantor of Western security and as a leading defender of the economic system of the free world." In this context America's technological preeminence and its high-technology industries take on strategic importance, and the maintenance and protection of a broad technological base becomes a "vital element of national security policy."[23] Accordingly, it is not surprising that huge quasi-industrial policy programs have been set up by the Department of Defense (e.g., the VHSIC program)[24] in order to regain technological superiority in areas which are perceived to be vital and endangered.

From a West German perspective this has raised two sets of problems. The first is of a purely economic nature. It is obvious that such American efforts enhance its ability to compete internationally, although there have been doubts about the spillover effects of such military-oriented efforts. The security-related problems, however, pose even more difficult problems because these efforts call for increased secrecy rules. The increasing dependence of U.S. industry on defense contracts adversely affects the ability of U.S. companies to cooperate technologically with foreign partners.[25] There have been reports about scientific conferences closed to non-U.S. citizens, about limited access of scientists to certain research institutions, about additional security regulations for non-American companies or simply a refusal when they wanted U.S. advanced technology,[26] and reports that the access to technical data banks in the United States had been curbed.[27] Most of these studies were quick to point out that the curbs were determined by purely security considerations. However, they do have an economic impact and influence the relative competitiveness of the countries concerned.

West German Responses

Unfortunately, the actual impact of U.S. security-tightening efforts on West-West economic relations cannot be measured exactly. Taking into consideration access to the large American market and the readiness of powerful U.S. companies to continue to cooperate economically and technologically, West German companies tend to avoid public discussion of these difficulties. Because a large part of economic interaction among the United States and the other industrialized countries, including West Germany, takes place without any friction, it would be an exaggeration to assume a change in the political-psychological climate, or even a change of perception in the West German business community, of the United States. Nevertheless, West German companies have become increasingly cautious in using advanced technologies of U.S. origin. And they are well aware that access to the U.S. market or the use of U.S. high technology requires an acceptance of its export control regulations. This limits their range of choice, not just with respect to their potential trade with the East, but also with the rest of the world economy, particularly with those regions in the Middle East and in Central America which are perceived as a security threat by the United States but not necessarily by West Germany. The comprehensive U.S. control efforts challenge governments and firms to review their technological cooperation with the United States and induce them to cut back their technological dependence on the United States by initiating their own technological programs. Efforts in Europe such as ESPRIT and EUREKA are cases in point.

Obviously the U.S. administration has become sensitive to these effects and has announced a variety of changes in the procedures governing the sales of U.S. technology to Western nations.[28] This is certainly not just the result of increasing domestic pressure in the United States, but also due to the pressure from Western Europe and West Germany.[29]

Consequences and Prospects

Although there has recently been some progress in adjusting American and West German regulations on export controls, there is still much potential for future conflict. This is not just a consequence of existing differences in the regulations, but also a result of the different underlying philosophies. The West Germans fear that U.S. action could limit their range of policy options with regard to Ostpolitik and *Deutschlandpolitik*, and adversely affect their economic and, as a consequence, political relationships with the United States. The West Germans are interested in reducing the barriers between the two antagonistic blocs in Europe and emphasize cooperation and the intensification of contacts—cultural, political, economical, and technological. (Indeed, a number of agreements to expand such contacts were signed by GDR leader Erich Honecker during his historic visit to the FRG in September 1987.) Thus, the West Germans tend to reject the imposition of punitive economic sanctions and prefer a positive linkage policy. With regard to the security implications of these relations, they accept export controls for military reasons and cooperate in COCOM, although they refuse to conduct economic warfare. The experience of the late 1970s and early 1980s has contributed to West German awareness that it pays to pursue political and economic continuity rather than "light-switch diplomacy." Taking into consideration recent modifications of the U.S. position, this seems to have been justified.

A new problem is likely to come up shortly when members of the European Community realize their pledge to create a market within the EC without customs controls in the early 1990s. COCOM and its security export controls are not covered by the EC treaty although, mainly as a result of re-export regulations for U.S. high technology, some kind of controls within the community will still be necessary. Thus, any effort to shift export controls to the outside borders of the EC (which includes non-NATO, non-COCOM Ireland) has to take into consideration the possibility of the diversion of militarily relevant high technology to the East.

West Germans feel that the current discussion about the harmonization of Western export control rules should concentrate on three issues: the scope of U.S. export controls, the necessity of re-export licences, and the question of extraterritoriality.

The West Germans doubt the necessity to employ U.S. export controls for national security reasons over and above COCOM controls. They view the existence of the more extensive U.S. Commodity Control List (CCL) as superfluous. After all, effective Western export controls can be reached only through cooperation of all the countries involved, and the existence of different lists has always been a source of friction and conflict.

This issue is closely connected to the necessity for non-American firms to apply for re-export licenses; e.g., when they have used U.S. goods or goods produced under U.S. license. The West Germans advocate the removal of this regulation when such goods and technologies leave COCOM countries under COCOM rules.

Finally, the West Germans oppose the extraterritorial extension of the U.S. export control regulations. The pipeline controversy of the early 1980s is a case in point. Although the 1985 Export Administration Amendments Act made it more difficult for the U.S. government to impose export controls for foreign policy reasons and called for consultation with the allies, the United States still claims that its export control regulations can be applied to companies abroad.

Thus, there are still different philosophies between the FRG and the United States and, therefore, areas of potential conflict. But, as has been pointed out by West German government officials, when the United States is prepared to renounce the use of unilateral measures and to accept dialogue, cooperation, and pragmatic solutions, conflict might be reduced in this field.[30]

However, the history of the conflicts which have taken place so far allows for some skepticism about the likelihood of such changes. It is true that the United States and West Germany are integral parts of the Western alliance and share the conviction that Western security should be preserved. Controversies between both countries can easily occur, however, and are likely to recur in the not too distant future. Policy and strategic differences between the United States and the Western European countries, particularly with regard to the communist countries, are conceivable, especially if Gorbachev's new course in the Soviet Union actually leads to significant human rights improvements, the reactivation of the economy, and arms control agreements. This would require a serious reevaluation of the perceived Soviet threat and the appropriate Western response to it. One can quite easily envision different reactions in the United States and in West Germany which, again, would bring up the subject of appropriate export controls.

6

Controlling East-West Trade in France

Marie-Hélène Labbé

Introduction

Like other Western countries that have economic relations with the communist East, France faces a dilemma: how to foster East-West trade while safeguarding national security. While these objectives are not necessarily incompatible, they are difficult to balance. The French dilemma is compounded by the fact that France wants to be a full member of a Western alliance in which the United States is obviously dominant and has a prevailing voice. So the French dilemma is how to reconcile three objectives: (1) to promote East-West trade; (2) to protect national security; and (3) to maintain good relations with the United States.

It is not always easy to follow the decisions of an ally whose policy seems to fluctuate as much as that of the United States. After having warned of the "hemorrhaging" of Western security, chastised its allies for lax export controls, and taken significant domestic measures to curtail the eastward flow of strategic technology in the early 1980s, the Reagan administration appeared in 1987 to shift its policy toward a relaxation of controls. The French realize that it is risky not to take notice of American policy, both when it is control-oriented, because of France's dependence on U.S. technology, and when it is pro-trade, because of the keen competition for markets in the East.

Table 6.1.   French-CMEA Trade, 1970–85 (current French francs, billions)

	1970	1971	1972	1973	1974	1975	1976
French exports	3.6	4.0	4.7	5.8	7.7	11.1	13.0
French imports	2.5	3.1	3.6	4.4	6.4	7.2	9.5
Trade balance	+1.1	+0.9	+1.1	+1.4	+1.3	+3.9	+3.5

Source: French Customs statistics.

Having placed France's East-West trade and export control policies in historical perspective, this chapter will describe and examine the structure, processes, and actors involved in the French export control system. It will then describe and explain some significant changes that have taken place in French export control policy in the 1980s.

French East-West Trade in Historical Perspective

In the 1950s there was relatively little trade between France and the CMEA countries. It was only later, with the political opening to the East which characterized détente, that a strong basis for economic cooperation was established. Long-term agreements were signed and permanent joint commissions created to encourage French-Soviet cooperation. A similar policy was pursued vis-à-vis the smaller CMEA countries; indeed, Romania and Poland were France's two most important communist trading partners for many years. In a further effort to expand its East-West trade France lifted import restrictions on about 960 CMEA items in 1966.[1]

Until 1980 France enjoyed a trade surplus with the USSR, but since then it has run an annual deficit because of the increased price of oil imports and a decrease in its exports to the Soviet Union (see table 6.1). Although trade with the USSR accounted for only about 2 percent of French exports and 3 percent of imports in 1981, CMEA trade is very important to some industrial sectors and some companies in France. For example, the CMEA countries accounted for 50.4 percent of steel pipe exports in 1980, 41.3 percent of compressor exports, 30 percent of steel strips, and 75.6 percent of metallurgical

1977	1978	1979	1980	1981	1982	1983	1984	1985
13.5	13.1	17.1	19.5	21.0	18.4	25.4	25.8	26.3
10.9	11.5	14.1	22.2	26.5	28.2	30.7	33.4	33.7
+2.6	+1.6	+3.0	−2.7	−5.5	−9.8	−5.3	−7.6	−7.4

testing machines.[2] Large companies like Pechiney, Rhône-Poulenc, Creusot-Loire, Thomson-CSF, Dresser-France, Alsthom-Atlantique, Vallourec, and Technip all have a significant stake in East-West trade. It has been estimated that East-West trade guarantees some 200,000 jobs in France.[3] This figure that cannot be ignored by French politicians. Indeed, in a speech to the National Assembly in July 1982, Foreign Minister Claude Cheysson argued that economic warfare against the Soviet Union would be conducted against France's own work force. The figures and speeches suggest that there are powerful reasons and interests in France for maintaining and promoting good economic relations with the communist East.

French East-West trade policy has been and is directed by the highest levels of the executive branch of government. The president, the prime minister, and the bureaucracy play important roles in policy making. The president sets the tone for the conduct of French-CMEA trade and is often active in the formulation of East-West trade policy. His official visits to Eastern Europe, especially Moscow, provide opportunities for trade promotion through various commercial agreements. The prime minister is responsible for the implementation of presidential directives concerning East-West trade through the relevant ministries. The president and the prime minister are usually of the same party and tend to share similar views on East-West trade. The latter held true even during "la cohabitation" of socialist President François Mitterrand and conservative Prime Minister Jacques Chirac.

President Charles de Gaulle (1958−69) used East-West trade as a means to achieve one of his key foreign policy goals—to maintain independence from the two superpowers. Good relations with the

Soviet Union were designed to counteract U.S. influence. At the same time France's position between the superpowers allowed it to play an important role in international events. De Gaulle's concept of a Europe that stretched "from the Atlantic to the Urals," and his motto, "détente, understanding, cooperation," suggest that East-West trade was extremely important to him. His commitment to East-West trade was exhibited as early as 1964, when the first five-year trade agreement was signed. Later, in 1966, the French-Soviet "*Grande Commission*" was created, and the first general agreement on scientific, technical, and economic cooperation was signed during de Gaulle's state visit to Moscow.

After Georges Pompidou's tenure as president (1969–74), during which France lost some ground to its European competitors for East-West trade, a strongly pro-trade government came to power. As well as recognizing the great economic potential of East-West trade, President Valéry Giscard d'Estaing (1974–81) and Prime Minister Raymond Barre (1976–81) believed that there could be important long-term political spin-offs, and so even if their policies were not radically different from those of previous governments, the underlying assumptions and hopes were. Giscard's views were strongly influenced by those of his adviser, Samuel Pisar, who saw trade as a "weapon of peace."[4] Giscard's views on the role of East-West trade are apparent from the foreword that he wrote to Pisar's book, *Coexistence and Commerce: Guidelines for Transactions between East and West*, when he was finance minister: "Who can say today if the difference between East and West that occurred after World War II will not appear as an episodic classification of the present world political and economic systems? With this uncertainty prevailing, doctrine and pragmatism combine themselves in an attempt to implement international guidelines promoting first trade and economic relations, then, human and cultural links."[5] Barre professed similar functionalist views of East-West trade, once publicly quoting John Stuart Mill's belief that "it is trade that makes war obsolete."[6]

It was in the second half of the 1970s, after America had more or less rejected détente, that France gained a reputation within the Western alliance as being "soft" on export controls. During this period the French government apparently saw COCOM as an outdated relic of the Cold War. France's lax policy took several forms: export licenses were routinely granted;[7] COCOM was often bypassed; and France frequently took advantage of America's unilateral controls to take business away from U.S. firms. In 1977, for example, a U.S. company, Cyril Bath, received a request from the Soviet Union for some stretch-forming presses. An export license was denied by the U.S. Commerce Department, which argued that the presses could be used for aircraft construction. At the same time, without submitting their case to COCOM, the French government granted an export license to Creusot-Loire for the sale to the Soviet Union of comparable presses, arguing that they were for automobile manufacture and did not constitute advanced technology.[8] McIntyre and Cupitt make the point that the Cyril Bath case was a prime example of a differential interpretation of the COCOM rules.[9] Similarly, in 1978 a French firm picked up part of the contract that Sperry-Univac lost for a computer system for TASS because of restrictions that the Carter administration imposed for Soviet human rights violations.

Giscard d'Estaing and his prime minister remained true to their free-trade principles (and to France's economic interests) when they offered only lukewarm support for American sanctions against the Soviet Union for its invasion of Afghanistan in 1979. Indeed, some would argue that France (and the other allies) actually undermined the sanctions. For example, France did not boycott the Moscow summer Olympics, and just two and a half months after the invasion it signed a new general credit agreement with the Soviet Union at interest rates below those established by the 1978 OECD export credit arrangements. French firms again picked up orders lost by U.S. firms as a result of the embargo, and Creusot-Loire profited when Armco was denied the right to fulfill its contract for a steel mill at Novolipetsk.[10] The French foreign minister declared that "France was sticking to détente, especially in the field of trade relations, and was not ready to jeopardize good political relations with the Soviet Union by ordering sanctions."[11]

Giscard's policy toward the Soviet Union was a key issue of the presidential elections of 1981. Socialists and conservatives alike accused him of complacency and criticized his "lightning visit" to Moscow in May of 1980 to meet with Leonid Brezhnev and Edward Gierek, calling him "the little telex boy." *Pravda* gave Giscard the kiss of death by indicating its support for him and thus providing France's socialists with the unique opportunity of denouncing a conservative as "the candidate of Moscow."

The tone of French-Soviet relations changed with the election of socialist François Mitterrand. Mitterrand had been elected due to a socialist-communist coalition and he had appointed four communist ministers; consequently, unlike his predecessors, he did not have to coddle Moscow in order to have a moderating influence on the French communists. But because of the presence of communists in his government, Mitterrand felt obliged to demonstrate his commitment to the Western alliance—particularly for America's sake. This may partially explain the Mitterrand government's export control policy in the mid-1980s, which will be examined later.

The saga of the Urengoi natural gas pipeline illustrates some significant aspects of French policy, including the agreement between conservative and socialist presidents on the undesirability of foreign policy export controls. The negotiations for the purchase by France of 8 billion cubic meters of Soviet gas per year over twenty-five years were initiated by the state-owned Gaz de France in July 1980, and were wholeheartedly supported by Giscard and Barre.[12] While the economic benefits were great, the Reagan administration and even some inside the French government, such as Mitterrand's foreign and foreign trade ministers, were deeply concerned about the risk of dependency and the possibility of Soviet leverage over French policy. Moreover, after the imposition of martial law in Poland in December 1981 there were calls, especially from trade unions like the *Confédération Française et Démocratique du Travail*, for a suspension of the gas contract negotiations. Despite the government's strong opposition to martial law, it did not believe that economic sanctions against the USSR were an appropriate or effective means to express disapproval. Consequently, the protests from both within the government and outside were ignored by Mitterrand, who authorized the signing of the gas contract just six weeks after martial law was declared.[13] Pierre Mauroy, Mitterrand's first prime minister, echoed the sentiments of his conservative predecessor when he justified the decision to go ahead with the pipeline deal by arguing that "economic warfare leads to war,"[14] and that "it would be unnecessary to add to the tragedy of the Poles, the tragedy that a cut in their gas supply would represent for the French."[15]

As the pipeline drama unfolded, the French stuck to their anti-embargo position. Along with the British they were the strongest opponents of the U.S. extension of export controls to West European–based U.S. subsidiaries and licensees. Throughout the summer of 1982 the French made their position quite clear. The government declared that "French contracts concerning the Urengoi pipeline have to be respected" and "what has to be delivered in 1982 will be delivered in 1982."[16] On August 23 the French government used "blocking" legislation to order French-based firms, such as Dresser-France, Thomson-CSF, Alsthom, and Creusot-Loire, to fulfill their contractual obligations vis-à-vis the pipeline.

France's East-West trade policy has traditionally been pro-trade for both political and economic reasons. De Gaulle used East-West trade to promote his foreign policy objectives. As a pragmatic economist, Giscard d'Estaing favored trade for economic reasons while recognizing the important, long-term political benefits. And in the 1980s, while being cautious in his dealings with the Soviet Union, François Mitterrand (like Giscard) rejected American attempts to forge a Western embargo on trade with the Soviet Union. Yet, like other members of the Western alliance, France has recognized the need for some controls on strategic exports to the communist East. We now turn to a description and examination of France's export controls.

French Export Controls

Legal Bases and Procedures

French export controls are not codified in any specific regulation or legislation such as the U.S. Export Administration Act.[17] In France there are five different administrative procedures dealing with East-West trade. A brief review of each provides a useful introduction to the legal bases and procedures governing French export control policy.

The first, COCOM, or "final destination" controls (CDF), as they are known in France, are applied via a 1944 decree which created a set of general controls on imports and exports. These controls are published in France's equivalent of the *Congressional Record*, the *Journal Officiel*, as *"Avis aux importateurs et aux exportateurs"* (advice to importers and exporters).[18]

The French export control list reprints all the items included on the COCOM International List. It has been updated in 1948, 1955, 1967 and, most recently, in December 1985. In the latest *Avis* there was for the first time a description of the CDF licensing procedure, and the technical characteristics were specified for each item that would allow an "administrative exception" to be made (i.e., an exception to the export controls made at the national level).

Second, war matériel exports are controlled by a specific procedure based on a 1939 decree-law (i.e., an administrative regulation which has force of law). The basic list of war matériel is contained in a 1971 decree which is regularly updated. License applications for military exports are carefully reviewed by a special commission, the Interministerial Commission for the Study of Military Materials Exports (CIEEMG), which is chaired by the prime minister's *Secrétaire Général de la Défense Nationale* (SGDN), and composed of representatives of the Ministries of Finance, Foreign Affairs, and particularly Defense, which provides the technical expertise.

Third, nuclear exports are governed by a 1973 decree referring to the 1944 decree, which also sets the basis for CDF controls. The list of products is published in the *Journal Officiel* and regularly updated. The control procedure was set by prime ministers' unpublished directives in 1975 and 1979. Applications for nuclear exports are examined by an ad hoc committee called the Interministerial Restricted Group (GIR) composed of representatives of the Ministries of Foreign Affairs, Defense, Industry, Finance, and the SGDN. If the GIR cannot settle a case, it is forwarded to the prime minister.[19]

A fourth French procedure, called the "national procedure," was implemented in October 1981 by a prime minister's directive which has never been published. Although this procedure is confidential, it is known that it concerns a hard core of high technologies—not products—submitted to more scrutinized controls. The technologies are probably microelectronics, computer hardware and software, fiber optics, robotics, and advanced switching systems. The countries affected by the national procedure are the COCOM-controlled countries and some "sensitive" countries, such as Syria, Iran, and Libya. Getting an export license for these countries is particularly difficult because of the Defense Ministry's input (which will be described later).

The last French procedure concerns the distribution licenses. On January 13, 1986, France established a procedure for a single license for multiple transactions, similar to the U.S. distribution license. The French license, called LIDIS, is granted for twenty-four months. It could apply to parent-subsidiary or exclusive distributor relationships, and to other regular clients if they are final end users.[20] The distribution license which frees the exporter from obtaining "import certificates" and "delivery verification certificates" can be granted only to firms which give written assurance that they will set up strong internal controls to prevent any diversion.[21] The system was set up in December 1986, and by October 1987 over thirty-five firms had been granted a LIDIS.

The Licensing and Review Processes

Just as in other COCOM countries, the responsibilities for the formulation and implementation of French export control policy are shared by various departments (see figure 6.1). The principal departments

Figure 6.1.   Governmental Actors Involved in French Export Control Policy

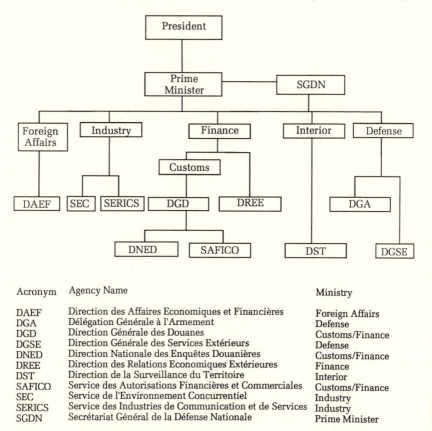

Acronym	Agency Name	Ministry
DAEF	Direction des Affaires Economiques et Financières	Foreign Affairs
DGA	Délégation Générale à l'Armement	Defense
DGD	Direction Générale des Douanes	Customs/Finance
DGSE	Direction Générale des Services Extérieurs	Defense
DNED	Direction Nationale des Enquêtes Douanières	Customs/Finance
DREE	Direction des Relations Economiques Extérieures	Finance
DST	Direction de la Surveillance du Territoire	Interior
SAFICO	Service des Autorisations Financières et Commerciales	Customs/Finance
SEC	Service de l'Environnement Concurrentiel	Industry
SERICS	Service des Industries de Communication et de Services	Industry
SGDN	Secrétariat Général de la Défense Nationale	Prime Minister

involved in the licensing process are the Ministries of Industry and
Defense, and Customs. In the list review process (i.e., consideration
of additions to and deletions from the control list) the principal
ministries are Industry, Foreign Affairs, and Defense.

Customs, which is part of the Ministry of Finance, administers the
licensing process from beginning to end. When a French business
wants to export a product or a technology it has to submit an application form to a Customs office called SAFICO (Financial and Commercial Authorizations Office, see figure 6.2). After technical input from
the Ministry of Industry the license comes back to SAFICO, which

Figure 6.2.   French Export Licensing Process

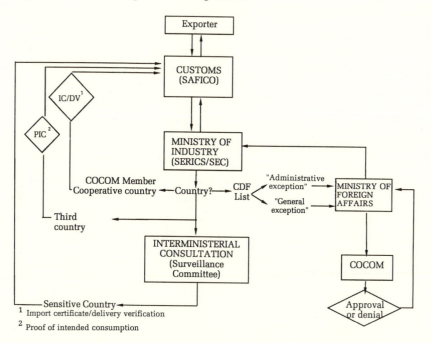

1 Import certificate/delivery verification

2 Proof of intended consumption

delivers it to the exporter. Depending on the destination of the export, Customs will ask for other documents. For COCOM member countries and cooperative countries (e.g., Austria, Finland, Hong Kong, Sweden, Switzerland, and Yugoslavia), Customs delivers the license after presentation by the exporter of an import certificate (IC). After the sale the exporter will have to give Customs a delivery verification certificate (DV). For third countries proof of intended consumption in the importing country is required before delivery of the license.[22] Customs also checks that the goods that cross the border are those for which the license has been granted. It is tempting for exporters to apply for a license for a non-strategic item and use it to export a more critical item.

Within Customs the *Direction Nationale des Enquêtes Douanières* (customs inquiries) is primarily responsible for export control enforcement, and can be helped by the intelligence services—the

Interior Ministry's *Direction de la Surveillance du Territoire* (DST) and the Defense Ministry's *Direction Générale des Services Extérieurs* (DGSE).

While Customs administers the licensing process, the Ministry of Industry has the important task of reviewing and assessing the technical aspects (and therefore the licensing status) of every application. SAFICO sends the license application to Industry's Office of Competitive Environment (SEC) which, after classifying the product, forwards it to the appropriate technical experts. The SEC sends all the licenses concerning electronics or microchips to the Office of Communication and Service Industries (SERICS). About 80 percent of license applications go to SERICS, which employs a number of full-time professional engineers.[23] Of the remaining 20 percent of applications, those relating to nuclear materials are dealt with by the SEC itself, and those relating to other categories of products (e.g., machine tools and chemicals) are the responsibility of various experts who have other (non-COCOM) responsibilities. The Ministry of Industry's function is to review the technical characteristics of every item for which a license has been requested and assess whether it falls under the CDF controls. If the product is controlled the Ministry of Industry's experts will determine whether, given its technical characteristics, the product is eligible for an "administrative exception," similar to the British "national discretion."[24] At this stage the ministry will, within the limits set by security considerations, work with individual firms to make the items under consideration licensable. This would save the application from going to COCOM for a "general exception."

If the application must be referred to COCOM, the Ministry of Industry sends it to the Ministry of Foreign Affairs. Within Foreign Affairs, the Directorate for Economic and Financial Affairs (DAEF) is responsible for CDF controls. The French delegate to COCOM and his assistant belong to the directorate. If necessary the French delegate to COCOM will request a "general exception" from the other COCOM members. Though COCOM decisions are not legally binding on member states, in practice the Ministry of Industry generally abides by them. However, France requests relatively few general exceptions from COCOM. The reason for this, according to a former SGDN official, is that the French government takes a favorable view of "administrative exceptions."[25] This is especially so in regard to exports to the PRC in the 1980s.[26]

The invasion of Afghanistan and U.S. accusations that French export control policy was excessively lax led free-trader Raymond Barre to ask his services in 1980 to strengthen French control policy; (the official directive, creating the national procedure, was actually signed by Barre's successor, Pierre Mauroy, the following year). The national procedure increased the role of the Ministry of Defense in the licensing process and created the Surveillance Committee. Before 1981 the Ministry of Defense was not formally involved in the licensing process. With the national procedure the Ministry of Industry cannot grant a license without the approval of the Ministry of Defense. In case of disagreement the case is submitted to a special committee, the Surveillance Committee. This committee (which is probably similar to Britain's SXWP in structure and function)[27] is composed of top representatives of the SGDN and of the Industry, Foreign Affairs, Finance, and Defense ministries. It is chaired by the general secretary of the government, who reports directly to the prime minister. The composition of the committee (like that of the SXWP in the United Kingdom) suggests that it is designed to act as a restraint on the pro-trade Ministry of Industry. If agreement cannot be reached in the committee, the dispute is decided by the prime minister. In practice, very few cases are appealed to the prime minister. Indeed, few cases are even submitted to the Surveillance Committee. One source reported that less than twenty cases per year have been submitted since 1982.[28] Moreover, the committee has met only once at the directeur level (as of mid-1987); issues usually are resolved at lower levels of the bureaucracy. These facts suggest that both formal and informal inter-departmental dispute-resolution mechanisms work well in France. This in turn suggests that there is considerable consensus within the French government on East-West trade and export control issues.

A more recent development affecting the licensing process and the nature of the government-business relationship in it is the INFOCOM initiative. This was designed and introduced by experts in the Ministry of Industry and accepted by an inter-ministerial body in January 1987. INFOCOM is intended to make information on the French licensing process more easily available to exporters, especially to small and medium-sized firms. Large French businesses usually employ a legal expert to deal with COCOM matters but small firms, even if they know that certain exports to communist destinations are subject to controls, often do not know exactly what the regulations and procedures are and where they can seek advice. Moreover, supposing that they have a copy of the *Avis*, they will probably be discouraged by its complexity and sheer length. The Ministry of Industry therefore edits a more readable text that is available to firms through the widely used MINITEL computer network.

The INFOCOM project should also be of use to France in its dealings with COCOM. When making a good, justifiable case for a general exception, the French delegation needs to know the "case law." Were similar projects accepted or refused in the past? Which country "objected" or expressed reservations? Computerizing this information will help the Ministry of Industry to advise French businesses with better accuracy and help the Ministry of Foreign Affairs make better exception cases in COCOM.[29]

Apart from Customs the actors in the licensing process are also actors in the review process, i.e., the updating of the COCOM lists. The Ministry of Industry is the key actor in the list review process within France. It is responsible for reviewing the characteristics of particular products and technologies. The ministry often solicits business's input about possible items for decontrol and consults with particular firms about their products, about the COCOM regulations, and about the possibility of redesigning products to make them licensable. This dialogue between government and business is usually initiated by the government. Unlike in the United States, French businesses affected by export controls have not formed lobbying groups to influence political decision-makers.

Although representatives of the Ministry of Foreign Affairs present items for review and possible decontrol to COCOM, the ministry receives considerable input from other government departments. Technical input is provided by experts from the Ministries of Industry and Defense. Within Defense, the *Délégation Générale à l'Armement* (DGA), the Atomic Mission, the Directorate of Electronics and Electrical Materials, and the intelligence service (DGSE) are all involved in various aspects of review work—deciding, for example, if dual-use items could or would be put to significant military use. The Directorate for External Economic Relations (DREE) in the Ministry of Finance reviews possible items for decontrol from an economic viewpoint. Before any final decisions are made about review items, an interministerial group, set up in 1978 under the authority of the SGDN, studies the problems associated with the export of these materials and technologies. Like the British, the French generally resolve interdepartmental differences—if there are any—before COCOM meetings, preserving what the British call the "seamless robe" of government.[30]

The Essentials of French Export Control Policy

A number of general observations can be made about France's export control policy making from the above description. First, French export control policy is a complex affair. This complexity arises from the fact that there is a gamut of regulations and procedures which sometimes overlap and are—at least for three of them—based on wartime regulations. According to a former French official, "reference to wartime publications may not be appropriate."[31] Moreover, the French export control procedure is surrounded by secrecy. Some procedures have even not been published in the *Journal Officiel*; such was the case for the national procedure whose existence was revealed, by chance, by the minister of defense during a press conference.[32] The complexity of the policy area and the secrecy that surrounds it increase the power of the French bureaucracy; (knowledge and information are, after all, important sources of power). Consequently there has been little incentive to publicize and formalize the export control process in the past. Opposition to the creation of a French equivalent of the U.S. Export Administration Act has been especially strong in the Ministry of Foreign Affairs, where it is feared that public debate on East-West trade could damage diplomatic relations with Eastern Europe.[33]

Second, French export control policy is a consensual affair. Within the French bureaucracy consensus is rather easily reached, helped by the fact that a relatively small number of bureaucrats (perhaps as few as twenty) control this policy. If agreement cannot be obtained through inter-ministerial consultations, the French regulations have established administrative mechanisms to resolve disputes—inter-ministerial committees such as the Surveillance Committee, the GIR (for nuclear exports), and the CIEEMG (for war matériel exports). Relations between business—especially big business—and the French bureaucracy are also rather consensual.

A third and final general observation concerns the role played by business in this policy area. Essentially it is a limited and reactive role. Although the INFOCOM project may change things, it seems that only a small number of large firms are involved in the policy-making process, and even these are not particularly active. Unlike American and, to a lesser extent, British industry, French industry does not organize itself into an effective lobby to attempt to influence export control policy. Instead, French businesses prefer to work with the authorities through the contacts established between their legal experts and export managers and a relatively small group of government officials. This type of relationship with the government may exist because French businesses see themselves primarily as competitors rather than allies against the government, or for the simple, pragmatic reason that French industry has no need to pressure its government; that is, business lobbies are not emphasized because, to use the statist terminology of Elliott's chapter, a long-term "happy convergence" of interests exists between the government and business which obviates the need for an extensive and expensive anti-control assault upon the government, as in the United States.

Taken together, these observations are consistent with the orthodox textbook characterization of French politics as hierarchical, highly centralized, and elitist. The complexity and secrecy that surround French export controls and the fact that a relatively small number of bureaucrats control this policy area reinforce this characterization. Some of these issues will reappear in the next section of this chapter, which examines and explains some important changes in French export control policy in the 1980s.

Changes and the Forces of Change in the 1980s

There have been some significant changes in French export control policy in the 1980s. French policy has changed from being lax regarding East-West export controls, to being more security oriented, and then toward establishing greater balance between economic and security interests.

France's strong pro-East-West trade attitudes, and its purported opportunism in picking up lost U.S. business throughout the 1970s and into the 1980s has already been described. However, after 1981 France shifted to a more security-conscious approach. There were many public statements emphasizing the change in policy: Foreign Minister Claude Cheysson, for example, made it clear that the French "accept like the other allies some constraints in our economic relations with Eastern Europe where it is proved that those relations could reinforce the Soviet military potential."[34] Henri Conze, deputy director of international affairs at the Defense Ministry, suggested that France was "much more restrictive than COCOM on the transfer of security-related technology and in some cases, even more so than the United States";[35] and François Heisbourg, international security advisor to the minister of defense, stated that "as a result of the national procedure, France has not had a single controversial new case for a couple of years."[36] While some of these claims were perhaps overstated, there were some practical changes that did indeed suggest that the French were beginning to take export controls more seriously. Most significant was the increased role of the Ministry of Defense in the making of export control policy. Its institutional powers were, of course, increased with the creation of the national procedure in October 1981, and it was reported that Defense used these powers to oppose Industry on numerous occasions within interministerial committees, almost always getting its way. Moreover, for the first time since 1958 the defense minister, Charles Hernu, was a political rather than a technical minister. He had excellent relations with and easy access to President Mitterrand who, as we shall see, became very sensitive to the security costs of East-West trade in the early 1980s. Internationally, Hernu and Heisbourg established good contacts with their U.S. counterparts, Caspar Weinberger and Richard Perle. Such contacts and the appointment of a number of pro-U.S., security-conscious export control officials (including the new COCOM delegate in 1983) resulted in closer cooperation between France and the United States, especially in their intelligence services' efforts to curb illegal technology transfer. Also of significance was the support that France gave to the United States in the creation of the Security and Technology Experts' Meeting (STEM). The idea of a military committee attached to COCOM had been rejected originally by the allies when the United States first proposed it in 1982. However, with Defense in its new position of influence, France became an important ally of the United States in getting the initiative accepted in 1985.[37]

All this is not to say that France and the United States were suddenly seeing eye to eye on every export control issue. France was still strongly opposed to more extensive controls, foreign policy controls, and anything that seemed like an infringement of its national sovereignty. And despite the 1984 COCOM agreement to prohibit the sale of sophisticated telecommunications equipment until 1988, the French continued negotiating and even signing such contracts as long as actual delivery was not scheduled until after 1988. This loose interpretation of the COCOM agreement led the French government to allow Thomson-CSF to sell an important telephone exchange system to Bulgaria (something that British companies had been forbidden to do). U.S. officials were peeved, complaining that such activity contravened "the spirit, if not the letter" of the COCOM agreement.[38] Nevertheless, given France's deserved reputation as the maverick of COCOM in the 1970s, the increased attention to the security implications of East-West trade in the early 1980s represented a significant change in policy.

These changes took place within the broader context of changing French-Soviet relations. As mentioned earlier, the inclusion of communists in Mitterrand's government meant that he could not afford to have as close a relationship with the Soviet Union as his predecessors and needed to demonstrate continued commitment to the Western alliance. A toughening of policy toward the Soviet Union was evident in the French government's support of the deployment of Euromissiles and the expulsion of forty-seven Soviets from France on suspicion of espionage in April 1983. However, perhaps the specific catalyst for change in French export control policy was the revelation of the "Farewell" affair. In the early 1980s a KGB officer provided the French intelligence services with official Soviet documents that detailed how the Soviet Military Industrial Commission, the VPK, was engaged in a systematic effort to acquire militarily useful technology from the West.[39] Farewell had a tremendous effect on French officials responsible for export control policy. Indeed, the impact of the event went all the way up to President Mitterrand who, according to one report, "became a hawk on technology protection overnight."[40] In this respect it is important not to neglect events as determinants of policy.

The period since 1985 has been marked by movement toward a new balance between trade and security in France—a new effort to resolve the basic dilemma of East-West trade. A number of developments have called attention to this shift. First, there was the publication of the COCOM list in the *Journal Officiel* in December 1985; this helped exporters by making the export control regulations more accessible and supposedly clearer.[41] Second, there was the creation of the LIDIS distribution license system in January 1986. This is particularly illustrative of the shift in policy because it eased the administrative burden of controls on exporters if, and only if, they set up strong internal controls to prevent any diversion of exports to proscribed countries. This license was created to ward off American attempts to oversee the activities of French firms benefiting from U.S. distribution licenses. An agreement signed between the French Foreign Affairs Ministry and the U.S. Commerce Department in September 1986 is likely to have included acceptance that U.S. officials would not audit French firms, even if they were U.S. subsidiaries, without the presence of French Customs. Third, the INFOCOM project of January 1987 can also be seen as an attempt to promote France's economic interests in East-West trade. And finally, the debate about the appropriateness of a comprehensive export control law has sharpened in the late 1980s, with the position of the Ministry of Foreign Affairs being increasingly criticized by Industry and by the prime minister's SGDN.

The changes taking place in France's export control policy in the mid and late 1980s parallel those taking place in the United States where, given the broader context of the growing U.S. trade deficit, there has been increasing concern about the economic costs of export controls. These trends in the United States have influenced the export control debate within the French bureaucracy. This debate, in turn, has been taking place within the economic context of a deteriorating trade balance for France vis-à-vis the Soviet Union. In 1986 the trade deficit stood at FF 6.7 billion.

In conclusion, we can say that French policy results from the complicated interaction of both international and domestic forces and factors. Internationally, both superpowers have, in different ways, influenced French policy. In the 1980s the French have been reassessing their relationship with the Soviet Union and the role of trade and technology transfer in that relationship. The Farewell affair was a particularly important event in this process. Within the Western alliance France continues to guard against American initiatives that would infringe on its sovereignty. However, as a member of COCOM and, less selflessly, as a dependent on U.S. technology, France has been and will continue to be influenced by U.S. concerns and policy initiatives in the export control area. Domestic forces and developments also have considerable influence on French policy. Most important perhaps is the pro-trade consensus that exists in France and, more specifically, the economic benefits derived from East-West trade. Also, given the concentration of decision-making power in this policy area, individuals, such as Mitterrand, Hernu, and Heisbourg, can have a significant influence over policy—much more than if power were more widely distributed. This partly explains the profound influence of the Farewell documents on French export control policy; that is, it was necessary to convert only a few key decision-makers to "hawks" on export controls to bring about a major change in policy. Efforts to understand and explain past, present, and future French controls on East-West trade and technology transfer must be sensitive to the complex interplay of these international and domestic forces.

—————

Controlling East-West Trade in Britain: Power, Politics, and Policy

———

Gary Bertsch and Steven Elliott

Introduction

As a trading nation Great Britain has generally been reluctant to restrict its international economic relations. This attitude has certainly influenced its approach to controlling East-West trade in the postwar era. In addition, seeing its significant market share of Western trade with the East slip substantially in the 1970s and 1980s, the pressures to export and to avoid excessive control grew even stronger. At the same time the United Kingdom's "special relationship" with the more control-oriented United States, and the conservative views of the two countries' leaders, made the British more susceptible to American pressures to tighten controls in the early 1980s. As a result, when examining Western policies to control trade and technological relations with communist countries, Britain represents an interesting case and differs in important ways—in politics and policy—from both the United States and its West European neighbors.

This chapter begins by putting the British case in its proper historical context. In so doing it will briefly examine the level and importance of British trade with the Soviet Union and East European countries and the nature of its political relationship with the United States in this policy area. Subsequently it will describe the control authority and the conduct of British export controls. It will examine the governing legislation (the Export of Goods [Control] Order of 1985), the British licensing and review processes, and British participation in the Coordinating Committee for Multilateral Export Controls (COCOM). We shall then address the issues and relationships surrounding power, politics, and policy in Britain today, identifying the major actors and their interests, involvement in, and impact upon the policy-making and implementation processes. The final section of the chapter will compare and summarize the British experience in reference to the American, German, French, and Japanese cases addressed by the preceding chapters.

Although the chapter focuses primarily on domestic factors and the role of the United States in determining British export control policy, it should be noted at the outset that British trade policy with the East is also, to a considerable extent, a function of Britain's involvement in, and attempt to contribute to, what Michael Clarke calls a "Western world order."[1] This Western world order involves Britain's attempt to uphold the Atlantic alliance, stabilize East-West relations, and contribute to European Community affairs. While this is of course true, and should be recognized when putting the British effort to control East-West trade in its broader context, there are still some additional domestic and bilateral (U.S.-U.K.) sources of British policy that will be singled out for consideration in this chapter.

The Historical Context

Current British policy surrounding the control of East-West trade is deeply influenced by a broad and historically stable consensus that economic relations with the East are in the country's interest. This consensus, encompassing all governments, parties, and interest groups, grows out of Britain's long history as a trading nation.

Britain's economy has traditionally been dependent on its trading capabilities, and as a seafaring nation it has sought out sources of necessary imports and markets for its manufactures in many faraway places, including those countries to the East. From the mid-sixteenth century Britain has sold to Russian foreign trade monopolies large quantities of manufactured goods, such as textiles, in return for food and raw materials—especially, timber, flax and hemp, grain, and oil.[2] Despite some occasional setbacks this mutually beneficial, complementary pattern of trade flourished from the time of Ivan the Terrible until a downturn following the Bolshevik Revolution and the ensuing civil war.[3] The downturn was temporary, however, because the Bolsheviks needed British technical goods and, more important, access to London's financial markets, and because severe post–World War I unemployment in Britain made the prospect of an Anglo-Soviet trade revival, in the words of George Kennan, "not a negligible consideration."[4] Under David Lloyd George's guidance an Anglo-Soviet Trade Agreement was signed in March 1921.[5] This provisional agreement provided for the establishment of de facto relations between Britain and the Soviet Union, the removal of "all obstacles hitherto placed in the way of the resumption of trade," and for the nondiscriminatory treatment of such trade "as compared with any other foreign country."[6] The significance of the agreement was that it represented the first Western initiative to formally recognize the new Bolshevik regime. In addition to other important elements, the agreement, in effect, granted most favored nation (MFN) status to the Soviet Union. Ramsay MacDonald, Britain's first Labour prime minister, attempted to consolidate Lloyd George's achievements and regularize Britain's relationship with the Soviet Union by extending full de jure diplomatic recognition in February 1924.[7] This action set a precedent and many other Western nations followed suit; (the United States did not formally recognize the Soviet Union for yet another decade).

Despite Stalin's preference for an autarkic economic policy and the upheavals of World War II, Anglo-Soviet trade survived and intergovernment agreements continued to provide its framework. In 1947 the Protocol of Agreement on Questions of Trade and Finance was signed, which provided for the British import of grain in return for the export of locomotives, generators, heavy machinery, and precision scientific and laboratory instruments. Earlier that year the British had sold the Soviets fifty-five gas turbines and an unspecified number of aircraft. Due to U.S. concern with the possibility of rapidly expanding British and West European trade with the Soviet Union, the United States sought and obtained allied participation in a multilateral system of strategic trade controls (COCOM).[8] With further deterioration in East-West relations in the late 1940s, the allies supported, although in some cases reluctantly, the U.S. policy of economic warfare against the Soviet Union and East European countries. However, with the Korean armistice and the improving East-West political environment in the mid-1950s, the British and European governments pressured the United States to loosen the COCOM trade controls; this allowed the British greater freedom to pursue their traditional trade interests with the Eastern countries.

Between 1955 and 1972 Britain signed a number of trade agreements with the CMEA countries (table 7.1). One of the historically most significant agreements was signed on May 24, 1959, with the Soviet Union. The Anglo-Soviet Long-Term Trade Agreement of 1959 was the first postwar long-term agreement the Soviet Union signed with any Western nation. This five-year agreement was followed up with similar agreements in 1964 and 1969, which led the way in expanding East-West trade and in which contemporary trading practices are reflected. Once again, while these and agreements with other CMEA countries were not necessary preconditions for trade, they provided an important, agreed-upon framework within which British exporters could develop their CMEA markets. Such agreements originally put British firms in a strong position in Soviet bloc trade vis-à-vis their West European competitors.

Anglo-Soviet and Anglo–East European trade remained strong in the 1960s. No longer threatened by the "Sword of Damocles" provisions of the U.S. Battle Act,[9] Britain was able to press for a further normalization of East-West economic relations. In 1964 Britain encouraged East European imports by abolishing its severe quota system in favor of a more flexible trade-inducing policy. Also, quantitative controls were lifted on all imports from Poland, Czechoslovakia, Romania, Hungary, and Bulgaria under the "open general license" system. In order to try to counterbalance the expansion of CMEA imports, the government also approved a fifteen-year credit of $300 million to

Table 7.1.   Inter-governmental Trade Agreements between Britain and
CMEA Countries, 1955–72

CMEA Country	Trade agreement	Long-term
Bulgaria	1955, 1959, 1963, 1965	1970
Czechoslovakia	1956, 1960, 1962, 1964, 1967	1972
Hungary	1956, 1960, 1963, 1964, 1968	1972
Poland	1957, 1960, 1963, 1964	1971
Romania	1960, 1963, 1968, 1969	1972
USSR		1959, 1964, 1969

Source: Malcolm Hill, *East-West Trade, Industrial Cooperation, and Technology Transfer* (Aldershot, U.K.: Gower, 1983), pp. 7–8.

build turnkey factories in the Soviet Union as part of the new five-year trade agreement. Britain further encouraged CMEA imports when the Board of Trade[10] expanded the criteria governing remaining country quotas; in May 1967, for example, this more than doubled the volume of importable Soviet consumer goods.

Between 1967 and 1974 the inter-governmental framework for business contacts was further extended through a series of agreements for cooperation in the fields of applied science and technology, including one with the Soviet Union in 1968. This 1968 agreement was augmented in the following year when the two governments, "noting with satisfaction the considerable expansion of trade between the Soviet Union and the United Kingdom," entered into another long-term trading agreement whereby they agreed to "facilitate the exchange of goods and services . . . subject to the essential security interests of each country."[11] This agreement was extended for another five-year period to December 31, 1975, after which it would be extended annually unless either government gave notice of termination.

Whereas the U.S. government has tended to erect barriers impeding U.S.-Soviet trade, the British government has played a role of facilitation. Indeed, inter-governmental arrangements were instrumental in Britain's export performance in the 1960s. Although exports to CMEA countries accounted for only 3 percent of total export business in the late 1960s, Britain was the most important exporter to

Eastern Europe in the European Free Trade Association (EFTA). Unhindered by American competition in this period, British companies such as the British Aircraft Corporation, Leyland Motors, and ICI competed favorably against their West European rivals in the fierce contest for CMEA business. The success of British firms at this time is exemplified by that of English Electric Computer (known as ICL after 1968), which exported the first computers to the Soviet Union in 1966.

From 1973, however, the form of Britain's bilateral trade agreements with the Soviet bloc countries began to change to conform with a new European Economic Community (EEC) East-West commercial policy. Britain's latitude to promote trade was restricted by EEC policy because, for one thing, tariffs and quotas on Eastern Europe could no longer be amended by EEC member states unilaterally. Despite this restriction Britain continued to sign bilateral trade agreements with CMEA states by replacing expired "trade" agreements with long-term agreements on "economic, scientific, industrial and technological co-operation." As with previous bilateral agreements, these were seen as umbrellas for trade, acknowledging formal government support for the firms and agencies involved.

Britain's superiority in East-West trade deteriorated sharply in the 1970s. Its share of the developed market economies' exports to the CMEA countries fell from 11 percent in 1963, to 8.6 percent in 1970, to 5.4 percent in 1978. The reasons for the loss of the CMEA market share are multifarious. Although there was an overall decline in British industrial productivity and competitiveness which affected trading performance, British exporters also faced increased competition from their West European counterparts, who began to exploit their market proximity and traditional trading links with Eastern Europe. British exporters were also reluctant to involve themselves in the countertrading and export consortia which were increasingly accepted practices and forms of East-West trade on the Continent. Another event which influenced Anglo-Soviet trade was the expulsion from Britain in 1971 of 105 Soviet trade officials for alleged industrial espionage and other offenses. This happened a day before the arrival of a high-level Soviet trade delegation and resulted in the loss of important contacts and contracts—which were difficult to regain despite the offering of generous credit lines in 1972 and 1975—of £200 million and £950 million, respectively.

Britain's interest in expanding its trade with the East in the 1970s brought it into occasional conflict with the United States. In 1970, for example, Britain threatened to veto all U.S. license requests to COCOM until America removed a two-year block on ICL's request for a license to export more computers to the Soviet Union. Even after the United States lifted its ban on the license the Nixon administration tried to prevent ICL's sales by invoking provisions of the 1969 Export Administration Act (EAA) to prohibit the re-export of American components in ICL computers.[12] Such experience with American attempts to implement the provisions of the EAA to apply export controls extraterritorially both here in 1971, and again in the 1982 pipeline sanctions dispute, helps explain Britain's opposition to extraterritoriality pursuant to U.S. export control efforts.

Britain's declining share of trade with the Soviet Union (as indicated in figure 7.1 and in specialized U.K.-CMEA trade statistics) has troubled those concerned with U.K.-Soviet relations. Although Britain attempted to promote its East-West trade vigorously in the 1960s and 1970s by matching its competitors' credit conditions, encouraging East-West trade commissions and other initiatives to facilitate trade, and seeking to loosen further the COCOM embargo, it was unable to reverse its declining trade performance with the East.

Seeing its market shares decline in relation to those of its major competitors, some in Britain wondered about the desirability and growing costs of British controls on East-West trade. Although many other factors were influencing the British decline and its competitors' rise, the possibility of COCOM controls unfairly restricting British exports was a convenient explanation for some. Table 7.2 illustrates the magnitude of adjustments that were rapidly occurring in the OECD's market shares of total trade turnover with the Soviet Union. While Britain slipped from 14.4 percent and first in the OECD market share in 1965, to 6.4 percent and seventh in 1975, to 3.8 percent and

Figure 7.1.   U.K. Share of Soviet Turnover with Industrial West (percentages).

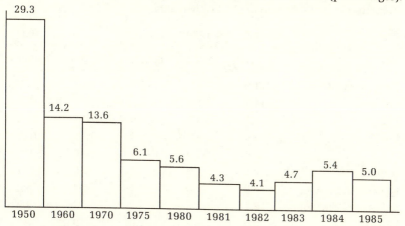

Source: Great Britain, Parliament, Second Report from the Foreign Affairs Committee, Session 1985–86 (UK-Soviet Relations), HC 28-I, p. cxii.

eighth in 1983, West Germany went from 11.0 percent, to 19.3 percent, to 18.7 percent during the same period.

Even during the more recent period, following the significant drop in Britain's market share relative to its major competitors, the percentage of British exports going to the East continued to decline. Table 7.3 illustrates the declining percentage of British exports going to the Soviet Union and other CMEA countries as a percentage of total British exports from 1975 to 1983. Although the drops from 1.1 percent to 0.8 percent in exports to the Soviet Union and 3.0 percent to 1.6 percent in exports to all European CMEA countries may be viewed by outsiders as relatively minor, they were viewed in Britain as troubling signs of the continuation of Britain's deteriorating trade performance with the East.

In view of the declining trade performance and growing American pressures to control East-West trade more tightly in the early 1980s, British officials and exporters wanting to expand trade in the East had a great deal to do. However, unlike in the United States, there were few if any influential leaders or interest groups in Britain actively opposed to trade with the East. Moreover, major trade-related groups

Table 7.2.   U.K. and Major Competitors' Shares of Total OECD Trade
(Exports and Imports) with the USSR (percentages)

	1965	1970	1975	1980	1983
U.K.[1]	14.4 (1st)	14.1 (2d)	6.4 (7th)	6.2 (6th)	3.8 (8th)
West Germany	11.0	14.0	19.3	18.0	18.7
Finland	14.2	11.2	11.3	12.4	13.9
Italy	8.7	10.8	8.9	9.4	11.5
France	6.8	8.7	9.0	13.0	10.6
Japan	12.6	15.0	13.1	10.0	9.0
Netherlands	2.5	1.9	2.4	3.8	6.7
U.S.A.	2.8	3.5	9.8	4.2	5.0
Belgium/Luxembourg	2.1	2.4	3.0	3.7	3.8
Canada	5.9	1.9	2.0	3.0	3.1
Austria	3.4	3.0	2.5	3.2	3.0
Australia	2.9	1.4	1.7	2.5	1.0

[1]U.K. market position in parentheses

Sources: OECD Monthly Statistics of Foreign Trade (series A); OECD Historical Statistics of Foreign Trade (series A).

like the British-Soviet Chamber of Commerce, the London Chamber of Commerce, the Confederation of British Industry, the East European Trade Council, and others made their concerns about the future and growing costs of declining East-West trade quite clear. The banking lobby was also deeply concerned about what the decline would do to London's reputation as a world financial center. Having considerable stake in vigorous and stable East-West economic relations, the banks were loathe to see Britain adopt restrictive policies such as those proposed by the United States in response to Soviet complicity in the Afghanistan and Polish crises. Although generally neutral on the issue, British trade unions were also aware of their stakes in East-West trade and often sought to take positions supportive of them. Some unions have been upset by cases of "unfair" competition that have resulted from economic relations with the East,[13] but most have favored trade with the East. Unlike its partner in the "special relationship," deteriorating East-West relations and political events in

Table 7.3.   Exports to CMEA (Europe) as a Percentage of Total British Exports

	1975	1976	1977	1978	1979	1980	1982	1983
USSR (exports)	1.1	0.9	1.0	1.1	1.0	0.9	0.6	0.8
(imports)	—	2.1	2.1	1.7	1.7	1.5	1.1	1.0
Total CMEA (Europe)								
(exports)	3.0	2.5	2.5	2.6	2.2	2.2	1.5	1.6
(imports)	—	3.3	3.4	2.9	2.9	2.4	1.9	1.9

Source: East European Trade Council.

the late 1970s and early 1980s (such as the Afghanistan and Polish crises) did little to weaken the British consensus in support of East-West trade. British reactions to American efforts in the 1970s and 1980s to place pressure on the Soviet Union through the imposition of East-West trade controls clearly reflected the pro-trade consensus and the deep-seated opposition to using export controls for political purposes. When President Carter protested Soviet human rights policy by denying the American exporter Sperry Rand a license to ship a computer to TASS for the 1980 Olympics, the British company ICL picked up part of the contract. A few years later, when President Carter sought British participation in a panoply of economic sanctions to protest the Soviet invasion of Afghanistan, Britain's support was lukewarm. The British responses were largely symbolic and none were undertaken which were judged to be more costly to Britain than to the Soviet Union. The credit line was discontinued, for example, but the government had already considered this action because the credit was not fully utilized and was becoming a source of embarrassment. Also, although Britain has always been willing to listen and has usually been sympathetic to American proposals to tighten export controls for national security reasons, it is generally unsympathetic when American restrictions are judged to be responses to political events. British reactions to American efforts to tighten domestic and multilateral controls in the aftermath of the Soviet invasion of Afghanistan reflected its distaste for foreign policy controls. Britain also opposed American proposals to expand the COCOM mandate to control Western "process know-how" going to Soviet "defense related industries." The British were also adamant in opposing a major upgrading of COCOM, which might take more export control authority away from London and the other national capitals and open the possibility of its being increasingly usurped by a U.S.-dominated COCOM in Paris.

Finally, Britain's strong pro-trade consensus remained intact in the face of American efforts to punish the Soviet Union for its complicity in the Polish crisis. Dissatisfied with the lack of allied support for U.S. East-West economic policy in general, and hoping to get the allies to withdraw from the major Urengoi pipeline project with the Soviets, the United States extended its controls extraterritorially to prohibit subsidiaries of U.S. firms from exporting non-U.S. oil and gas equipment and technology to the Soviet Union; and to prohibit export to the Soviet Union of products made abroad using technology either exported from the United States or made under U.S. license prior to the imposition of U.S. controls. The European response was unanimously critical. The British condemned the extraterritorial extension of U.S. control as a violation of international law. Lord Cockfield, the British secretary of trade, declared the extension "an attempt to interfere with existing contracts" and "an unacceptable extension of U.S. extraterritorial jurisdiction which is repugnant to international law."[14]

The government invoked the provisions of the Protection of Trading Interests Act, and the secretary of state for trade issued seven directives under section 1 (3) of the act, forbidding certain United Kingdom companies from complying with the U.S. embargo. This act had been passed in 1980 as a measure to protect companies and individuals in Britain against attempts by other countries to impose their legislation and regulations outside their own territory. Specifically, it was designed to combat what was considered the unjustified extraterritorial application of U.S. antitrust laws, which had long offended the British sense of sovereignty and territoriality, and which had a history of formal British protests. Thus, in August 1982 the act was unexpectedly useful when it was invoked to protect

British interests by prohibiting British-based American subsidiaries and licensees from adhering to the Reagan administration's trade sanctions. On August 2 the government used the act to safeguard four British contracts totaling £137 million, which represented over half the value of total U.K. orders won for the pipeline at the time. Similarly, in September the government directed John Brown Engineering Limited, a turbine-producing company, to ignore the imposed sanctions. In a demonstration of government, business, and trade union solidarity against the American demands, Mrs. Thatcher had visited the John Brown company and declared: "We will stick to our deal. We want to deliver. We will deliver!"[15]

Therefore, although Britain has long had a special relationship with the United States, and although both governments were led by conservative, anti-communist leaders in the 1980s, the British were unwilling to yield passively to U.S. export control directives. At the same time their opposition to U.S. policy was not as strong and their efforts to control East-West trade more rigorous than their allies on the European continent. As a result, and as we shall see below, the British position on the control of East-West trade falls somewhere between that of the more control-oriented United States and the more liberal allies discussed in the previous chapters.

Structure and Processes of British Export Control

The principal statutory instrument regulating U.K. exports is the Export of Goods (Control) Order. This is made under the Import, Export, and Customs Powers (Defence) Act of 1939. Under section 1 (1) of this act the secretary of state for trade and industry "may by order make such provisions as" he thinks "expedient for prohibiting or regulating . . . the importation into, or exportation from, the United Kingdom . . . of all goods or goods of any specified description." The order of 1985 incorporated the COCOM regulations agreed upon in late 1984.[16] The order, however, is not simply a reproduction of the COCOM embargo lists. For one thing, it also embodies a range of unilateral U.K. controls on items from nuclear goods to livestock to antiques.[17] Moreover, the COCOM regulations include a number of judgmental decisions (on the exercise of national discretion, for instance) which are not suitable for legal or enforcement purposes and are therefore omitted from the national regulations.

Just as in other COCOM countries, the responsibilities for export control policy in Britain are divided among various branches of government. The principal U.K. departments involved are the Foreign and Commonwealth Office (FCO), the Department of Trade and Industry (DTI), the Ministry of Defence (MoD), and Her Majesty's Customs and Excise. While Customs is responsible for enforcing policy under the 1979 Customs and Excise Management Act, the other departments are involved, in varying degrees, in the licensing and list review processes (commonly referred to as "casework" and "review work").

The DTI is the central actor in the licensing process (see figure 7.2). License applications for the export of controlled items to "proscribed destinations" are handled by the DTI's Security Export Control Section (SEC, informally referred to as the "COCOM division").[18] SEC is responsible for granting or denying licenses for the export of controlled industrial items to proscribed destinations. When SEC receives the initial export license application, it registers it and passes it on to the appropriate technical experts within the DTI.[19] The first task of these experts is to assess the embargo status or "licensing level" of the item in question. There are three basic licensing levels: at the first level is the self-explanatory "not embargoed, no license required"; at the second level the item is "caught" (i.e., embargoed) and a license is required, but the application need not be submitted to COCOM for consideration; rather the licensing decision is left up to "national discretion";[20] at the third licensing level the item is again caught, but the application must be referred to COCOM. At this third level the DTI is careful to point out that it "seeks" the views of its COCOM partners rather than having them imposed, because COCOM decisions are not in themselves legally binding on member states and the DTI would certainly not want to give British business the impression that it is dictated to by other states. In practice, however, COCOM's decisions are rarely overridden.

Figure 7.2. U.K. Security Export Control: Licensing Process

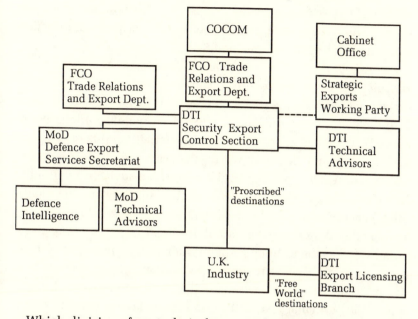

Which division of DTI technical experts the license application is sent to depends on the nature of the technology in question. Some 80–90 percent of license applications go to the Electronics Application Division (LAID).[21] As of December 1986, LAID employed sixteen or so full-time professional engineers and fourteen administrative assistants. This division handles all license applications having anything to do with electronics or microchips. The remaining 10–20 percent of applications concerning, say, avionics or chemicals are the responsibility of six or seven experts who have other (non-COCOM) responsibilities, and can devote only as little as 20 percent of their time to COCOM issues.[22]

At the same time that SEC sends license applications to these DTI technical experts, it also sends copies to the Foreign and Commonwealth Office (FCO) and the Ministry of Defence (MoD). Sending copies of individual license applications to the FCO is largely a formality. Although the possible foreign policy implications of high-technology exports to communist destinations have to be considered, it is rare for SEC to receive any feedback from the FCO. The FCO is more interested in broader foreign policy issues (e.g., liberalizing trade with China), and the export of goods to politically sensitive "middle destinations" such as Libya, Iran, and South Africa.[23]

The role of the MoD in the licensing process is an important one. Broadly speaking, its task is to consider the national security implications of high-technology and other exports to potential adversaries in the communist world (and about fifteen non-communist countries). The Defence Export Services Secretariat (DESS) is responsible for export control licensing within the MoD (like SEC in the DTI).[24] The MoD forwards those applications on which advice is required to its technical experts in the Chief Scientific Advisory and to Defence Intelligence. The task of the MoD intelligence experts is to determine, among other things, whether or not the prospective importing country already has the technology in question. Since any export license application that reaches the MoD is for an item that is on the COCOM list, it has already been determined that the item has some strategic value. The particular task of the MoD's technical experts is to assess that item's potential military application and the implications of allowing the technology to be exported to the particular destination for which the license is sought. Unlike most of the DTI's technical experts in LAID, the MoD's experts have various responsibilities and work only part-time on COCOM issues. Consequently, they will occasionally seek advice from civilian or military R&D establishments.

By law the MoD's decision on a license application is purely advisory because the DTI is responsible for granting and denying licenses, and therefore has a veto over the MoD's decision. In practice, however, the DTI rarely overrides the MoD's recommendations outright. Disagreements over licensing decisions are usually resolved quietly in interdepartmental working groups. Unlike in the United States, such disagreements rarely surface in public.[25]

The highly secretive Strategic Exports Working Party (SXWP) is an inter-departmental group that warrants special attention. It was set up in July 1983 in the aftermath of some harsh Pentagon criticisms of British controls and a visit by U.S. Defense Secretary Caspar

Weinberger.[26] The SXWP reports to a Cabinet Office committee, thus giving the prime minister the possibility of directly and specifically influencing the licensing process (see figure 7.2). It is chaired by the MoD and includes representatives from the DTI, the Joint Intelligence Committee (Whitehall's top intelligence watchdog), MI5, MI6, and Customs. Although little is known about the SXWP, it coordinates export control policy among the various departments and is thought to be responsible for beefing up export control enforcement and dealing with particularly sensitive license requests over which there are some inter-departmental disagreements. Despite the presence of the DTI, the composition of the group suggests a pro-control orientation. If this is so, it would not be surprising that the group maintains a low profile, given the strong pro-trade consensus and lobby in Britain. Moreover, despite the DTI's legal jurisdiction over the licensing process, it has been reported that the SXWP "has the right of veto over any proposal on equipment Britain puts to COCOM."[27] It is conceivable, of course, that the group is merely a cosmetic measure to appease the Pentagon's security concerns and really has little meaningful involvement in the licensing process.

Both the DTI and MoD are also involved in "review work"; that is, reviewing and working to update the COCOM lists to ensure that they continue to serve their strategic purpose without causing unnecessary difficulties for British exporters. A review of all items was previously conducted once every four years. However, this was inadequate, given the rapid pace of technological change, and it put the responsible authorities in each member state under considerable pressure; so, to improve the process, new procedures were agreed upon in COCOM to conduct review work on an ongoing basis, with one-fourth of the list being reviewed every year.

The relationship between government and business in this policy area is close and, generally speaking, is about as understanding and cooperative as can be expected in a situation where the objectives of each are largely incompatible. There is considerable consultation with industry in both casework and review work. Regarding casework, if a license application is caught, the typical reaction of the exporter (a "knee-jerk" reaction according to DTI officials) is to say that it should not be controlled. This reaction, even before it is known whether the license is granted or denied, is understandable given the delays and uncertainties that the licensing process causes.[28] If an application is caught or refused the DTI will very often explain the decision to the exporter, who will then be given an opportunity to challenge it. At this point the DTI (and its technical experts) and the exporter will often work together to try to improve an application's chances of success.[29] This could be done by trying to redefine the COCOM list category or "repackage" the product. While the former option is difficult and time consuming, the latter often involves redesigning the product downward (i.e., "downgrading"). This obviously has commercial disadvantages since the customer is unlikely to accept a technically inferior product.

Consultation between the government and business is even more important in conducting review work. The DTI maintains close contact with a number of large corporations, trade associations, and other interest groups on a fairly informal basis.[30] In an effort to assist exporters by minimizing unnecessary controls, the DTI actively seeks business's views on the COCOM industrial list. The feedback that it receives, especially from the more credible trade associations, may provide the government with important ammunition in arguing for a liberalization of controls on certain items within the COCOM forum. Many British businessmen, however, feel that their government does not do enough. They believe that the British government enforces the COCOM rules much more rigorously than other members and that, as a result, they are put at a competitive disadvantage. Registering concern over Britain's alleged restrictiveness, one member of Parliament suggested that Britain was "batting by the rules of cricket while our competitors are actually playing baseball."[31]

For many years Britain has been thought to occupy the "middle ground" in COCOM, between the restrictive, pro-control stance of the United States and the more liberal, pro-trade position of some of the other West Europeans. As early as 1953 one Foreign Office official described Britain's position as being "between the cynicism of the Continentals and the desire for outright economic warfare on the part of the Americans."[32] To some extent this represents the tension between Britain's perceived "special relationship" with America and its more recently realized role as a "European" nation. More relevant perhaps, its centrist position reflects, on one hand, its traditional commitment to free trade and, on the other, its appreciation of the need for some strategic controls.[33] This makes Britain less predictable than other member states. Sometimes it will clash with the United States on individual license applications (such as ICL's in 1970), or it will take the lead in calling for a liberalization of COCOM controls, as it did, along with France, during the 1950s and 1960s. Yet at the same time Britain has consistently recognized the need for strategic controls and has supported U.S. calls to strengthen COCOM and close existing loopholes; various reports suggest that, despite earlier opposition, it has also followed the American lead in regulating the flow of technical information.[34]

The balanced composition of the British delegation to COCOM reflects the middle ground it occupies. Although the delegate and his assistant (from the FCO) are the only permanent British representatives in Paris, technical experts from the DTI and MoD attend COCOM list review meetings.[35] However, it is relatively unusual to have technical support at the table on a regular basis. Although some other West European member states and Japan have trade department representatives, they generally bring in technical support only when a major commercial project is at stake. It is even more unusual to have technical experts from the defense establishment, as the United States does.[36]

Just as the British government tries to present a united front at home, so it does in COCOM. The trade and defense experts attempt to come to a consensus on agenda items well before the COCOM meetings. While there are differences of opinion among government departments, officials do not believe that Paris is the place to air them.[37] Consequently, the "seamless robe" of the British civil service is preserved.

The Making and Implementation of
British Export Control Policy

In this section we shall examine how the laws, orders, and regulations that constitute British export control policy are made, and how the policy is implemented to control British trade and technology transfer to the East. We shall proceed by considering the power of the groups involved in export controls, the politics of policy making and implementation, and the policy itself. Figure 7.3 illustrates our analytical framework and indicates the results of the analysis.

As the diagram indicates, there are both multilateral and national dimensions to policy making and implementation. In the multilateral dimension we are particularly interested in the influence of the United States on British export control policy. Indeed, one of our tasks will be to assess the degree of autonomy that Britain has over the making and implementation of its export control policy. In the national dimension we shall examine the power and political interaction of the various British governmental and business actors, and the impact they have on Britain's export control policy.

The Multilateral and National Dimensions
of Policy Making

Multilateral Power, Politics, and Policy. Britain's strong support of and participation in COCOM since its inception in 1949 result from its commitment to the Western alliance and the premise that export controls are vital to Western security. This commitment, and the COCOM regime more generally, represent historical influences of primary significance on the making of British export control policy.

More tangible, and worthy of special consideration, is the influence of the United States over British policy. In the early 1950s the United States dominated COCOM, specifically through the implicit threat of the Battle Act. However, as West European economic dependence on the United States declined and as the Cold War thawed, American

Figure 7.3. The Making and Implementation of British Export Control Policy

Dimensions of the policy process	Power	Politics	Policy
Policy making			
Multilateral	COCOM U.S. dominant ("first among equals")	Declining U.S. hegemony. Bargaining, conflict, and compromise	British policy reflects COCOM compromise
National	U.K. government U.K. business	Consensus and cooperation: "corporatism"	Acceptance of COCOM compromise: "incrementalism"
Policy implementation			
National	DTI, FCO, MoD, SXWP, U.K. business	Consultation and cooperation: corporatism	Strict interpretation of Control Order
Multilateral	COCOM and United States	COCOM veto; bargaining and reciprocity	Faithful implementation of COCOM compromise

hegemony weakened. As early as 1957 Britain unilaterally withdrew from the trade embargo on China (CHINCOM), and throughout the 1960s it successfully pushed for a liberalization of controls, indicating that the United States was no longer in complete control. Nevertheless, the perception and fact remain that the United States is still the single most powerful member of COCOM, and many British traders believe that it dominates that organization.

COCOM operates on the basis of unanimity, not majority rule. This gives each member, from the biggest to the smallest, a possible veto over all decisions. Technically, this veto power makes COCOM a body of equals. However, just as the British prime minister is the "first among equals" in the cabinet, so is the United States in COCOM. This is, of course, largely because of America's superpower status, but also partly because of its greater propensity to use its COCOM veto and partly because the veto is not the only power resource that can be used in COCOM. Information and expertise are also important and, with a larger team at COCOM and considerable support staff at home, the United States is well placed to influence technical debates. America's traditional pro-control stance on most COCOM issues also provides it with some power advantage because the burden of proof most often lies with those who wish to have an exception or something taken off the list. In this regard, notification about items on the COCOM agenda is generally received well in advance, giving the defense-oriented U.S. team plenty of time to prepare a strong case against decontrol should it wish to add some credibility to its use of the veto.

An acceptance of the need for strategic controls provides the basis for a strong political consensus among members of the Western alliance, and Britain is quite willing to work within the COCOM framework. However, there is a "control threshold" beyond which Britain will react to and resist what it considers to be excessive controls. The foreign policy controls that the United States has occasionally tried to foist upon its allies certainly fall beyond this threshold and, consequently, have been resisted. Moreover, at the periphery of the consensus on controls, where definitions of "strategic" vary, the political process in COCOM is also highly conflictual. The politics surrounding policy making are well illustrated by reference to the review of controls on computers.

During the 1982–84 review of the COCOM list the computer issue was perhaps the most fraught with difficulties. The United States (and in particular Richard Perle and the DOD) initially wanted to control all computers over eight bits because of their potential military application; (it was pointed out, for example, that the United States used the Apple 2 to target nuclear weapons). Britain and others, however, thought that this would be unenforceable and favored fewer but tighter controls on computers. The political interaction among the antagonists consisted of a number of compromises in three related areas: computer hardware, computer software, and telecommunications switching equipment. According to an American official in Paris, the compromise was "worked out to everyone's satisfaction"; and, reflecting their commitment to the "Western world order," British officials called it "a blow [i.e., a victory] for alliance unity."[38]

Without going into the specifics of the "horse trade," a number of points can be drawn from this case. For one thing, the compromise package came as a blow to Plessey and GEC's bid to sell "System X" telecommunications equipment to Bulgaria. Despite their financial resources and strong political connections (for example, GEC's chairman was Lord Carrington), the influence of these companies over the government was, apparently, no match for that of the United States. Also, in a revealing statement, a DTI official said that Britain had been unable to resist the U.S.-inspired telecommunications controls as much as some other COCOM members because its industry was more dependent on U.S. technology.[39] This was certainly true for the computer industry which, by one estimate, was 80 percent dependent on U.S. technology.[40] Moreover, the United States was ready to exploit this dependence. In June 1983, for example, it had threatened to cut supplies of American high technology to Britain unless Britain tightened up its export control enforcement practices.[41] This was not an isolated incident, but was rather part of an overall strategy to put pressure on the allies to toe the American line on export controls. It was clear to many observers that the Reagan administration linked progress in COCOM (i.e., an expansion and tightening of controls) to changes in controls on U.S. trade with COCOM countries.[42] One must conclude, therefore, that Britain agreed to the compromises not only for the sake of alliance unity, but also for more pragmatic economic reasons which transcended the interests of any particular firms, no matter what their resources.

Events, from the British withdrawal from CHINCOM to the latest computer list review, indicate that U.S. hegemony over COCOM is not complete and it is obliged to compromise occasionally. However,

Britain's dependence on American technology and, more generally, the importance of its trade with the United States (especially compared with its East-West trade), quite obviously puts it at a disadvantage when haggling with America in COCOM and obliges it to go the extra mile in making concessions.

National Power, Politics, and Policy. We know that, broadly defined, the principal actors at the national level are British business and the British government. Interested British business groups include exporters, trade and users associations, and other business interest groups such as the Confederation of British Industry (CBI). The main governmental actors were discussed in the previous section—the DTI, MoD, FCO, Customs, and inter-departmental working parties such as the secretive SXWP. In addition, there are a number of groups that bridge the gap between business and government—for example, the Inter-governmental Joint Commission, the East European Trade Council (EETC), and the Sino-British Trade Council (SBTC).[43] It is important to remember that members of Parliament also bridge this gap. Some, such as Paddy Ashdown (Liberal) and Spenser Batiste (Conservative), have championed business's cause by bringing export control issues onto Parliament's agenda and generally raising the level of consciousness about problems associated with export controls. Both Ashdown and Batiste have been especially concerned about the degree of American influence in COCOM and over British policy.

The DTI appears to be the *single* most powerful actor in making policy at the national level because of its central role in the export control list review. Other government departments make only a marginal contribution to this process. There are, however, two qualifiers. First, although the FCO may not take a direct and consistent interest in the review process itself, it does shape the broad foreign policy framework within which export control policy is made. For example, the DTI would not have pushed for a liberalization of trade with China without some Foreign Office assessment of the political changes in China and the future of Sino-British relations. Thus, the DTI makes export control policy within the broader foreign policy parameters set by the FCO and British participation in and commitment to the

Western alliance. Second, although the DTI has an institutional power advantage, having primary responsibility for policy making, it is highly dependent on business for much of its technical information. Thus, business can and does use its expertise to exert some influence over the government.

There are considerable power differentials within the business sector. For example, the DTI is much more likely to have established contacts with large corporations, such as Plessey, GEC, and Rank Xerox, than with small businesses. Having a larger share in East-West trade, large corporations are willing (and able) to contribute more time, money, and expertise to the review process. They are much better placed to influence policy than small firms. Trade associations are in even a better position to contribute to policy making. The DTI meets with key trade associations in working groups about four times a year to discuss list review issues.[44] It is because these trade associations represent a large number of firms, and therefore have a fairly broad view of industry's needs, that they have a special consultative relationship with the DTI.[45] Trade associations and large corporations also have more input into formulating policy options and making policy because, generally speaking, they accept the basic need for some strategic controls and are more willing to work within the established COCOM framework. Smaller firms, whose very existence may rest on the approval of an export license, are less tolerant of controls and tend not to have such a close working relationship with the DTI. It is also easier, of course, for the government to deal with a few large businesses than hundreds of small ones.

It is important to note here, in a discussion of power, that the government sets the rules of the game and industry must play by them or risk exclusion. The government's ability to do this is a powerful tool because it means that it can set the agenda and control different groups' access to the policy-making process. As far as input is concerned, the government is in a buyer's market and tends to co-opt only "team players" into the policy-making process; that is, those, to continue the analogy, who will "play ball."

Another advantage that the government has over business in conducting the review process is that much of the detailed consultation goes on under the constraints of official secrecy.[46] This denies business any leverage that it might otherwise gain by publicizing its arguments through the media. In short, although operating under some constraints, it appears that the DTI has certain advantages over business in making policy at the national level. The government solicits business's input in a selective manner and seems to use only that which is not inconsistent with Britain's interests and participation in the COCOM process.

The politics of policy making in Britain is, by and large, a consensual affair. Decisions are made with a minimal amount of conflict. Certainly all parts of the government work together to make policies that serve Britain's long-term security interests, which include economic as well as military goals. These interests are shared by many in the business community; those who see Britain's interests differently are largely excluded from policy making.

Despite the business groups mentioned above, it seems that most groups involved in East-West trade seldom get actively engaged in the formulation of export control policy options. The DTI, for example, has been disappointed by the minimal response to its efforts to solicit industry's input into the list review process. Spenser Batiste, M.P., has chastised these groups for their apparent reluctance to influence policy through Parliament, and has suggested that they only have themselves to blame for restrictive legislation.[47] Some in industry acknowledge this criticism. For example, representatives of the 48 Group of British Traders with China conceded that they had not made enough effort to persuade Parliament to promote Sino-British trade. This was in marked contrast to the situation in 1957, when industry bombarded Parliament with hundreds of cases and questions relating to the anomalies of CHINCOM.[48] Also, apart from some questions raised in Parliament by Ashdown and Batiste, there was little public debate surrounding the revision of the Export of Goods (Control) Order in 1985—a situation very different from the prolonged conflict over the passage of the U.S. Export Administration Act.[49]

Whether relevant interest groups are excluded by the government or exclude themselves because of apathy or lack of political efficacy, it seems that the consensual politics of British export control policy making is partly a result of the limited number of actors involved. If more groups were active the process might well be more conflictual. As it is, the making of British export control policy seems to be "corporatist" in nature. Although the government controls the policy-making process, business actors have some power and give governmental decisions a degree of legitimacy as reflections of industry's interests. Consequently, the government incorporates cooperative business actors into the policy-making process. Because all actors share some basic interests and understandings, and are interdependent (albeit asymmetrically), the politics of export control policy making is characterized by consensus and cooperation. This means that without the input of less enchanted groups who may, for example, see all controls as excessive, British policy is "incremental" and not far removed from that which results from the political processes in COCOM.

The Multilateral and National Dimensions of Policy Implementation

The implementation of export control policy refers, of course, to the licensing process addressed earlier in this chapter. We shall begin here by examining the power and politics of licensing policy on the national level, and then follow the process to the multilateral level to examine what impact the COCOM process has upon British licensing policy. To talk of policy here may be slightly misleading because it refers not to the laws, regulations, and orders that constitute export control policy, but rather to the consequences of the implementation of those laws.

National Power, Politics, and Policy. As noted above, the DTI implements the Export of Goods (Control) Order with the advice and participation of the MoD, FCO, and Customs. As in other countries, interdepartmental or ministerial differences do exist. The MoD tends to be more control oriented and emphasizes national security considerations. The FCO tends to be more foreign relations oriented and emphasizes diplomatic considerations. However, unlike the American process, these bureaucratic differences are seldom made public and are usually resolved quietly through interdepartmental meetings.

A big question in the mid-1980s concerning the distribution of power within the government at the licensing stage surrounds the role of the Strategic Exports Working Party (SXWP). Although the DTI is nominally the ultimate arbiter on "national discretion" licensing decisions, there is the possibility that the SXWP has some sort of de facto veto power.[50] If this is so, and if the SXWP has a pro-control bias (which its composition suggests), the implications for the power, politics, and policy surrounding British export control may be significant.

One of the most salient features of the politics surrounding the implementation of national policy is, in a sense, the relative lack of politics. Politics, by most standard definitions from Lasswell to Easton, involves making hard choices, and this implies dissension and conflict. While it would be foolish to say that the implementation of export control policy in Britain is apolitical, it is certainly far less adversarial than in the United States and in this sense is less political.[51] This is especially so for inter-departmental politics which, in turn, reflect some fundamental differences between the British and American government bureaucracies.[52] The internecine nature of bureaucratic politics in America has been addressed in John McIntyre's chapter in this volume. This is very different from the apparent consensus and deference displayed in the British bureaucracy; (hence the term *civil* service perhaps!). Although different government departments have different responsibilities, their interests and concerns overlap. Again, this is not to say that there are no differences among government departments, simply that the differences are not irreconcilable and they rarely surface in public.[53] The appearance of consensus, of the "seamless robe," seems to be vital—perhaps to the legitimacy and therefore continuity of national policy made chiefly by the bureaucracy.

The relationship between government and industry at the licensing stage of policy making is understandably somewhat more political. No matter how appreciative a firm may be of the need for strategic controls, that appreciation disappears when the firm applies for an export license and a potentially conflictual situation arises. However, despite business's typical "knee-jerk" reaction when an application is "caught," and despite grumblings about American influence over British policy, the politics here is characterized by a high degree of consultation and cooperation. Where feasible, and within limits defined by British participation in COCOM and the "Western world order," the DTI will work with individual firms to make a particular item licensable.

There have been times, of course, when some business groups have been unhappy with the licensing process. At one point, for example, delays in the licensing process became so bad as to be considered an "official handicap for UK high-tech exports."[54] One reason for the delays was that the volume of applications more than doubled between 1983 and 1985,[55] and the DTI simply did not have the staff to cope. The problem was aggravated by the confusion and extra work created by the new control regulations. In a paper submitted to the House of Commons Foreign Affairs Committee in May 1985 the East European Trade Council (EETC) reported that the "growing groundswell of anxiety among British manufacturers [about] delays in the issue of export licences in accordance with COCOM requirements had reached an alarming level."[56] It further claimed that the backlog of pending applications had reached "overwhelming proportions."[57] This outcry from British business had some effect because by the time the DTI gave evidence before the same committee in November 1985, considerable improvements were reported. Significant staff increases meant that whereas in January only 34 percent of applications were determined within two months, by August 65 percent were.[58]

Although this episode indicates that a concerted effort by industry can have some effect on policy, it also illustrates an acceptance of the prevailing consensus by industry. The business groups involved did not challenge the existing framework of export controls but rather tried to make it more efficient. Moreover, the episode was only a partial success because it treated the symptoms rather than the underlying causes of the long delays; most important, it failed to resolve the problem of extraterritorial U.S. controls which were resulting in additional delays of at least six months.[59] This situation had to await an American initiative.

Within the business sector trade associations are not as involved as individual businesses in the licensing process. It is only the prospective licensees who can adequately explain the exact nature of the items they wish to export. Again, big businesses are likely to have a decided advantage over small businesses when applying for licenses. For one thing, they are more familiar with the intricacies of the licensing process and are thus better players; they are also likely to have more contacts within the DTI and are able to devote more legal and technical resources to their application requests. They are more able, therefore, to influence policy implementation in the sense of getting their applications approved at the national level; as was seen in the case of Plessey and GEC, though, this by no means guarantees success.

Multilateral Power, Politics, and Policy. The veto that all members of COCOM have over individual license requests represents an important source of power in the licensing process. As was suggested above, U.S. power in this regard is particularly relevant simply because of America's pro-control orientation and its traditional propensity to use its veto quite frequently. However, the use of the veto on exception cases is restrained to some extent by the need to follow precedents in order to avoid charges of discrimination. And should this restraint be insufficient, the politics of the COCOM licensing process dictate that the veto cannot be used excessively for fear of a tit-for-tat strategy whereby one's exception requests may be vetoed by those whose requests were vetoed earlier. Inevitably the unanimity rule means that some restraint must be exercised in using the veto and, although COCOM decisions are made in strict secrecy, our interviews with delegates suggest that the political process at the licensing stage in COCOM involves considerable bargaining, compromise, and reciprocity.

There are other ways in which the United States is believed to have considerable influence over the implementation of export control policy. For example, some in Britain perceive an indirect American influence over "national discretion" licensing decisions and believe that America was directly involved in the establishment of the SXWP. Certainly those who criticize the present Thatcher government as an "American poodle" hold this point of view.

A more tangible source of American power over policy implementation in Britain lies in the extraterritorial extension of U.S. export controls. This is undoubtedly the most contentious export control issue that exists in Britain in the mid-1980s, and yet it is one that the British government has found difficult to tackle, despite its strong stand against American extraterritorial controls in the past. Until early 1987 British companies wishing to re-export U.S. goods or export goods with U.S. components had no choice but to apply to the U.S. Commerce Department for a license. Not only was this a time-consuming process, but a large number of applications were returned without action (RWA)—an implicit rejection. The DTI warned traders that, although these regulations were not legally binding in Britain, "the US authorities commonly penalize foreign companies which do not comply, by denying them access to US goods or technology in future [sic]."[60] This situation infuriated many traders, but despite the parliamentary efforts of Ashdown, Batiste, and others, the government did little. In February 1987 the British government allowed U.S. auditors to inspect U.K. importers of American technology at the importer's request.[61] By subjecting themselves to a U.S. audit, British firms could get "approved consignee" status that would obviate the need for a U.S. license in some instances. As well as the administrative advantages of the new arrangements for traders, the government had secured some concessions from the United States which made the inspections slightly more tolerable. For example, the audits were to be voluntary and, more important perhaps, U.K. companies would not have to furnish the U.S. Commerce Department with a complete list of their customers—information with considerable commercial value. Yet, despite these concessions, the new regulations relieved the problem of extraterritoriality at the margins only. Although individual U.S. licenses are not required to re-export national discretion items to other COCOM countries, they are still needed to re-export from other COCOM countries to third countries. Also, U.S. licenses are required to re-export goods with U.S. content over 10 percent for the East and over 25 percent for the West; percentages, some would say, that are exceedingly difficult to calculate. The policy outcome shows that the boot was, once again, quite securely on the American foot; the United States was able to tighten West-West controls on technology transfer at the expense of British economic and political autonomy.[62]

In conclusion, although the DTI is nominally the key actor in the political process surrounding export licensing, it is sensitive to, and at all times influenced by, input from other actors inside and outside the British government. Inside, others such as the MoD and SXWP are potentially important actors who, under certain circumstances, can and do influence licensing decisions. Outside the government, businesses have some access to and influence over the licensing process by virtue of their expert knowledge of the technology. Although the process is not a highly politicized, visible one, business does have some impact on both the nature of the licensing process (e.g., in reducing processing delays), and the licensing decisions themselves. Finally, for those licensing decisions that must be taken to COCOM, the United States and other COCOM members always have the veto power to make their presence known. Furthermore, the United States can exert its influence over the British licensing process outside of the COCOM framework—most importantly through its extraterritorial controls. These sources of power have had and will continue to have an important impact on British licensing outcomes.

British and Allied Export Control Policy in Comparative Perspective

To summarize and conclude, we wish to address comparatively some of the central themes in this book. The first has to do with the broader political environment in which trade policy and, more specifically, East-West trade and export control policy, is made and implemented. There are some important contrasts involved among the countries we are addressing in parts I and II of this book and, significantly, between the United States and the four allied states in particular. In the four allied states, and certainly in Britain, governmental and non-governmental actors interested and involved in trade policy are operating in and wield power within a political environment that is distinctly more pro-trade than that found in the United States, or perhaps we should say in the United States of the past. Because of this pro-trade environment, most actors with power in Britain, continental Western Europe, and Japan emphasize the benefits of promoting and the costs of controlling trade with the East. These broader political environments and general attitudes about East-West trade tell us something important about who will have power to make and implement policy controlling East-West trade.

Accordingly, in comparison with the United States, there are more actors with power in the British, West European, and Japanese democracies who are in favor of doing what they can to promote rather than control East-West trade. Although all national leaders and most public officials in the allied states go along with the controls called for in the compromises reached in COCOM, they oppose extending them to a broader list of dual-use technologies as many powerful actors in the United States wish to do. It is extremely hard to find political personalities in Britain, or in any of the other West European or Japanese democracies, who favor controls on East-West trade in the way that Ronald Reagan, Caspar Weinberger, Jesse Helms, or Richard Perle have done in the United States in the 1980s. Furthermore, there are no agencies or institutions in the allied governments that have pursued an aggressively active anti-trade, pro-control campaign as has the Department of Defense in the United States. In fact, the preceding chapters reveal very few actors in the allied states with or without power, in or out of government, who are calling for strict controls on economic and technological relations with the East. While the 1987 Toshiba affair spawned a variety of pro-control initiatives in Japan, considerable evidence suggests that these represented the political exigencies of the moment rather than any fundamental change in Japanese politics and policy.

The chapters in this section (and indeed those in the previous section on the United States) have shown that power in the area of export controls is concentrated in the executive branch of government. The principal bureaucratic actor in all countries is the trade ministry, which is also responsible, of course, for trade promotion. In Britain and France, however, unlike Japan and the FRG, the defense ministries also have a significant role to play in the policy-making process.

The power of business groups in this policy area varies somewhat from country to country, although it is important to remember that they all operate within strong pro-trade environments. In Japan and the FRG business groups have considerable interest in and access to the policy-making process; indeed, in Japan it is sometimes difficult to distinguish between government and business, given the exchange of key personnel between the two. In Britain and France these groups are still interested in pro-trade policies, of course, but are less active even though the opportunities for greater participation exist.

Little debate takes place in the parliaments on the issue of export controls, but when it does it is often in opposition to the pro-control, anti-trade initiatives that the United States has attempted to impose on the allied governments. Debates related to export control policy in European parliaments in the 1980s generally focused on the need for the national governments to resist the extraterritorial impositions of the U.S. superpower. Because of the intensity of the domestic sources of power in Britain and elsewhere, the United States was frequently obliged to make deals and compromises with allied governments on export control issues. However, the debates within the parliaments, and broader societies, do call attention to the powerful role played by the United States in the export control policies of its European and Japanese allies. Although the United States is no longer a hegemonic power able to get what it wants all the time, no one would ignore its role in continuing to influence the making and implementation of export control policy in the allied countries.

The politics surrounding the implementation of export control policy also varies considerably between the United States and its British, West European, and Japanese allies. In comparison with what has been traditionally a more adversarial business-government relationship in the United States, the allies provide a relatively open and explicit form of exporter access to the licensing bureaucracy. The relationship between the government agency in charge of licensing and those exporters applying for licenses has tended to be a cooperative one. Certainly, many pro-control spokesmen in the United States claim that the relationship has been too cosy and that the licensing authorities have been too willing to accommodate business. They allege that this has resulted in practices that have undermined the Western embargo. Clearly the pro-trade politico-cultural environments, power structures, and policy-making and implementation processes have brought about policy outcomes in Britain, continental Western Europe, and Japan that are quite different from those in the United States.

In summary, although agreeing to control militarily significant trade and technology transfer as part of their participation in the Western alliance and COCOM, the allies are reluctant and, for the most part, unwilling to consider policy changes that they interpret as an expansion of the COCOM embargo. Their national export control policies, and the implementation of these policies, are of a minimal nature in that they represent an inclination to do no more than is necessary to restrict the eastward flow of militarily significant technology. These policy outcomes contrast markedly with the traditional maximal (doing everything necessary to "play it safe") approach of the United States.

Although predictions are always risky, we do not foresee any major changes in British or allied policy. There may, of course, be occasional incidents resulting in temporary concern about the need to tighten export controls in some of the countries, as there was in Japan in 1987 in the aftermath of the Toshiba affair (discussed in

Gordon Smith's chapter). However, the politico-cultural environments, power structures, and processes are such to resist major changes that might move their policies more in line with the more restrictive U.S. approach. As noted in the chapters that follow, these realities have important consequences for the power relationships, political processes, and policy outcomes characterizing the issue of controlling East-West trade within the Western alliance.

III

The Management of East-West
Trade and Technology Controls
within the Western Alliance

8

The Management of Alliance Export Control Policy: American Leadership and the Politics of COCOM

Michael Mastanduno

Introduction

Throughout the postwar era America's military and geopolitical competition with the Soviet Union has contained an explicit economic dimension. One of its central features has involved an effort by U.S. officials to deny or delay the Soviet acquisition of civilian technologies and products of military relevance (so-called "dual-use" items). U.S. officials have pursued that objective nationally by utilizing an extensive peacetime export control apparatus, and internationally through the multilateral coordination of export controls with members of the Western alliance (including Japan) in COCOM.

Since 1949 the Western allies have used COCOM to construct and administer lists of items to be restricted from export to the East for reasons of national security. It has been the primary, albeit informal, mechanism through which the allies have attempted to reconcile the conflict between economic benefits and security risks inherent in trade with potential adversaries. As a "gentlemen's agreement," COCOM's decisions have always been viewed as recommendations to member governments; compliance is dependent on the will of those governments rather than on multilateral procedures and penalties.

The fact that the allies have participated in COCOM, however, tells us little about the nature and extent of their cooperation and how it has changed over time. COCOM's relative strength or weakness as an embargo instrument can vary, depending on such factors as the scope and coverage of the control list, the commitment of alliance members to the enforcement of their controls, the frequency with which embargo exceptions are granted and, generally, the attitude of COCOM members with regard to the national security significance of their multilateral control efforts. Judged by these factors, COCOM exhibited considerable weakness during the 1970s. Enforcement was lax, exceptions were routine, and the interpretation of the control list by member governments lacked uniformity. Since 1980 it has been partially strengthened, yet simultaneously it has faced (and currently faces) a number of problems and conflicts that, taken together, threaten to undermine the renewal of commitment that has emerged. Thus, the picture since 1980 has been mixed: while COCOM members have reached and acted upon a consensus that national security export controls should receive greater priority, that consensus is subject to pressures and strains that call into question its ability to endure over the longer term.

The purpose of this chapter is to document and explain the evolution of COCOM since 1970. What accounts for the relative strength or weakness of COCOM and its ability to maintain the former over time? The central argument is that more than changes in the relative distribution of power in the Western alliance, or in East-West economic conditions, the key factor influencing the effectiveness of cooperation in COCOM is the attitude of and role played by the United States. Over time the United States has tacitly acquired a special set of responsibilities in COCOM. These include responsibilities to maintain the integrity of the control process, set a domestic example, minimize the administrative burden of controls, and obtain the cooperation of key non-COCOM suppliers. The willingness of other Western states to cooperate fully in COCOM has been contingent upon the willingness and ability of the United States to carry out those responsibilities. The failure of the United States to do so during the 1970s was the key factor contributing to the weakness of COCOM. Since 1980 U.S. officials have taken on some of the responsibilities of COCOM leadership but have neglected or abused others. A somewhat strength-ened, yet still troubled COCOM has been the result.

The inability of the United States to carry out, consistently and fully, the tasks required of it in COCOM can be traced to distinctive features, both in terms of substance and process, of America's national export control policy. In particular, the tendency to entangle national security controls with foreign policy considerations, the complex and fragmented nature of the export control process and, with spe-cial relevance to the post-1980 period, the rise of the Department of Defense (DOD) as an export control actor have proven to be significant constraints on the ability of the United States to undertake a clear leadership role in COCOM. Moreover, to the extent that these factors are "structural"—i.e., embedded in U.S. control policy and likely to endure—even a strengthened COCOM will continue to be plagued by controversy.

A major theme in this volume concerns the relationships among power distributions, politics, and policy outcomes. The argument of this chapter suggests that while the decline of American power has made effective cooperation in COCOM more essential, since the United States no longer enjoys unilateral control over a wide range of civil-ian technologies of potential military significance, it has not ren-dered it unattainable. Despite having declined in *relative* terms, the United States continues to possess sufficient power and prestige in *absolute* terms to promote the realization of effective cooperation. This is largely due to the fact that the potential for effective coopera-tion in COCOM is still strong. While particular disagreements cer-tainly exist, there is less fundamental conflict between the United States and its allies over the purpose and necessity of COCOM's strate-gic controls than there is, for example, over controls intended to hinder the Soviet economy or influence Soviet political behavior. Consequently, the realization of cooperation does not require the United States to possess an overwhelming preponderance of re-sources to be used systematically to force the compliance of recal-citrant allies. Instead, American officials need to perform the leader-ship tasks noted above, consistently and predictably, in order to maximize the incentives for other COCOM members to participate faithfully.

Since the extent to which American officials perform such tasks is affected by the distinctive features of America's own export control system, the fate of multilateral export control policy is necessarily tied up with American national policy. Thus, efforts to reform or strengthen COCOM must consider and incorporate those aspects of U.S. policy that weigh heavily on the multilateral mechanism.

The next section of this paper provides a brief sketch of COCOM prior to 1970 and describes the distinctive responsibilities of the United States in COCOM and how they relate to the export control preferences of America's Western allies. The third section provides a discussion of what is meant by COCOM effectiveness. The fourth and fifth sections examine the politics of COCOM and the U.S. role in COCOM in the 1970s and 1980s, respectively. The conclusion elaborates on the argument and its implications.

COCOM: West European Preferences and the Special Role of the United States

The first decade of COCOM's existence (1949–58) was characterized by an ongoing alliance conflict over the broad parameters of the embargo effort.[1] While both the United States and its Western allies accepted the necessity of national security export controls and the need to coordinate controls multilaterally, they differed profoundly with regard to the scope of controls and the criteria that should be used to govern construction of the control list. West European governments favored what might be called a strategic embargo, involving restrictions only on those civilian items that would be of direct military utility to the Soviet Union.[2] Such an embargo would entail some degree of economic sacrifice, but would be sufficiently narrow in scope to allow the restoration of "peaceful" trade with the East. U.S. officials, in contrast, sought restrictions not only on exports of direct military significance but also on those that would contribute significantly to Soviet economic recovery and development. As put forth in NSC-68, they presumed that the primary function of the Soviet economy was to serve the needs of the military sector and thus reasoned that Western trade that enhanced the Soviet economy indirectly contributed to Soviet military power.[3] West European officials were wary of accepting this logic and of participating in a broader economic warfare strategy, on the grounds that it was both economically costly and politically provocative to the Soviet Union.

This alliance conflict was muted only in 1950–52, when the outbreak of the Korean War and the sense of military vulnerability it created in Western Europe worked to shift West European preferences in favor of a more comprehensive embargo.[4] COCOM maintained this broader embargo until 1953, when West European leaders, reacting to the receding threat of East-West conflict and the acceleration of economic recovery, began to press the United States for a significant reduction in the COCOM control list. By 1954 U.S. officials reluctantly acquiesced, and COCOM adjusted its criteria and controls to that of a narrow strategic embargo. The United States managed, temporarily, to maintain COCOM support for the continuation of comprehensive controls on exports to China, but by 1957 this so-called "China differential" was also formally abandoned following the unilateral defection of Great Britain. A second general round of list reductions occurred in 1958, and by its completion the multilateral embargo unambiguously reflected the preferences of Western Europe, while the United States was left to practice economic warfare unilaterally.

Compared to the first decade of its existence, the most striking feature of COCOM in the 1958–69 period was that it was no longer an issue of "high politics" in the Western alliance. There were no great debates over the purpose and direction of the embargo, and relations among COCOM members were not marked by the atmosphere of conflict that had prevailed during much of the previous decade.[5] COCOM delegations carried out the detailed, technical work of administering the embargo without major controversy.[6] List reviews were carried out periodically and became a matter of routine; marginal additions to and deletions from the list reflected military-related technological progress in the West and the USSR. The number of items on the list remained fairly constant, fluctuating only within a relatively narrow range.[7]

Two factors accounted for the relative harmony in COCOM relations during the 1960s. First, despite continued differences at the level of national policy, the issue of control criteria ceased to be one of alliance contention. With some reluctance U.S. officials accepted that COCOM controls, which focused only on civilian items of direct military significance, would be less comprehensive than U.S. controls, which continued to restrict items of economic significance as well. Second, adherence to COCOM controls did not significantly constrain West European states from pursuing trade with the East. Throughout the 1960s West European firms managed to expand significantly their exports of industrial machinery and equipment, as COCOM controls affected only a relatively narrow range of civilian traded goods.[8]

The fact that COCOM controls were narrowly conceived and compatible with expanded East-West trade should not be taken to imply that they were perceived as strategically inconsequential. On the contrary, U.S. officials in particular considered the multilateral control system to make a meaningful, if modest, contribution to U.S. and Western security. While export controls clearly could not prevent the Soviet Union from becoming a major military power, U.S. intelligence officials estimated in the mid-1960s that COCOM controls had helped to retard Soviet military capabilities that were dependent on a range of advanced technologies. A relaxation of multilateral controls would give the Soviet military "an improved ability to perform its basic missions."[9] U.S. officials came to recognize that while COCOM could not deny outright the Soviet acquisition or development of militarily significant technologies, it could help to delay that process and thereby contribute to the preservation of U.S. lead time in the application of technology to military purposes. Since the mid-1960s the use of export restrictions to help preserve U.S. strategic lead time has endured as COCOM's primary objective.[10]

More important for the purposes of this chapter, the first two decades of COCOM's existence witnessed the emergence of the general conditions under which multilateral cooperation in pursuit of that goal could be effective. Those conditions involved the relationship between West European export control preferences and the special role played by the United States in COCOM. An understanding of that relationship is vital to understanding the strengths and weaknesses of COCOM in the 1970s and 1980s.

Special responsibility for ensuring the effectiveness of cooperation in COCOM falls upon the United States for two reasons. First, as leader of the Western alliance the United States has always assumed primary responsibility for ensuring the adequacy of alliance deterrence and defense. Consequently it has a stronger interest than other alliance members in ensuring that Western technology does not contribute inadvertently to Soviet military capabilities. This is not to suggest that other COCOM members are unconcerned, but the United States by necessity is more concerned. It has the most invested in military systems and technology and is most responsive, in terms of defense expenditures and commitments, to improvements in Soviet capabilities. Not surprisingly, West European governments have tended to be passive in this aspect of COCOM, and the great majority of proposals for extending or enforcing controls have originated in the United States.

Second, the history of COCOM demonstrates that West European governments have been willing to cooperate effectively in the multilateral export control regime only if certain conditions are met. Items under control must be clearly "strategic," that is, shown to be directly useful to the Soviet military and likely to enhance Soviet military capability. The exercise of controls with the intention of weakening the Soviet economy or influencing Soviet political behavior has been considered beyond the purview of COCOM. U.S. efforts to use COCOM for such purposes generally have met with resistance. Moreover, each government has been willing to control those items accepted as strategic only if assurances are provided that all other suppliers—COCOM and non-COCOM—are similarly restricting the items in question. America's counterparts in COCOM have been reluctant to deny their firms the opportunity to export items that are available to the East from other sources. Taken together, these two conditions suggest that

West European governments are willing to accept the economic sacrifices only of those controls that are justifiable on narrow national security grounds and are likely to have an impact on Soviet capabilities. This reflects the fact that West European governments and firms place considerable value on the economic benefits of trade in general and East-West trade in particular.

The combination of America's preponderant and Western Europe's contingent interest in COCOM controls makes it imperative that the United States exercise leadership responsibilities in COCOM. For Western Europe, where economic interests are a primary concern, effective cooperation requires that certain assurances be provided and conditions met. For the United States, where security interests are dominant and require multilateral cooperation to be realized, there is great incentive to see to it that such assurances are provided and conditions satisfied. Effective cooperation in COCOM can be realized only if the United States creates an environment within which other members have incentives to participate fully and faithfully. Specifically, maximization of West European participation and COCOM's effectiveness requires that U.S. officials undertake the following four responsibilities.

First, the United States must take the lead in maintaining the integrity of the control process. Although in principle all COCOM members share this task, in practice the United States bears primary responsibility for bringing control proposals to COCOM and establishing their strategic merit. More so than other members, the United States possesses and employs the intelligence resources necessary to determine which civilian items are likely to be of military significance in Western and Soviet systems. In judging strategic merit, COCOM has come to rely heavily on U.S. technical assessments; when U.S. officials can offer clear and specific evidence of an item's military relevance, other members are generally receptive to adopting controls.[11] The legitimacy enjoyed by the United States, however, can be compromised if other members suspect that U.S. proposals are driven by political rather than strategic considerations. In that event the incentives to cooperate diminish, as evidenced by Britain's and Japan's refusal to abide by the China differential in the mid-1950s.[12] As a general rule, maintaining the integrity of the control list requires that the United States refrain from using COCOM as a political instrument, consciously or inadvertently.

Second, U.S. officials can foster cooperation by setting a domestic example. The United States has been called the "conscience" of COCOM, suggesting that American behavior sets a standard for others to follow.[13] If U.S. officials expect other members to adopt and enforce controls faithfully, they must ensure that American firms are denied strategic trade with the East and that U.S. enforcement efforts are exemplary. As discussed below, considerable discontent has been generated in COCOM by the perception that U.S. policies at times enable American firms to gain competitive advantages in Eastern markets. Their veracity notwithstanding (indeed, American firms have been more disadvantaged by controls than their West European counterparts), as long as such perceptions are widespread the incentives for cooperation in COCOM diminish.

Third, it was noted above that West European COCOM members are willing to control strategic items as long as they can be assured that other potential suppliers, COCOM and non-COCOM, are applying similar restrictions. The provision of such assurances, particularly with respect to non-COCOM suppliers, has generally fallen upon the United States. During the 1950s U.S. officials struck bilateral export control agreements with Sweden and Switzerland; more recently they have sought to strengthen those arrangements and to initiate others with newly industrializing countries such as India and Singapore. The existence of foreign availability outside COCOM has the potential to frustrate and render COCOM controls pointless, and thus it is imperative that this task be accomplished.

Finally, the United States can enhance COCOM cooperation by working to minimize the administrative burdens of the export control system. Specifically, this means working to keep the control list as short as possible by decontrolling items at the lower end that are readily available to the East either indigenously or through non-COCOM sources. It also calls for timely responses to West European requests for exceptions to the embargo or re-export licenses. Administrative feasibility is a critical issue to West European governments and firms. The more comprehensive the list, the more difficult it is for governments to administer and enforce it, and the greater the licensing delays, the more difficult it becomes for firms to compete effectively for export markets. While these factors are relevant in the U.S. context, they tend to weigh more heavily for America's trade-sensitive allies. As the lead actor in COCOM, the manner in which the United States handles the administrative tasks of the regime bears significantly on the overall cooperative effort.

By undertaking the above tasks the United States will not ensure absolute harmony or the absence of conflict in COCOM. Disagreements over the strategic utility of certain items will always exist. Similarly, member states will continue to exert pressure to liberalize strategic items when economic incentives are particularly high. Nevertheless, by carrying out its leadership responsibilities fully and effectively, and by negotiating compromises in COCOM over items at the margin, the United States can maximize alliance support for an effective strategic embargo.

In short, the potential for cooperation in COCOM has traditionally depended on a tacit arrangement between the United States and its allies. The allies accept the economic and administrative burdens associated with export controls, while the United States accepts responsibility for providing the strategic justification for controls and ensuring that burdens are minimized and shared equitably. During the 1970s the United States did not perform its leadership role adequately, while during the 1980s it has done so only partially. The reasons underlying this behavior and its impact on COCOM are explored later in this chapter. The next section provides a working definition of COCOM strengths and weaknesses and briefly examines alternative explanations for the evolution of COCOM since 1970.

COCOM Strength: Definition and Explanation

As others have observed, determining precisely the "strength" or "effectiveness" of COCOM is a complicated task.[14] Data are not always available, and often judgments must be made that are somewhat subjective or arbitrary. Ideally, it would be useful to evaluate the ability of COCOM to achieve its ultimate objective—the preservation of U.S. (and Western) lead time over the Soviet Union in the application of technology to military systems. This might involve a measurement of the U.S.-Soviet technology gap across a number of weapons systems over time. If the (cumulative) gap grew larger, it could be taken as a sign of COCOM's strength; if it grew smaller, of COCOM's weakness. An obvious problem is that export controls are not the sole factor influencing the technology gap; of equal or greater importance are considerations such as the efficiency of the U.S. weapons procurement system, the indigenous technological capabilities of the Soviet Union, and the ability of the Soviets to absorb and diffuse Western technology. An assessment of the relative importance of these factors in determining the extent of the technology gap is beyond the scope of this chapter.[15] Furthermore, even if one were to make that determination and isolate the impact of export controls, there are additional difficulties in ascertaining whether Western technology actually finds its way into Soviet military systems, and if so, how significant a contribution it makes. Even government agencies with access to the best available information are sometimes unable or unwilling to render definitive judgments on the significance of individual or cumulative acquisitions.[16] Finally, even if the significance of Western technology's contribution could be established, the most imporant transfer mechanisms (e.g., espionage) might be beyond the ability of the export control regime to influence.[17] COCOM might be very effective and yet Western technology might nevertheless contribute significantly to Soviet military capabilities. In light of these considerations it is not surprising that a persuasive assessment of COCOM's impact on the technology gap has yet to be made.

A second, though less broad, approach is nevertheless useful and is adopted in this chapter. Rather than assessing the impact of COCOM controls on Soviet military power and the technology gap, it focuses more narrowly on the utility of COCOM as a mechanism for coordination.[18] In this approach COCOM's strength or weakness is assessed in terms of the faithfulness with which COCOM members formulate, implement, and administer their multilateral controls. Given COCOM's control criteria, how seriously or scrupulously do members commit themselves to ensuring that items judged to be strategic do not reach the Soviet defense sector? While by itself this approach does not enable assessment of COCOM's impact on Soviet capabilities, its advantages lie in directing attention to the internal political dynamics of COCOM and helping to shed light on the conditions under which effective cooperation can take place.[19]

An assessment of COCOM's relative strength—defined in terms of the commitment of members to maintaining their strategic embargo —can be made by examining such factors as embargo exceptions, enforcement, the coverage and interpretation of the control list, and the general attitude of member governments regarding the embargo effort. While these indicators do not lend themselves to precise measurement, they can provide a general, though somewhat rough picture of COCOM's strength at a given point in time.

For example, the extent to which member governments take pains to enforce their national controls is a useful indicator of the embargo's strength or weakness. Signs of strength include an ability to prevent or hamper the illegal acquisition of controlled items, or at least a willingness to devote additional effort and resources to that task in the face of evidence that it is required. Signs of weakness might include the existence of significant or routine diversions, and inaction by member governments in the face of it.

Second, COCOM rules include an exceptions procedure that allows members to request and (if approved) undertake a onetime sale to the East of a controlled item on the grounds that it will be used for peaceful (i.e., non-military) purposes. In and of itself the granting of exceptions should not be taken as a sign of weakness, and in fact the selective use of this procedure could help the embargo to function more smoothly in instances where economic interests are pressing and the risks of diversion minimal.[20] However, if exceptions granting becomes a matter of routine (and hence is no longer, strictly speaking, "exceptional"), and if it takes place without strict assurances that the items in question will not be directed to military use, this should be taken as a sign of embargo weakness. From the perspective of the embargo, as a general rule the less exceptions the better; the more there are, the more likely it becomes that items judged to be of military significance will reach the Soviet defense sector. Moreover, the routine use of exceptions may also weaken COCOM by legitimizing, in the eyes of governments and firms, trade in strategic items.

A third indicator involves the manner in which members construct and interpret the control list. It is a sign of regime weakness if items of direct military significance are left off the control list, either consciously or inadvertently. The same judgment can be made if members interpret the control list differently, meaning some governments allow sales that others presume to be restricted. Conversely, the undertaking of list revisions that lead to the addition of items of military significance or of policies that lead to uniformity in interpretation can be taken as indicators of regime strengthening.

The failure to decontrol items that are no longer strategic is by itself not a sign of embargo weakness. However, such a practice is likely to contribute to weakening the embargo to the extent that it strains the credibility of the embargo and increases either the burden of enforcement or the demand for exceptions. Thus, the failure to decontrol should be taken as a sign of indirect, or potential embargo weakness.

Finally, the attitudes of member governments toward COCOM are relevant, since the strength of the embargo depends significantly on the willingness of national governments to publicize, administer, and enforce controls. If government officials tend to view COCOM as either a futile or trivial undertaking or, more cynically, as an instrument to be used for economic advantage, their incentive to cooperate is likely to be dampened. Alternatively, governments are likely to comply more effectively to the extent that they perceive COCOM as a necessary and integral part of national security strategy.

An aggregate assessment of these factors suggests considerable weakness in COCOM during the 1970s. The enforcement of controls was not a high priority, and in retrospect it becomes apparent that the

Soviets routinely acquired strategic items illegally, particularly in the area of semiconductor manufacturing equipment. COCOM members processed and approved large quantities of exception requests, notwithstanding doubts as to whether they could adequately ensure that such items would not be diverted to military uses. Also evident was a lack of uniformity in interpreting COCOM controls, leading some members to export items others believed should be restricted. Finally, in terms of general attitudes COCOM was a source of controversy, as the allies questioned each others' motives and commitments, accused each other of hypocrisy, and at least at times wondered whether COCOM could continue to serve effectively as a strategic embargo instrument.

Since 1980 COCOM has been partially strengthened. The control list has been expanded, providing increased coverage in some areas and extending it to others not previously under control. At the same time members have sought to harmonize their interpretations of the control list. Efforts also have been made to improve enforcement; some governments have devoted additional resources to the task and have sought to increase awareness of the diversion issue in the business community. Diversions still occur, yet when they do and are exposed (for example, as in the Toshiba-Kongsberg case), member governments have become far more likely to respond by adopting significant corrective measures.[21] The granting of exceptions for the Soviet Union has been curtailed, and while the overall volume has remained high, the great majority of exceptions, especially prior to 1985, have been for exports to China. In general there appears to be greater concern among member governments regarding the risks of diversion and the significance of multilateral coordination.

COCOM's strength, and its ability to maintain it, should not be exaggerated. Enforcement efforts of some members continue to lag and illegal acquisition remains a significant problem in an absolute sense. The length of the control list and failure to decontrol less strategic items have placed pressure on the COCOM consensus and threaten to compromise the improvements in enforcement that have been made and the existing commitment to minimize Soviet exceptions. Perhaps most important, there still exists considerable discontent among some officials in both the United States and Western Europe regarding the export control practices of the other, which threatens to undermine the renewal of commitment. Thus, an overall characterization of COCOM for the period since 1980 as somewhat stronger, yet still troubled, seems apt.

Common explanations for the evolution of COCOM since 1970 focus on market conditions or international power considerations. A market explanation, in Odell's terms,[22] would emphasize the pressure placed on the COCOM embargo by the intensification of Western competition for Eastern export markets. Those markets, and others, became more attractive in light of the oil shocks and slow growth that characterized the 1970s. Governments, responding to economic pressures and incentives, weakened their commitment to COCOM. This interpretation appears to have been accepted by Dean Rusk, who argued in 1978 that "COCOM has withered away under the pressure of the NATO allies to sell to the East."[23]

Clearly, economic competition has played some role in straining the COCOM consensus. As a general explanation, however, a focus on market conditions is not fully adequate. For example, the COCOM list has remained fairly selective and narrow since 1958, suggesting that the expansion of export competition can, at least in principle, be compatible with the maintenance of a strong strategic embargo. During the 1960s the rapid expansion of Western Europe's trade with the East occurred without compromising the strategic embargo. Thus, for the 1970s what requires explanation is why export competition "spilled over" and affected COCOM. As suggested below, the reason has less to do with the enhanced importance of Eastern markets and more with the fact that during the 1970s the United States entered Western competition, and did so in a manner that compromised the strategic embargo. More important, unless one presumes that economic interests declined rather suddenly after 1980, it is difficult for a market explanation to account for the strengthening of COCOM. The early 1980s witnessed a sharp recession in the West, as well as a pipeline confrontation in which West European governments defended the access of their firms to Eastern markets. Notwithstanding incentives for and evidence of continued export interests, COCOM members agreed to bolster the strategic embargo.

A second possible explanation might focus on the relative distribution of power within the alliance. Some versions of the hegemonic stability argument, for example, hold that the maintenance of strong regimes depends on the existence of a dominant state, whose officials possess a preponderance of resources and use them to persuade or coerce other states to comply.[24] As U.S. power resources have declined relative to those of its allies since 1970, the ability of the United States to maintain strong regimes has become problematic. This argument can be applied to the export control regime: the weakness in COCOM since 1970 can be traced to the inability of the United States to maintain the compliance of others due to the fact that it no longer enjoys an overwhelming preponderance of resources.

This argument is useful in that it directs attention to the critical role of the United States in accounting for COCOM's effectiveness. However, its explanatory power is also somewhat limited. Again, unless one is willing to accept that America's relative power decline suddenly reversed itself after 1980, it is difficult to account for the strengthening of COCOM's strategic embargo since then. Moreover, given the (contingent) interest of West European governments in an effective strategic embargo, the possession by the United States of preponderant resources, relative to other states, is not required to sustain effective cooperation. While such cooperation is not automatic, the existence of essentially compatible interests makes it attainable even in circumstances of declining power. Even a non-hegemonic United States possesses sufficient resources to undertake its leadership responsibilities and to bargain forcefully in COCOM to sustain an effective strategic embargo.

On the other hand, where there does exist a fundamental conflict of interests over the purpose and necessity of trade controls, the United States most likely will be unable to obtain the compliance of its alliance partners. America's inability to gain alliance support for foreign policy controls in general, and the abandonment of the trans-

Siberian pipeline project in particular, attest to this fact.[25] In such circumstances the decline of American power is clearly more consequential.

The 1970s: U.S. Policy and COCOM's Decline

An adequate explanation of COCOM's strengths and weaknesses can be found more in the interaction between American export control policy and the multilateral regime than in economic pressures or the relative distribution of alliance power. For reasons discussed earlier the key factor concerns the extent to which the United States undertakes a special set of responsibilities in COCOM. During the 1970s the United States tended to neglect those responsibilities and no longer played an unequivocal role as the "conscience" of COCOM. Specifically, the United States failed to set a domestic example, ensure the integrity of the control process, or minimize the administrative burden of controls.

The primary reason can be traced to a profound shift that took place in America's national export control policy during the early 1970s. U.S. officials continued their pursuit of a strategic embargo, nationally and multilaterally. The United States remained, relatively speaking, the COCOM member most concerned with trade restrictions. At the same time, however, U.S. officials developed and utilized a strategy of trade expansion designed to achieve political objectives, and in particular to influence Soviet behavior. (The use of East-West trade expansion to further economic interests was at best a secondary concern; in fact, American firms were consistently hindered throughout the 1970s by the complexity and unpredictability of the U.S. export control process.) The linkage of American trade to "responsible" Soviet behavior was of course an integral component of America's overall détente strategy; particularly during the Nixon administration U.S. officials considered the rewarding of U.S. economic assets to be among their most powerful sources of political leverage.[26]

The question of whether trade was indeed an effective political instrument has been addressed elsewhere and is not of concern here.[27] What is crucial for our purposes is that the strategy of trade expansion became entangled with, and took precedence over, the pursuit of the strategic embargo. Within the U.S. government the potential foreign policy (and to a much lesser extent economic) benefits of East-West trade took on primary significance, while narrowly defined national security considerations, traditionally dominant, were still important, though no longer an overriding priority.

This shift in priorities is suggested by the fact that during détente U.S. officials permitted not only exports that would enhance Soviet economic capabilities, but also those which were likely to be put to military use and/or had potential military significance. The two most infamous cases involved Kama trucks and Bryant Grinder ball bearings. In the former case the Nixon administration granted numerous licenses and approved the full participation of U.S. firms in the massive project, despite strong evidence that some of the trucks produced might be used by the Soviet military.[28] The Bryant Grinder case was of potentially greater strategic significance in that it involved the export of machines that could mass produce precision ball bearings, which could be used to improve the guidance mechanism of MIRVed missiles. Whether or not the Soviets needed or actually employed the machines for that purpose is still a matter of debate.[29] What is important for our purposes, however, is that the United States allowed the sale despite the potential risks. And while Kama and Bryant are the most celebrated cases, others, detailed in a GAO report, similarly suggest a less vigilant attitude with respect to potentially strategic trade.[30]

A more general indication of the shift in U.S. policy concerned the willingness of U.S. officials to approve exports of potential military significance (i.e., COCOM-controlled items) if it could be demonstrated that the items in question would be used for peaceful purposes. The question of whether to rely on "end-use" determinations in American-Soviet trade became highly controversial during the late 1970s. The Commerce Department generally defended their utility, while other officials expressed considerable skepticism, particularly with regard to technology exports. They argued that once manufacturing know-how is transferred and absorbed, its initial end use is irrelevant and further applications cannot be controlled.[31] Moreover, detecting the diversion of items from civilian to military use is frequently difficult; in 1982 a high Defense Intelligence Agency official described the U.S. ability to do so as "woefully inadequate."[32] Another U.S. official frankly conceded that end-use controls were of limited utility but claimed it "made us feel good" to receive the written assurance of the end user.[33]

It must be emphasized that whether items were actually diverted to military use, and if so whether they proved to be militarily significant, is relatively unimportant for our purposes. Indeed, the military significance of American-Soviet trade during the 1970s has likely been exaggerated, particularly by Reagan administration officials.[34] Nevertheless, the fact that the United States was willing to accept what was traditionally considered strategic risk in the interest of broad foreign policy considerations is critical, given the traditional role of the United States in COCOM. This shift in orientation could not help but have a major impact on the calculations and attitudes of other Western states, which were pursuing trade liberalization for their own reasons.

The clearest link between the shift in U.S. policy and the change in the COCOM regime is found in the issue of COCOM exceptions. During the 1950s and 1960s the United States requested exceptions only very infrequently, and never for exports to the Soviet Union. As table 8.1 indicates, however, during détente the United States became the undisputed leader of the COCOM allies in making requests. It requested more exceptions than any other COCOM member, and in some years (1976–78) more than the total of all other members combined. As a percentage of total requests, U.S. requests climbed steadily and reached a peak in 1978, when five out of every eight requests were made by the United States.

Not surprisingly, as U.S. requests increased so too did those of other COCOM members. Given the traditional role of the United States as the conscience of COCOM, its change in behavior constituted tacit

Table 8.1.   COCOM Exception Requests

Year	Total requests	U.S. requests	United States requests as percentage of total
1962	124	2	1.6
1966	228	29	12.7
1970	544	133	25.6
1971	635	186	29.3
1972	1,085	415	38.2
1973	1,268	519	41.0
1974	1,369	567	41.4
1975	1,798	798	44.4
1976	1,039	593	57.1
1977	1,044	539	51.6
1978	1,680	1,050	62.5

Source: Statement of Lawrence Brady, in *Transfer of Technology to the Soviet Bloc*, p. 62.

approval of the extension of Western export competition into the realm of COCOM-controlled items. The United States essentially "opened the door," and legitimized the routine use of the exceptions mechanism.[35] And since COCOM decisions are sensitive to precedent, requests by one member to export a particular item not previously allowed prompted other members to make similar requests.[36] As a result, exception requests mounted rapidly, from a few hundred during the 1960s to over 1,000 annually in the 1970s.

The majority of COCOM exception requests were approved. Between 1974 and 1977, for example, out of over 5,000 total requests only 101 were denied, about 2 percent.[37] Interestingly, virtually none of the cases denied involved requests by the United States. If the United States wished to export items on the COCOM list, the allies, reflecting their general passivity in COCOM, were more than happy to oblige. On the other hand, virtually every denial made came as a result of the exercise of the U.S. veto.[38] The upshot of this pattern, predictably, was discontent on the part of the allies. For the United States to deny the exceptions of others on strategic grounds while it abstained from export competition was tolerable. However, to deny requests while at the same time submitting for approval more than any other member not surprisingly generated resentment in COCOM.[39]

Even more disturbing to the allies than denials were delays. The United States took significantly longer than other COCOM members to process exception requests and frequently flouted COCOM's procedural rules, which set limits on the amount of time allowed each member to review the requests of others.[40] The problem was compounded since the United States was the only COCOM member to impose re-export control requirements. This meant that requests submitted to COCOM that contained U.S.-origin components or technology were for some time subject to a double review. The COCOM request was processed by the State Department, while the re-export request —essentially the same thing—was handled by Commerce. Such cases, 25 percent of all allied exception requests, were subject to the longest delays.[41] To Western Europe and Japan the additional re-export review implied a lack of trust on the part of the United States of the COCOM process. Equally important, the uncertainty associated with U.S. delays hampered the ability of the allies to meet Eastern demand. The resentment of COCOM members reached its peak in 1978, when U.S. exporters complained that their exception requests were being held hostage in COCOM until the U.S. government granted approvals for other states.[42]

The combination of U.S. trade expansion and its occasional denial and frequent delay of other members' cases generated suspicion among the allies regarding U.S. motives in COCOM. The belief spread that U.S. denials and delays were less a matter of legitimate strategic concerns, and more the result of commercial considerations. The United States was perceived as abusing its privileged position in COCOM to advance its economic interests by providing its firms with a competitive advantage. When the United States objected in COCOM in 1975 to West German plans to build a $600 million nuclear power plant in the USSR, the West Germans suspected that the underlying U.S. motive was to manipulate the global competition between Kraftwerkunion and the U.S. firm Westinghouse.[43] Similarly, when the United States objected to a proposal by Lucas Aerospace of Britain to sell an advanced electronic fuel-control system to the Soviets for use in their version of the Concorde, Lucas contended that the real reason for denial had nothing to do with Western security but was intended to assist American aircraft parts manufacturers who competed with Lucas.[44] In a case involving the French firm Thomson, a French Foreign Ministry official scoffed at the suggestion that the United States was genuinely concerned that a sophisticated digital switching system could enhance the command and control capabilities of the Soviet military. Rather, he claimed, the United States was bitter over Thomson's success in marketing a system which AT&T had discarded earlier as lacking commercial promise. The real issue behind the U.S. objection was the global struggle for high-technology market shares between the United States and France; "there are no angels in this game, and in a fight even a hit below the belt is a good one, if you can get away with it."[45]

European accusations notwithstanding, it is doubtful that U.S. officials were sufficiently Machiavellian or unified to use COCOM systematically to advance American commercial interests. The delays in responding to COCOM exception requests were more likely a result of the same cumbersome bureaucratic procedures which frustrated U.S. exporters.[46] Nevertheless, that the *perception* existed that the United States was motivated in COCOM by economic rather than strategic considerations demonstrated the cynicism with which the NATO allies had come to view COCOM. In an informal organization based on the mutual trust and shared expectations of its members, such attitudes were a serious problem and could only reduce incentives for compliance with the rules. That the United States did little to allay the concerns of its allies reflects the lack of appreciation at the highest levels of the U.S. government for COCOM's problems.[47]

In light of the proliferation of exceptions and liberal application of end-use standards, it is not surprising that the United States and its major allies came into conflict over how strictly the multilateral embargo should be interpreted and applied. These conflicts demonstrated (as did American use of the exceptions veto) that the United

States, despite its own shift in policy, nevertheless was concerned with the potentially strategic trade of other Western states. In this sense the United States continued to play its traditional COCOM role. Given its own trade expansion, however, it was difficult for the United States to be credible in urging its allies to accept economic sacrifices in the interest of collective security.

Between 1967 and 1972 the United States attempted to resist pressure from Britain and France to allow the provision of equipment and technical assistance necessary to enable Poland to mass produce integrated circuits.[48] Poland desired the capability in order to increase its output of television sets, desk calculators, and small computers. U.S. objections were based on the fact that the integrated circuits produced could also be used in military equipment, and more important, the technology provided could serve as a starting point from which Poland (and the USSR) could progress to the production of more advanced circuitry with more important military applications. By 1972, with the onset of détente and America's own barrage of exception requests, the Nixon administration could no longer credibly resist. Nixon was persuaded by British Prime Minister Heath, against the advice of the Defense and Commerce departments, to remove U.S. objections. Exceptions were granted and the French won the sale.

Another well-known case was brought to light by the American machine tool manufacturer Cyril Bath.[49] In 1977 its application to sell a metal-stretching machine tool to the USSR was denied by the United States. Although intended for civilian use, U.S. officials decided that the machine in question could be used to enhance the performance of Soviet aircraft production. At the same time a French firm accepted an order for nine metal-stretching machines, virtually identical to those of Cyril Bath. Although the item was on the COCOM list, the French government never brought the case before COCOM as an exception request. When questioned, the French COCOM delegate claimed the machines were for automotive use and thus did not require COCOM approval.

A third case involved the Japanese sale of a huge floating dry dock to the Soviet Union, to be used for the servicing and repair of large ships at sea.[50] The Carter administration objected, claiming the dock to be militarily significant (despite the fact that it was not on the COCOM list at the time), and considering it likely that it would be diverted to military use. With a capacity of 80,000 tons it would be the only dock in the Pacific fleet area large enough to accommodate the Kiev-class aircraft carrier. The Japanese firm defended its sale, claiming that since the dock would be used primarily for civilian purposes it did not require export control approval. The Japanese government apparently concurred, since it declined to block the sale. In response to U.S. criticism, a spokesman for the firm stated that "we have nothing to do with the use to which this dock will be put, and if such a way of reasoning is applied, even foodstuffs can be used for military purposes . . . it was a floating dock we built gladly, as there are no orders for new ships."[51]

A final, critical indicator of COCOM's weakness concerns the laxity with which, in retrospect, export controls appear to have been enforced during the 1970s. A GAO study published in 1979 found that inadequate resources were devoted to enforcement efforts in the United States, reflecting its low-priority status in the eyes of U.S. officials.[52] For example, the Compliance Division of the Commerce Department, which had primary responsibility for enforcement, relied upon spot checks to discover and seize dual-use technology leaving the country illegally. Its coverage, however, was uneven; 88 percent of the checks were conducted at New York exit points, where only 55 percent of controlled shipments left the country; while only 4 percent of the checks were made in California, where 25 percent of controlled commodities exited.[53] Moreover, inspections were rarely made at nights or on weekends, despite the frequency of flights at those times, due to a lack of overtime pay for inspection personnel. In an earlier study in 1976 the GAO had found the Compliance Division to be "unable to effectively determine compliance with export control regulations," and to have "limitations on its ability to investigate alleged violations."[54] A Senate staff investigation completed in 1982 reached a similar conclusion, finding the Compliance Division to be "understaffed, ill-equipped and underqualified," and recommended transferring responsibility for enforcement to the Customs Service of the Treasury Department.[55] During the early 1980s both Commerce and Customs sought to take lead responsibility for export enforcement; during détente, however, neither was especially concerned with the problem.

To protect against the re-export of U.S. technology the United States relied upon the cooperation of its allies. This system was similarly less than airtight. The allies' willingness to cooperate was hindered by their opposition to the extraterritorial reach of American controls and by their resentment at the delays encountered in obtaining re-export licenses from the United States. According to the GAO's 1976 study, "the re-export of United States-controlled commodities without United States approval is the most significant form of illegal diversion to Communist states."[56]

In light of trade expansion and the cynicism that pervaded COCOM, it is not surprising that West European governments considered enforcement even less of a priority than did the United States.[57] The prevailing attitude in Europe appeared to be that since the Soviets could obtain virtually anything for which they made a determined effort, major efforts to prevent illegal sales were not worthwhile. Moreover, very little in U.S. behavior suggested that such an attitude constituted a threat to Western security.

An unclassified version of a CIA study and hearings conducted by the Senate Permanent Subcommittee on Investigations in 1982 brought to light some of the abuses of the control system during the 1970s.[58] The most dramatic case involved a syndicate of U.S. and German firms acting as illegal intermediaries between U.S. electronics firms and Soviet purchasing agents. Between 1977 and 1980 enough equipment was apparently shipped illegally—piece by piece, from Silicon Valley through Western Europe to the Soviet Union—to put together at least one entire integrated circuit manufacturing plant. According to the CIA, the ability of the Soviets to achieve large-scale integration and to apply it to their most advanced weapons systems can be traced directly to combined legal and illegal acquisitions from the

West. The general impression that emerges is that the Soviet Union encountered little difficulty in obtaining illegal items it desired for military purposes.

This section has traced the weakness that existed in COCOM during the 1970s to the failure of the United States to play its traditional leadership role. By the manner in which it expanded its own trade the United States failed to set a domestic example, thereby creating little incentive for others to minimize exceptions, adhere to a strict interpretation of the control list, or devote priority attention to enforcement. By subjecting exception and re-export requests to significant delays, the United States exacerbated the administrative burden of the control system and raised suspicions regarding the integrity of its own motives in COCOM. By failing to acquiesce in the decontrol of less strategic items, the United States increased the pressure for exceptions and reduced the incentives for enforcement. Finally, by allowing foreign policy considerations to become entangled with COCOM controls, the United States failed to maintain the integrity of the control process and thereby diminished its legitimacy as a necessary strategic instrument.

The 1980s: A Partially Strengthened, Yet Unstable COCOM?

The period since 1980 witnessed yet another significant shift in U.S. export control policy. The Soviet invasion of Afghanistan, the abandonment of détente, and most important, the growing concern among U.S. defense and intelligence officials regarding the strategic consequences of technology transfer to the East led the United States, beginning in the last year of the Carter administration, to tighten export control policy. The U.S. control list was extended, a policy of no exceptions on COCOM-controlled items for the Soviet Union was adopted, and a highly publicized effort to prevent the illegal diversion of technology to the East was put into place by the Customs Service. In recognition of the fact that in order to be effective controls must be multilateral, U.S. officials made the strengthening of COCOM a major priority. They sought to expand the COCOM control list, to improve enforcement, and to give more public prominence and a greater organizational presence to COCOM.

The response of America's COCOM allies was mixed. On one hand, Western Europe and Japan were unreceptive to any U.S. effort, in both the Carter and Reagan administrations, to extend COCOM controls to items of indirect strategic (i.e., economic) significance.[59] They also were wary of U.S. efforts to bolster or reshape COCOM organizationally. Western Europe and Japan resisted the intent of some Reagan administration officials to convert COCOM to treaty status and similarly refused to agree to the creation of a permanent military subcommittee on COCOM.[60] On the latter issue they ultimately accepted a compromise that created a body called STEM (Security and Technology Experts' Meeting), which could advise COCOM but had no formal role in it.

The response of West European governments to the initiatives described above reflects the endurance of their preferences regarding the purpose and nature of COCOM. As during the Cold War, the allies continue to support only those control proposals narrowly conceived and targeted directly at the Soviet defense sector and to prefer that COCOM remain an informal agreement with minimal publicity.

On the other hand, COCOM members have been more receptive to U.S. initiatives in the areas of exceptions, list additions, and enforcement. First, the allies acquiesced in 1980 to the U.S. policy of not granting COCOM exceptions to the Soviet Union. Given the routine use of the exceptions procedure to export controlled items to the Soviets during détente, the "no-exceptions" policy represented a significant development in COCOM. It had the effect of strengthening the embargo in that it reduced the access of the primary target to controlled items. As discussed below, however, the no-exceptions policy also created problems in COCOM, given the manner in which it was implemented.

Second, and more important, as a result of the 1982–84 list review, COCOM members accepted a significant expansion of the control list. Negotiations were protracted and difficult, but the outcome reflected a serious commitment on the part of the Western states to extend strategic export controls. In the first two rounds of the review tighter controls were agreed to on the export of electronic-grade silicon, printed circuit boards, and oil and gas technology that met the narrow criteria of dual-use items with direct strategic significance. Other significant list additions included large floating dry docks, a response to the Japanese sale of 1978, and certain industrial robots and the technology to produce them.[61] The final round of negotiations proved the most difficult, involving computers, software, and digital-switching telecommunications equipment. Computers had been at the center of COCOM debate since the mid-1970s; since that time no agreement had been reached to update the control parameters. The United States pushed in 1982–84 for very comprehensive controls, which the allies were reluctant to accept. A compromise was finally struck in July 1984 in which the United States exchanged some degree of liberalization on computers for new restrictions on software and telecommunications technology.[62]

In addition to expanding COCOM coverage in critical areas, the new restrictions entailed economic sacrifices for Western Europe and Japan. Shortly after the agreement was made, for example, the Soviets began to test it by pressing Japan officially for the export of robotics, computers, and telecommunications and semiconductor manufacturing equipment. The Japanese government—to the disappointment of some Japanese firms—quietly affirmed its adherence to the COCOM agreement and even attempted to have the Soviet request removed from the official communiqué of the meeting.[63]

In the telecommunications sector competition for sales to the East had become especially intense. Due to pressure from commercial interests, Britain and France initially resisted the COCOM compromise. The British firms Plessey and GEC had landed a £50–100 million contract to sell their "System X" to Bulgaria, its first significant overseas sale. The COCOM rules forced them to abandon the deal. The British government warned, however, that its firms would reconsider if non-COCOM suppliers threatened to replace the sale. The United States, taking responsibility for the preservation of the agreement, forced the major non-COCOM supplier, Sweden's Ericcson, to observe informally COCOM's new rules.[64] Similarly, West Germany's Standard Electrik Lorenz (SEL) was awarded a letter of intent from Hungary for a digital exchange system, and was promised follow-up contracts in the Hungarian market. The German government tested COCOM by agreeing to submit an exception request for the sale. The United States vetoed it and SEL at that point decided to await the outcome of COCOM's 1988 review.[65] Finally, while the French government sold switching equipment to the Soviet Union and Bulgaria prior to the 1984 agreement, it has apparently observed the new COCOM restrictions since then.

Third, COCOM members have been responsive (though in varying degrees) to U.S. concerns regarding the illegal diversion of controlled technology. Enforcement has been given greater priority at the multilateral level, with an emphasis on targeting technologies and third countries susceptible to diversion, and on harmonizing the import certificate/delivery verification system.[66] At the national level the British government increased its commitment, as evidenced by the establishment in 1983 of a team of nine customs investigators and three technology specialists to monitor illegal technology transfers to the Soviet bloc.[67]

At the urging of the United States, Japan similarly increased the resources of its customs service, with priority attention directed to COCOM-controlled items. In 1983 the Japanese government required for the first time that importers submit end-use documentation as a way to deter the illegal re-export of technology to the Soviet bloc.[68] In the wake of the Toshiba incident, and in response to U.S. pressure, Japanese enforcement efforts are likely to be strengthened further. With regard to France, the most important manifestation of improved enforcement efforts was the dramatic expulsion of forty-seven Soviet officials in 1983. The impetus for that decision came when French intelligence officials obtained the so-called "Farewell" papers, which documented the systematic, and successful, effort by the Soviets to acquire illegally militarily significant Western technology.[69] Finally, the West German government has worked to increase the awareness of private firms of the technology diversion problem and has been willing to devote some additional resources (yet not enough to satisfy the United States) to the enforcement effort. German officials stressed that their efforts were heavily dependent on the United States, since only the United States possessed the resources and networks necessary to "do the brainwork" and track down potential diversions.[70]

The commitment of America's principal COCOM allies to improve the enforcement of controls has been uneven, with Japan and West Germany appearing to lag behind Britain and France. Moreover, the improvements that have taken place have not halted the Eastern acquisition of relevant Western technology. Enforcement remains a significant problem on COCOM's agenda. Nevertheless, by frustrating a number of potentially significant diversion attempts, Western governments appear at least to have complicated and increased the difficulty of the Soviet effort.[71]

Indeed, the same point can be made regarding the general strengthening of COCOM, as evidenced by the apparent shift in attitude among Eastern bloc officials. During détente those officials hardly acknowledged the existence of COCOM, much less complained that its controls stifled trade. Since the completion of the list review in 1984, however, complaints have become a matter of routine, suggesting their concern and frustration over the strengthened regime. At a 1985 meeting of the West German–Soviet Economic Commission Soviet negotiators emphasized that the two countries could not advance their trade relationship to a qualitatively higher stage without the removal of COCOM obstacles. Similarly, Soviet officials formally expressed their concern over U.S. attempts to draw Sweden and Austria into conformity with COCOM, and warned Sweden that compliance would not be favorable to Soviet-Swedish relations, or to Sweden's neutrality. Czechoslovakia went further and registered a formal complaint with the General Agreement on Tariffs and Trade (GATT), claiming that COCOM was in effect a non-tariff barrier to the free flow of trade.[72]

The partial strengthening of COCOM during the first half of the 1980s suggests that, given the adoption of a leadership role by the

United States, other COCOM members are willing to commit themselves to a stronger embargo, even if it involves a degree of economic sacrifice. Since 1980 the United States has set a domestic example in the areas of exceptions and enforcement, has taken the initiative in seeking to tighten COCOM restrictions, and has accepted primary responsibility for keeping non-COCOM suppliers in line.[73] Other COCOM members have been generally receptive, even if they have not always accepted U.S. proposals.

Yet while it has taken on some aspects of a leadership role, at the same time the United States has continued to abuse or neglect other aspects and, as a result, the renewed consensus in COCOM has been placed under strain. For reasons discussed below the United States has continued to exacerbate the administrative burdens of the control system and compromise the integrity of the control process.

First, the 1984 agreement notwithstanding, U.S. officials continue to exert what some West European officials refer to as "relentless pressure" to extend the COCOM list. For many Europeans the list is already too long and its coverage too wide, and the United States appears too eager to add and too reluctant to remove items. In particular, other COCOM members fear that the integration of the Defense Department's Militarily Critical Technology List (MCTL) into the existing U.S. Commodity Control List (CCL) will result in even more comprehensive U.S. controls, and subsequently in even more persistent U.S. efforts to achieve multilateral coordination. The widespread perception in Western Europe is that U.S. officials ultimately will never be satisfied and that they are fundamentally disinterested in the legitimate trading needs of their allies.[74]

The maintenance of an unnecessarily comprehensive control list threatens COCOM's stability in that there exists a trade-off between the coverage of the list and the willingness of government officials to administer it. As the list becomes more comprehensive, it becomes more difficult to enforce and harder to respond in a timely fashion to license requests. For both governments and firms the incentives for compliance thus tend to diminish. Moreover, U.S. pressure is particularly troubling in light of the 1984 list review. West European officials feel they have already done much to accept their share of the burden, but rather than acknowledging it, the U.S. response has been to return with greater demands.[75]

Second, U.S. officials continue to compromise the integrity of the COCOM process by manipulating controls for foreign policy purposes. For example, the no-exceptions policy for which the United States gained COCOM acquiescence in 1980 may have contributed to the effort to tighten controls on strategic trade with the USSR, but also caused considerable discontent in COCOM as the control list became more extensive. The United States exacerbated the problem by using its veto against previously agreed-to "exceptions to the no exceptions" (e.g., for spare parts), and by extending the no-exceptions policy to Poland in 1982, again through the questionable use of the veto.[76] According to a French Foreign Ministry official, some COCOM members who resented being forced to align, in effect, with U.S. foreign policy positions retaliated by selling controlled items to the Soviet Union without bringing the cases to COCOM.[77] Moreover, since for foreign policy reasons the no-exceptions policy applied only to the Soviet Union and not to Eastern Europe, the possibility that strategic goods might be shipped to the Soviets from their Warsaw Pact allies vitiated further the potential strategic benefits.

The manipulation of COCOM controls for foreign policy reasons also created discontent in the case of China. During the Reagan administration China has been allowed to purchase technology at increasing levels of sophistication.[78] Seeking to maintain flexibility so as to influence future Chinese behavior, the United States during Reagan's first term sought not to shorten the COCOM list for China but to maintain the same control list and use the exceptions procedure. The result was a proliferation of exception requests—mainly American —that surpassed even the liberalization of the early 1970s. From 1981 to 1983 COCOM handled approximately 2,000 cases annually, with 70–80 percent of them for exports (mostly American) to China. The situation reached crisis proportions in 1984 with the United States alone requesting 3,122 exceptions, 89 percent of which were for China.[79] Since in a "good" month COCOM can decide only about

100 cases, the existence of frequent and protracted delays, ranging from six months to well over one year, should come as no surprise.

In effect, COCOM experienced a recurrence of the damaging problem of the early 1970s, with China as the focus rather than the Soviet Union. The United States appeared to use the exceptions mechanism to further its own trade and political objectives, while delaying and reserving the right to veto the requests of others. Accusations were again made that the United States was abusing its special role in COCOM to advance its commercial interests at the expense of its competitors. One British firm threatened to violate COCOM's rules, claiming its requests in COCOM had been held up while U.S. firms sold similar equipment through non-COCOM subsidiaries. At the same time U.S. firms complained that their own requests were being stalled by other COCOM governments as a measure of retaliation.[80]

The general implications are clear. COCOM works best if it is depoliticized; the more the allies consider it a purely technical exercise, the more likely they will agree to controls and enforce them faithfully. By injecting political considerations into COCOM, the United States calls into question whatever proposals it makes, even those justifiably guided by strategic considerations. It also threatens the long-run stability of the regime in exchange for possible short-run foreign policy gains.

Finally, the United States has created significant discontent in COCOM by tightening its controls on technology transfers to other Western states. By increasing restrictions on so-called West-West trade, the United States has made it more difficult for its allies to acquire advanced American technology. By increasing re-export restrictions, the United States has hindered West European exports to the East (even those not subject to COCOM controls) that are products of American technology or that contain American components. This shift in American export control strategy has brought forth accusations of "technological protectionism" and "technological imperialism" from other COCOM members and has led some West European firms to reconsider their longstanding reliance on U.S. firms as sources of supply.[81]

For the United States, West-West restrictions are both a response to the perceived inadequacies of the control systems of other Western states (COCOM and non-COCOM) and a bargaining instrument designed to induce improvements in those systems. With regard to the latter the United States has had some success, particularly in relations with non-COCOM suppliers. In the COCOM context, however, while West-West restrictions provide additional leverage, they also raise a number of significant problems. First, by creating delays and uncertainty they increase the burden of the control system for private firms on both sides of the Atlantic (and the Pacific), thereby diminishing their incentives to cooperate in control and enforcement efforts. Second, to the extent that such controls involve the extraterritorial application of U.S. authority, they pose a challenge to the sovereignty of allied governments. The depth of West European officials' concern is suggested by their hostile reaction to the extraterritorial provisions of the Export Administration Act of 1985 and to recent U.S. efforts to audit West European firms that are distributors of American products. It is difficult for Western governments to be receptive to U.S. initiatives in COCOM if at the same time the United States is perceived to be coercing Western firms in violation of international law. Third, American restrictions suggest a vote of no confidence in the control efforts of other COCOM members and signal a preference on the part of the United States to handle the export control issue unilaterally. If such a perception endures, it is unlikely that effective cooperation can be sustained.

In the interest of prompting other COCOM members to improve their controls, an alternative to extending West-West restrictions would be an American initiative to decontrol or reduce the coverage of strategically less significant items on the COCOM list. By reducing the administrative burdens of the control system, such an initiative would increase the manageability, and most likely the effectiveness, of other COCOM governments' enforcement efforts. It would also increase the incentives of private firms to comply with the regime. While the Reagan administration does not object in principle to reducing the control list in exchange for tighter enforcement, as of early in 1987 it had done little to foster such an arrangement.

Given the importance attached by the Reagan administration to COCOM, what accounts for the tendency of U.S. policy to work at cross-purposes with the multilateral regime? Two considerations suggested in the discussion above are central. The first concerns what might be called the "sanctions habit," or the tendency for U.S. officials to use export controls for foreign policy purposes. As an alternative to diplomacy or military activity, the manipulation of trade relations has become an increasingly attractive instrument of American statecraft. The problem is that such an instrument becomes all too easily entangled with the multilateral regime when the targets of U.S. foreign policy controls are COCOM-controlled destinations, and when the sources of leverage include COCOM-controlled items. Moreover, since foreign policy controls require multilateral coordination to be effective, to U.S. officials COCOM offers a seemingly handy forum for that purpose. Thus it is not surprising that the United States injected foreign policy considerations into COCOM intentionally following the Soviet invasion of Afghanistan and the imposition of martial law in Poland. Foreign policy concerns can also become entangled with COCOM unintentionally, as when the export of American technology as a "reward" to China required that COCOM exceptions be granted. In either case American policy works at cross-purposes with the requirements of leadership and the stability of the regime.

The second factor concerns the rise of the Defense Department in the U.S. control process. Since the mid-1970s DOD officials have enhanced their role and authority and currently occupy a position far more prominent than their counterparts in other COCOM states. Moreover, during the Reagan administration the DOD has become a prominent actor not only in the United States but in the multilateral context as well, and the implications for alliance coordination have been profound. On one hand, Defense officials have contributed to strengthening multilateral control policy by increasing awareness in the United States and COCOM of the strategic significance of Western technology and by lobbying hard for more effective restrictions. Yet more significantly, they have been responsible for certain American initiatives and policies that have worked to the detriment of COCOM. DOD officials sought to undermine the State Department and force other COCOM members to comply with American positions, thereby jeopardizing the compromise that ultimately completed the 1982–84 list review.[82] They have also been largely responsible for American unwillingness to decontrol less strategic items, and for American restrictions on technology transfers to COCOM members. In general, the Defense officials who gained positions of prominence in U.S. export control policy were less willing to compromise in COCOM and more inclined to seek unilateral solutions to export control problems. Ironically, in their quest to deny strategic technology to the Soviets, Defense officials took initiatives that threaten to undermine the stability of the multilateral instrument designed to achieve the very same purpose.

Conclusion

This chapter has put forth a two-step argument to account for the evolution of COCOM since 1970. First, I have contended that the strength and stability of COCOM depend critically on the role played by the United States, and in particular on the willingness of U.S. officials to undertake a specific set of responsibilities. That the United States must play such a role is dictated both by the structure of American and West European interests in COCOM and by shared expectations, i.e., the fact that the United States played such a role prior to 1970. In terms of the larger themes of this book, both the politics of COCOM and policy outcomes (i.e., effective cooperation) depend critically on the extent to which the United States exercises effective, consistent leadership.

Second, I have claimed that the ability of the United States to carry out its responsibilities has been affected most critically by distinctive features of America's own export control policy, in particular the tendency to politicize strategic export controls and, more recently, the rise of the DOD in the control process. During the 1970s the entangling of foreign policy considerations with the strategic embargo, as part of a broad shift in American policy toward the Soviet Union, caused the United States to neglect key aspects of its leadership role; as a result, COCOM weakened. The shift in U.S. export control policy after 1979 prompted the United States to recover some aspects of its leadership role, while others continued to be neglected for the reasons described above. The result has been a somewhat stronger COCOM, yet one whose underlying consensus is subject to considerable strain.

A major implication of this argument is that there is at least the potential for effective cooperation in COCOM despite the relative decline in American economic power. While that decline has made cooperation in COCOM more essential, and perhaps more difficult, it has not rendered it unattainable, due to the existence of essentially shared interests between the United States and its major alliance partners in an effective, albeit narrowly conceived strategic embargo. The United States continues to possess adequate resources to perform the tasks critical to COCOM cooperation—setting a domestic example, ensuring the integrity of the control process, minimizing the administrative burdens of controls, and obtaining the compliance of non-COCOM suppliers. As the recent National Academy of Sciences study notes, performing the latter task promises to be increasingly difficult in coming years, as advanced technology is diffused to more non-COCOM countries. Nevertheless, recent U.S. agreements with Sweden, Austria, India, Singapore, and Spain (prior to its joining COCOM) suggest that even a non-hegemonic United States continues to possess considerable leverage through the threat of denial of American technology. Moreover, to the extent the control list can be narrowed, the problem of alternative suppliers can be minimized; newly industrializing countries are more likely to be competitive at the lower, rather than the higher end of the technology scale.

One might argue, of course, that the relative decline of American economic power has contributed indirectly to COCOM's problems since 1970 by bringing about the developments in American export control policy that have affected the multilateral regime. Specifically, the shift to a "pro-trade" orientation in American policy could be explained as a function of America's need, in a period of decline, to pursue export markets in the East. The shift in American policy, however, was motivated more by political considerations, namely, the desire to use economic assets to shape Soviet behavior, than by economic concerns. If economic concerns had been paramount it would be difficult to explain why American firms were consistently placed at a disadvantage by U.S. government policy in the competition for Eastern markets, even after 1970. Overall, the developments in American export control policy that had significant consequences for COCOM appear to be more a function of changes in America's relationship with the Soviet Union than of the decline in American economic power.

Given the close link between the two, efforts to enhance the future stability of COCOM should focus as much, if not more, on U.S. policy than on COCOM itself. Insulating COCOM from the effects of U.S. foreign policy controls is likely to do more for COCOM than would granting it treaty status or giving it more publicity. Similarly, relegating the DOD to a technical advisory role and allowing the State Department to manage the COCOM process would be more useful than creating a military committee in COCOM or assuring more defense participation on the part of member countries. This also implies, of course, that to the extent that politicization of strategic controls and the prominence of the DOD prove to be enduring features of U.S. policy, COCOM's strength and stability are likely to face persistent challenges.[83]

If such features do prove enduring, the future stability of COCOM may be enhanced by the willingness of the United States and its major allies to strike a bargain similar to that struck in 1954.[84] At that time the allies agreed to specific improvements in enforcement, while the United States accepted a reduction in the control list and relaxed West-West restrictions. A similar deal would enhance COCOM's effectiveness today, and would be even more attractive if West European states were committed to assisting the United States in ensuring the cooperation of non-COCOM suppliers in Europe and Asia. The need for such a deal to be struck will grow more urgent as the combination of counterproductive U.S. initiatives and the West European response in COCOM threatens not only the stability of the export control regime, but also other matters of alliance concern.

9

Western Control of East-West
Trade Finance: The Role of
U.S. Power and the International Regime

Beverly Crawford

Introduction

One of the most difficult tasks NATO countries have faced in recent years has been the negotiation of joint policies to regulate East-West trade finance. When the Carter and Reagan administrations attempted to put tighter collective restrictions on credit to the East in the aftermath of the Soviet invasion of Afghanistan and the Polish declaration of martial law, their efforts were blocked by recalcitrant West European allies. More recently, a conflict over French loans to the Soviet Union was the last straw in the trans-Siberian pipeline dispute, leading to U.S. retaliation and direct conflict between the United States and its European allies.

These political controversies highlight the importance of finance in the politics of East-West trade. In fact, successful policy coordination to regulate financial flows is the key to NATO's control of nonstrategic trade with the Soviet Union and Eastern Europe. When Western states regulate the flow of credits they control Eastern demand for Western goods. Because their currencies are not convertible and because their industrial goods are not yet competitive in Western markets, finance is essential if the Council for Mutual Economic Assistance (CMEA) countries are to import from the West.

Despite its obvious importance, however, the issue of finance is treated only peripherally in most scholarly analyses of East-West trade.[1] Scholarly debates have been organized largely around an assessment of the politics of control over the *supply* of Western goods to the East. Regulating finance, however, involves a different set of institutions and actors regulating Eastern *demand* for Western goods. Political actors in the United States have long recognized the importance of the West's capability to control this demand and the potential for trade finance to become a diplomatic instrument in East-West relations. The precise purposes and ultimate effectiveness of that instrument, however, depend on the ability and willingness of all Western governments to coordinate their credit policies toward the East.

This chapter analyzes the evolution of these policy coordination efforts among NATO countries in an effort to assess the conditions for stable and effective cooperation. By "stable" cooperation I mean joint arrangements to which all participants are committed, which are resiliant in crisis and flexible enough to adapt to new situations, and which are effective in achieving joint goals.[2]

Stable policy coordination has been difficult to achieve among the NATO countries with regard to East-West trade finance. Whereas the United States has pursued policies of *denial* and *leverage* since the 1930s, West European governments have long pursued policies of *export promotion* through subsidized credits. These policies conflict with one another, and negotiated coordination is required to reduce alliance tension.

Two alternative theoretical perspectives on the conditions for stable policy coordination can be employed to analyze the West's cooperative efforts to control East-West trade finance: the "realist" and the "institutional" views.[3] Whereas the realist approach argues that the ability of states to coordinate their policies varies with the *organization of power* among them, the institutional perspective is concerned primarily with how the norms, rules, and procedures of *international "regimes"* can foster more stable dispute settlement processes. To be sure, the distinction between the two approaches is artificial; many students of international politics have argued that the organization and exercise of power are important causal variables explaining the creation, maintenance, and demise of international regimes. Nevertheless, it is useful to separate the two approaches here because I wish to emphasize that the organization and exercise of power—in particular hegemonic power—are less important in explaining stable policy coordination than the norms, rules, and procedures of regimes. Despite the fact that international regimes as political institutions are the result of power struggles among participants, there is evidence that they can take on a "life of their own" in shaping the politics of bargaining and negotiation and the final policy outcomes of those processes.[4]

I will go so far as to argue that in this case the finance regulatory regime has worked to attenuate the effects of power, in much the same way that laws can work to attenuate power in domestic society. This is not to say that the distribution and exercise of power is unimportant (either in domestic or international society) but simply to say that power does not solely determine outcomes. Although the argument is made for the case of East-West trade finance, there is evidence that the framework developed here can be applied usefully to other areas of alliance policy coordination in East-West trade as well.

The discussion begins by summarizing the two perspectives and making a case for the institutional approach. It then outlines the goals governments can pursue with the instrument of trade finance and describes the conditions under which these goals may conflict. It then moves to an analysis of the goal conflicts among Western states in their East-West trade finance policies. The analysis traces the interplay between the exercise of U.S. power and institutional norms, rules, and procedures in NATO's postwar struggle to resolve the conflict and coordinate conflicting trade finance policies. This evidence suggests that the institutional approach does better in explaining stable policy coordination than the realist perspective.

The Realist Approach

The realist approach to international stability begins with the claim that cooperation in world politics is difficult, and long-term cooperative relationships among states are all but impossible. Because the international system is anarchic, that is, it lacks a central governing authority over states to enforce their agreements, states can defect from those agreements with impunity. States are insecure; without the protection of a central authority their chief concern is to amass enough power to ensure their survival and maintain their sovereignty. Because they will never recognize a legitimate authority over them, states compete, often violently, for power. Competition and confrontation best characterize states' interaction under anarchy.[5]

Even among states that seem to share common interests, such as allies and trading partners, cooperation is always the second-best alternative to going it alone. Thus, a commitment to agree is hard to get because it may mean giving up some unilateral control over policy decisions. Defection from cooperative arrangements is easy, and the possibility of cheating and deception hovers over every agreement. From a realist perspective states have little incentive to coordinate their policies because such coordination usually implies the relinquishing of some aspect of sovereignty.

Thus most arguments from this perspective hold out little hope for stable cooperation. When states do enter into negotiations to coordinate their policies the realist approach explains the negotiated outcome and predicts the odds for stability by examining power asymmetries among the negotiating parties.[6] One strand of realist theory argues that hegemonic power is the key to international stability.[7] Robert Keohane's definition of hegemony is generally the accepted one: hegemony simply means the preponderance of control over power resources. As applied to the international political economy, this would mean control over raw materials, sources of capital, markets, and competitive advantages in the production of highly valued goods.[8] Hegemonic stability theory claims that because states under anarchy always prefer to prevail in an international dispute rather than compromise or come together, the substance of any stable agreement conforms most closely to the preferences of the most powerful state. This is because the dominant state can use its power to change the preferences of others and enforce commitment to its preferred goal. With regard to policy coordination on East-West trade, one analyst has stated hegemonic stability theory succinctly: "To get even allied nations (who are also commercial competitors) to march in tandem requires an extraordinary expenditure of power on the part of the alliance leader."[9]

How is power exercised to change preferences and ensure commitment to the hegemonic goal? The strategies dominant states use can be divided into three categories: (1) the exercise of "leadership"; (2) compensation; and (3) coercion.[10] Leadership is usually exercised through a symbolic action designed to be highly visible and to underline commitment to a line of argument which justifies the hegemon's interests. The intent is to signal to other parties that the leader means business and that they should follow. With regard to East-West trade, for example, the United States has exercised leadership by restricting more goods to the Soviet Union and Eastern Europe than it expected its allies to embargo. Although elements of the American business community have always grumbled about this inequality, it has been intended as a signal to Europeans that they should change their preference for trade promotion and tighten their own export control regulations.[11]

Compensation is a strategy of escalating commitment to the achievement of compliance. Pursuit of this strategy requires the expenditure of resources, i.e., "carrots," in order to compensate for losses incurred through compliance. The effectiveness of this strategy depends primarily on the level and type of resources committed. In the early postwar period the United States offered to compensate European countries for their loss of the Eastern market if they complied with the U.S. preference for a wide embargo on the supply of goods to CMEA countries. It offered Marshall Plan funds, discrimination against its own exports, and ample reserves for the European Payments Union, not only to build up Western economies but to cut off old trading patterns with the East. More recently, the United States offered defense contracts to firms whose governments would agree to restrict the sale of technology to the Soviet Union. And recent U.S. agreements with Britain, the FRG, Italy, and Japan which permit those countries to participate in joint SDI research are conditional upon the tightening of their export controls to bring them in line with U.S. perceptions of a strategic embargo.[12] Compensation has permitted Europeans to continue pursuit of export promotion by simply switching markets.

Coercion is the most costly strategy, and it may be pursued in addition to the other two or when they fail. As the other side of the compensation coin, it involves the use of "sticks," that is punishment for noncompliance. Here the dominant state threatens to withdraw needed resources if others do not comply, thus inflicting pain if original preferences are pursued. The U.S. Mutual Defense Assistance Control Act of 1951 (the Battle Act) stipulated that all aid to states that exported strategic and even non-military goods to communist nations would be curtailed. The Export Administration Act of 1985 incorporates provisions for a coercive strategy in the form of the extraterritoriality principle. Here the United States extends its own export control policy to cover re-export of goods and technology from European firms. If these firms engage in re-export to communist countries they are denied goods and technology from the United States. Some business interests in Europe who do not want their U.S. technology imports curtailed are pressuring their governments to tighten export controls.[13] For coercion to be effective in this case, Europe's pain of losing Western markets must be greater than the pain of losing Eastern markets. If the pain is greater, it is argued, preferences of the coerced parties will change.

Despite the fact that hegemonic powers believe their strategies can achieve policy coordination on their terms, there is evidence that cooperation achieved through compliance is likely to be unstable. When goals conflict and the cost of following the leader is perceived to be too high, parties to an agreement may defect or demand compensation for compliance. But by extracting compensation, dominant powers do not fundamentally alter the preferences of others.

Compensation is really just a sophisticated form of bribery; compliance will last only as long as compensation is assured. When compensation is no longer forthcoming others begin to pursue conflicting goals.[14]

Coercion can produce similar results. Since coercion threatens the overall tone of the relationship and reduces the potential for agreement in other issue areas, it is the most costly and destabilizing way to achieve agreement, particularly within an alliance. Coerced parties may learn that they can do without the withheld resources, or they may search for alternative ways to achieve their original goals. Incentives to defect and to cheat are high; thus coercive policies are ineffective in the long run. Particularly when coerced parties lessen their dependence upon the resources controlled by the hegemon or when his control over needed resources declines, coercion loses its effectiveness. Indeed, all three strategies lose their effectiveness when power shifts; policy coordination on these terms tends to break down in the face of hegemonic decline because power resources dry up and there is no central authority over states to enforce earlier agreements.[15]

Preliminary evidence on NATO efforts to control East-West trade jointly indicates that stable agreements have not been achieved when they depended solely on the hegemonic leadership, compensation efforts, or coercion of the United States. This was true not only after overall U.S. economic power began to decline, but during the hegemonic period as well. To be sure, for a brief time—until 1955—compliance with U.S. preferences was achieved and East-West trade declined while total Western trade expanded. Cheating, however, had been in evidence all along; in 1950 the U.S. Commerce Department blacklisted 1,500 firms that transshipped goods to the Soviet Union. Most of them were European. The Battle Act, however, was never enforced. By 1955 U.S. economic and military aid to Western Europe began to decrease. With the decline in compensation and the recovery of the West European economies, trade between Western Europe and the CMEA began to expand. Nonetheless, the United States continued to attempt coordination for joint restrictions. For example, in the early 1960s the United States pressured its allies not to supply the Soviet Union with large-diameter pipe for the transport of oil to Eastern Europe. By 1965, however, the agreement broke down. And in the early 1980s the United States used all three strategies to halt Western construction of the trans-Siberian pipeline in the Soviet Union; the Europeans rebuffed each of these efforts, and the pipeline was built to supply Western Europe with Soviet natural gas.

In short, despite the claims of the hegemonic stability theory, the realist approach offers few prescriptions for stable agreement among states in their policy coordination efforts with regard to East-West trade. Below I will explore in detail how compliance strategies have been used in Western efforts to control finance of that trade and assess their effectiveness. First, however, I will outline the institutional perspective and argue that international regimes can manage power relationships and shape bargaining and negotiation processes in ways that may hold the key to stable policy coordination.

The Institutional Approach

The institutional perspective begins with the assumption that nations exist not only under anarchy, but in relationships of complex interdependence.[16] Interdependence means that the actions of states affect others, whether intended or not. For example, a nuclear accident in the Soviet Union affects the price of American wheat; the price of the dollar affects interest rates in Europe. And because of the requirements of an interlocking international banking system, one nation's default can destabilize the entire system of international finance. The fact that states' policies affect one another, particularly the policies of those states that have chosen the "strategic interdependence" of an alliance, means that, for better or worse, they participate in a set of relationships which are difficult to break. For the sake of certainty, stability, and the "national interest," the terms of those relationships must be negotiated. These negotiations are intended to resolve the conflict between original preferences and the preference for managing or preserving the relationship.

International institutions represent the outcome of those negotiated relationships. They are composed of mutually accepted norms, rules, and procedures which provide a structured political environment and a set of guidelines for negotiations within a particular issue area. The institutions in which these rules and procedures are embedded are commonly called international "regimes."[17] International regimes intervene between the anarchic structure and organization of power in the international system on one hand, and the process of policy coordination on the other. They thus mediate between power capabilities and international outcomes. Their primary task is to provide guidelines of interaction for the negotiating parties. Their norms, rules, and procedures perform the same function for states as boiler-plate language in labor negotiations. They assure that every aspect of a new cooperative arrangement need not be renegotiated from scratch. Above all, international regimes institutionalize a commitment to agree among their members, enhancing expectations for a negotiated settlement of disputes.[18] They thus provide models of cooperative behavior that members can adopt in new situations.

There are three related reasons why states adhere to agreements negotiated within regimes. First, stable agreement within interdependent relationships is most likely to emerge when negotiators believe that they have a future together. If they value their future interactions, the incentive to reach agreement in the present is high. Thus a direct connection between present negotiating behavior and anticipated future benefits of interaction is established. Expectations of future interactions are enhanced by the institutionalization of the relationships within international regimes. Because regimes provide a forum for ongoing discussion in which negotiators know they will meet one another again, they enhance the importance of the long-run, or lengthen the shadow that the future casts on present negotiations.[19]

Second, regimes can provide important information and technical expertise to the negotiating parties. This information can open up possibilities for creative solutions to substantive problems. Often, if information is generated by the parties themselves it can be distorted by self-serving interests and is thought to be a biased instrument of persuasion. If the facts surrounding a problem are gathered by experts in a "neutral" organization, their credibility is enhanced. Agreement on the facts provides important consensual criteria for arriving at shared meanings of important terms and for evaluating a negotiating problem. Such agreement can also allow for the discovery of overlapping areas in which interests can converge and can even modify the preferences and goals of the negotiating parties.[20]

Third, international regimes can provide a set of rules and procedures that limit the demands of the negotiating parties when such demands would threaten common interests. States submit to rules which restrict their behavior because they want others' behavior to be restricted as well. By institutionalizing this "reciprocity principle," regimes constrain states' behavior and mediate the role of power in determining the outcomes of substantive negotiations.[21] Regime norms, rules, and procedures protect a negotiated relationship by providing limits on competition among negotiating parties for limited resources. They thus provide a framework for dispute settlement on specific issues within which destabilizing coercive tactics can be minimized.

The institutional approach to the assessment of NATO's policy coordination in East-West trade is appropriate, since there are a number of indicators that a Western East-West trade regime has emerged in the postwar period. The regime began with COCOM, an informal group created to coordinate Western states' policies on restricting the supply of strategic goods to the East. As new East-West trade issues such as countertrade, energy dependence, and finance became salient on the policy agendas of Western industrialized countries, the regime grew and changed to manage their effects. The expanded regime was "nested" chiefly within the OECD.[22] In sum, the institutional approach offers a number of prescriptions for stable policy coordination which have emerged from recent studies of international regimes. Further, there is ample evidence that an East-West trade regime has grown and developed in the West. Therefore the approach would seem to hold promise for an analysis of the conditions for stable Western policy coordination in East-West trade finance.

The remainder of this chapter analyzes the postwar history of Western joint regulation efforts in East-West trade finance. It focuses both on U.S. compliance strategies and West European responses and the evolution and role of international regimes in the process of negotiating coordinated policies. To anticipate the chapter's conclusions, the empirical material suggests that the achievement of stable policy coordination depends on the convergence or coexistence of actor preferences. When goals on a particular issue essentially conflict among interdependent states, hegemonic power and compliance strategies are less effective in changing the preferences of other actors to achieve goal convergence and coexistence than the norms, rules, and procedures of international regimes. The discussion shows how the institutional approach to stability may have useful implications for the analysis of other Western policy coordination efforts in East-West trade.

State Goals in Trade Finance

Trade finance can be used as a tool of statecraft in three different ways to achieve broader foreign policy goals. These goals are *trade promotion*, to improve foreign relations; *leverage*, to extract political concessions from a potential borrower; and *denial*, to signal displeasure with the borrower's political behavior.

The use of finance to achieve trade promotion demands that exporting governments undertake much of the risk of lending. Normally, if states decide to assume financial risk, they do so in order to stimulate exports. But the means established to assume risk can actually become an instrument to achieve broader political goals, namely, improving foreign relations. Government officials rather than private traders can decide which borrowers should be favored for what purposes. When states assume all or part of the financial risk of lending they reduce the cost to exporters of financing trade and thus make their exports attractive to potential importers. The cost of borrowing will be reduced because when governments assume risk, interest rates, which reflect risk calculations, are below what the borrower would have to pay under normal market conditions. This serves the broader commercial interests of the lender. But also, by assuming all or part of the financing risk, governments use trade as a foreign policy instrument by providing incentives to lend to otherwise risky borrowers and incentives for risky borrowers to buy from them.

There are two ways in which governments can assume that risk, be it for political or purely economic objectives: they can grant direct credits or they can provide export credit guarantees and insurance policies.[23] Most industrialized countries created agencies to supply credits and credit guarantees in order to promote exports in the interwar period. Italy began even earlier by establishing the Istituto Nazionale delle Assieurazioni (INA) in 1912. Britain established the Export Credits Guarantee Department (ECGD) in 1919, and in Germany HERMES Versicherungs AG was created in 1926. The French government began to provide official export credits in 1929 but did not establish the Compagnie Française d'Assurance pour le Commerce Extérieur (COFACE) until 1946. In 1934 the Export-Import Bank was established in the United States, and in 1950 the Export-Import Bank of Japan was created. These agencies have continued to provide export subsidies in the form of credits and guarantees and they have come to play an important role in trade promotion.[24]

A second goal is that of leverage. When a policy of leverage is pursued, governments will release trade credits to potential borrowers *only* when political concessions are made. The United States used trade finance as an instrument of leverage, for example, when it denied official credits to Poland in 1982 until certain political concessions were forthcoming.

A final goal is trade denial, through denial of trade finance. States may wish to deny trade finance as a punitive response to undesirable behavior on the part of the would-be borrower. Or denial may be the response when leverage does not achieve the required concessions from the borrower. A policy of denial requires that states place strict legal constraints on the activities of both exporters and trade-promoting institutions. For example, states can enact laws which forbid private lending and deny official credit altogether. Partial denial is also possible. Lending can be denied for certain goods, or the government can place lending "ceilings" on borrowers which cannot be exceeded. The discussion below of the Stevenson amendment to the Export-Import Bank Act of 1974 provides a good example of the attempt to use trade finance as an instrument of denial. It placed a ceiling on the amount of credit available to the Soviet Union and put particular restrictions on the finance of U.S. energy exports to the USSR.

When exporting states pursue these policies two kinds of conflict can arise. First, if one state enacts policies of leverage or denial with the intention of changing the political behavior of the borrower, while another pursues a policy of trade promotion to expand exports or improve overall political relationships, the effect of a denial or leverage policy will be dissipated as the borrower switches to a more congenial trade partner. The state attempting to deny trade credits may try to persuade other lenders to coordinate their policies with its in order to impose multilateral sanctions on borrowers. Second, if a number of states pursue policies of trade promotion, they may face the unintended consequence of export credit competition and dangerous trade wars. The experience of those consequences may lead to negotiations on a joint policy to harmonize interest rates and the length of loan maturities in order to minimize competition.

Seeds of Conflict and Early Policy Coordination in the 1930s

Both kinds of conflict and the impulse for policy coordination among trading states had their origins in the political and economic crises which swept the world in the 1930s. While the United States pursued a policy of denial with regard to trade finance to the Soviet Union after the 1917 Revolution, other industrialized countries took steps to promote their exports abroad, including exports to the Soviets. By the late 1920s the British, German, French, and Italian governments all attempted to remedy their deepening trade deficits by subsidizing their export industries with official export credits. One by one they established export credit agencies to implement their general export promotion goals. Trade promotion was pursued for its own sake and not as an instrument of political influence in these states' foreign relations.

This was not the case in the United States. In 1934 the U.S. Export-Import Bank (Eximbank) was created, but almost immediately it became a bargaining chip in negotiations with the Soviet Union. Roosevelt's objective was to provide U.S. Eximbank credits in exchange for Soviet political support in opposing German and Japanese aggression. But others, including Secretary of State Cordell Hull and Eximbank president George Peek, wanted to restrict the bank's ability to subsidize all trade and dangle U.S. credits in front of the Soviets only if they would be willing to change their political system and alter their international behavior. Their views prevailed over Roosevelt's and the Soviets balked at their demands. As a result, negotiations with Soviet officials broke down over the terms of credit extension in the spring of 1935, and for the next thirty-nine years Eximbank credits went unused in U.S.-Soviet trade.[25] In addition, the Johnson Debt Default Act of 1934 forbade governments in default on their debt payments to float loans in the United States. A disputed tsarist debt put the Soviets in default.[26] As a result, the Soviets turned away from the United States as a trading partner and toward European governments, who were more than eager to expand industrial exports through competitive trade finance. In 1930 the USSR imported 46 percent of its machinery and transport equipment from the United States; by 1936 that figure had dropped to 30 percent. In those same years Soviet imports from the German Reich jumped from 33 percent to 50 percent of total imports.[27]

Despite clear policy differences with Europe in regard to Soviet trade, the issue was placed on the back burner as the worldwide depression deepened. Increasingly, many leading figures in industry, finance, and government came to view competitive export policies and expanding trade wars as a threat to national economic health. Export credit competition was recognized as part of that threat. In an effort to control the negative effects of competitive export subsidies, the United States joined with twenty-three government and private credit insurance organizations in 1934 to establish the Union d'Assureurs des Credits Internationaux in Berne, Switzerland. The institution came to be known as the Berne Union. Its rules of association amounted to a loosely drawn gentlemen's agreement regarding limits on government guarantees on private supplier credits. Members agreed to insure only those export credits with maturities up to five years. If they intended to break this "five-year rule," they obligated themselves to inform other members and justify their actions. Members could not agree, however, on limits for official credits and loans, and thus the regime rules restricted discussion to credit guarantees. The Berne Union never achieved the status of a binding legal agreement, yet it was an important forum for the exchange of information on credit policies and regulation of some forms of competition.[28]

This international agreement, however, did not prevent the seeds of policy conflict between the United States and Europe over East-West trade from growing in the aftermath of depression and war. As the following discussion will show, the Berne Union was not strong enough to prevent future disputes over trade subsidies; competitive finance of Soviet trade would trigger larger conflicts over trade subsidies in general. And the United States would not be content to stand by while European non-strategic trade with the Soviet Union increased.

The Growth and Resolution of Conflict in the Postwar Period

Strategies of leverage and denial which had come to dominate U.S. East-West trade finance policy in the 1930s intensified in the postwar period. Rivalry with the Soviet Union after World War II created a new mission for the Eximbank as an instrument of statecraft within the context of global anti-communism. Immediately after the war Congress increased the bank's lending authority from $700 million to $3.5 billion. In 1945 the bank began to provide reconstruction loans for Western Europe before the Marshall Plan was formulated. After the revolution in China in 1949 it offered development loans to Asia, Africa, the Middle East, and Latin America. These loans were part of an overall strategy of trade promotion aimed at speeding up the economic and political development of less developed countries (LDCs) to prevent their fall to "communist domination."[29] It offered supplier credits as inducements for exporters who would otherwise have little incentive to trade with these nations. Throughout the 1950s the U.S. government used the Eximbank as one weapon in its arsenal against the global expansion of communism.

Meanwhile, West European countries rebuilt their own economic strength and began to reconstruct their severed financial ties with the Soviet Union and Eastern Europe. European export credit agencies were never legally barred from extending credits and guarantees to communist countries, and their governments had eschewed the use of export subsidies as an instrument of political leverage vis-à-vis the Soviet Union. As the Soviets began to press for more credits in their trade with the West, Europeans responded by providing greater credit support for East-West trade than for their overall trade.[30] In fact, as we shall see below, once agreement between the United States and Europe was reached that the sale to the East of non-strategic goods was permitted, West European countries began to compete vigorously to provide the most favorable credit terms.

By the late 1950s competition over the length of loan maturities had begun. The Soviet Union had pressed creditors for longer maturities since it was most interested in purchasing capital goods from the West, for which longer credit terms are the rule. It also wanted to buy entire turnkey plants, which would involve long construction and repayment periods. It is important to note here that until the expansion of Euromarket borrowing, long-term financing was qualitatively different from medium- or short-term loan relationships.[31] Commercial banks were reluctant to make long-term loans at fixed rates of interest because of the risk involved. Thus government credit agencies usually took the risk of providing long-term credits to foreign countries. The less risky medium- and short-term loans were provided by banks with credit guarantees and interest rate support from the government.

By 1958 the U.S. government had recognized the conflict between its own restrictive policy on the finance of trade with the Soviet bloc and the liberal policies of Western Europe. In order to curb the expansion of West European trade with the East the United States pursued two strategies: it took the lead in its own policy and appealed to the norm of the Berne Union, limiting competition among exporters. Within the Berne Union the United States attempted to persuade members to adhere strictly to the "five-year rule" with regard to both official direct credits and guarantees in financing trade with CMEA countries. The United States also asked Berne Union members to require from the Soviet Union a cash down payment of at least 20 percent of the purchase price of all imported goods. Since U.S. officials recognized the East's intense need for long-term trade finance of capital goods, they hoped that this limitation would adequately restrict trade with the adversary. In negotiations with Berne Union members the United States argued that credit support was a "virtual extension of financial aid, which enabled communist countries to divert more of their own resources to investment in military and other strategically significant areas."[32]

Because Japan was not a member of the Berne Union, CMEA countries turned to that country to obtain credits with maturities of longer than five years. West Europeans feared a potential decline in their trade with the East, and one by one they began to violate the five-year rule. Britain was the first to defect. In response to increasing Soviet and East European requests for long-term loans, the British ECGD introduced in 1960 what it called a "matching policy." By this it meant that it was prepared to meet the financing terms provided by any foreign competitor for any specific sale for long-term financing (over five years). The ECGD also began to finance sales by foreign subsidiaries of British firms in order to enhance its competitive position.[33]

In direct competition with Britain, Italy's export credit agency, IMI, began in 1961 to extend lines of credit to socialist countries with possible maturities of up to twelve years. Italy's liberal credit terms were an important factor influencing Fiat's favorable negotiations with Soviet officials in the mid-1960s over the construction of the Togliatti automobile plant. In that case credits extended over a period of fourteen years. In contrast, Fiat had expressed the desire to purchase $50 million worth of machine tools for the plant from American firms. The Joint Chiefs of Staff and several cabinet officers testified before Congress on behalf of the Fiat purchases; the U.S. machine tool industry suffered from surplus capacity, and the companies involved had expressed strong interest in the sale.[34] Despite this pressure Congress held the Eximbank to its restrictive policy; the companies were denied credits from the Eximbank for the sale because the financing requests exceeded the five-year rule. The United States was clearly exercising leadership in the hope that the five-year rule would hold.

Until 1964 the FRG had followed the United States in the denial of trade and finance to Eastern Europe and the Soviet Union. It had further persuaded its EEC partners not to exceed a five-year limit on loans to the GDR. Competition from Italy and Britain in lending to other East European countries, however, pushed West Germany to allow HERMES to extend credit guarantees to other CMEA countries. Although the West German government provided no official direct credits, it agreed to guarantee commercial loans for up to five years on exports to those CMEA countries willing to exchange trade missions with the FRG. By 1965 it approved credit guarantees to those same countries for up to eight years. Shortly thereafter Germany resumed its prewar position as a major promoter of trade and a major lender to the Eastern bloc countries.[35]

In 1964 France also took steps to expand its share of the Eastern market by offering increasingly competitive credit terms. It began to provide loans with five- to seven-year maturities for the export of French capital goods. By 1974 two-thirds to three-fourths of all French capital goods shipped to the USSR were financed through official loans with seven- to eight-and-one-half-year maturities.[36]

Thus, while West European export credit facilities grew to be robust and competitive trade promotion institutions during the 1960s, facilitating trade with the East, the U.S. Eximbank remained stunted by restrictive legislation. It remained a political instrument to promote trade with non-communist LDCs and deny trade to communist countries.

Recognizing the conflict in these goals, the United States had attempted to exercise leadership in an effort to coordinate a restrictive policy, in the hope that its allies would follow. It had also asked its allies to observe the Berne Union rules in order to restrict the specific long-term financing most desired by the Soviet Union and Eastern Europe. Although in a position of hegemonic dominance within NATO as a result of preponderant military power, both strategies failed and the United States was not able to sustain a joint commitment to finance restrictions on the part of its allies. The allies grumbled that the United States, in an uncompetitive trade position, was simply trying to dampen trade competition from other industrialized nations. After all, they argued, the five-year rule applied only to credit guarantees and not to official direct credits.

The late 1960s and early 1970s saw a U.S. attempt to ease trade restrictions and move toward a trade promotion policy with the Soviet Union as part of its new détente strategy. These efforts, however, suffered two blows from Congress which moved U.S. policy back to leverage and denial. By 1974 the Jackson-Vanik amendment to the Trade Act had effectively curtailed the administration's trade promotion efforts. Passed in 1974, the Jackson-Vanik amendment stipulated that trade concessions to the Soviet Union and other communist countries would be subject to the condition that those countries allow free Jewish emigration. Soviet leaders would never concede to this condition and the U.S.-Soviet Trade Agreement, which would have significantly expanded trade between the two countries, was never signed.

The Stevenson-Jackson amendment to the Eximbank bill was the second blow to administration proposals for trade promotion. In essence this amendment limited the amount of new Eximbank credits to the USSR to $300 million. Furthermore, any single project requiring Eximbank credits would be subject to congressional approval. Specific official credit limitations were imposed on energy-related exports to the Soviet Union. The most that could be granted for energy research and exploration was $40 million, and no credits would be available for energy production and processing.[37] The amendment was accepted by Congress, and after 1974 the Eximbank operated under these new restrictions. A policy of denial was firmly in place.

With these new restrictions and the weakening of Berne Union norms, the conflict between U.S. and European policies was intensified.[38] The United States, however, continued to press for policy coordination on its terms. It now turned to a loosely knit group which had formed within the OECD in the early 1970s. The group's purpose was the same as that of the Berne Union—to avoid destructive trade competition—but this time with regard to official direct credits as well as guarantees. Similar to the Berne Union procedure, members exchanged information and consulted with one another before they made any changes in interest rates or official credit support.

It was no secret, however, that the United States chose this OECD forum to focus efforts to reduce official support of export credits to the Soviet Union and Eastern Europe.[39] In defense of their position on loans to CMEA countries U.S. officials made three arguments. First, they argued that the volume of credit should be reduced because overextended banks would become channels of Soviet influence with their own governments. Second, they argued that it made no economic sense to subsidize the Soviet economy with low-interest loans and endless credits when such a high proportion of its resources was devoted to military spending. Finally, they feared that the East would have a bargaining advantage in the debtor-creditor relationship.

These arguments, however, did not persuade the Europeans to focus on credit denial to CMEA countries. They stood firm on their position that the objective of the group was to reduce dangerous export credit competition and not reduce the amount of credit available to the CMEA. Having learned from their increasing competition in the 1960s, they recognized that for this objective to be realized the regime would have to be strengthened. Many members believed that it should be upgraded from a forum for information exchange and consultation to a set of agreements which would actually coordinate export credit policy. Early negotiations focused on defining the problem: members favored certain trading partners with lower interest rates and longer loan maturities. In order to reduce competition members would have to harmonize interest rates and the length of loan maturities granted to all importers, as well as find acceptable criteria by which countries could be grouped for differing levels of credit support.[40]

By 1976 the first negotiations had been completed, and in 1978 the Arrangement on Guidelines for Officially Supported Export Credits, or the "consensus," was formed. Its rules of association were the same as those of the Berne Union; members were not legally bound to the agreements and met primarily to exchange information on their own credit policies. They agreed to follow a set of guidelines to harmonize their interest rate support according to "objective" criteria. In that way no one country's preferred trading partners would be favored. If they decided to deviate from the guidelines they would report the deviation to other members. Interest rates would vary according to whether the borrower was classified as rich, middle income, or poor. Borrowers were placed in one of the three categories through a process of bargaining and compromise among members rather than according to rational criteria.

The United States, for example, wanted to use these categories to reduce lending to the East; U.S. negotiators took the position that CMEA countries should be squeezed by being placed in the category of "rich" countries with shorter maximum maturities. But because CMEA countries were important trading partners for Germany and France, negotiators from these countries wanted them placed in the more favorable "intermediate" category. European consensus members won on this issue; CMEA members were initially classified as intermediate countries. They benefited particularly from a clause in the agreement which allowed lines of credit agreed to before 1976 to continue at the same (lower) interest rate until they lapsed.

The Soviet invasion of Afghanistan in December 1979 led the U.S.

government to press for a joint leverage policy, i.e., multilateral sanctions against the Soviets. These were to include stiff credit sanctions. Publicly, Washington asked NATO allies to cut in half all official export credits to the Soviet Union. The response was overwhelmingly negative. In defending their recalcitrance, the Europeans argued that the U.S. request violated guidelines set in the multilateral consensus agreement.[41] Paradoxically, resistance to U.S. leadership for restriction was bolstered by the decision of an institution it had helped to build.

But by 1982 two important events led the United States to once again pursue compliance strategies for policy coordination on its own terms, both within the consensus and in ad hoc negotiations outside the regime. The first event was the debt crisis in Poland and the imposition of martial law there on December 13, 1981. The second event—which was eventually linked to the first—was the deepening dispute between the United States and Europe over the construction of the trans-Siberian pipeline. It is to these two events that our discussion now turns.

The Polish Crisis

Between 1977 and 1981 the Polish external debt nearly doubled, from $14 billion to $26 billion. Most of that debt was held by West German banks.[42] By April 1980 the Polish government openly admitted that it lacked both the export potential and the hard currency reserves to meet even its interest payment obligations. The central bank attempted to put together a syndicated commercial loan of $550 million, led by Bank of America, but by that time most banks had recognized that their previous loans had not been invested in ways that would help the Poles service their debt. These banks refused to participate in new loans unless the Polish government initiated strict economic reform measures.

In response the Gierek government implemented an austerity plan, focused chiefly on Polish workers. These austerity measures were crucial in creating widespread support for the general strike in August

1980 under the leadership of the Solidarity union. Even with these new measures, however, Poland had only been able to raise a $325 million loan for seven years.[43] This, Polish officials admitted, would not be enough to even service the existing debt.

The Polish economy continued to decline. In April 1981 Poland was forced to negotiate with its major creditors on debt relief. Fifteen major Western government creditors—including the United States—agreed to reschedule 90 percent of the Polish official debt, and an agreement was also later reached to reschedule commercial loans. Meanwhile, Poland had requested membership in the IMF in the hope of a major loan to ease the crisis. IMF membership, too, would raise the incentives of commercial banks to continue lending.[44]

The declaration of martial law on December 13, 1981, however, led the U.S. government to again seek a major policy change within the alliance. One faction within the Reagan administration, led by Defense Secretary Caspar Weinberger and supported by right-wing groups headed by the Conservative Caucus, sought a declaration of default on Poland's official debt to the U.S. government.[45] Those in favor of this option made two arguments for it:[46] first, a declaration of default would put financial and political pressure on the Soviet Union and deprive the Communist bloc of the infusion of credit it had enjoyed in the 1970s. Thus the Soviets would have to use their own precious hard currency to bail out Poland.

Second, a declaration of default would put pressure on the recalcitrant West European allies, who were flaunting their "business as usual" policies in the face of increasing tensions between the Soviet Union and the United States. A particular thorn in the side of the Reagan administration was the trans-Siberian pipeline construction, which the administration had attempted to block. Responding to the Polish declaration of martial law, President Reagan had imposed sanctions on American oil and gas technology destined for the Soviet Union. The United States had hoped that the Europeans would follow the lead and impose their own sanctions on the export of energy equipment, but they refused. One way to coerce them, conservative forces argued, would be to declare Poland in default. A declaration of

Polish default would trigger cross-default agreements, which would dry up future loans earmarked for the pipeline. West European governments, supported by the U.S. Treasury and State departments, argued strongly against a U.S. declaration of default, stating that such an option would trigger an international financial crisis: default would force Western governments to make good on their commitments to honor credit guarantees and lead to massive write-offs of the non-guaranteed portion of the debt. This would drastically reduce the banks' assets and interrupt their stream of profits.[47]

Ultimately, West European governments were able to strike a tacit bargain with the United States to avoid a declaration of Polish default. Throughout 1981 it became clear that the Polish crisis was part of a much larger international debt problem. Within the IMF the United States lobbied for support for a debt restructuring package for Mexico, which also was tottering on the edge of default. West Europeans, particularly the West Germans, would not support the loan for Mexico until they had assurance that the United States would not place West European banks in danger. The United States backed down and agreed not to declare Poland in default.[48] The Polish default option was simply not viable, given the interests of West European banks and governments in East European stability and solvency and U.S. interests in protecting its own banks' interests in Mexico's solvency and stability.

Since default was now out of the question the Reagan administration sought alternative means to pressure Poland's military government through the instrument of Western trade finance. Quickly four unilateral measures, combining elements of leverage and denial, were decided upon: a freeze on all new official credits, suspension of debt rescheduling negotiations, opposition to Poland's membership in the IMF, and suspension of Eximbank's line of credit insurance for Poland. Now the United States hoped for policy coordination in pursuit of these goals. As a symbolic act, other NATO governments agreed to suspend negotiations on further official debt rescheduling. And because Poland's creditworthiness was now in question, they cut in half all new official credits to Poland. The United States wanted these measures to remain in effect until the Polish government put an end to martial law, released all political prisoners, and resumed talks with the Solidarity union.[49] European officials, however, stated that because the suspension of restructuring negotiations was purely symbolic, they would resume even if these demands were not met. And credits would be granted on the basis of financial decisions, not Polish "politial concessions."[50]

This joint policy of leverage may have been partially effective. In July 1984 the Polish government declared amnesty for all political prisoners, and in response the United States lifted its objection to Poland's application for IMF membership.[51] There were, however, a number of unintended consequences that had weakened commitment to the policy. As long as official debt restructuring talks were suspended Poland made no payments to Western governments. This eased the payments burden and allowed Poland to make substantial payments to private banks, gradually enhancing its creditworthiness in their eyes.[52] Meanwhile, in the United States, since no official payments were being made the Reagan administration had to reimburse U.S. banks for $71.3 million in credit guarantees.[53]

Commercial bank confidence increased as Poland continued to make interest payments on its unguaranteed loans. Already by April 1982 Poland had formally reached agreement with Western banks on rescheduling. And by the close of 1983 Western governments reopened negotiations on further rescheduling so that they would not have to make good on their guarantees.[54] By that time Poland had reduced imports from the West by 50 percent and the debt crisis appeared to be in remission.[55]

The Polish crisis clearly demonstrated once again the divergence of policy goals between the United States and its European allies. While the Europeans stubbornly adhered to the norm of "financial caution" in their dealings with Poland in the wake of the debt crisis, strong factions within the Reagan administration took the lead in pursuit of leverage and denial, attempting to coerce the allies into policy coordination with the threat of Polish default. Given its own entanglement in the international debt crisis, however, the United

States simply did not have the power resources to carry out that threat. Europeans briefly conceded to a joint policy of leverage, but the concessions were weak and symbolic, and lasted only until financial conditions in Poland appeared stable. By February 1987 key figures in both the Polish Solidarity union and the Catholic church had appealed to the United States to end its unilateral sanctions, and U.S. State Department officials conceded that the economic penalties were conflicting with efforts to promote better relations with the Polish government.[56] By the end of the month U.S. sanctions were lifted.

The Trans-Siberian Pipeline Dispute

Despite the fact that agreement had been reached to exercise these joint policies of leverage and denial vis-à-vis Poland in early 1982, the pipeline dispute still simmered. Arrangements for financing the pipeline construction provided a perfect focus for changes the United States wanted in overall East-West trade credit arrangements. Interest rates for the sale of pipeline equipment were set at 7.8 percent by France and 8 percent by Italy and the FRG, while the prevailing market rate was 11 percent. These specific credit arrangements were a perfect target for U.S. complaints about imprudent trade subsidies to the adversary, and "evidence" of Soviet bargaining advantage in trade with the West.

Although the allies had resisted U.S. pressure for the pipeline embargo, they appeared willing to negotiate over the issue of credits. Consistent with their views on how to treat Poland, they insisted that joint decisions could be based on sound business practice without considering the "political" dimension of lending. In early February 1982, at the European Security Conference in Madrid, European foreign ministers had told Secretary of State Alexander Haig that credit was the East-West trade issue most likely to get allied agreement. A majority of the EC governments agreed in principle to increase the minimum interest rates on official export credits to the Soviet Union and stated that they would be willing to negotiate the terms within the OECD consensus.

But negotiation on credits within the regime was not enough to placate the United States with regard to the pipeline construction. In the spring of 1982 Reagan administration officials warned the Europeans that the sanctions which had been imposed six months earlier would be extended to European firms if voluntary compliance with an embargo was not forthcoming. The United States flatly demanded a joint policy to curtail the supply of pipeline equipment, reduce the amount of credit available to the East, and halt further subsidies on loans to the USSR.

Europeans, however, balked at these demands. Pipeline equipment continued to be shipped, and European governments refused to cut the volume of Soviet credits. On the issue of credits in general, Europeans stated that they would be willing to raise interest rates on official credit, since the goal was sound financial practice and the reduction of competition rather than political influence vis-à-vis the Soviet Union.[57] They continued to argue that this should be done through negotiations within the export credit regime and that the issue of credit subsidies should be delinked from the pipeline dispute.

Failing to persuade its allies in ad hoc negotiations, the United States agreed to discuss the issue of credits within the consensus. But now its demands would be constrained by the norms, rules, and procedures of the regime. And by May 1982 member countries had negotiated to actually strengthen the rules. The new agreement was not confined to credit policies toward the Soviet Union and Eastern Europe, but did include them. The agreement had three parts. First, members agreed to reclassify borrowers according to objective criteria. Countries with per capita GNP greater than $4,000 (1979 data) were classified as "relatively rich." Countries receiving International Development Agency credits or countries on the U.N. list of "least developed countries" were classified as "relatively poor." All other countries were classified as "intermediate." By this criterion the Soviet Union now fell into the "rich" category. Second, minimum interest rates were greatly increased for the "rich" countries and increased to a lesser extent for the "intermediate" countries. Rates for the "poor" countries remained unchanged. Finally, participants pledged not to deviate from these minimum interest rates and maximum repayment terms. Recall that in the 1978 agreement members agreed only to notify others if they planned to deviate from the guidelines. Thus this new agreement considerably strengthened the regime.[58]

Clearly, two concessions were made to the United States. First, the "prior commitments" clause was changed so that the terms of prior commitments could apply for only six months after a change. Second, the new arrangement raised interest rates for official credits to the Soviet Union. Instead of paying interest as low as 7.8 percent with a maturity on loans of eight and one-half years, the consensus agreed to charge between 12.15 percent and 12.49 percent, with maturities restricted to five years. This agreement actually brought the cost of official export finance to the Soviet Union into alignment with commercial interest rates, which were at the time moving downward, at least in Britain and the FRG. Under these market conditions West European states could be assured that financial transactions would not dry up.

Aware that the new agreement would not significantly cut Western exports to the CMEA, the United States wanted more than an increase in official export credit interest rates. Officials in the Reagan administration still wanted coordination on a policy of denial. They wanted Europeans to restrict their East-West trade by restricting finance. To achieve policy coordination on these terms the United States pursued alternate strategies of coercion and compensation *outside* the confines of the consensus regime.

The United States raised the issue at the Versailles summit in June 1982, one month after the completion of the consensus agreement. Here the United States pressed European governments to cut the volume of official credits to the Soviet Union and to reduce further the periods the Soviets would have in which to repay the loans. The Europeans again balked at this demand and clung to the terms of the consensus agreement.[59] The United States did manage to extract an agreement from France to tighten its credit restrictions on trade with the Soviets in exchange for more U.S. intervention in international financial markets to stabilize exchange rates. The closing statement at the summit, however, was a much weaker joint commitment to denial than the United States wanted. It included an agreement by all parties to offer loans to the Soviets at prevailing market interest rates. Since the rates on official loans had now reached market rates, and since the Soviets were borrowing heavily on Eurocurrency markets as market rates moved downward, this did not represent a commitment to reduce the volume of credits.[60]

Even the agreement reached between the United States and France was short-lived. Summit negotiators later revealed that the United States never believed that international monetary stability could be achieved through intervention in financial markets and that France was not prepared to back out of important credit negotiations with the Soviet Union. In the wake of the meetings President Mitterrand commented that "France would not support economic warfare against the Soviet Union," and it was not bound by the summit declaration to cut the amount of credit it extended to Moscow. Following the statement, France added injury to insult by revealing a secret bilateral agreement with the USSR on credit. U.S. officials were now fed up. Shortly after Mitterrand's revelation the Reagan administration extended the pipeline sanctions to cover products sold by European subsidiaries and licensees of U.S. firms.

Crisis Resolution and the Strengthening of the Regime

Despite the fact that these crises were not resolved the way many Reagan administration officials desired, an overall U.S. objective was reached. Europeans agreed to study further the central problems which the United States perceived East-West trade raised for the Western allies. These studies would be conducted within the East-West trade regime. All parties believed that the resulting technical information could provide a factual basis for a joint policy.

The studies' conclusions, however, did not support the leverage and denial policies preferred by the United States. Instead they supported the European preference for regulating competition. The communiqué published at the conclusion of OECD ministerial meetings in May 1983 stated that "East-West trade and credit flows should be guided by the indications of the market. . . . Governments should exercise financial prudence without granting preferential treatment," and keep East-West trade under "close observation."[61] This meant that Western governments should not intervene, either to deny or to promote East-West trade.

The consensus regime was considerably strengthened throughout this crisis, however, and its norms of reducing dangerous trade finance competition, rules for grouping borrowers into categories, and harmonizing interest rates on official credits have also been strengthened. Before 1982 members had simply informed the group when they wished to negotiate loans outside the guidelines. As indicated above, after May 1982 they agreed to adhere to the guidelines set by the organization. In 1983 consensus members established a system to set minimum rates automatically for official credits, which would be tied to average market rates and adjusted every six months. Thus, in contrast to the period before 1983, changes in official rates would not have to be continually renegotiated.

Conclusion

This chapter has presented an argument for the institutional basis of stable policy coordination in East-West trade finance when goals among the actors conflict but policy coordination is perceived as necessary by all. The thrust of the argument is twofold. First, U.S. hegemonic power and compliance strategies were ineffective in changing the goals of European governments. Second, the regime which emerged was effective in modifying both Europe's goal of trade promotion and U.S. goals of leverage and denial to achieve stable policy coordination.

The argument is illustrated by an examination of the interplay of U.S. compliance strategies, European responses, and regime development in the postwar period. The dominant U.S. strategies of leadership and coercion to coordinate policies for leverage and denial were sometimes effective but never stable. In its own restrictive export credit policy the United States attempted to exert leadership vis-à-vis the allies. But even though the United States adhered to the Berne Union "five-year rule," its leadership proved ineffective. The rule itself did not prove to be stable. Leadership was effective only once, in persuading the allies to cut credits to Poland after the imposition of martial law. And then Europeans argued that they did it because financial considerations so dictated. In the 1980s, the United States twice used coercion or threat of coercion to extract compliance. The threat to declare Poland in default was resisted by the counterthreat of withholding an IMF loan for Mexico. Europeans also resisted coercive pipeline sanctions and the U.S. demand to cut the volume of credit to the Soviet Union made in conjunction with those sanctions. Throughout the postwar period the United States has failed to achieve lasting coordination on East-West trade finance policies in pursuit of its preferred policies. And the norms of leverage and denial were never institutionalized in the regime.

Perhaps a strategy of compensation would have been effective with regard to trade finance, but it was never tried. During the hegemonic period it appears that the United States hoped that "leadership" would be successful. With the onset of hegemonic decline in the 1970s, material resources for compensation began to dry up. And, as the story suggests, resources for coercion were lacking. It can be argued that the United States never possessed the control over the sources of credit needed to exert hegemonic power over its allies in this issue area. Like the Eximbank at the government level, U.S. commercial banks have historically played a minor role in meeting the Soviet Union's credit demands.

In contrast, the international regime created to regulate competition in export credits has grown to be robust and effective in facilitating stable policy coordination without hegemonic dominance. What explains members' willingness to adhere to regime norms, rules, and procedures? What explains the increasing strength of the institution? One explanation suggested by the empirical material is that over time state actors began to recognize the unacceptable costs of their trade promotion strategies. Unbridled export promotion within interdependent relationships leads to dangerous trade wars. The regime norm was to permit trade promotion but prevent excessive competition. States joined the regime because it helped them achieve their original goal within the limits agreed to by all members. The institution of the reciprocity principle greatly facilitated regime strength. If everyone agreed to limit their trade promotion activity, no one state would have to take the "sucker's payoff" and forgo profits by initiating unilateral limitations. Although the regime had no enforcement mechanism, the rules were largely self-enforcing when they helped members meet their own goals. Although the Berne Union "five-year rule" eventually broke down, it was effective for thirty years, and the competition management norm upon which it was based was incorporated into the consensus.

Eventually the United States had to act within the regime because compliance strategies were poisoning interactions within the alliance relationship. The way the issue was resolved and the fact that it was resolved within the regime suggest that the future of alliance unity loomed larger than "winning" on the specific credit dispute. Thus, U.S. incentives to negotiate within the regime for its East-West trade preferences increased. And those preferences were not entirely neglected by the joint policy decisions. Over time, as the rules became stricter, the joint activities needed to reduce export subsidy competition also made it more difficult for CMEA countries to obtain official credit.

The information generated within the regime about the preferences of the members and about international financial markets helped the negotiation process, which led to policy coordination. The initial function of the regime was information gathering. When states knew the policies of other states and the effects of those policies on competition, limits were easier to agree upon. Information on "overlending" to CMEA countries permitted agreement on higher interest rates. The United States had to settle for higher interest rates as a symbol of tighter credits for the Soviet bloc.

The story also suggests that the Europeans had an interest in strengthening the regime because its norms, rules, and procedures provided a buffer to U.S. demands. Each time the United States pushed for joint policies of leverage and denial, Europeans protected themselves by calling upon the regime rules—rules to which the United States was committed. The consensus regime in particular protected the negotiated relationship on trade finance and minimized the effectiveness of U.S. coercive tactics. Thus, even when the United States exercised compliance strategies within the regime, its preferences were successfully resisted by others who called upon the regime's norms, rules, and procedures to support their positions.

This discussion of the evolution of Western efforts to control East-West trade finance is not intended to be a rigorous test of the argument presented here. It does, however, suggest that the argument is a viable one. An examination of Western negotiations over technology transfer to the East or European energy imports from the Soviet Union would seem to reinforce the explanatory and prescriptive utility of the institutional approach. Indeed, an East-West trade regime has clearly emerged in the postwar period, not only to restrict trade but to promote it and regulate competition. A further specification of the evolution of that regime and its impact on policy coordination is both possible and useful.

10

The Western Alliance and East-West Energy Trade

Bruce W. Jentleson

Memories (not to mention scars) of the early 1980s controversy over the Urengoi natural gas pipeline have yet to fade away totally. This was the most serious conflict over an issue of East-West trade in the history of the Western alliance. However, it was not the first time that American and West European policy had conflicted over East-West energy trade. In fact, over the years no sector of East-West trade has caused more West-West conflict than the energy sector.[1]

This chapter has four principal purposes. First, I present a basic analytic framework for explaining the changes over the postwar period in the Western alliance politics of East-West energy trade policy. Second, I apply this framework and establish past patterns through a brief review of three key periods and cases: the early cold war period (1949–54), with its strict trade controls in the energy and most other sectors; the growth of East-West oil trade in the late 1950s, culminating in the controversy over the Friendship oil pipeline (1962–63); and the growth of East-West energy trade in the 1970s.

Third, I assess recent trends as manifested in the Urengoi pipeline controversy and its aftermath. Never before had such bitter rhetoric been hurled across the Atlantic, or such punitive countersanctions been resorted to by the United States against its own allies. Yet never before had the United States exerted so little leverage over its allies' policies. On the other hand, even after the Reagan countersanctions had been rescinded the actual growth in East-West energy trade was less than originally projected. This was true with regard both to imports of Soviet natural gas and exports to the Soviet Union of energy equipment and technology. The key interpretive question, then, is whether (as is often asserted by the Reagan administration) the allies finally came around to more restrictive policies, or whether (as I argue) the limited growth in East-West energy trade is attributable to the conjuncture of highly unfavorable economic conditions— i.e., a function of markets more than politics.

Finally, I consider the future prospects for East-West energy trade and for intra-alliance relations on this issue. The key question here is whether, as market conditions change—as ultimately all market conditions do—East-West energy trade may once again become a major source of conflict within the Western alliance.

U.S. Power and the Western Alliance Politics of East-West Energy Trade Policy

Historically, the most frequent and most formidable constraint coercer states have faced in seeking to use economic sanctions for anything other than symbolic purposes has been the *alternative trade partner dilemma*.[2] Its nature and its essence are succinctly stated by Albert Hirschman in his classic 1945 work, *National Power and the Structure of Foreign Trade*: "A country menaced with an interruption of trade with a given country has the alternative of diverting its trade to a third country; by so doing it evades more or less completely the damaging consequences of the stoppage of its trade with one particular country. The stoppage or the threat of it would thus lose all its force."[3]

There are both economic and political reasons why alternative trade partners play such a critical role. In economic terms, even if a premium must be paid or some efficiency is lost in trading with an alternative partner, the actual impact of sanctions on the economy of

Table 10.1.   Exports to the Soviet Union of Energy Equipment and
Technology by COCOM Countries (in $ million)

	1975	1979
United States	$ 284.7	$ 237.6
Japan	904.4	1,097.1
Western Europe[a]	1,420.8	1,879.2
Other[b]	156.7	213.1
Total	$2,766.6	$3,427.0

[a]West Germany, France, Italy, United Kingdom.
[b]Principal countries in this category: Canada, Netherlands, Norway, Sweden, Switzerland.
Source: Office of Technology Assessment, *Technology and Soviet Energy Availability* (Washington, D.C.: Government Printing Office, 1981), p. 174.

the target state is reduced substantially. With regard to the Soviet energy sector this is particularly important because, as documented in the 1981 study by the Office of Technology Assessment of the U.S. Congress, there are very few energy-related equipments and technologies in which the United States still monopolizes world production.[4] Thus, even if certain American exports are more advanced than those available from Western Europe or Japan, the costs to the Soviet economy are far less than if the embargo were multilateral. Similarly, on the other side of the trade ledger, given that the United States imports hardly any Soviet oil and no Soviet gas, while Western Europe imports substantial quantities of both, a unilateral American boycott makes little dent in Soviet hard currency earnings.

Tables 10.1 and 10.2 illustrate these points. Had 1980s figures been used in table 10.1, the American share of Western exports of energy equipment and technology to the Soviet Union would have been even smaller. The 1979 figures predate the nearly comprehensive sanctions on energy-related exports imposed by the Reagan administration, although they do include the effects of the Carter administration policy of requiring prior governmental review (i.e., licensing) of equipment and technology for oil and gas exploration and production. The 1976 figures predate the Carter licensing policy,

Table 10.2.   Imports by Non-communist Countries of Soviet Oil and
Natural Gas (in $ million, 1985)

	Oil	Natural gas	Total
United States	$ 8	$ 0	$ 8
Japan	150	0	150
Western Europe[a]	9,062	3,156	12,218
Other	4,920[b]	668[c]	5,588
Total	$14,140	$3,824	$17,964

[a]West Germany, Italy, France, the Netherlands, Belgium, Greece, United Kingdom, Denmark, Spain
[b]Principal countries in this category: Finland, India, Sweden, Switzerland
[c]Principal countries in this category: Austria, Finland
Source: *Oil and Gas Journal*, September 8, 1986, p. 49.

yet even then we see that the American market share was only 10 percent. On the import side (table 10.2) the United States is seen to be virtually a non-actor. Even Japan has not been much of a market for Soviet oil and no market at all for Soviet natural gas. Western Europe, on the other hand, imported over $12 billion of Soviet oil and natural gas, a figure equal to 68 percent of total Soviet oil and gas exports outside their own bloc.

The negative political effects of trade provided by alternative partners are more subtle but in certain ways even more consequential. When the coercer state's own allies act as alternative trade partners, economic sanctions lose much of their credibility. The signal sent to the Soviet adversary is not a particularly convincing one if the process of sending it highlights a lack of alliance solidarity. Instead, doubt is cast on the threat to sustain the sanctions—and perhaps even on other Western commitments for collective action. Economic sanctions thus can end up detracting from, rather than reinforcing, the overall Western deterrence posture.

Therefore, if energy trade sanctions are to have any chance of economic or political impact on the Soviet Union, the United States must be able to get its allies, particularly Western Europe, to collaborate. Yet, as noted above, intra-alliance conflict on this issue has been greater than in any other sector of East-West trade. Moreover, not only has such conflict been a recurring phenomenon, it also has been an intensifying one.

Before reviewing specific illustrative cases, it is important to establish a more general analytic framework. In this regard three factors are key: (1) foreign policy strategy; (2) economic interests; and (3) American power.

Foreign Policy Strategy

While united in their pursuit of collective security (the core basis for NATO), the United States and its West European allies often have differed over the optimal strategy for achieving this objective. At its most basic level the dispute can be expressed as being over whether détente and defense are complementary or contradictory strategies for relations with the Soviet Union. Generally speaking, European governments have tended to be more disposed to the complementarity view. They always have agreed that the Soviet Union is a common and formidable adversary. Their differences with the United States have come over assessments of the nature and severity of the Soviet threat and, accordingly, how best to counter this threat.

Differences over trade sanctions have reflected, and in turn often contributed to these broad differences over foreign policy strategy. As a general rule, the degree of consensus within the Western alliance on embargoing a particular export to the Soviet Union has varied with the military significance of the export in question. Through COCOM a common policy has been forged that deals fairly consistently on arms, munitions, nuclear-related exports, and those dual-use items whose military applications are both direct and highly significant.[5] Agreement has been more difficult, however, on those exports whose military significance is indirect, peripheral, or otherwise not quite self-evident. On these issues, in keeping with their respective overarching views of East-West relations, the United States has tended to push for a broad construction of military significance, while the allies have tended toward a narrower interpretation.

Trade in the energy sector not only fits this characterization of indirect military significance, but raises issues that go two steps farther. First, beyond just the military significance of particular exports there is the broader strategic significance of the energy sector in the overall context of the East-West rivalry. As the two OPEC crises of the 1970s demonstrated all too graphically, the energy sector is of vital importance to all industrialized economies. This is arguably even truer for the Soviet Union which, in addition to being an industrialized economy, by the early 1980s also had come to rely on energy exports for 80 percent of its hard currency earnings. In this regard the broad constructionist view (the American tendency) stresses the strategic benefits of trying to weaken such a key sector of the Soviet economy. In the narrow constructionist view (the European tendency) such strategic considerations are given even less weight than indirect military significance.

Second, the flow of trade in the other direction (i.e., imports from the Soviet Union) has been more of a foreign policy issue than any other sector of East-West trade. The American position repeatedly has been that energy imports from the Soviet Union risk political vulnerability. The Europeans, in turn, have argued that their trade agreements did not put them in any kind of dangerously dependent position. Which position has been the more valid is less important for the present point than the fact that in no other sector has there been a comparable debate over the foreign policy implications of imports from the Soviet Union.

Economic Interests

A second source of intra-alliance conflict has been the divergence in the economic interests at stake in East-West energy trade. Here, too, there are both export and import dimensions—and on both dimensions the allies have stood to lose much more than the United States.

Two general statements, both of which are supported by the data in table 10.3, can be made about Western exports to the Soviet Union.

Table 10.3.   Divergent Economic Interests: Exports to the Soviet Union
(1983)

	(1) Exports to USSR as percentage of total world exports	(2) Export share index (U.S. = 100)	(3) Exports to USSR as percentage of GNP[a]	(4) GNP share index (U.S. = 100)
United States	1.0	100	0.06	100
United Kingdom	0.7	70	0.14	233
West Germany	2.6	260	0.67	1,117
France	2.4	240	0.44	733
Italy	2.6	260	0.52	867
Japan	1.9	190	0.24	400

[a]Calculated as column one multiplied by total world exports as percentage of GNP or GDP (GNP for United States, West Germany, and Japan; GDP for United Kingdom, France, and Italy). Figures: U.S. 6 percent, U.K. 20.1 percent, West Germany 25.9 percent, France 18.3 percent, Italy 20.19 percent, and Japan 12.7 percent.

Sources: Export data from United Nations, Statistical Office, Yearbook of International Trade Statistics (1983); GNP and GDP data (except France) from Organization for Economic Cooperation and Development, Main Economic Indicators: Historical Statistics, 1964–1983; France GDP data from United Nations, Statistical Office, Monthly Bulletin of Statistics (July 1985).

First, consistent with columns one and three, we see that for all major Western nations the *absolute* value of the Soviet market is not particularly high. At most, exports to the Soviet Union amount to less than 3 percent of total world exports and less than 1 percent of GNP. Second, as the indexes in columns two and four indicate, the differences in the *relative* value of the Soviet market to the allies as compared to the United States are quite substantial. The export share index ranks only the United Kingdom below the United States. The export share index for Japan is almost double the U.S. index, and those for West Germany, Italy, and France are all around two and one-half times greater. The differences in the GNP share index are even more pronounced. On this index the United Kingdom also ranks higher than the United States, while the differences for West Germany, France, Italy, and Japan are of much higher orders of magnitude than in the export share index.

Thus, while not excessive, the costs incurred by anti-Soviet export embargoes are nevertheless distributed highly unequally. The United States bears much smaller relative costs than do Western Europe or Japan. (Had grain exports to the Soviet Union been factored out —which, after all, would be consistent with the policy approach of the Reagan administration—the relative differences would have been even greater.) In addition, there are sectoral and cyclical factors which do not show in the aggregate data but which can further increase the relative value of the Soviet market. For example, as Marie-Hélène Labbé reports in this volume, in 1980 50.4 percent of French exports of steel pipe and 41.3 percent of compressor exports went to the Soviet bloc. The same pattern holds true in these sectors for both West Germany and Italy. Moreover, when recessions have hit, as a very severe one did in the early 1980s, the marginal economic value —and the absolute political value—of any and all markets have increased even more.

On the import side, with particular regard to East-West energy trade, economic interests have diverged even more sharply. As table 10.4 shows, there are very sharp differences within the Western alliance between those countries that can produce their own energy supplies domestically (i.e., energy producer states) and those that must rely primarily on imports (i.e., energy consumer states). In the 1950s and early 1960s, when primary reliance was on coal, all the major Western nations except Italy qualified as energy producer states. However, with conversion to oil in the 1960s and to natural gas in the 1970s came a dramatic decline everywhere except in the United States in the percentage of energy consumption that could be satisfied by domestic production. The discovery of oil and natural gas in the North Sea in the 1970s allowed Britain to recapture its position as an energy producer. But West Germany, France, Italy, and Japan all were able to make only incremental reductions in their dependence on foreign energy supplies. The projections for 1990 and 2000 do not indicate any

Table 10.4.   Energy Producers versus Energy Consumers (domestic energy production as a percentage of total energy consumption)

	1950	1960	1973	1982	1990	2000
United States	100+	97	86	91	87	91
United Kingdom	100	78	56	100+	100+	94
West Germany	100+	90	46	48	51	52
France	68	62	21	25	—	—
Italy	24	34	16	17	22	28
Japan	96	56	9	11	22	27

Source: Data for 1950, 1960, 1973 from United Nations, *World Energy Suppliers: 1950–1974* (New York, 1976), table 2; 1982 from United Nations, *Energy Statistics Yearbook: 1983* (New York, 1985), table 1; 1990 and 2000 from International Energy Agency, *Energy Policies and Programs of IEA Countries: 1984 Review* (Paris, 1985).

significant change away from their positions as energy consumer states.

Thus, it is not casual calculations of commercial advantage as much as fundamental differences of position in the structure of the international energy economy which are at work in the divergent valuations of Soviet exports of oil and natural gas. Especially in the wake of the two OPEC shocks, energy consumer nations have had an obvious interest in diversifying their suppliers in order to enhance their economic security. "No one can tell me," as one West German official put it, "that the Straits of Hormuz are a safer energy channel than a gas pipeline from Russia."[6] For energy producer nations supplier diversification is a much less compelling need.

In addition, in what might be called the "geoeconomics" of East-West natural gas trade, West Germany, Italy, and France are located within construction range of pipelines from the rich Soviet oil and gas fields in western Siberia. Pipelines are much less feasible to Japan and are simply not possible to Britain or the United States. When gas trade has been discussed with these countries it has been in terms of liquefied natural gas (LNG), an industrial process and mode of transportation which carries a host of its own environmental and commercial problems.

American Power

The ideal scenario for a coercer state is one where there are no differences over foreign policy strategy and no divergences of economic interests between it and those states which are potential alternative trade partners for the target state. However, as usually is the case in international relations, the reality rarely corresponds to the ideal. In situations such as East-West energy trade, in which a coercer state needs the collaboration of other states whose own interests (foreign policy and economic) point to trade rather than trade controls, a third factor enters into the policy equation: the *power* that the coercer state can bring to bear as leverage over those states that are in a position to be alternative trade partners.

One possible source of leverage is for the coercer state to have sufficient economic resources to compensate other states for the economic costs of forgoing trade with the target state. This economic compensation may be through substitute supplies of goods which otherwise would be imported from the target state, substitute purchases of exports which otherwise would be exported to the target state, or through more indirect forms such as economic aid linked to trade controls collaboration. Alternatively, economic power may be flexed more punitively. States which refuse to collaborate may be targeted for trade and other economic countersanctions intended to increase the costs of noncollaboration. Either way the basic strategy here is, in effect, to make divergent economic interests converge.

A less tangible but often more useful power resource, especially in relations among allies, is political prestige; i.e., the status and reputation which engender what in a broader political-sociological context Harold Lasswell and Abraham Kaplan call "deference values."[7] Energy trade falls mostly outside the domain of the COCOM export controls regime. Nor does it have even the degree of consensus on basic rules and norms which, as Beverly Crawford points out in her chapter, characterizes the finance sector. The extent to which the United States can draw on its own prestige to enhance its authority, and avoid having to resort to more blatant measures, thus has been especially important with regard to alliance East-West energy trade policy.

We therefore should expect to find a relationship between the leverage that the United States has been able to bring to bear through these power resources and the extent of allied collaboration with controls on East-West energy trade. With this basic framework established, we turn to a brief historical review.

Past Patterns: Historical Summary

Early Cold War Period, 1949–54

Even during the early years of the Cold War the allies did not go as far as the United States wanted in controlling trade with the Soviet Union. They agreed to the creation of COCOM as an export control regime, but they sought to keep it a weak regime by limiting both its policy and its policing authority.[8] Whereas American exports to the Soviet Union fell to miniscule levels (e.g., $15,000 in 1952), exports by European COCOM members never fell below $71 million.

Nevertheless, the extent of alliance collaboration achieved during this period was both substantial in its own right and greater than would ever again be seen. European exports to the Soviet Union may have been greater than American exports, but they were much less than both traditional prewar levels ($1.41 billion in 1938) and the immediate postwar years prior to the creation of COCOM ($118 million in 1949). Moreover, most of the trade that did continue involved items with little significance even for the Soviet industrial base, let alone for Soviet military capabilities. The original COCOM lists placed 144 categories of exports under total embargo, 27 under partial embargo, and 6 under strict reporting requirements. By August 1954 these lists had grown to 320, 92, and 102 items, respectively—an increase of almost 300 percent.[9]

This high degree of overall alliance collaboration on export controls can be explained quite well using the analytic framework just delineated. The first point is that the European allies largely concurred with the United States on the utility of export controls as part of the overall Western deterrence posture against the Soviet Union of Stalin. In the face of the Czechoslovakian coup of 1948, the Berlin crisis of 1948–49, the successful Soviet A-bomb test in September 1949, and the Korean War, the Soviet threat was no less clear and present to Western Europe than to the United States. While the Europeans stopped well short of inflicting upon themselves a trauma akin to McCarthyism—as David Caute observes, the British managed to fight the Cold War without an "un-British affairs committee"[10]— intra-alliance disputes over foreign policy strategy were minimal during these years.

Second, with regard to economic interests, European motivations for trading with the Soviet Union at this particular time were minimal. Exports had been growing rapidly without Soviet or East European markets (e.g., a 30.1 percent average annual growth in West Germany in 1950–54). As table 10.4 shows, with their economies still coal-based, most West European countries were energy self-sufficient. Moreover, even if they had wanted to trade, the Russians under Stalin did not. They created the Council on Mutual Economic Assistance (CMEA) in 1949 to turn themselves and Eastern Europe inward toward regional autarky.[11]

Reinforcing these inclinations toward export controls was American power. At a time when self-defense was no longer possible, the United States stood as Europe's protector. In more intangible but still quite potent ways, the combination of the still-fresh memories of World War II and the beneficence of the Marshall Plan imbued the United States with the leverage that comes with such extremely high political prestige. In addition, in 1951 the U.S. Congress had passed the Mutual Defense Assistance Control Act (the Battle Act) linking Marshall Plan aid (which between 1949 and 1953 totaled $15 billion, 87 percent of which was in outright grants) to European collaboration with export controls. The Truman administration had opposed this legislation, and neither it nor the Eisenhower administration ever invoked the Battle Act to cut off aid. But the threat that it could be invoked was always there, particularly if the McCarthyite Congress forced the issue. Thus, when West European officials were asked by the Swedish author Gunnar Adler-Karlsson why they stuck to such strict controls in the early 1950s, "the answers invariably referred to the U.S. aid as the overridingly important reason."[12]

The 1950s Soviet "Oil Offensive" and the Friendship Oil Pipeline, 1962–63

Among those exports which had been put under total embargo by COCOM were "all basic specialized equipment for the exploration, production and refining of petroleum and natural gas." The Soviet Union held rich and vast deposits of oil and natural gas. In fact, at the turn of the century Russia was the world's leading oil producer. Since then, however, decades of revolution and war had taken their toll on actual Soviet production capacity. By the early 1950s the situation was such that, according to a study by the CIA, without Western supplies of oil industry equipment and technology "the Soviets cannot be expected to make any spectacular improvements in the near future."[13]

However, when the COCOM embargo lists were cut back in 1958, at European insistence and over American objections, oil industry equipment was among those exports decontrolled.[14] Of particular significance was the decontrol of wide-diameter pipe. Contrary to the CIA's prognostications, and despite the COCOM embargo, the Soviets had managed major increases in oil production (100 percent between 1953 and 1958). One of the key bottlenecks they still faced, though, was their limited capacity to produce the wide-diameter pipe necessary for the planned major expansion of their pipeline system, including the construction of the "Pipeline of Friendship," a 7,500-kilometer pipeline through which oil was to be exported in vastly increased quantities to Eastern and Western Europe. The lifting of the COCOM controls made it possible for the Soviets to import much of the wide-diameter pipe they needed from West Germany in particular (867,000 metric tons), as well as from Italy (240,000 tons) and Japan (25,000 tons).[15]

The United States had opposed the original 1958 decision to decontrol wide-diameter pipe and even more vehemently opposed the particular project of the Friendship oil pipeline. One reason, as delineated in a State Department memorandum, was that the Friendship pipeline would "facilitate and improve relative military, strategic and economic strength of USSR." A second reason was that it would "permit Soviets to intensify oil offensive to non-bloc countries."[16] On this point the United States had economic as well as political motivations. The Soviet Union already had increased its oil exports to such energy consumer countries as West Germany and Italy by over 400 percent since 1956. In so doing they were taking away markets from the Middle Eastern operations of such major American oil multinationals as Standard Oil of New Jersey. Moreover, in cases such as Italy, where the Soviets had gained upward of a 20 percent market share, there was growing concern in Washington about the potential political consequences of a NATO member depending upon the Soviet Union for such a large share of such a vital resource.

Thus, in late 1962 the Kennedy administration sought to bring its leverage to bear for a wide-diameter pipe embargo and a scaling back, if not boycott, of Soviet oil. While not totally successful these efforts did achieve their major immediate objectives. West Germany, the principal wide-diameter pipe exporter, went so far as to cancel existing contracts on which delivery was pending. Italy and Japan followed suit by turning down new contract orders the Soviets brought to them. Italy also scaled back its imports of Soviet oil to the point where, by 1965, the Soviet share of the Italian oil market had shrunk to about 10 percent.

With West Germany the principal source of American power was the still high American political prestige. The primary West German motivation in exporting wide-diameter pipe to the Soviet Union had been economic. As far as foreign policy was concerned, West Germany still for the most part uncritically followed the American lead. Thus, as Foreign Minister Gerhard Schroeder put it during the Bundestag debate: "My heart is completely with the iron and steel industry, with full employment and the full utilization of our capacity. . . . But I must choose here between the interests of foreign policy and the interests of our economy. Thank God in a limited sphere. So I am choosing foreign policy."[17]

With Italy the United States relied more on economic power resources. It follows from the earlier discussion that Italy, an energy consumer country, would be the most interested in Soviet oil. Foreign policy came into play slightly more than in the West German case, but what most attracted Italy to Soviet oil was its low price. Accordingly, the State Department worked closely with Standard Oil of New Jersey and other major American oil companies (whose market shares the Soviets were moving into) to combine political pressure with a de facto compensatory economic offer of low prices and other commercial benefits.[18]

Energy Trade and Détente in the 1970s

In 1972 the United States for the first time began loosening its controls on energy equipment and technology exports. President Richard Nixon and National Security Adviser–Secretary of State Henry Kissinger saw American-Soviet energy trade as an integral component of their strategy of using the inducements of economic relations to help build détente with the Soviet Union. Of particular priority in this regard were the multibillion-dollar North Star and Yakutsk projects (the latter with Japanese partnership in the consortium) for the development of Soviet natural gas reserves and their export as liquefied natural gas to the United States and Japan. The joint communiqué issued at the June 1973 summit by Nixon and Soviet leader Leonid Brezhnev singled out these projects for endorsement. To promote them the U.S. Export-Import Bank proposed over $2 billion in loans and loan guarantees.

However, as with much of American-Soviet trade, these projects fell victim to the restrictions imposed by Congress through the Trade Act of 1974. The Jackson-Vanik amendment linked most favored nation (MFN) status for all Soviet exports to a U.S.-set quota for emigration of Soviet Jews. The Stevenson-Church amendments, also passed in late 1974, restricted lending to the Soviet Union by the U.S. Export-Import Bank. The overall ceiling on new lending was set at $300 million, but credits related to energy research and exploration were subjected to a subceiling of only $40 million and an outright ban was imposed on any lending related to the production, processing, or distribution of energy. Thus, while not directly prohibited, the North Star and Yakutsk projects lost any chance of becoming commercially viable.

During the Carter administration, as part of what George Shultz (then a private citizen) dubbed "light-switch diplomacy," further restrictions were placed on East-West energy trade.[19] In July 1978 new regulations were promulgated requiring that all exports of equipment and technology for oil and gas exploration and production be subjected to executive branch licensing.[20] As an immediate matter, the planned export by Dresser Industries of a $144 million turnkey factory for manufacturing sophisticated rock-drill bits was suspended. The timing of these actions was in retaliation against the arrest of a number of prominent dissidents (including Anatoly Shcharansky) on charges of crimes against the state and also of an American businessman on charges of black marketeering. At a more strategic level these tightened export controls also reflected the debate engendered by a CIA study the previous year predicting the imminent decline of Soviet oil production.[21] Thus, when in early September the Soviets released the American and some of the dissidents, the sanctions on the Dresser sale were lifted but the general licensing requirement was kept on the books.

Interestingly, over the ensuing sixteen months virtually every application to export oil and gas exploration and production equipment and technology was approved. The total value of such exports reached $161.1 million in 1979, more than double the 1978 figure.[22] When the Soviets invaded Afghanistan, however, policy changed once again. In January 1980 all existing licenses for energy equipment and technology exports were suspended and all new license applications were subjected to a presumption of denial.[23]

No such politically motivated gyrations characterized West European–Soviet energy trade in the 1970s. To the extent that foreign policy did enter in, it was as another factor in favor of increased East-West trade, in particular for the Ostpolitik of West Germany and the Gaullist Independent foreign policy of France. The fluctuations that did occur were economically motivated. For example, West European imports of Soviet oil increased following the 1973 OPEC oil shock, then leveled off in the mid-1970s, only to increase again following the 1979 OPEC shock. Similarly, while over the course of the decade West European exports of energy equipment and technology grew significantly, there were short-term downturns such as in 1977, when the Soviets were forced by hard currency shortages to cut back on their imports.

The most substantial growth was in natural gas trade. The basic terms of trade were analogous to those in West European–Soviet oil trade: Soviet exports of the energy raw material and West European exports of equipment and technology (wide-diameter pipe once again, and also the turbine-powered compressors needed for efficient pipeline transmission). Also, as in the oil sector, trade developed selectively, with the energy consumer countries of West Germany, Italy, and France in the lead. A first round of natural gas trade agreements had been signed by Italy and West Germany in late 1969 and early 1970. A second round of agreements was signed in the wake of the 1973 OPEC oil crisis, this time also including France. Following the 1979 OPEC crisis, negotiations were begun on a third round of agreements—agreements which when signed in 1981–82 became the basis for confrontation with the Reagan administration.

Recent Trends: The Urengoi Pipeline Controversy and Its Aftermath

To be fully understood the Reagan administration's sanctions against the Urengoi natural gas pipeline have to be placed in the context of its overall strategy of cold war–style economic coercion. The Soviet economic system, according to Defense Secretary Caspar Weinberger, was "fatally flawed," condemned to inefficiency and ultimately decline because "their system cannot be reformed without liberalizing Soviet society as a whole." Thus, by providing "constant infusions of advanced technology," Western trade not only saves the Soviet industrial base from "cumulative obsolescence," but also "helps preserve the Soviet Union as a totalitarian dictatorship."[24]

From this perspective the very centrality of East-West energy trade made sanctions in this sector especially important. Over 80 percent of total Soviet hard currency earnings came from oil and gas exports. Western equipment and technology, while not absolutely essential, played an important role in Soviet energy projects. Moreover, there was the fear, as in the early 1960s with Italian imports of Soviet oil, of Western countries becoming too dependent on the Soviet Union for their energy supplies. Thus, when West European–Soviet discussions on the Urengoi pipeline began in 1980, the Carter administration had taken a position of "muted skepticism."[25] The Reagan administration's position, however, was both more skeptical and less muted. It was forcefully and unequivocally articulated by Assistant Secretary of Defense Richard N. Perle. In testimony before a congressional committee on November 12, 1981 (i.e., one month and one day *before* martial law was imposed in Poland), Perle laid out his views:

> First, it [the Urengoi pipeline] will generate substantial hard currency earnings for the Soviet Union that will finance a number of Soviet developments inimical to our interests. With the pipeline in full operation, several billion dollars annually will flow into the Soviet treasury. . . .
>
> Second, the revenues available to the Soviets will help to forge an economic link with Europe that will inevitably increase Moscow's influence among our allies. And where jobs and profits emanate from Moscow, it would be naive to believe that politics will stay far behind. . . .
>
> Third, we believe that Europe will incur a dangerous vulnerability to the interruption of supplies of natural gas from the Soviet Union. . . . Even in the absence of a crisis severe enough to lead to a Soviet cutoff, there is the day-to-day influence that

must flow, like the gas itself, through a pipeline to which there will be no practicable alternative. . . .

Is there any doubt that our allies listen more carefully to kings and rulers who supply them with energy than to those who do not?[26]

The imposition of martial law in Poland thus was the proximate but neither the only nor the most significant cause for the sanctions against the Urengoi pipeline.[27] The problem for the Reagan administration, though, was to get the allies to go along. After all, it was the Europeans who were putting up the hard currency for Soviet gas, who held most of the export contracts, and whose security allegedly was being endangered.

In the European policy of refusing to go along with the American sanctions and the inability of the United States to either persuade or force them to do so, we see the culmination of the historical shifts in the alliance politics and power relationships of East-West energy trade.

First, the Urengoi pipeline embodied a much broader dispute over foreign policy strategy. On this as well as other issues the differences alluded to earlier over whether détente and defense were complementary or contradictory had come to full intensity. The Europeans did not dismiss the Soviet threat, but they did reject what one official labeled "the thesis prevalent in the [American] administration that the West is in a state of permanent conflict with the Soviet Union."[28] Herein lies the logic as to why they were prepared to bolster the NATO defense posture with the Pershing and Cruise nuclear missiles despite extensive public opposition, and why (as Michael Mastanduno and the authors in part II of this book point out) they cooperated in tightening controls on high-technology exports, yet they would not end energy trade with the Soviet Union. Moreover, they rejected and were affronted by the Reagan administration's contention that they were allowing themselves to become too dependent on Soviet gas. Quite the contrary, they saw their security being enhanced in its economic component by this lessening of their dependence on OPEC.[29]

They further stressed that safeguards already were being planned and implemented against possible emergencies (with greater progress in a shorter time, it was often noted, than the United States had made with its own strategic petroleum reserve).

Second, the intra-alliance divergence of economic interests was now wider than ever before. The contrast in structural positions between the United States as an energy producer state and most of Western Europe as energy consumers was both starker and more central to policy following the second OPEC crisis and amidst the Iran-Iraq War and other sources of continuing instability in the Persian Gulf and Middle East regions. The decision by the Reagan administration to lift the grain embargo against the Soviet Union added to European resentments, as it was seen as assisting the one interest group in the United States with a major economic stake in trade with the Soviet Union. Some Europeans even speculated that the hidden agenda of the whole American sanctions strategy was to take away a market in which the Europeans had a competitive advantage and which, if it continued to grow, could help them generate revenues, gain experience, and develop economies on a scale which could increase their overall international competitiveness. As Michael Mastanduno notes, whether or not this was true was less important than that the perception existed.

Third, given these major differences, the Reagan administration would have needed to bring American power to bear in substantial form to bridge the gaps. It tried persuasion as early as the July 1981 Ottawa summit, but to no avail. A few months later a State Department delegation went to Western Europe with a compensatory economic package, but this, too, proved inadequate to the task. Finally, on June 18, 1982, the administration resorted to more punitive tactics. It claimed extraterritorial jurisdiction for American sanctions over European subsidiaries of American corporations, European companies producing under license from American firms, and European companies using American-made parts. In effect, it sought to impose through American power a policy on which it could not get political agreement.

In response the leaders of Western Europe exhibited unusual unity, not only across national lines but also across party lines within each nation. One after the other, France, Italy, Britain, and West Germany went ahead with their exports; and one after the other, the Reagan administration slapped countersanctions on the offending countries and their firms. The *New York Times* editorialized against "pipeline machismo," warning that "incompetent American diplomacy has turned the disagreement into a battle over sovereignty that mocks the unity of the Atlantic alliance."[30] French President François Mitterrand and British Prime Minister Margaret Thatcher held a joint news conference to express their mutual outrage. Newly elected West German Chancellor Helmut Kohl alluded to American grain exports to the Soviet Union in his remark that "one should not demand of the other what one would not like to have demanded of oneself."[31]

Finally, after almost five months of this imbroglio, and with new Secretary of State George Shultz leading the way, the United States lifted the countersanctions against its own allies. The official American position was that a compromise agreement had been reached and that, as President Reagan put it, "there is no further need for these sanctions and I am lifting them today."[32] The reality, though, was that the United States had done far more conceding than leveraging. As part of the November 1982 agreement the Europeans agreed to participate in a study of gas import vulnerability directed by the International Energy Agency (IEA). The Reagan administration had hoped to use this process to legitimize and institutionalize strict limits on imports of Soviet gas. Its goal was a *binding* maximum ceiling at 30 percent of total gas consumption. But while advancing general principles about avoiding undue dependence on any single supplier, the IEA study stopped well short of any binding policy strictures.[33] As table 10.5 shows, West Germany and France both were importing much more Soviet gas in 1985 than in 1980. Italian imports actually had fallen in the short-term, in large part reflecting some bilateral commercial disputes, but by 1990 Italy, like France, was projected to be over the 30 percent mark.

It is true that these levels of gas imports were less than those

Table 10.5.   Western European Imports of Soviet Natural Gas, 1980–1990

	1980		1985		1990 (projection)	
	Volume[a]	Share[b]	Volume	Share	Volume	Share
West Germany	10.8	15.0	12.0	25.9	15.0	28.2
France	4.1	11.7	6.4	22.6	9.2	32.0
Italy	7.2	27.6	5.8	18.5	12.4	33.4

[a]volume in billions of cubic meters
[b]share as a percentage of total natural gas consumption
Sources: 1980 data from Statistical Office of the European Communities, Eurostat: Hydrocarbons, Monthly Bulletin (January 1982): 18; and U.S. Department of Energy, Energy Information Administration, 1981 International Energy Annual (Washington, D.C., 1982), p. 70; 1985 and 1990 data from Commission of the European Communities, Communication from the Commission to the Council on Natural Gas (December 11, 1986): appendixes 3 and 4.

originally projected. Italy had dragged out its negotiations until the Soviets agreed to smaller volumes and lower prices. Both France and West Germany renegotiated their already-signed agreements for both lower prices and lower volumes. Countries such as Belgium and the Netherlands, which originally expressed interest, decided against Urengoi pipeline gas. This has meant as much as a 50 percent short-fall between actual and projected Soviet hard currency earnings. However, while the Reagan administration often cited such statistics as evidence of the success of its sanctions policy, far more accurate is the analysis expressed in the subtitle of an article in Forbes: "American diplomacy couldn't cut Russian export earnings from natural gas, but it looks like the market can."[34]

What actually happened was that a number of market forces, all highly unfavorable to East-West energy trade, came together in the 1982–85 period. The early 1980s recession caused an overall decline in West European demand for energy, which for gas amounted to an 8 percent drop in total consumption between 1979 and 1982. The plunge in world oil prices came on top of this already unfavorable macroeconomic trend. As a result, the aggregate increase in West European natural gas consumption for 1979–85 was only 5 percent, compared to 49 percent for the previous six-year period. Moreover, a 1986 IEA study scaled back the projections for 1990 (made in a 1982 study) by 18–25 percent.[35]

On top of reduction in demand, competition increased from the three other major natural gas suppliers. The Netherlands, which since the mid-1970s had been intentionally reducing its gas exports in order to guard its reserves, reversed its policy in September 1983.[36] This had both an immediate impact, as Dutch gas exports increased 7.7 percent in 1985, and an effect on future markets, as instead of zeroing out by the year 2000, Dutch exports now were forecast at 20–25 billion cubic meters (bcm) per year. Norway also began moving toward a similar shift away from a restrictive gas export policy. This culminated in an agreement in December 1986 with France, West Germany, Belgium, and the Netherlands to develop the giant Troll fields in the North Sea. The plan is for Troll gas to begin flowing in 1993 and to continue through the year 2020, reaching its peak of 20 bcm by the year 2000.[37] Algeria, a supplier of both LNG and pipeline gas to France and Italy, whose hard-line commercial tactics (e.g., insisting on high prices and reneging on contracts when its demands were not met) had in recent years been costing it markets,[38] recognized the extent to which conditions had changed to a buyer's market and now was taking a much more businesslike approach in an effort to be more competitive.

On the Western exports side of the trade relationship the limited actual growth in trade was also more for economic than political reasons. Once the American countersanctions had been lifted in November 1982, the West European firms fulfilled their original export contracts for the Urengoi pipeline. When over the ensuing six months the Reagan administration again tried to get multilateral export controls on energy equipment and technology, the allied governments once again resisted. In February 1983 the United States proposed that COCOM adopt some two dozen new sanctions on oil and gas equipment and technology (including the same turbine-powered compressors which had set off the 1982 imbroglio). The few sanctions which dealt with dual-use items (e.g., geophones) were adopted by COCOM.

But as regarded the fundamental notion that oil and gas equipment and technology exports should be controlled, the allies responded with "an unusually strong protest expressing their 'deep abiding concern' over the new American proposal."[39] The Reagan administration next sought to use the May 1983 Williamsburg summit to press for these added sanctions and, according to some reports, for a moratorium on Western participation in all future Soviet energy projects. But when the allies once again opposed such moves, the administration had little choice but to settle for the vague and toothless statement that "East-West economic relations should be compatible with our security interests." This gave at least the political form of a compromise but with very little policy substance.

Accordingly, in the first five months following the November 1982 settlement, West European firms signed $1.5 billion in new contracts for additional wide-diameter pipe, gas turbine components, and for such new projects as sulfur-extraction and gas treatment equipment for the Astrakhan gas fields. Both the allies and the Soviets seemed to be making statements through the timing of these contracts. In the months that followed numerous other deals were reported in the popular and trade press, including major new contracts for additional wide-diameter pipe, pipe-layers and spare parts for oil-field equipment.[40]

This did not lead, however, to any sort of lasting boom. After an initial post-sanctions spurt, Western exports of oil and gas equipment and technology to the Soviet Union sagged. Wharton Econometrics estimated a one-third drop in 1984 in EC exports of energy equipment and technology, and another 18 percent drop in 1985. One factor was the fruition of the crash compressor-building program initiated by the Soviets in response to the 1982 sanctions.[41] A second and more pervasive factor was the overall hard currency shortage the Soviet Union was suffering amidst plunging world oil prices. In the 1970s, with earnings from oil exports riding the OPEC crest, hard currency earnings had been much less of a problem. Between 1972 and 1974 the volume of Soviet crude oil exports to the West actually dropped 5 percent while their earnings increased over 400 percent.[42] Their windfall following the 1979 oil shock was a 96 percent increase in hard currency earnings (from $5.7 billion in 1978 to $11.2 billion in 1981) despite a 15 percent decrease in total volume. It also is worth noting that the $11.2 billion earned by oil exports accounted for 58.3 percent of total Soviet hard currency earnings. Combined with the $4 billion from natural gas exports, this meant that almost four out of every five dollars earned were from energy exports.[43]

When oil prices first fell in 1981–82 the Soviets kept their hard currency earnings up by substantially increasing the volume of their oil exports to the West. They were able to do this through a combination of a 10 percent cut in oil supplies to Eastern Europe, greater conservation and conversion measures at home, and a 375 percent increase in oil imported from Libya, Iraq, and other states, largely as barter payment for increased arms sales.[44] Moreover, their own oil production was slowing down but had not yet begun to fall. Hard currency earnings from oil exports thus increased to $14.1 billion in 1983 (and a 64 percent share of total hard currency earnings). But by 1984–86 this gambit was no longer working. Supplies to Eastern Europe could not be cut further without possible political risks. Conservation and conversion within the Soviet Union were proceeding, but only so rapidly. The arms-for-oil barter was still going on, but at lower levels. Most important, prices were plummeting—from a peak of close to $40, Urals crude was going for $11.50 on the spot market in June 1986.[45] Moreover, for the first time since World War II oil production was falling—from 616.5 million metric tons in 1983, to 611 in 1984, and to 595 in 1985. With both prices and export volume falling, hard currency earnings fell to $10.8 billion in 1985 and, based on available estimates, to as little as $4–6 billion in 1986.[46]

Summary

To a great extent, then, the economic constraints that were a function of the particular market conditions of the early 1980s masked the more fundamental changes which had occurred in the alliance politics of East-West energy trade. Whereas in 1962–63 the Kennedy administration had been able to lure Italy away from Soviet oil with attractive economic compensations, the compensatory package offered Western Europe by the Reagan administration in 1981–82 proved insufficiently attractive. Similarly, the juxtaposition of the images of the adulation given John F. Kennedy in West Berlin in 1963 and the stormy protests which greeted Ronald Reagan in Bonn in 1982 communicates a very graphic sense of the diminution of American political prestige. And while threats and punishments may have brought the United States some leverage in the early 1950s, in the early 1980s they infused trans-Atlantic relations with a "politics of resentment."[47] Thus, temporarily overridden as it may have been, the political reality was one of more contentious intra-alliance politics, diminished American power, and correspondingly major disputes over East-West energy trade policy.

Future Prospects: American Power, Alliance Politics, and East-West Energy Trade Policy

What does the future hold? The answer depends primarily on American policy. If the United States once again seeks to use its power to impose energy trade sanctions, renewed intra-alliance conflict is highly likely, for the same basic fault lines continue to mark the alliance politics of East-West energy trade policy.

It is true that in the early 1980s there was a certain receptivity in Western Europe to the Reagan hard-line foreign policy strategy. Amidst the Soviet invasion of Afghanistan, the crackdown on Solidarity in Poland, and the continued deployment of SS-20s, the Soviet threat appeared more ominous than at any time since the days of Stalin. Moreover, the Soviet leadership made a number of diplomatic blunders, including the walkout from the Geneva arms control negotiations and the all too blatantly heavy-handed propaganda campaign against the Pershing and Cruise deployment. However, since the accession in March 1985 of Mikhail Gorbachev, the Soviet Union has shown itself at least to be more adept at cultivating favorable international perceptions. As of the end of 1987 there continues to be significant movement toward some form of revitalized East-West détente, both between the superpowers and in Europe.

Short of a drastic transformation of this foreign policy context, any argument by a U.S. president about the need for controls over East-West energy trade is unlikely to be greeted by the allies as either credible or legitimate. To the contrary, the energy sector often is highlighted as one of the key areas for developing the kinds of economic relations that can have at least some positive influence on East-West political relations. This line of reasoning is not to be taken too far, but by the same token it does not warrant being dismissed out of hand. It may well be, as I have suggested elsewhere, that trade alone is not a sufficient condition but is still a necessary one for substantial and enduring improvements in East-West political relations.[48] Moreover, one is likely to find more support in Western Europe for this proposition and the foreign policy strategy it implies than for another round of pipeline sanctions and the like.

The economic future of a sector in which world prices have gyrated as extremely as have energy prices is understandably unpredictable.[49] Nevertheless, what can be said with some certainty is that East-West energy trade is unlikely either to return to the boom days of the late 1970s and early 1980s or to stay mired in the stagnation of the mid-1980s. European natural gas consumption is expected to grow at about 1 percent per annum through 2010, faster than the expected rate of growth in overall energy demand. It may grow even faster if countries like Sweden decide to reduce their use of nuclear power.[50] The competition among suppliers is more extensive now, and OECD countries like Norway and the Netherlands have a certain inherent advantage over the Soviet Union. But intra-OECD natural gas trade never has been conflict free. In the past consumer countries were less than pleased with the Dutch and Norwegian policies of limiting their exports. The Dutch company Gasunie has been known to resort to export cuts in instances of price disputes.[51] Uncertainties, both financial and technological, still shroud the prospects for the Norwegian Troll fields.[52] For these and other reasons the gas consumer countries have a stake in keeping the Soviets in the marketplace.

The same is true for Soviet oil. Energy planners and analysts, while enjoying the short-term benefits of low oil prices and the weakening of OPEC, remain concerned that through either market forces or Persian Gulf–Middle East political instability supplies could tighten in the future and re-empower OPEC.[53] In late 1986, with world oil prices plummeting, the Soviet Union cooperated to a greater degree than ever before with OPEC in an effort to boost world prices. At other times, though, it has undercut OPEC prices and even clandestinely made itself available as an alternative source of oil for countries embargoed by OPEC.[54] The problem of lagging Soviet oil production does remain, although after two years of decline production began increasing again in 1986.[55] For this and other reasons there is a great deal of debate among analysts as to how much oil the Soviet Union will be able and willing (two separate issues) to export to the West in the future. Thus, while uncertainty also prevails here, the reality is likely to be somewhere between the extremes of major decreases and major increases.[56]

Western exports of energy equipment and technology also stand reasonable prospects for future growth. The energy sector was singled out for special priority in the economic address delivered in June 1986 to the Twenty-seventh Party Congress by Premier Nikolai Ryzhkov. The Twelfth Five-Year Plan calls for a 47 percent increase in state investment in the energy sector, including six new natural gas pipelines, offshore drilling in the Barents and Caspian seas, efficiency improvements in the western Siberian oil fields, a giant coal slurry pipeline, and other major projects.[57] Under the Gorbachev regime's unprecedented emphasis on economic reform and technological development, the Soviet energy industry has made significant production strides of its own, as in its increased capacity in the wake of the Urengoi pipeline sanctions to produce turbine-powered compressor stations for gas pipelines. Nevertheless, as recent studies by the OECD and the CIA concluded, especially in the immediate future Western equipment and technology remain important to any chance for reaching the energy targets of the Twelfth Five-Year Plan.[58]

For Western Europe and Japan—and for the United States—this can mean important potential export markets at a time when, given the depressed state of energy industries in many other parts of the world, few other such markets exist. Soviet purchasing power remains constrained by a shortage of hard currency, but with the decline of world oil prices seemingly arrested, and with new loans being extended by Western banks, this may be less of a problem.[59] In addition, Western energy companies have been among those most involved (e.g., Occidental Petroleum, Dresser Industries) in discussions concerning possible joint ventures under the new Soviet reform law which took effect in 1987.

Thus, if the United States were again to seek to mobilize its power and exert leverage over its allies in an effort to get them to forgo East-West energy trade, the results likely would be even more damaging to the Western alliance than the Urengoi pipeline imbroglio was. For in addition to the sources of conflict having become greater, the political and economic power resources on which the United States can draw are much less. The celebrations in the spring of 1987 of the fortieth anniversary of the Marshall Plan brought out, however unintentionally, the extent to which American political prestige among its allies has waned. This is not something that was caused exclusively by the Reagan administration (although perhaps exacerbated). It is more of a secular trend, and thus something that any successor will have to face.

Nor is American economic power any longer sufficient to compensate other nations for the costs incurred by embargoing exports of energy equipment and technology to the Soviet Union or by boycotting imports of Soviet oil and natural gas. The United States cannot offer exporters alternative markets at a time when its own manufacturers are stricken with their own enormous surplus capacity. The United States also is unable either directly through its own resources or indirectly through brokering compensatory trade arrangements involving third parties to assure the European allies of reliable and competitive supplies of oil and natural gas as substitutes for Soviet exports. In these respects, Bruce Russett's arguments about America's continued margins of relative power notwithstanding, the decline in absolute terms of both its hegemonic power and its hegemonic status has diminished the capacity of the United States to influence its allies' East-West energy trade policies.[60]

The United States is left with countersanctions and other punitive measures. In this respect American power does remain formidable. European firms do feel the pinch if they lose export privileges to the American market, or if U.S.-manufactured components are embargoed. But what distinguishes hegemonic power and status is the ability to exert influence without having to resort to baldly coercive measures. The Urengoi pipeline episode should have left few doubts about the dangers which American efforts to exercise unadulterated coercive power over its allies have for long-term alliance cohesion.

Even more to the point of the central concerns of this book is the fallout effect of intra-alliance conflicts over East-West energy trade on efforts to achieve cooperation on export controls in other sectors of East-West trade. Ambassador Hillenbrand, Bill Root, Hanns-Dieter Jacobsen, Marie-Hélène Labbé, Gary Bertsch and Steve Elliott, and Mike Mastanduno all stress the poisoning-of-the-atmosphere effect that can make (and has made) alliance cooperation more difficult in those sectors truly vital to Western security.

Fortunately, in this light, over the course of 1986 and 1987 the Reagan administration gradually moved away from its previous policy of energy trade sanctions. Undoubtedly the wreckage of past policy and the realities of the present contributed to this shift. Domestic pressure also played an important role. A major lobbying effort was launched by the Petroleum Equipment Suppliers Association (PESA) in conjunction with the National Association of Manufacturers (NAM) and the U.S. Chamber of Commerce.[61] PESA represents 218 companies who together account for 90 percent of the annual sales of an industry which has been suffering hard times. Earnings of the eleven largest companies had gone from a $2.2 billion annual average profit to an average annual loss of $500 million. Employment was down to 246,200 from its 1981 peak of 611,300. Exports had shrunk from $5.3 billion to $2.5 billion.

In January 1986 the Reagan administration shifted its policy marginally by allowing case-by-case review instead of a presumption of denial in cases of oil and gas exploration and production technology. Then in January 1987, after what one participant called a "textbook case of lobbying," the Commerce Department announced total decontrol of all oil and gas exploration and production equipment except those with military applications. It is too soon to tell how much this will affect actual levels of American-Soviet trade. Other factors, not the least of which will be the overall state of American-Soviet relations, also will enter in.

More certain, though, is that this kind of policy will substantially reduce West-West conflict over East-West energy trade. To the extent that U.S. policy continues to move in this direction, the Western alliance will be that much better off.

IV

Implications and Prescriptions
for the United States
and the Western Alliance

11

Changing Perspectives toward the Normalization of East-West Commerce

John P. Hardt

Introduction

For most of the postwar period East-West economic relations have been considered uniquely oriented to political and security policies and divorced from normal practices in the world market and international economic community. While political and security factors may continue to be present in trade, significant economic changes in both the East and the West, and in the international economy, suggest that we may see in the decades ahead a trend toward greater East-West commercial normalization and expanded economic interchange.

The controls on East-West commerce that developed after World War II were influenced strongly by the U.S. view that Soviet military strength should not benefit from Western technology, and the Soviet view that increased trade with the West led to unacceptable dependence. However, over the years U.S.-Soviet trade varied with the cycles of political cooperation and confrontation between the superpowers. During the same period Western and Eastern countries other than the superpowers tended to support trade on commercial grounds, and a normalizing trend toward increasing economic interdependence developed, especially within Europe. This contrast between the ebbs and flows of the superpowers' relationship and the normal development of commerce among their respective allies has led to recurrent and expanding frictions within each alliance system on just how policies on trade and security, and trade and diplomacy should be balanced in East-West commerce.

The amplitude of superpower trade policy generally found the leaders of the United States and the Soviet Union alternatively pressing for more or less commerce than their respective allies supported. Thus, the superpowers went further in facilitating trade during the apogee period of economic détente (1972–74), and in restricting commerce during the policy perigee in response to the Afghanistan invasion, Polish martial law, and the "pipeline dispute" of the early 1980s.

In the West the continued U.S. predilection for the use of foreign policy export controls has kept open the embargo option, at least outside the grain trade, suggesting an indifference to the need to compete or to develop stable, predictable, competitive economic relations. The Europeans, though, eschewing the dominance of politics over economics in East-West economic relations, have chosen to continue to build wider bridges for normalized commerce and exchanges. This broadening and deepening of East-West interchange significantly raised the cost of superpower interventions in the normalization pattern reflecting politically driven cycles of U.S.-Soviet relations.

The mechanisms of economic exchange have also broadened and deepened, complicating East-West economic policies and further exacerbating differences in both alliances. In the immediate postwar period short-term trade on a cash-and-carry basis was the norm, with the East focusing on key industrial imports to overcome specific bottlenecks in exchange for raw materials (oil, timber, furs, grain, gold). In subsequent decades, however, the exchanges have broadened and deepened and the mechanisms of East-West exchange have become more complex. Now a variety of factors has become important: balance of payments criteria, including credit terms, have an increasing influence; the structure of trade has widened to include all manner of goods and services; barter or countertrade mechanisms have developed; and the emphasis on illegal trade and espionage has increased. Transfer of capital goods and turnkey plants have led to long-term commitments and system changes, and people transfers through contracts, consultation, and exchanges have increased. With long-term commitments in manufactured goods and energy trade, Western Europe has been increasingly interrelated with the East in a pattern of long-term manufactured goods agreements. The intra-German trade is a special example of East-West normalization. As these developments suggest, difficult adjustments on bridging the different systems to normalize long-term commerce have added to divisiveness in both the Eastern and Western alliances. Nevertheless, consensus may be found in the mechanisms of economic interchange if, as in trade proper, a common multilateral alliance policy on economic relations is developed.

During the first Reagan administration (1980–84), when superpower relations on East-West economic exchanges were at a decidedly low ebb, the United States emphasized security concerns in a reported effort to reform the system by placing more focus on controlling critical technologies, more highlighting of espionage losses, and more attention to indirect diversion of sensitive exports through third countries. The differences between the United States and its COCOM allies widened and deepened during this period to the point where some West Europeans began to talk of a "progressive divorce" between America and its allies. In this regard the unilateral control system of the United States became more active in this period in controlling West-West commerce.

However, a qualitative, more thoroughgoing change in U.S. export control policy may have begun with the growing recognition in the United States in 1985 of its serious global financial and commercial problems, highlighted when the United States attained debtor nation status with deep and long-term trade imbalances. The need to strengthen competitiveness and to reform global trading practices would appear to be the driving force behind a new American consensus for more narrowly defined security controls, a change that would move U.S. policy closer to the trade-facilitating postures of its allies. Concurrently, the Soviet Union under Gorbachev has adopted a policy of increased global interdependence and promotion of exports to the West. Gorbachev's and Reagan's declared intent to develop inter-national interdependence and globalism in order to be more competitive calls to mind revival of the Bretton Woods wartime concept of international economic cooperation and East-West normalization of commerce.

These important changes in the superpowers' positions suggest a tendency toward convergence in East-West commercial policy with a possibility that the past cycles of U.S.-Soviet trade will be moderated to match the more predictable, stable course of their allies' East-West commercial policies. If the United States and the Soviet Union begin, for the first time, to place East-West commerce in a newly developed global commercial policy deemed critical to the domestic performance of each economy, the superpowers may move with their allies toward a trend of long-term normalization. By moving closer to the East-West trade policies of their allies, the United States and the Soviet Union may not only gain commercial benefits for themselves, but also remove a major source of recurrent friction within their respective alliances. For the United States the contentious issues of trade, credit, and technology transfer may be taken off the agenda of divisive policy issues in COCOM, NATO, and the OECD. Moreover, a process of normalization of U.S.-Soviet economic exchanges might be joined with an arms limitation process and improved bilateral relations in general.

Cycles in East-West Trade

Over the course of communist governance the economic relationship of the USSR with the Western economies has been alternatively adversarial and cooperative. Ideologically, the conflict of capitalism and communism provided the centrifugal political impetus. Pragmatically, the development of the Soviet economy and the opening of its market provided a measure of mutual economic interest that stimulated the overall centripetal force toward selective economic interdependence. On the Western side the modern export control system emerged after World War II to manage the balance between security concerns and trade interests, and to carry out the NATO strategy of maintaining a substantial technology lead over the Soviet Union instead of numerical parity in conventional weapons. Over the course of the past forty years, however, changes in the pace and dispersion of technological development, and continuing efforts by the Soviet Union to close the military technology gap, have complicated the task of controlling militarily significant technology.[1]

In contrast with the cyclical pattern of U.S.-Soviet trade, non-superpower East-West commerce has moved steadily toward normalization and interdependence since the 1960s. In the immediate postwar period the United States and the Soviet Union dominated the respective commercial policies of the West and East. However, with increasing dispersion of technological, economic, and political power in both West and East, alliance consultations replaced domination, especially in the West. As the Cold War thawed, and particularly after the NATO pipeline embargo of 1964, the consensual Western policy toward the communist world began to unravel. In Western and, to a lesser extent, Eastern Europe there were greater prospects for independent action and an increasing diversity of commercial and scientific opportunities for East-West cooperation.[2]

Regarding Soviet East-West trade policy, certain periods have been conducive to economic isolation and others to some interdependence. A special economic relationship had developed between the superpowers during World War II, but the pendulum swung away when restrictive Stalinist economic development was resumed after the war. Autarky once again became a central feature of the system, making that period a low point in economic relations. The Cold War worsened during the Korean War and up until Stalin's death. This was followed by de-Stalinization in the USSR and a reopening to the United States from the 1950s to the mid-1960s. But the Vietnam War and the invasion of Czechoslovakia acted as centrifugal forces in U.S.-Soviet relations, while the allies continued to trade with the East, not permitting politics to dominate economic relations.

This downturn in superpower commerce in the 1960s was soon followed by a change in U.S. East-West trade policy when the Export

Administration Act (EAA) of 1969 replaced the cold war Export Control Act. The new legislation sought to restrict only exports that might directly enhance the military capability of potential communist adversaries as opposed to exports that would enhance the overall economic viability of these countries. With the policy of the Brezhnev regime of selective economic interdependence, highlighted by large-scale automotive deals, a mutual basis for cooperation returned in the form of economic détente.

The period 1972–74 was the high tide in U.S.-Soviet commercial relations after World War II.[3] This was a time in which both the expectation of expanding commercial relations and the willingness to compromise on outstanding economic, political, and systemic differences was greatest in both countries. For the United States this period was characterized by a willingness to settle old credit and tariff issues and to develop means for bridging differences between the two divergent systems. For the Soviet Union the perceived need for Western goods and technology, especially American, was at its apogee. To obtain them the Soviet Union indicated a greater readiness to negotiate and be flexible on outstanding economic and political issues. Acceptance of a degree of mutual dependency was the hallmark of this period.

The Soviet Union and the United States became willing to consider industrial cooperation during this period in massive natural gas development projects, with the direct involvement of American engineers and technicians, American plans for construction, quality control in performance, and product output in repayment.[4] The degree of Soviet systemic flexibility was greatest in the length of contractual commitments and systemic transfers over time. Significantly, both superpowers favored greater and faster trade facilitation than their respective allies. During this heyday settlement terms of Lend Lease debts were agreed to and large-scale U.S. government credits were proposed and accepted in principle. But, while provisional agreement was reached on large-scale cooperation, credit, debts, and tariffs, economic détente was quickly ended with the passage of the 1974 Trade Act containing the Jackson-Vanik and Export-Import

Bank Act revision, including the Stevenson-Church amendment. Based on this restrictive legislation linking trade privileges to Soviet emigration policy, the provisional U.S.-Soviet trade agreements did not go into force.

It was as if a dialectic process were operating during this period —for each new thesis in commercial relations, an offsetting political and security antithesis arose. For example, Soviet restrictions on the degree of Western involvement based on concerns over increasing dependence and alien impact on their socialist system tended to cool their negotiations. Thus, while long-term trade commitments were being arranged, simultaneous efforts were under way from both the Soviet and the American sides to restrict and even terminate trade.

U.S.-Soviet trade continued to fluctuate in the 1970s and into the 1980s as a result of political pressures.[5] It was affected significantly by President Carter's human rights foreign policy, the Soviet invasion of Afghanistan, martial law in Poland, and the election of an ardently anti-communist administration in the United States.[6] And yet, by the mid-1980s there appeared signs of significant changes in U.S. perceptions of international, including East-West, economic relations.[7]

The growth of America's international debt and trade deficit was instrumental in increasing U.S. awareness of the global nature of the country's economic problems. With specific reference to East-West trade, there was a greater awareness of the broader context of U.S.-Soviet trade, of the need to reach consensus on export control policy in COCOM, and of the need to strike a more fruitful balance between economic and security interests.[8] The awareness was reflected and nourished in two important studies: the National Academy of Sciences's (NAS) *Balancing the National Interest* and the President's Competitiveness Initiative.

The NAS study was part of a debate in the United States on export control reform that began in 1986.[9] The debate was shaped largely by the recognition of significant changes in the world economy that were reducing U.S. technological dominance and, with the growing U.S. trade deficit, appeared to challenge American economic security. Mindful of the broader contexts of export competitiveness and alliance unity, the reformers wanted to reduce the burden these controls placed on U.S. exporters and, at the same time, reduce the potential for further conflict within the Western alliance by focusing controls more on multilaterally agreed, military-related transfers.[10]

The economic importance of East-West trade had long been recognized in Western Europe and Japan. Where industrial sectors and geographic regions were significantly dependent on communist markets, East-West trade issues came up in local elections and occasionally prompted visits to the regions by national leaders. It was only in the 1980s, after the impact of the grain and pipeline embargoes, that the economic importance of East-West trade began to be recognized in the United States. With the loss of important contracts and market share as a result of U.S. foreign policy export controls, it became apparent that trade with the Soviet Union was a vital factor in determining acceptable levels of production, employment, and profitability for American agriculture and certain industrial sectors. This was reflected in the great importance that American farmers attached to the 1983–88 U.S.-Soviet Long-Term Grain Agreement. (It should also be noted that this issue determined the outcome of several congressional races in grain-producing states.)

The economic interdependence of the superpowers is likely to increase in the late 1980s and beyond, and the economic significance and potential of East-West trade for the U.S. economy will be increasingly recognized. In a global buyer's market continued Eastern requirements for energy equipment, metal products, agricultural technology, and automotive equipment will bring very competitive suppliers throughout the West vying for shares in the Eastern and global markets.[11] And, being such potentially large markets, communist countries represent special magnets for key exporting sectors in the West whether or not there is policy agreement on the appropriate response to the economic demands of communist states.

This interpretation of the history of U.S.-Soviet economic relations has emphasized the cyclical nature of the relationship. These cycles have been driven by political phenomena from the Cold War to the Reagan-Gorbachev summits. If this process continues we should expect another upswing in U.S.-Soviet economic relations in the late 1980s and early 1990s, followed by a downswing. However, the pattern may be changing. The magnitude of the economic problems that both superpowers have may be leading them into an economic relationship similar to that of the non-superpower East and West; that is, one of increased economic normalization and interdependence. The slowly emerging globalism of trade policy in both superpower camps suggests this possibility and is reinforced by the view that U.S.-Soviet trade may be less susceptible to major interruptions through politically motivated embargoes in the future. However, to achieve interdependence and therefore some degree of independence from the political realm, and to fully realize the economic benefits of U.S.-Soviet trade, effective mechanisms for economic interaction and greater policy agreement that will serve to bridge systemic differences must develop on both sides. Just as differences between superpowers in international security and political affairs overrode the potential benefits of normal international trade, systemic changes in the broader aspects of increased interdependence influenced the political and economic systems of the respective countries involving dependencies on market forces.[12]

Increasing Commitment to Normalization and the Rising Cost of Superpower Political Intervention

As the trend toward normalization and the superpower cycles continued over time, more attention needed to be given to the longer-term and broadening systematic and institutional requirements of effective economic relations. Normalization—the movement toward the pattern of economic interchange in the world market—is a process that accentuates the economic benefits of a global market mechanism and minimizes its costs. As East-West economic interrelations burgeoned, East-West relations were increasingly woven into the fabric of West-West relations. With each successive political cycle in superpower relations the cost of interrupting this normalization process has grown. Normalized relations increasingly accepted by both superpowers as reflecting broad world market forces suggest the rising importance of economic, technological, and scientific relations in mutually advantageous exchange. Moreover, capital goods transfers reflecting comparative advantages especially need stability over time to be profitable to both sides. Also, increasing opportunities have been expressed in people transfers, including scientific and technical exchanges. These cumulative requirements accentuate the problems caused by interruptions in relations for foreign policy or political reasons, e.g., the so-called "light-switch" approach that has come to characterize the American application of foreign policy controls on capital goods exports.

On the Eastern side Soviet restraints on the direct involvement of Western partners in the installation, testing, operation, quality control, and other effective mechanisms of technology transfer restricted the beneficial impact of Soviet economic interchanges with the West. Furthermore, the Soviet Union and the East in general have been restricted in expanding economic interchange based on comparative advantage due to limited hard currency earnings, which result from the absence of significant Eastern exports of manufactured goods.

Western Europe and Japan have become increasingly involved over the last few decades in capital goods sales requiring long-term contracts and closer inter-country relations. Such relations are especially disrupted by the U.S. propensity to use foreign policy criteria for restricting trade. In this regard the allies were especially disturbed by the U.S. extension through extraterritorial control of third-country transfers to restrict West-West trade within and outside COCOM.[13]

The Soviet Union and the United States have set up mechanisms to implement policies designed to alternatively facilitate and restrict commercial, technological, and scientific exchanges. In facilitation, steps have been taken toward normalization by moving toward the use of the commercial practices and institutions of the world trading community. New mechanisms, such as agreements on levels of annual trade, bilateral balancing, and long-term contracts, have been used to bridge the systemic differences between a market system and a centrally planned economy. The U.S.-Soviet Long-Term Grain Agreement, assuring embargo-free grain trade, represents one such trade-facilitating mechanism. Policies of facilitation and restriction have existed simultaneously in both the United States and the USSR; accordingly, relations have been characterized by either long-term agreements or extended embargoes.

Moreover, the Soviet use of normal commercial mechanisms has expanded over time. Nikita Khrushchev rediscovered the international division of labor, or comparative advantage, as a criteria of trade with the West. Necessary imports under Stalin were limited largely to industrial goods to overcome short-term bottlenecks, a policy based on absolute advantage. In 1963 Khrushchev broke with the Stalinist pattern by importing grain from the United States; later, under Leonid Brezhnev, corn and other feed grains were imported to provide for the needs of the newly important feed-grain livestock sector. The break with Stalin's policy of grain independence echoed the English acceptance of Ricardo's argument more than a century earlier that the importation of grain from the continent was economically desirable, even if trade raised political concerns of dependence on possibly hostile foreign sources. Acceptance of comparative advantage as dictated by market forces was a major Soviet step toward normalized foreign economic relations.

Despite this movement toward some interdependence, the Soviet Union continued to avoid large-scale borrowing to support its trade. In conformance with this credit policy the preferred industrial cooperation strategy for the Soviet Union with the West under Brezhnev was barter—pay-back arrangements such as that discussed in the U.S.-Soviet negotiations on the North Star pipeline, a gas-for-pipe arrangement. (This kind of deal was concluded with the Europeans for the export gas line opened in 1984 as part of the Soviet-German long-term agreement.) The Soviet-American project was to involve the U.S. company directly in construction, operation, and management. The later European arrangements did not include such direct involvement, in part as a result of the pipeline dispute of the 1980s.[14]

More recently the Soviet Union has moved away from investment in large new complexes to renovation or modernization of existing plants. Gorbachev's preferred strategy for commercial relations with the West appears to be more carefully targeted to these kinds of specific needs—more effective in application and comparably more productive of value-added manufactured goods.[15] Soviet trade institutions are being reformed to make possible direct contact between foreign suppliers and Soviet end users, and to allow joint ventures in production, construction, and management in ways that permit the Soviets to develop competitive manufactured or processed goods for exports. New forms of interaction tying together enterprises in the centrally planned and market systems are being developed within the international trading and financial institutions and in bilateral East-West contracts.[16] Although participation in the full Bretton Woods system has not been revived,[17] some forms of multilateral cooperation, such as the shelved International Trade Organization, are being discussed anew.[18]

Scientific communications have also become important mechanisms for promoting economic relations. These have been encouraged through a variety of channels, including normal government exchanges, for example, those covered under the umbrella U.S.-USSR Agreement on Scientific and Technology Exchange of 1972. Under this agreement participation of Soviet scientists in international meetings and through international institutions such as the United Nations has been expanded. The agreement also established programs in chemical catalysis, electrometallurgy and materials, microbiology, physics, computer applications to management, science policy, and scientific and technical information. It also served as a model for other agreements signed during 1972 and 1974 that dealt with energy, atomic energy, space, public health, artificial heart research, housing, transportation, environmental protection, the world oceans, and agriculture. The net benefit to the United States of these programs, if resumed, would likely be assessed according to the view that, in these specific areas, the United States and the Soviet Union both gained more by having the bilateral programs than by prohibiting them, the analog of the logic of mutual benefit of international commerce. Certainly through most of the 1970s, and until the bilateral programs were interrupted after the invasion of Afghanistan, these exchanges were largely considered a mutually beneficial interaction between the Soviet Union and the United States.[19]

Because fairly stringent national security controls are placed on East-West trade, technology transfer, and scientific communication, efforts to reduce the scope of controls may prove to be an important trade-facilitating measure. What appears to be a growing consensus on export controls is how, not whether, to achieve a reduction in the scope of controls. Implicit are both philosophical and practical questions. First, what is to be our definition of what is militarily critical and important? To a large degree the decision of what to control depends upon our information as to what exactly the Soviet Union needs and would be capable of applying for military benefit. Second, control decisions also reflect judgments about whether technology transfer can be more effectively inhibited through controls on commercial transactions, through counterespionage efforts, or some combination thereof.[20] Where the emphasis is on counterespionage, is the export administration system relevant or are counterintelligence agencies more appropriate?[21]

Many Western observers argue that illegal transfers of technology have played a significant role in the qualitative improvement of the Soviet military arsenal. Some in the United States, looking at both product and critical technology systems transfer, still say that "when we see the Soviet weapons system, that is actually ours or a derivative of ours." While industrial espionage for core military programs is undoubtedly critical for relieving military bottlenecks, available information does not support the contention that broad Soviet military advances have been wholly or even primarily a product of clandestinely obtained technology.[22] A new effort to better assess actual Soviet needs and use of industrial intelligence may focus and improve the effectiveness of multilateral controls, thus minimizing their restrictiveness and allowing trade, technology transfer, and scientific exchanges to help bridge systemic differences between the superpowers.

Management disagreements over the West's trade policy are primarily over West-West control mechanisms. For example, the first Reagan administration advocated reforms intended to tighten controls on Western high-technology exports through the extraterritorial extension of U.S. unilateral controls.[23] Also, while Europeans did not oppose U.S. calls for new COCOM restrictions on selected high technologies of direct military relevance, they were generally against additional controls, especially those on older—less than state-of-the-art—technologies which they saw as readily available in the world market. They also opposed restricting the mechanisms of normal exchange of scientific information and technical expertise. On the contrary, they favored fostering systemic interaction to improve the quality and volume of all forms of East-West commerce.

The imposition of U.S. export controls in the West-West context will remain a highly controversial issue in the Western alliance if not successfully addressed by the COCOM countries. An agreed control protocol on increased discipline, intelligence exchanges, and indigenous penalty procedures to ensure that incidents such as the Toshiba-Kongsberg sale of propeller-machinery equipment do not erode Western defenses will be necessary. Moreover, increasing foreign availability of technologies on the U.S. unilateral control list in European non-COCOM industrialized nations and the newly industrialized countries of Asia—e.g., South Korea, Taiwan, Hong Kong—have accentuated the need for an even broader multilateral consensus.

Another type of export control to be examined and reassessed if systemic differences are to be bridged by trade is foreign policy controls. As noted in part II of this book, many Western countries maintain that the explicit use of foreign policy criteria in economic interchanges is inappropriate; others feel that while economic contacts can be used as instruments of diplomacy, their effectiveness is highly questionable. U.S. economic policy toward the Soviet Union in this regard has shifted from a balanced policy of rewards and penalties, as practiced in the 1960s and 1970s, to a policy that in the late 1970s and 1980s was based primarily on penalties to punish the Soviets for maltreatment of dissidents, the Afghanistan invasion, Polish martial law, arms buildup, and adventurism in Africa, Central America, and other regions. Meanwhile the Europeans have continued to value trade with the East for economic more than political reasons. When trade is used politically the Europeans tend to consider incentives over the long-term as more effective than sanctions and embargoes, and tend not to make the linkage between trade and politics explicit.

In contrast, the United States has tended toward the explicit withholding of commercial relations as a means to influence Soviet domestic and foreign policy. The U.S. Congress has facilitated this use of embargoes and sanctions by including "foreign policy criteria" in trade legislation (i.e., the revised Export Administration Acts of 1979, 1981, and 1985, and the 1974 Trade Act), thus permitting the use of export controls and the withholding of trade benefits as a response to human rights violations as well as foreign policy infractions.

As noted in William Long's chapter, export licensing to communist countries is regulated under the EAA in accordance with U.S. national security interests, foreign policy objectives and, to a lesser extent, limitations on domestic supplies. It was the EAA that empowered Presidents Carter and Reagan to restrict U.S. commercial relations with the Soviet Union in 1980 and 1981–82. In the latter case, the "pipeline dispute," European commercial relations with the USSR were also affected. And, as noted in Elliott's and Jentleson's chapters in this volume, this occurred when foreign policy criteria for restricting the exportation of domestically produced U.S. energy equipment were extraterritorially extended to include U.S. subsidiaries and foreign affiliates and licensees.

According to the Europeans, contract sanctity was breached by that U.S. action and extraterritoriality was applied retroactively. As noted in part II of this volume, U.S. law was brought into direct conflict with some European laws (e.g., Bertsch and Elliott's chapter notes that Prime Minister Thatcher directed John Brown, Ltd., to give precedence to the laws of the United Kingdom rather than acknowledge U.S. extraterritorial jurisdiction). After settlement of the pipeline dispute, FRG Economic Minister Bangemann threatened German blocking legislation similar to that of the British in response to a controversial restriction of a German sale of telecommunications equipment to Eastern Europe. In defense of its extraterritorial controls the United States maintained that American technology had been obtained under certain policy and contractual understandings, and these contracted obligations were violated by European exports to the USSR and East European countries.

The U.S. Export Administration Amendments Act of 1985 dealt with the issues of contract sanctity and extraterritoriality but did not settle them. Business critics of U.S. policy argued that continued uncertainty about contract sanctity would reduce U.S. competitiveness worldwide and would weaken the effectiveness of necessary controls. Moreover, they argued that further extension of extraterritoriality would weaken alliance unity and the competitiveness of U.S.-based multinationals. Others believe, however, that the Western countries will close ranks in order to retain access to U.S. technology and out of common concern about Soviet military and economic advances.

Each recurrent superpower political cycle restricting or facilitating economic interchanges has been accompanied by greater U.S. efforts to enforce alliance unity due to the increasing importance of foreign availability of products and processes in non-superpower nations. The unilateral efforts to attain consensual actions through extraterritorial intervention by the United States in allied commerce has aggravated the Western alliance and imposed costs on the allies in their domestic and foreign economic relations. The growing realization that only multilateral action is effective and that U.S. views on national security and foreign policy controls were at variance with the rest of the alliance brought the issue of reform in U.S. control policy to the forefront.

Globalization of U.S. and Soviet Commercial Relations

With the transition of the United States from a longtime creditor nation to the greatest debtor nation in history, and with an acceptance that major policy changes are needed to regain global competitiveness, East-West trade has become an element of American global trading policy.[24] As evidence of this change, debate over U.S. export control policy was renewed in 1987 in the larger context of concern about overall U.S. trade policy and competitiveness in the omnibus Trade Act of the One Hundredth Congress. The NAS study on national security export controls and the President's Initiative on Competitiveness both contributed to the formulation of new trade legislation. Responding to the burgeoning U.S. monthly trade deficit, which reached $15 billion for the month of February 1987, on top of a total of $170 billion in 1986, Congress sought to develop omnibus trade legislation addressing the perceived causes of the significant increase in the trade deficit that had occurred since 1980. Within this broad spectrum of trade issues, export control policy reform was raised as one means of improving U.S. competitiveness in the world market and thus contributing to the reduction of the U.S. trade deficit.

At the same time Mikhail Gorbachev's strategy of openness and interdependence was designed to move the Soviet economy toward joining the commercial policies and mechanisms of the world market. Traditionally the Soviet Union considered the world market and the multinational institutions set up after World War II to be U.S. dominated and inimical to Soviet interests.[25] According to these earlier beliefs, the growth and stability of the world market and the international monetary system were all Western objectives. Political instability and unsettled economic conditions that would further political change beneficial to the Soviets were considered central to Soviet interests. However, in recent years, as the Soviet Union became a major creditor country it became more interested in the health of the world economic community in general and more interested in global price stability in particular.[26] The Gorbachev regime seems to have developed a stake in the stability and health of the international monetary system.[27]

Ironically, pressure that could push Gorbachev toward more openness and interdependence and to make the necessary systemic changes may be generated by the United States in the form of the economic and technological threat of the Strategic Defense Initiative (SDI). Only by very basic, long-term changes can the Soviet Union keep up in the scientific and technological race to keep open the prospect of becoming an economic superpower. Gorbachev is known to be concerned about the widening technological gap between the Soviet Union and the West.[28] Moreover, in view of the dynamic character of military technology, falling further behind in the civilian scientific and technological revolution would erode the long-term security of the USSR as a military superpower.

If Gorbachev continues to establish and solidify his domestic power, he may also be expected to reexamine the issue of Soviet control over Eastern Europe. His announced policy in CMEA is to have his allies follow his lead on economic transformation at home and greater interdependence with the West.[29] The Soviet Union, like the United States, can more easily persuade its allies to adhere to a policy of trade facilitation than one of trade restriction. Moreover, Gorbachev's policy on Eastern Europe seems to be more performance oriented than economically interventionist. It is recognized that East European countries must rely more on economic relations with the West to modernize and improve living standards.[30] The collective CMEA view will become increasingly important as Soviet leverage over Eastern Europe through energy supplies is weakened and the value of their East European machinery imports increases. Thus, Gorbachev's policy tends to strengthen the CMEA consensus on the importance of normalizing East-West economic relations.

The new Soviet globalism reflects an adjustment to its increased influence and dependence on the international economy. The USSR is an important factor in world energy and commodity markets and a major creditor nation—albeit mainly in the socialist and Third World countries. Moreover, domestic reforms aimed at reducing subsidies and their inflationary gap require a move toward domestic goods convertibility, greater public disclosure (glasnost), and improved quality and disclosure of economic statistics. These domestic developments in monetary and information disclosure policy would facilitate the "globalization" of Soviet economic policy, including some movement toward foreign currency convertibility and accurate economic reporting, which are basic technical requirements for joining most international economic organizations.

As a true superpower, the Soviet Union has been recently intent on becoming an actor in all elements of global affairs.[31] Since the cold war fracturing of the Bretton Woods process, the Soviets have not participated in international economic forums but, just as they value their role in the political institutions of the United Nations, they also wish to be a significant "player" in the international financial and commercial community.

As the pattern of interrelations between superpowers broadens and deepens, trade relations may become more a part of a pattern of commercial, financial, scientific, political, and security intercourse, with some longer-term commitments built in. The increasing importance of the allies and other power centers has diminished the prospects and raised the costs of the continuation of political cycles of superpower relations. The non-superpower countries of Europe and Asia have favored a trend of normalization over cycles of confrontation and cooperation and now have more power to bring this about. The traditional strengths of the United States in technology, credit, and competitiveness have eroded substantially, leaving other Western nations with an edge in the third technological-information revolution; U.S. debt and trade deficits have increased the influence of Japan and the European Community in controlling credit policy. The shift under Gorbachev toward more reliance on economic factors in international relations, and the increased need for interdependence is moving the Soviet Union toward a more stabilizing posture in the global economic arena; the increasing East European multilateralist influence and stability in global relations have been enhanced.

With the broadening, normalizing, and stabilization of East-West relations, the Soviet Union may place more reliance on effective commercial technology transfer and exchanges and less on their unconventional means of transfer through espionage. On the Western side, American concern about global competitiveness and a normalization with the Soviet Union would have the effect of reducing the

U.S. unilateral use of controls and sanctions. While competitiveness in the global market may sharpen due to the imbalance of supply over demand and balance of payments deficits, the divisive force of unilateral U.S. trade policy seems likely to be ameliorated in the alliance.

While economics remains a small part of the broad power balance of the superpowers, the fact that commercial relations represent the major area of mutual benefit, and increasingly an area of interest group concern, makes both either uniquely positive forces or visible sources of irritation in bilateral relations. As East-West economic policy has become interwoven with the issues of global competitiveness and commercial deficits, the economic factor in East-West commerce has been given new weight in both the United States and the Soviet Union.

Conclusion

By 1947–48 the postwar pattern of East-West commercial relations was set as the Soviet Union turned down the Marshall Plan and the Cold War began. Both superpowers followed a policy of independence, isolating their allies from the other camps largely on political-security grounds. The United States was concerned with maintaining a technological edge that offset massive Soviet military forces; the Soviet Union was concerned with avoiding dependence on the technologically superior West. Initially this policy of mutual isolation and independence provided a stable East-West economic relationship based on superpowers' domination over their allies. The mechanisms for the minor economic exchanges that did take place were simple and direct (i.e., limited Western-manufactured goods sales to relieve absolute Eastern bottlenecks on a cash basis from export of materials).

Over time this mutual independence and isolation were moderated by superpower political cycles, a rising multilateralism in commerce, and a growing complexity in economic relations as non-superpower exchanges moved steadily toward economic normalization. But at the same time the economic importance of East-West commerce rose, friction in the respective alliances increased due to the domestic economic costs of politically inspired variations in commercial policy. These costs were especially exacerbated by the "light-switch" character of U.S. export control policy.

However, in this increasingly complex commercial environment, U.S. unilateralism proved ineffective in controlling multilateral commerce and stemming espionage losses. Furthermore, the United States and the Soviet Union each faced a rising need for global interdependence and trade deficit management that was impaired by unilateral East-West policy controls. Indeed, in the mid-1980s superpower economic policy was adjudged ineffective and inappropriate throughout the Eastern and Western alliance systems.

Given these developments, a new, more stable basis for West-West and East-West commerce may be attainable. Major issues likely to be considered by the United States and within the Western alliance include: (1) emphasis upon multilateral controls in COCOM, the OECD, and among Asian NICs in place of an emphasis upon unilateral controls by the United States; (2) focus on security controls related to specific weapons systems with heightened intelligence exchanges among Western industrial economies; (3) increased discipline and indigenous penalty procedures in each Western industrial country related to inadvertent supply of militarily relevant technology; (4) multilateral Western policy to discourage effective use of Eastern espionage by whatever means may be effective; and (5) more selective and effective use of foreign policy criteria resulting in more infrequent use of embargoes and sanctions.

Western agreement on these issues is more likely if the United States and the Soviet Union agree on the following: (1) comprehensive joint ventures and long-term agreements that ensure conditions of mutual benefit in commerce and broad exchanges; (2) Soviet limitations on espionage outside of the core military programs; (3) U.S.-allied moves toward effective focus and concentration on transfers directly related to Soviet core military programs; and (4) joint participation in international and multilateral institutions to enhance global economic health and improve bilateral economic interests.

The use of commercial and other forms of economic interchange for political purposes in the superpower relationship has been costly and largely ineffective. Global balance of payments, competitiveness issues, and alliance cohesion have become increasingly important. A continuation of old politicosecurity-dominated superpower policy is possible but likely to be increasingly costly to each participant. The broader trends of interdependence and globalism are likely to persist and increase in importance. At the same time the need for alliance consensus on effective multilateral control policies will remain. Political pressures in both the United States and the Soviet Union to tie economic interchange to great power political cycles may be increasingly ineffective and costly, though persistent. If a process of military balance management through arms control and weapons systems reduction becomes a centerpiece of U.S.-Soviet relations via summitry, then a process of facilitation and economic normalization may be its companion in the summitry process. Positive superpower initiatives toward the normalization of economic interchange fit the global needs of the superpowers and the trend of normalizing East-West relations. Some four decades after the breakup of East-West economic development, the process of normalization may be resumed.

12

East-West Economic Relations,
Export Controls, and
Strains in the Alliance

Martin J. Hillenbrand

American attempts to bring our European allies into line with our more rigorous export controls on trade with Eastern Europe, including the Soviet Union, have been a continuing source of strain in European-American relations during much of the postwar period. The differences of approach that have arisen reflect important differences in both the analysis of trends in Eastern Europe and how best to influence those trends in directions more favorable to Western interests. The least troublesome years in this context came during the era of Nixonian détente, when the U.S. government itself accepted the view that expanding trade and economic relations with the East could produce positive political consequences.[1] As the United States moved away from détente, however, particularly after the Soviet invasion of Afghanistan, the old attitudes and strictures reasserted themselves in Washington, while a commensurate reevaluation did not take place in Western Europe.[2]

At the psychological level American and West European officials have tended to have basically different attitudes toward Eastern Europe. Ever since the origins of the Cold War, to Americans Eastern Europe has been essentially hostile territory dominated by the Soviet Union. To the Europeans it has been still a part of Europe in historical heritage and culture, and at some admittedly indefinite point in the future destined to rejoin the states of the West in a greater whole. The Federal Republic of Germany, part of a former greater Germany, particularly has felt the strains of division and the fundamental impermanency of the postwar settlement in central Europe. The customary official formula, "two German states within a single German nation" has reflected this, as has the special treatment accorded to trade between the German Democratic Republic and the Federal Republic as intra-German trade. A protocol annexed to the treaty establishing the European Economic Community stipulates that "since exchanges between the German territories subject to the Basic Law for the Federal Republic of Germany and the German territories in which the Basic Law does not apply are part of German internal trade, the application of this treaty requires no amendment of the existing system of such trade within Germany."[3] This, in effect, means that the German Democratic Republic (GDR) was incorporated for trade purposes within the European Economic Community.

Recognition of this contrast in outlook between Europe and the United States, as well as sheer geographical propinquity, lies at the bottom of the prevailing sentiment in West Germany and other European countries that their governments and private businessmen know better how to deal with Eastern Europe than the geographically remote and, in this respect, relatively unsophisticated American government. I have observed this sometimes irritating feeling of superiority over the years and must grant that there is a considerable basis for it. At the same time one cannot help noting the peculiarly schizoid European fear of Soviet aggression, and the corresponding reliance since 1949 on the American deterrent within NATO to provide basic security. To the degree that a new generation of Europeans no longer has this fear—a clearly observable trend—not only does this ultimately have consequences for the structure of the alliance, but obviously also for a further diminution of European willingness to accept controls on trade with the East. The growing appeal, at least among intellectuals, of a European Peace Order (*Europaische Friedensordnung*) from which both superpowers would be excluded, is symptomatic of thinking which may today seem unrealistic, but which may well grow in its appeal.[4]

A good example of this attitudinal difference and the related difference of emphasis was provided by the policy statement of West German Chancellor Helmut Kohl, made on March 18, 1987, setting forth the goals for his government's next four years. He called for a deepening of East-West ties, closer cooperation with the Soviet Union and the German Democratic Republic, and support for "realistic détente."[5] Here we have the conservative head of a conservative government expressing himself in terms hardly likely to be found in a conservative American president's State of the Union address. The chancellor was, of course, fully aware of what the German public and his own constituency wanted to hear.

European Restiveness

We can see some contradictory trends. As Professor Mastanduno notes in his contribution to this book, there is talk about the revitalization of COCOM under American pressure. At the same time there is continuing and even increasing restiveness among European members of COCOM—a restiveness expressed in the North Atlantic Assembly proposal of 1985 to create a new European agency to promote European technological independence and to bargain with the United States on technology transfer issues, and the 1986 resolution of the European Parliament criticizing unilateral U.S. technology controls. Any close observer of European opinion can see many other signs of European unhappiness.

It is worth noting in this context that the North Atlantic Assembly (the inter-parliamentary organization of member countries of the alliance) is made up of 184 North American and European parliamentarians who generally tend to be friendly toward the United States as the dominant contributor to security within NATO. The makeup of the European Parliament (which is now elected rather than appointed) is likely to be more varied in political affiliation and attitude toward the United States than the North Atlantic Assembly, but the majority of members are not normally anti-American. Their 1986 resolution called on the European Commission to investigate whether the 1985 amendments to the Export Administration Act eliminated the conflict between American re-export licensing requirements and the stipulations of the Treaty of Rome, which created the European Economic Community and which mandates unconstrained movement of goods within the community. The resolution went on to criticize U.S. controls on technology transfer and recommended development of an independent European technological capability that would rival that of the United States.[6]

Europeans have been aware, of course, that there have been deep cleavages within the American government and public about what should be appropriate policy on trade with the East, and about how much pressure should be applied to West Europeans to conform to U.S. practice, but they have noted that, in the final analysis, the hard line usually wins out. The well-publicized resignation and retirement in 1986 of William Root—the State Department official in charge of handling East-West trade matters—after the government adopted essentially the Pentagon position against his advice fell within this pattern. Mr. Root, who is one of the contributors to this volume, was widely regarded as a voice of moderation and sensitivity to European concerns.

It is, I think, generally true that our European allies will accept in principle the undesirability of sending anything to the East that clearly would be of direct assistance to the Soviet military effort, but they are disinclined to accept broader American definitions of what might constitute indirect assistance to that effort, specifically as to how much should be covered by International List I (dual-use items). These differences sometimes play themselves out within COCOM, but also sometimes at higher, bilateral levels. It is also unfortunately true that differences at the definitional and interpretative level have been accentuated at times by inept American diplomacy and blunderbuss attempts to pressure the Europeans into conformity with our various positions. Pronouncements from the Pentagon implying that we possess a higher quality of wisdom in such matters, and that Europeans must be incredibly naive not to see the force of our arguments, obviously have evoked only a negative response.

Responsibility for strained relations over issues of East-West trade does not, of course, lie solely on the American side. Europeans have sometimes seemed strangely insouciant to Washington about the need for stricter controls in COCOM and, in practice, about the sale of items that seem to U.S. officials clearly to have security implications. Nor have they failed to take advantage of competitive openings left by the withdrawal of export offers by American firms under stringent unilateral U.S. restrictions. Firms like Caterpillar Tractor Company, for example, have not enjoyed losing significant amounts of business to foreign firms and have made plain their unhappiness about market displacement. Rescission in December 1981 of a permit previously granted to Caterpillar for the sale of two hundred pipe-laying tractors to the Soviet Union came at a particularly difficult time for this American multinational and forced further layoffs at the main Caterpillar plant in Peoria, Illinois.[7] Needless to say, within the purely competitive context, our European and Japanese allies do not mind seeing the United States shooting itself in the foot.

If American diplomacy has at times tended to be heavy-handed, if not downright ham-handed, European diplomacy on the subject has sometimes come across as less than completely honest. The United States has at least avoided giving the impression that it tacitly allowed its exporters to do things surreptitiously that it was proclaiming against publicly and officially. Our behavior in the Iran affair, of course, went a long way toward destroying our own credibility in this context.

Whatever the actual degree of responsibility on either side, there is no denying the atmosphere of mutual distrust and resentment that beclouds this whole issue of East-West trade within the alliance. Given this fact, and the past record of discordant European and American attitudes with respect to export controls and technology transfer, as well as related issues such as extension of credits to finance exports to Eastern Europe or energy agreements bringing Soviet oil and natural gas to Western Europe, what can be done to remove, or at least reduce, actual and potential sources of controversy between the United States and its European allies? The answer to this question obviously involves judgments as to the likely course of future European-American relations in general, the importance of export control and related issues to those more general relations, and a reevaluation of specifically American interests in trade with Eastern Europe.

Desiderata and Difficulties

Among the considerations that one might have in mind in seeking a greater measure of European-American agreement on East-West economic relations, both within COCOM and more generally, would be:

1. The international marketplace has evolved to the point that global diffusion of technology, including that with military applications, is taking place at a rapid rate. At the same time American dominance over advanced technology is declining. Needless to say, this markedly reduces the amount of economic leverage that the United States is able to apply.

2. Another reality is the urgent need of the United States, with its mammoth negative imbalances on both trade and current accounts, to maintain and enlarge foreign markets for its products. It is important, therefore, to halt progressive de-Americanization of input into European products in order to nullify putative U.S. attempts to limit exports to the East through control over components. That such a process is taking place is, of course, impossible to quantify with any precision, but two fact-finding missions of the National Academy of Sciences panel to six West European countries came to the conclusion that U.S. foreign policy controls raised the specter of American industry as an unreliable trading partner and that this militated against buying from U.S. firms. A further negative factor was the cumbersome and inefficient administrative system connected with license applications that made compliance a major nuisance.[8] There is no obvious, ready-made

formula to turn around a process already under way that can be so damaging as this to important American economic interests, but one might suggest as a start reconsideration of the policies that have been the major causal factor.

Psychologically regarded, the problem of restoring confidence in American industry as a reliable supplier is not solely one of unilateral and sometimes erratic U.S. limitations on trade with the East. Although the U.S. government, especially at higher levels, is not noted for its institutional memory, some officials are undoubtedly still around who can certify to the deep scars left by the United States as a supplier of enriched nuclear fuel to West European countries. Although EURATOM (the energy authority created in 1958 to coordinate European Economic Community policy on nuclear power) has had a somewhat erratic record, the energy squeeze on Europe after the first oil shock of 1973 first brought home the need for an assured supply of nuclear fuel. European reliance on the United States as such a source received a rude blow in 1973 and 1976–77 with the tightening of American export controls as part of a revised nonproliferation policy. Although the European reaction on both occasions was partly rhetorical, if heated, some member countries, most notably the FRG, began to obtain a portion of their enriched uranium from the USSR.[9] This continues up to the present. Against this background American protestations during the natural gas pipeline dispute that the Soviet Union is an unreliable supplier inevitably had a somewhat hollow ring in Europe.

3. An important general goal of a sensible American policy should be the reduction of disagreements with our allies over East-West economic policy to the point where they do not threaten to corrode NATO political and security arrangements. This, as we shall see, is much easier said than done.

The Broader Economic Context

Realization of these goals will not be easy for a variety of reasons, largely having to do with generally unfavorable economic trends. East-West trade issues cannot be detached from the broader sweep of European-American economic relations resulting from the halcyon days of the Marshall Plan and other American postwar contributions to the economic reconstruction of Western Europe. The position of the American economy in the world has now fundamentally changed for the worse, and the process of restoring some measure of balance will inevitably be painful both to the United States and our principal trading partners. Apart from our internal budgetary deficit, with its spillover effect on our external economy, we have become the largest debtor nation in the world, sucking in foreign capital on a massive scale to pay for our huge deficits on trade and current accounts—this when according to all the rules of classical economics, as one of the rich countries of the world, we should be a net exporter of capital. We do not yet know how much the current depreciation of the dollar will rectify our external imbalances, but up to the point when this is being written the so-called J-curve has proved to have an extended trough. Moreover, many important trading partners, particularly in Asia, pegged their currencies to the dollar and let them float down with it, while Canada (our largest single trading partner) let its dollar depreciate against the U.S. dollar. Although some Asian countries have recently permitted their currencies to appreciate a bit, American deficits in value terms continue at unsustainably high levels.

In any event, as any observer who has recently traveled in Europe can attest, the result has been a loss of respect for the judgment of those making American economic policy—a psychological reality that makes European officials even less likely to respect our judgment on East-West trade issues. Many Europeans would agree with Felix Rohatyn that "the U.S. has been guilty of the most irresponsible fiscal behavior in its history during the last seven years."[10] It is in any event clear that the hegemonial era of American economic dominance in the world is over. We can no longer call the economic shots as we once were able to, despite the continuing reliance of the Europeans and the Japanese on our nuclear deterrent for their ultimate security.[11]

Another negative factor is that our running disputes with the European Economic Community (now the European Community) have helped to create a general climate of controversy. Differences over West-West trade and economic policies have come to be an important part of the background against which European-American relations play themselves out. The possibility of a trade war between the European Community and the United States is now the standard stock of journalists and economists; some have even questioned whether, with the breakdown of the traditional triangular balancing mechanisms of trade, the old economic complementarities between Europe and the United States still exist.

We really do not know what world economic prospects are likely to be, even for the years immediately ahead. There is little consensus among the warring schools of economists, who give conflicting policy advice to governments. One possible negative scenario sees the developed world moving into a period of growth stagnation. If, for whatever reason, this should prove to be the case (whether due to the working out of a Kondratief long-wave cycle, or because we are moving into a period of glut in the world productive cycle, or because of a permanent shift of comparative advantage across a broad front, or because of the breakdown of the international monetary and banking system due to excessive burdens of debt, or because of some combination of these), the consequences for European-American relations are bound to be bad.

What Needs to Be Done

Assuming a less dramatic movement of the world economy, in view of the many problems addressed in this book, there are still serious obstacles to be overcome in achieving greater European-American agreement on trade policy toward Eastern Europe and the Soviet Union, whether in COCOM or at other levels. The discussion that follows is not intended to be exhaustive, but to suggest a number of points that a sensible reconsideration of American policy might include.

Improving Our Arguments

We need first of all to improve the quality of our arguments. A record of taking extreme positions that do not seem intellectually respectable to our allies can only lead to loss of confidence in the judgment of those arguing for them. The Siberian natural gas pipeline imbroglio, which aroused such passionate debate and strong European resentment during the early years of the Reagan administration, provides a classic example of how a case based at least in part on ignorance can be self-defeating. The argument was made that construction of the pipeline would increase European dependence on energy deliveries from the USSR to a point where the Soviets could blackmail Europe by threatening to cut off the flow of natural gas to the West. Apart from the feelings of many Europeans, based on experience, that the Soviet Union was actually a reliable supplier of energy, this whole argument struck those who were knowledgeable about the nature of the West European integrated natural gas distribution network as superficial, if not irrelevant.

To begin with, a rise in European gas imports from the USSR would reduce the extent of dependence on OPEC oil, and it would be difficult to persuade European officials that the Soviet Union is a less reliable supplier of energy than countries in the turbulent Middle East. This, of course, is essentially a matter of political judgment. However, the essential basis of security, Europeans felt, was the integrated European gas pipeline grid of some 680,000 kilometers that connects almost all countries on the Continent (Sweden and Spain are the exceptions) with sources of natural gas supply in the Netherlands and Norway. With regular deliveries from the Soviet Union, this Western natural gas can, in effect, be preserved in part underground rather than gradually exhausted, to be drawn upon in the event of an interruption of supply from other sources. The author can recall discussing this whole question of a security reserve in the early 1980s with Dr. Dirk Spierenburg, who negotiated for the Netherlands a new upward price agreement with European distributing companies, such as Ruhrgas AG, to lower the Dutch financial loss from lower natural gas deliveries. His view was that the issue of natural gas security was a red herring.[12]

Anyone observing closely the dispute between Europe and the United States over the natural gas pipeline from the Soviet Union could not help but conclude that it quickly became essentially a dialogue of the deaf. The reality was, of course, that the United States could not make a case persuasive to the Europeans, and attempts to pressure them proved futile.

From the European point of view, a particularly irritating aspect of the whole business was the attempt to apply American regulations and sanctions extraterritorially. This has been a perennial source of difficulty with both our European and Canadian allies; there is a long record of acrid disputes over the extension of American antitrust legislation abroad. The worldwide activities of U.S. multinational firms seemingly beyond the regulatory authority of Washington have provoked many attempts by the U.S. Department of Justice to bring them within the scope of the Sherman and Clayton acts as well as other legislation. The response of foreign states has been uniformly negative. In the case of the natural gas pipeline dispute, the U.S. government tried on June 18, 1982, to enforce extraterritorial application of its export controls on a retroactive basis. Since all the major contractors had American ties as either parts users, subsidiaries, or technology licensees, the scope of the action taken was very broad. The European reaction was predictably strong, and in the final analysis the Europeans won out when Secretary of State Shultz managed to kick the issue under the rug after a patched-up and intrinsically ineffective agreement had been reached with the Europeans.[13] When the aroused passions of the moment had subsided, however, there were inevitably deep, lingering resentments at what to the Europeans seemed like just another particularly egregious and illicit attempt to extend American jurisdiction beyond its national boundaries.

In the light of past history and the more immediate outcome of the natural gas pipeline fiasco, it should be clear that we need to rethink our whole approach to the extraterritorial applicability of American laws and regulations. At the very least we should not blunder into any repetition of the 1982 experience without being aware of the price to be paid in terms of strains within the alliance and the possible stimulation of a mood of defiance inimical to the achievement of legitimate goals in the East-West trade context.

Improving Our Diplomacy

Our economic diplomacy obviously needs improvement. The U.S. government, as it operates in the 1980s, seemingly lacks the capacity to do this in any comprehensive way. Although I am aware that this will inevitably raise hackles in Washington, on the basis of long experience as an American diplomat I can only conclude that the best, and perhaps the exclusive, way to achieve coherence and finesse is to return a greater measure of supervisory responsibility for international economic affairs to the Department of State. If our international economic policy during the past two decades had had an unmitigated record of success, one might argue that the present diffusion of authority in the government is the best possible arrangement. But given the awesome negative international economic position of the United States described above, any argument for the status quo lacks credibility. Among the areas where this seems to be particularly apropos is that of East-West economic relations.

Without belaboring the point, I note that no other government in the advanced industrial world makes foreign economic policy with so little effective input from its ministry of foreign affairs. Why the Department of State has over the years lost a good deal of its competence in this area to the Department of the Treasury, the Department of Commerce, the Department of Agriculture, and even the Department of Defense in matters affecting East-West trade is a long story. The responsibility has been partly that of the Department of State itself, including the unwillingness of several secretaries of state who were not particularly interested in economic matters to combat the erosion of their authority. The standard argument heard in Washington has been that State is too concession-prone, always seeking compromises instead of adhering sternly to established positions. This common attitude, shared by some presidents, reflects a basic misunderstanding of the role of diplomacy in foreign relations and a failure to recognize that, with the ending of America's hegemonic international economic position, we cannot always dictate policy to our complete liking. Needless to say, I do not expect any significant shift of power in Washington in the direction indicated, but it would be well if it could become a reality.[14]

Understanding Differences of Assessment

I have already alluded to the important differences of approach and assessment between most American officials and West European officials with respect to the Soviet Union and Eastern Europe. Full agreement here is unlikely, but we need deeper insight in Washington into those differences and how they can lead to radically contrasting judgments about what is proper and desirable. Americans tend to view the division of Europe into East and West as a fact of life, regrettable but unchangeable. Even the efforts, sincere enough, that we made at various postwar conferences to find formulas that would end that division were never suffused with much hope that the Soviet Union would accept free elections and the installation of democratic regimes within its East European glacis. The splitting of Germany into separate states constituted the most dramatic symbol of a torn Europe—a Europe that could only view the historical and cultural ties between East and West as a basic reality and the Iron Curtain as unnatural and impermanent.

This difference between Europe and the United States is not only theoretical. It has practical consequences that evidence themselves in contrasting judgments and priorities with respect to economic relations with Eastern Europe. Apart from the heyday of Nixonian détente, most American officials have never given much credence to the argument that economic concessions to the Soviet Union will buy better behavior. This belief has had more enduring acceptance by West Europeans. The old shibboleth that a hungry (or thin) bear is more dangerous than a well-fed (or fat) bear sounds plausible enough if one accepts the premise that aggression is the child of frustration and want. During the middle 1960s, for example, German Chancellor Ludwig Erhard and his principal economic adviser, Minister of State Ludger Westrick, seriously considered making a very generous offer of aid to the USSR in order to improve Soviet behavior internationally, and specifically with respect to West Berlin.[15]

Although the Ostpolitik of Chancellor Willy Brandt a few years later was primarily carried out at the political level, the economic bait, particularly vis-à-vis the GDR, was always present in the background. The assumption that increased trade with Eastern Europe would inevitably follow resolution of border and territorial problems left over from World War II was very much a part of the Ostpolitik philosophy. Even conservative Germans would accept that East German behavior has been favorably influenced by West German swing credits and other economic concessions, and that alternatively the economic dependencies developed over the years constitute a formidable constraint on bad behavior. The obverse of this is a reluctance, shared by most Europeans as well as the Germans, to accept the logic of the argument sometimes advanced that anything that helps the economy of the Soviet Union ultimately contributes to the Soviet military potential by releasing assets to the military sector. If trade with the East is a good thing in itself, maximizing wealth and welfare, as Europeans tend to believe, then limitations on that trade should affect only the irreducible minimum.

The contrasting reactions in the United States and Western Europe, again particularly in the FRG, to the declaration of martial law and assumption of power in Poland by General Wojcieck Jarulzelski provide another good example of how differing perspectives can lead to differing conclusions. To Washington, Jarulzelski was essentially a stooge, pulling Soviet chestnuts out of the fire and obviating the need for a military invasion of Poland to reassert the authority of a crumbling Communist party. Hence sanctions seemed a natural and consequent reaction. To many Europeans, however, while the suppression of the Solidarity free-trade movement was highly regrettable, the assumption of control by the Polish military ran counter to the basic Marxist tenet that the party is the supreme authority within a communist state and confirmed its decline in Poland. Jarulzelski could, therefore, be regarded as a Polish patriot who, despite his Marxist background, had acted to prevent a Soviet military invasion. According to this interpretation, sanctions should be minimal and as much private aid as possible should go to the Polish people. Intertwined with this, of course, was the Polish debt crisis, which had dried up further extension of credits by the Western banking system. Some would claim that the European view was not dissimilar in essence from that taken by the Roman Catholic church in Poland.

A cynic might note that there is a great deal of wishful thinking on both sides of this issue. Whatever the role of prejudice and predilection in shaping conclusions, the fact is that American policy toward Poland has been carried out largely in blissful disregard of European views.

I have previously noted a certain schizoid quality in the West European approach to Eastern Europe. Within the alliance context the possibility of Soviet aggressive action against the West must still be entertained as justification for large defense expenditures and the preservation of NATO. At the same time the maximization of contacts and trade with the East in an effort to improve relations and ultimately to induce change becomes a basic objective. During the cold war era this conflict of goals did not appear much of a problem, but with the advent of détente the conceptual dilemma became more acute. It has remained up to the present. Even the Soviet invasion of Afghanistan and its aftermath did not really alter conflicting European attitudes, and the harsh posture of the first Reagan administration toward the Soviet Union provoked more concern than agreement.

Looking to the future, it would be foolhardy for the American government to ignore two trends in Europe that are relevant to East-West trade issues and to the larger complex of East-West relations:

the increased subtlety and effectiveness of Soviet propaganda under Gorbachev, and the perplexing problem of generational change (the so-called successor generation problem), as new leaders take over in both government and business who lack the formative personal experience of World War II and the early postwar years.

Whatever Gorbachev's ultimate objectives and the chances of his success (the international community of Sovietologists is far from unified on these points), the fact remains that he is something new on the Soviet leadership horizon. Comparisons with the early days of Nikita Khrushchev in power are interesting, but the latter obviously lacked Gorbachev's finesse in dealing with Western leaders, nor was he able to surround himself with as many able people willing to go in the same direction. In other words, West European attitudes are likely to be much more favorably influenced in the years ahead by blandishments from the East, which are likely also to create sentiment for ever more relaxation of trade controls. Gorbachev is hardly likely to emulate the major mistake made by Khrushchev in 1958 of unleashing a Berlin crisis that became a major preoccupation of Western leaders for nearly five years. A survey made in May 1987 by the United States Information Agency showed that West Europeans give the Soviets most of the credit for progress made up to that point on arms control; furthermore, the poll revealed that many Europeans do not believe that the United States can be trusted to keep its arms control commitments, but do believe that the Soviet Union can be trusted to so behave.[16]

One can attend a conference nearly every month somewhere in the West on the successor generation problem. Defining the problem is easy enough. How to instill in this generation the same values that governed political attitudes in the postwar era without the same shared experiences is a continuing and perplexing dilemma. What is particularly troubling is the tendency of many young Europeans to attribute equal responsibility to the United States and the Soviet Union for the military confrontation in central Europe and the failure to find a solution to the political division of the continent. Needless to say, if this interpretation of the postwar period is carried into government and business by significant segments of the successor generation, it will make even more difficult any attempt by the United States to impose the definitions and restrictions on trade with the East that it might favor. Early recognition of this impending reality will require, at the least, some important tactical adjustments.

American Interest in Trade with the East

Any reexamination of East-West economic relations must include a hard look at American trading interests with respect to the Soviet Union and the rest of Eastern Europe. While it would be unrealistic to expect that enhanced trade prospects with the East could make more than a marginal contribution to rectification of the enormous deficits on trade and current accounts that burden the U.S. international economy, the very existence of those deficits makes it imperative that we not overlook any possibility of expanding American exports within a sensible definition of our security interests. According to the National Academy of Sciences study already cited, "a reasonable estimate of the direct, short-run economic costs to the U.S. economy associated with U.S. export controls was on the order of $9.3 billion in 1985." This was a conservative estimate, and the report went on to say that if one were to "calculate the overall impact on the aggregate U.S. economy of the value of lost export sales and the reduced R&D effort, the associated loss for the U.S. 1985 GNP would be $17.1 billion."[17] If one also takes into account the longer-term, progressive de-Americanization of components in Western Europe already noted, then the overall loss to the economy, both short-term and longer term, is far from inconsiderable.

Even a major relaxation of American export controls would not, of course, automatically recapture lost markets in Eastern Europe. As we have learned from the experience of banned American grain exports during the Carter administration, or from the larger context of lost exports around the world from overvaluation of the dollar before the end of 1985, removal of the primary cause does not per se bring about speedy restoration of equilibrium on trade and current accounts. The question, nevertheless, arises whether the U.S. government does not need to factor in our overall trading requirements much more intensely, while taking a new look at the limitations we wish to impose on trade with Eastern Europe.

As ably discussed in Beverly Crawford's chapter in this book,[18] government trade finance or credit policy is an important aspect of trade policy. West European countries have traditionally followed more liberal credit policies than the United States with respect to their East European trade, and this question has been another source of continuing dispute within the alliance. American efforts to obtain European agreement to more restrictive credit policies involving observance of the Berne Union five-year rule generally failed, and self-imposed limitations on ourselves (some legislatively required) have merely damaged U.S. trading interests. Even the agreement of May 1982, which strengthened the rules on credit extension and brought the cost of governmental export credits in line with prevailing commercial interest rates, turned out to be a somewhat hollow victory since the East European countries were in any case moving away from Western governmental financing of trade to borrowing on the Eurocurrency market. So far as one can tell from IMF trade statistics there has been no distinguishable impact on West European trade with the East because of the tightening of governmental credit policy. Although we now seem largely to have eliminated competition for trade by extension of easy credit terms, the United States obviously needs to take a look at its own internal credit prescriptions with a view to eliminating those which reduce its competitiveness.

A final speculative question involves the degree of new trading opportunity that the possible, at least partial, success of Gorbachev's internal economic reform program might open up for the United States. If he actually succeeds in giving managers of enterprises in the Soviet Union the same kind of individual latitude that they already enjoy in Hungary, and thereby pumps new life into the Soviet economy, the Soviets may well show increased interest in East-West trade as well as Western financial markets.[19] Given the harsh international economic realities facing the United States, the prospect of expanding trade with the USSR, should it materialize, is not one that we should simply reject without examination.

COCOM Effectiveness and Non-member Countries

A recognizable development has been the growing technological competence of a number of countries that are not members of COCOM and have small intention of joining that organization or abiding by its rules. One can, of course, make a reasonable theoretical case for adoption of COCOM criteria by the newly industrializing countries that have developed some capacity in the production of high-technology items, provided the basic premises of the control system are accepted. That the latter condition is generally not met seems fairly obvious. The only practical way open to obtain compliance, as Henry Nau points out in his chapter in this volume,[20] is to have all COCOM members join the United States in exercising collective leverage by strictly controlling exports of technology to non-complying countries. Given the differing trading philosophies that we have already noted, such cooperation scarcely seems likely on any effective scale. Success in this endeavor would require considerably more skillful American diplomacy than we have displayed in the past, but if the whole system of controls is not eventually to collapse as non-member countries become technologically more advanced, the effort must at least be made.[21]

Conclusion

The reader will have concluded that I am not sanguine that a reasonable and effective system of export controls, consistent with both American economic interests and security concerns as we have traditionally defined them, can be achieved and maintained. As a former practicing American diplomat who has been observing Europeans at close hand during the entire postwar period, I am inclined to think that the issue of trade with Eastern Europe and the Soviet Union is one that we shall never resolve to our or their complete satisfaction.

We need a more sophisticated presentation of our views based upon a more realistic assessment of the desirable and the possible. Given all the other problems facing alliance political and economic relations, we cannot afford to leave this issue a running sore. Over the years I have been impressed with the intensity of European feelings on the subject, and the corresponding American indignation at what we regard as foolhardy noncooperation on the part of our allies.

Some Americans, perhaps given to hyperbole, might argue that we should threaten our allies with the possibility of an American pull-out from Europe if they do not comply with our desiderata on East-West trade. If one accepts the postulate that Soviet military power still constitutes a threat to the West—a necessary postulate if any controls on technology transfer to Eastern Europe are to be justified —then such talk is sheer nonsense. The reason the United States remained in Europe after World War II was fear of Soviet military aggression, or at least of Soviet political dominance of a kind that would have put Western Europe alongside Eastern Europe in the Soviet area of effective influence, thus forming an overwhelmingly superior combination vis-à-vis the United States. For anyone with a sense of history it is wrong to say that our continuing military presence in Europe is merely to protect the ungrateful Europeans. We are there to defend our own vital interest in avoiding any radical shift in the overall power balance to our disadvantage. We thus have a clear interest in preventing the kinds of strains within the alliance that, over time, could lead to its weakening or, under the worst of circumstances, even to its eventual dissolution.

One must accept that some Americans sincerely believe that Lenin was right in saying that capitalist nations would sell the Soviet Union the rope with which to hang the West. If one thinks this is what the West is doing, then emphasis is placed on claims that have appeared regularly in the 1980s, such as that "U.S. intelligence officials have identified more than 150 Soviet military systems that use American technology and materials," and that "from 1976 to 1984, Soviet agents are known to have obtained from the United States some 30,000 pieces of military-oriented equipment and 400,000 technical documents."[22] The obvious difficulty with this line of argument, from the European point of view, is that if such alarmist statements are true they indicate a fundamental weakness in American controls, whether unilateral or within a multilateral system. Moreover, as we have noted, our allies simply do not accept the evil empire image of the Soviet Union in the sense that every dealing with Soviet officials must be regarded as contributing to an accumulation of power that ultimately will be used against the West. Whatever the rhetoric may say from time to time, the U.S. government itself has seldom acted on any such assumption. Otherwise grain shipments would be just as much anathema as any other exports.

This being the case, a centrist position on trade and technology controls seem to make sense. While the recommendations made above will not completely bridge the gap, they will, if carried out, do much to ameliorate a bad situation. The fundamentally changed economic context to which we have called attention necessitates, in any event, a probing reexamination of the assumptions that have underpinned our policy. An important objective must be to improve West-West economic and technological cooperation aimed at building greater confidence in American industry as a reliable supplier. Recognition of today's realities is essential both to sound policy and to the elimination of avoidable differences that place serious strains on the alliance.

13

Export Controls and Free Trade: Squaring the Circle in COCOM

Henry R. Nau

The panel believes that the multilateral system is so essential to the effective denial or significant delay of strategic products and technology to the Soviet Union, and that the restrictions on West-West trade and technology exchange are sufficiently harmful to U.S. economic and Western security interests, that the United States ought now to pursue the objective of developing a *community of common controls in dual use technology* among cooperating Western countries. *This concept implies the construction of a common external "wall" of export controls to the East accompanied by a significant liberalization of controls within the West.* To be successful a community of common controls must in time include not only the industrialized allies but also a number of advanced or rapidly industrializing non-COCOM countries.

The panel recognizes that this objective will require major policy adjustments by both the United States and its major trading partners. Furthermore, there may be an incentive for one or more countries to remain outside the community as an island of unrestricted trading activity. This could only be *prevented by strict community control of exports to the noncomplying country.* Such contingencies need to be addressed in developing the community. *Nevertheless, recent improvements in COCOM and moderately successful diplomatic initiatives with European countries have made the concept of a community of common controls in dual use technology a realistic objective for U.S. export control policy.* (From National Academy of Sciences, *Balancing the National Interest*, 1987, pp. 135–36. Emphasis added.)

Trade serves different purposes in different strategic contexts. In relations among Western countries free trade is an expression of open societies and economic and political freedom. In relations between East and West trade is an element of deterrence to protect free societies.[1] Some fear that trade controls in the East-West context may interfere with free trade within the West, while others hope that free trade within the West may eventually spill over and create more open societies in the East, removing the need for trade controls. Neither expectation is realistic. Trade controls with the East do not have to interfere with the free exchange of trade and technology within the West and are likely to remain necessary as long as fundamental political values and geostrategic circumstances divide East and West.

Squaring the circle of export controls and free trade can begin with the recommendations outlined above in a study released in January 1987 by the National Academy of Sciences (NAS).[2] The study calls for a community of common controls in dual-use technologies among cooperating Western countries. Such a community would constitute, in effect, a "common market for export controls," embracing a common external wall of comparable trade controls vis-à-vis the East and a customs union or internal liberalization of licensing controls among cooperating Western countries. The stronger and more uniform the community is in its controls toward the East, the more liberal and free will be the flow of high-technology trade and transfer within the West. COCOM, the Western organization for multilateral export controls, is the framework of such a community. Thus, strengthening COCOM is the key to squaring the circle of export controls and free trade.

The NAS concludes that this community of common controls is "a realistic objective" for U.S. policy. The rest of this paper details a logic and strategy for achieving it. In the process it draws on and critiques the extremely useful papers in this volume dealing with both domestic and alliance aspects of export control policy issues.

The New International Environment
for Export Controls

Five features of the current international environment are relevant to the logic and maintenance of a multilateral community of common controls among Western countries:

1. The United States continues to enjoy a substantial lead over the Soviet Union in most types of dual-use technology—anywhere from 5–10 years—and the gap is not closing, according to the NAS study;[3]
2. The West continues to pursue a strategy of deterrence known as escalation dominance (see below), which depends on a Western qualitative lead in military, especially strategic technologies to offset a Soviet quantitative advantage in conventional systems;
3. The United States no longer enjoys a technological lead in many dual-use technologies within the West;
4. Commercial technologies with military significance are now emerging in world markets before military applications;
5. The Soviet Union has initiated a program of domestic economic reform and rapprochement with the principal Western international economic institutions that suggests a renewed interest in access to superior dual-use technologies in the West.

In 1986 the Defense Department estimated that the United States led the Soviet Union in thirteen out of twenty military-related technology areas, while the Soviet Union led in none.[4] A survey by Fortune magazine in October 1986 showed similar results. On a scale of 1 to 10, the Soviets ranked 1.5 in computer technology versus 9.9 for the United States, 1.3 in life sciences versus 8.9, 3.8 for advanced materials versus 7.7, and 3.6 in optoelectronics versus 7.8.[5] The Soviets do better in terms of operational weapons systems in the field. As the NAS study notes, "the strong Soviet emphasis on the development and production of military hardware has resulted in many items or equipment in the field that in many weapon system categories often are as modern as those deployed in the West."[6]

The Western lead in military-related technologies is not just a matter of scorekeeping, an American impulse to be superior. It is integrally related to Western military strategy for maintaining the peace. Since World War II the United States has relied on strategies of nuclear deterrence that threaten to escalate conflicts to higher and higher levels of offensive retaliation. Through doctrines of massive retaliation in the 1950s, flexible response in the 1960s, and escalation dominance in the 1970s and 1980s, the United States has put the Soviet Union on notice that, should it try to exploit its numerical advantage at any level of conflict in central Europe or other areas of vital Western interest, the West would retaliate at the next higher level of warfare, including strategic nuclear weapons. Escalation dominance, adopted by the United States in President Carter's famous PD-59, calls for such incremental escalation even at nuclear levels, that is, a capacity to fight, at least theoretically (since that is, after all, the purpose of deterrence), limited strategic nuclear wars. With its qualitative technological superiority the United States must be able to convince the Soviet Union that it could dominate (hence escalation dominance) at the next higher level of engagement—nuclear or conventional—regardless of the level at which the Soviets might choose to start a conflict. This strategy, as Michael Mandelbaum points out, requires that the United States "needs not just a handful of nuclear weapons that can rain destruction on Russia in response to an attack, but a varied, versatile military force capable of fighting at all the relevant levels of force."[7] Thus, Western deterrence strategy depends critically on the superiority of Western technological capabilities at all levels of potential conflict—nuclear, limited nuclear, or conventional. A qualitative technological lead is the linchpin of the entire structure of Western defense.

While the United States continues to lead the Soviet Union by a substantial margin in military-related technologies, it no longer enjoys a dominant position in these technologies within the West. The same *Fortune* survey noted above shows that Japan leads the United States in optoelectronics and runs a close second in other fields such as computers, life sciences, and advanced materials. In specific areas such as ceramics the Japanese probably lead, and in volume production of high-technology consumer products Japan is clearly the world's leader. The European allies also possess formidable dual-use technological capabilities, and even the newly industrializing countries are acquiring capabilities to utilize high-technology products from the industrialized countries, perhaps eventually to produce their own indigenous products in some of these areas. This diffusion of high technology with strategic implications opens up many more possibilities of transfer of strategic technology to the Soviet Union and thus complicates the task of export control to the East.

The new technologies further complicate this task because they often emerge first in civilian markets before their military implications become apparent. The technologies that emerged shortly before and during World War II were largely developed for military purposes under classified contracts or within defense laboratories—i.e., radar, jet engines, nuclear power, etc. Their entry into commercial markets could be carefully monitored and, if necessary, appropriately restricted (as was, for example, the development of civilian nuclear power). The new technologies—electronics and computers, biotechnology, materials, telecommunications, etc.—are being developed first for commercial markets outside the restricted environment of classified research and defense laboratories. These technologies may be widely available through industrial and scientific contacts, joint research activities, cross-licensing, and joint ventures. Controlling access to these technologies without interfering with the normal and necessary interaction of scientific and industrial personnel and products in open commercial markets poses new challenges for the United States and the West.

These challenges are likely to be made even more formidable by the Soviet Union. Frequently in the past the Soviet Union has turned to the West to acquire the leading-edge technologies that it lacks for its military as well as economic development.[8] Most recently, the "Farewell" papers revealed the extent to which the Soviet Union organized in the 1970s and early 1980s to "ransack" systematically Western markets for militarily useful technologies.[9] As Marie-Hélène

Labbé discusses in her chapter in this volume, these secret Soviet documents "opened many eyes" in France and the West in general to the Soviet appetite for Western technology. The NAS study concluded "that the Soviet technology acquisition effort is massive, well financed, and frequently effective."[10]

If anything, the new leadership in the Soviet Union under Mikhail Gorbachev seems poised to increase these efforts to tap into Western markets for needed military and commercial technologies. Gorbachev has launched a series of domestic reforms to revitalize the Soviet economy and upgrade existing production technology through imports and joint venture arrangements with Western companies. In addition, he has sought affiliation for the Soviet Union with major international economic institutions such as the General Agreement on Tariffs and Trade and the World Bank. This effort to access Western markets may focus particularly on Western Europe and Japan, exploiting the fact that leading technologies are now widely available within the Western world and putting added pressure on the Western system to control strategic exports to the Soviet Union.[11] In this volume Gordon Smith notes that Soviet balance of payments considerations have caused it to turn increasingly in recent years to Western Europe, more so than Japan, as the primary source of supply for machinery and equipment.

The New Policy Imperatives

Several policy imperatives would seem to follow from the five features of the current international environment discussed above:

1. The United States and its major Western economic partners have to maintain an aggressive and effective system of export controls on strategic trade with the East as long as Western security depends on a qualitative technological advantage over the Soviet Union;

2. The United States has to exercise the principal leadership toward this end both because it has the primary responsibility for West-

ern security and because it has the most at stake in terms of strategic defense investments;

3. The United States cannot rely on unilateral controls to the extent it did in the past because many dual-use technologies are now available from other Western countries, but the United States will have to continue to bargain aggressively with what technological leverage it retains to achieve multilateral agreement on essential controls;

4. Future export controls will have to license the users of dual-use technologies within the West rather than the individual transactions if commercial markets and free trade and technology flows with the West are not to be adversely affected.

In his contribution to this volume William Root correctly raises the question of the security rationale of export controls. Denying or delaying militarily significant strategic technology to the Soviet Union makes sense only in the context of a particular security policy. As noted above, however, Western security policy relies centrally on the technological superiority of offensive retaliatory systems. In this context export controls on superior technology, whether used in conventional (e.g., smart weapons) or strategic systems, remain necessary to protect the Western technological lead at all levels of potential strategic engagement. It makes no sense to export these technologies to encourage Soviet dependence unless one has an extraordinarily benign view of Soviet intentions or believes that these technologies would be so valuable to the Soviet Union that it would dramatically alter its domestic and foreign policies to conform to Western interests. If either of the latter two conditions prevailed, one might then ask why the Soviet Union would need a totally independent military establishment competitive with that of the United States. Moreover, if the export controls are administered properly they automatically result in Soviet dependence on obsolete technology because older technologies are removed from the control lists—and thus become available to the Soviet Union—as new technologies are added. It is also illogical to argue that because the Soviets eventually acquire these capabilities anyway through indigenous means the West should give it to them in the first place. The purpose of export controls is to protect a Western *lead*, not to deny these capabilities to the Soviet Union forever. The conclusion of the NAS study, that the Western lead in strategic systems remains substantial and may even be widening in certain areas, not only justifies strategic export controls but probably attests to the reasonable effectiveness of these controls over the past forty years.

If Western deterrent strategy should ever change, export controls would have to be reassessed in light of the new strategy. For example, the development of defensive strategic systems such as the Strategic Defense Initiative (SDI), coupled with the reduction of offensive retaliatory systems, could lead to what analysts have called a strategy of Mutual Assured Protection (MAP) or Mutual Assured Survival (MAS). Rather than depending on retaliatory capability, deterrence would rest on a capability to protect against strategic strikes. If only one side had such a capability it might be destabilizing. That side might be tempted to strike first, secure in the knowledge that it could defend against a retaliatory attack. In this situation, therefore, it may make sense to share defensive strategic technologies to ensure mutual capabilities to protect. At the moment these possibilities are a bit farfetched. No one knows if reliable and cost-effective defensive systems are feasible, let alone how such technology might be deployed or shared. Nevertheless, loose talk about sharing SDI technology with the Soviet Union, which President Reagan himself has engaged in, is not wholly nonsensical, even if a bit premature. Nor, it might be added, does such talk detract from the logic of *not* sharing strategic technologies with the Soviet Union as long as current deterrent strategy relies on offensive retaliation.

Michael Mastanduno has made a very persuasive argument in this volume that the United States has a special leadership role in the Western export control system. This role follows from the fact that the United States has primary responsibility for Western deterrence and defense and has the largest investment in strategic systems. Western Europe and Japan, as other chapters in this volume suggest, are not unconcerned about strategic controls but their concern is contingent on U.S. leadership and policy. Germany and Japan, two of the most advanced technological powers in the West, do not exercise independent responsibility for their security. Britain and France define their security interests somewhat less globally than the United States. It is inevitable, therefore, that the Western countries, while sharing a broad common interest in strategic controls, will tend to define "strategic" differently in specific export control decisions.

The differences in Western interests go beyond the strategic area. As Ambassador Hillenbrand suggests in his contribution, Western Europe has a different political and psychological orientation toward Eastern Europe than does the United States. It has closer historical ties in both the economic and cultural areas. Bruce Jentleson illustrates some of these economic differences in the energy section. Europe also has centuries of experience dealing with Eastern countries, including the Soviet Union, and feels that it is often better able to relate to these countries than the more remote and less experienced United States. Germany is a special case. As Hanns-Dieter Jacobsen points out, it has to contend with a divided country and a perilous geographic location. It is inclined to view economic and human contacts with the East, particularly East Germany, as absolutely vital to the preservation of its cultural identity as well as peace in Central Europe. Germany and other European allies are, accordingly, more likely to view trade as an element of cooperation in East-West relations and are more reluctant than the United States to use export controls for punitive or foreign policy purposes.

Thus, the structure of interests within the COCOM community is such that agreeing on specific export controls is likely to be a difficult task. This fact holds whether one views U.S. leadership in COCOM as destructive (see Root) or constructive (see Mastanduno). It is built into the geographic, historic, and contemporary strategic circumstances of the Western alliance. It is not helped, of course, by the inconstant role of the United States in COCOM (which both Mastanduno and Root criticize) or by the tendency of the Europeans to circumvent controls for commercial purposes and then insist that the United

States does the same (see Hillenbrand). But these differences are also not likely to go away simply by the United States cleaning up its act (as Mastanduno implies) or by the United States accepting the least common denominator of controls that the allies are willing to support (as Root favors because he believes differences exist largely because of U.S. unilateralism, not because of differences in the structure of interests). In my judgment the differences will persist and dealing with them effectively will require continuous and sometimes tough bargaining.

In such bargaining the United States will continue to have to exert leverage to achieve agreement on essential multilateral controls. Beverly Crawford, in her contribution to this volume, makes a distinction between power and institutional approaches to international bargaining. In her careful analysis of negotiations among the allies over controls on exports credits she concludes that the institutional or regime approach fits these negotiations best because the allies were able to agree on a strengthened consensus arrangement within the OECD but not on other aspects of East-West credits that were negotiated outside existing institutions (such as limits on the volume of credit). She downplays the use of power—leverage, denial, or compensation of benefits—to achieve these results and attributes outcomes instead to institutional or regime norms, rules, and procedures which are rooted in common interests such as the desire to contain the high costs of unbridled export credit competition. Similarly, in his chapter Michael Mastanduno argues that outcomes in COCOM depend less on American power or hegemony than on U.S. leadership to maintain the integrity of the control process. This implies, he argues, refraining from the use of coercion in COCOM and basing U.S. behavior instead on setting a domestic example for other COCOM members while offering persuasive, well-reasoned strategic arguments for controls. Bruce Jentleson argues that American leverage, even if used, is increasingly insufficient. In the pipeline case it did not alter behavior as much as markets did.

I have no quarrel with these arguments as far as they go. Both domestic example and institutional norms are important elements of effective bargaining, and American leverage is certainly less today than it was earlier. But carried too far the arguments become unrealistic. Power and institutions interact continuously in bargaining processes. From time to time the United States is going to have to exercise leverage within the alliance. This is likely to be particularly necessary when an institution is being created, as COCOM was in the late 1940s, or significantly strengthened, as COCOM was in the early 1980s. In the late 1940s and early 1950s the United States used both the positive incentives of the Marshall Plan and the negative incentives of the Battle Act to create COCOM and establish the norms, rules, and procedures of the export control process. (Both Jentleson and Jacobsen note the influences of these incentives in this period, especially on German policy.) After allowing the COCOM process to weaken in the 1970s, the United States exerted such leverage once again — positive incentives in the case of SDI technology and negative incentives in case of the pipeline controversy — to strengthen COCOM in the 1980s. While markets played a role in the outcome of the pipeline controversy, markets are not unaffected by policy. Recent decisions of West European governments and utilities to exploit Norwegian gas supplies rather than rely on Soviet exports reflect numerous policy adjustments, including subsidies, pricing formulas, and the like.[12]

Similarly, Crawford's analysis suggests that the United States used leverage to create the export credit arrangement in 1978 and again later to strengthen it. In the 1960s the United States sought to reconcile its restrictive credit policy with the more liberal policies of its European allies, first by setting an example in its own domestic policy and then by appealing to the Berne Union. When these efforts failed it turned to the OECD, where it established a new credit group which eventually negotiated the consensus arrangement in 1978. As Crawford notes, this initiative came after the United States had tightened its credit policies through the Stevenson-Church amendments, and, as she writes, "it was no secret that the United States chose the OECD forum to focus efforts to reduce official support of export credits to the Soviet Union and Eastern Europe." Thus, some leverage was implied in establishing the consensus arrangement, and it was clearly involved in U.S. efforts in 1982 to strengthen the consensus. After the Polish sanction of December 1981 the United States initiated the so-called Buckley group (named after James Buckley, the under secretary of state who led the U.S. negotiating team), to negotiate quantitative limits on export credits to the East. This effort was undertaken outside the OECD and, although it failed (confirming Crawford's thesis that power approaches may not be as effective as institutional approaches), it is also probable that the Buckley exercise contributed to the willingness of the allies to strengthen the consensus arrangement.

It is doubtful, therefore, that aggressive and effective bargaining within the alliance can always preclude the use of leverage. Perhaps the best one can hope for is continuity in bargaining. As Mastanduno's analysis points out, a shift in U.S. priorities weakening COCOM in the 1970s inevitably set up the alliance for a new crisis when those priorities shifted again, as they did in the 1980s. There is a limit, of course, to which COCOM can be insulated from shifts in foreign policy priorities. Even *strategic* export controls reflect general foreign policy conditions. When conflict wanes, as it has recently in U.S.-Chinese relations, for example, it is quite natural to relax export controls. As I argue at the end of this chapter, COCOM could be more effectively related to other alliance organizations to deal with these inevitable changes. However, it should also be accepted that alliance relations will not always be "reasonable and smooth" in an area such as export controls, where the structure of interests ensures important differences.

If leverage remains essential, does the United States still have enough of it to bargain effectively? Clearly, the days of the Marshall Plan and Battle Act are gone. Indeed, many now urge Japan, a clear leader in some sectors of high technology, to launch Marshall-type plans and exercise its new power. Nevertheless, as the *Fortune* survey cited earlier suggests, the United States retains important advantages in dual-use technologies. It cannot use unilateral controls to the extent it did earlier, but it can bargain with access to critical U.S. technologies, particularly militarily critical technologies such as SDI, to strengthen the control systems of other COCOM countries. It has even more leverage to urge important non-COCOM countries to tighten controls with the East.

Leverage, of course, should not be exercised in a high-handed or frivolous manner. The purpose of leverage is to facilitate eventual compromise or to create a set of institutional and regime norms which then permit bargaining to take place through more consensual means. The most useful form of leverage the United States might exert within COCOM and with non-COCOM countries is a willingness to liberalize licensing and hence access to and use of U.S. technology as these countries tighten their controls vis-à-vis the East. Toward this end the United States should encourage the use of general licenses which approve the user of the production technology involved rather than the individual exports or transactions. For example, recent U.S. legislation introduced the so-called G-COM license. This is a general license for all recipients within COCOM countries to receive low-technology items on the COCOM embargo list (items below the so-called AEN line) without an individual license. More recently, the U.S. Department of Commerce announced plans for G-FW and G-CEU licenses. The G-FW license offers the general license for low-technology items to recipients in all Free World countries (not just COCOM countries). The G-CEU license is a general license for certified end users (CEU) covering higher-technology items (above the AEN line). It will be offered initially to government agencies and government-controlled enterprises in COCOM countries, but eventually to private enterprises in these countries as well as government agencies and state enterprises in non-COCOM countries.[13] Licenses covering components, bulk transactions (distribution licenses), and technology transfer within multinational firms or networks of firms (the proposed comprehensive operations licenses) are also being developed or improved and more widely applied. These licenses are not only more consistent with the administration of export controls in a world market that is increasingly competitive and interdependent, but they also offer substantial incentives for other countries, especially important non-COCOM countries, to strengthen their systems for control of Western technology to the East. Non-COCOM countries, in particular, do not share common security objectives with COCOM countries, but these countries do have a growing interest in access to dual-use technologies that only the West can offer them.

A Negotiating Strategy for Common Controls

How does the United States convert the characteristics and imperatives of the current international environment considered in the previous two sections into an effective and consistent policy for achieving the "multilateral community of common controls" that the NAS study recommends? As we have noted, the United States can no longer direct this community unilaterally, as it may have in the early 1950s, nor can it settle for the lowest common denominator of controls acceptable to the allies. A bargaining process which permits outcomes to emerge somewhere in between these two extremes must be strengthened and institutionalized. The United States, by negotiating consistently and at times applying leverage, would insist on critical and particularly new technologies being added to the COCOM list even if they are available from other COCOM countries. Europe and Japan, on the other hand, would insist that lower-technology items be removed from the list in a timely fashion and that general license arrangements ease continuous access for the free flow of products and technologies among Western firms and countries. A stronger negotiating process, in short, would ensure both the continuous upgrading of controls to new items of technology and the more rapid decontrol of lower-level technological "commodities." Bargaining heightens the incentive to achieve a better balance between economic and security interests throughout the alliance and would benefit all parties equally.

To ensure a strong and resilient negotiating process COCOM must come "out of the closet" both physically and politically. The original agreement between the United States and the allies, which relegated COCOM to the basement of a building in Paris with no nameplate or official existence and shrouded COCOM proceedings in excessive secrecy and mystery, is no longer appropriate. In the early 1950s West

European governments were highly sensitive about the presence of communist parties in their own political systems and felt that they could not officially and openly acknowledge export controls with the East. Moreover, they hoped that by keeping COCOM small and secret they could resist U.S. pressures for what they viewed as excessive controls. Neither justification holds up in contemporary circumstances. Communist officials have served in European governments since the early 1950s, and communist parties in general have exercised much more independence vis-à-vis Moscow. Second, a small and weak COCOM, as Mastanduno shows convincingly, is a prescription not for avoiding serious conflict with the United States but ensuring it. COCOM cannot support a stable, aggressive negotiating process if it continues to exist without adequate staff, administrative (including computer) facilities, and more regular high-level political attention.

Accordingly, it is in everyone's interest to support the "coming out" of COCOM. This does not imply converting the COCOM agreement to the status of a treaty. Such a step is totally superfluous. It does imply continuing and accelerating the steps taken in recent years to increase staff, computerize operations, expand facilities, add military advice, and conduct more regular high-level meetings (which have been taking place now every two years since 1982).

Although some allied countries have resisted these steps, there is evidence that they, too, see the benefits of a stronger set of institutional arrangements in this area. The North Atlantic Assembly, for example, released reports in 1984 and 1985 which called for a new institution known as the Alliance Technology Agency to "establish the ground rules for intra-Alliance technology transfer . . . [and] also perhaps assume COCOM's duties."[14] At a conference in Brussels, Belgium, in February 1986, David Hobbs, director of committees and studies of the North Atlantic Assembly, called for a compromise on export controls which would establish "an agreed 'fence' around the Alliance so that fences inside it can be torn down." He noted that this would mean "making short-term sacrifices but would greatly facilitate technology sharing which should more than justify the sacrifices."[15]

A strengthening of COCOM should also entail more public analysis and discussion of COCOM activities and of national export control policies and procedures. It is noteworthy that this volume contains some of the only public analysis I know of dealing with British, French, Japanese, and German export control systems.[16] As these papers point out, there is little public discussion of export control issues in these countries and, relative to most other issues, also little in the United States as well. The University of Georgia has one of the few centers for systematic study of these issues in the United States, and the presence of four contributors to this volume from that university and the Georgia Institute of Technology testify to their invaluable role.

A stronger and more visible COCOM is not an end in itself; it is intended to serve three important objectives in achieving a "common market in export controls." The first is the continuous negotiation of the embargo list. List reviews are now held continuously but with only one-fourth of the list considered and acted upon in any one year. Hence items on the list are reviewed only once every four years. This may not be frequent enough, given the rapid pace of technological change. One benefit of enlarging COCOM capabilities would be to review all items every year. While this is a tall order, given the complexities of the list review, Western Europe and Japan should have an interest in this objective because it could contribute to more timely pruning of the list. In any case COCOM's staff must be enlarged even to keep pace with the current list review schedule.

Military advice, in particular, must be strengthened. The creation of the Security and Technology Experts' Meeting (STEM) in October 1985 is a start. This group meets informally outside COCOM to examine the military implications of various dual-use technologies. It refers its findings to the member governments rather than to COCOM. NATO is another potential source of military advice to COCOM but it has historically had no association whatsoever with COCOM. Some NATO members (e.g., France) object to establishing an economic dimension, which COCOM represents, to alliance deliberations. From one point of view this allergy in COCOM to systematic and adequate military advice is ludicrous. After all, how do you administer *strategic* export controls effectively without military advice? For the moment the requirement is to make STEM work effectively. If that proves difficult, the allies should establish direct military advisory capabilities within COCOM.

A second primary task for a strengthened COCOM is to harmonize export licensing and enforcement procedures. The papers in this volume suggest the diversity of licensing agencies and processes within the various COCOM countries. Britain and France have the most developed systems next to that of the United States. Germany and Japan, by contrast, have somewhat less systematic procedures. Indeed, the chapters on these two countries do not discuss at any great length exactly how licenses are processed, what follow-up paperwork is requested (e.g., import certification and delivery verification documents, or IC and DV, as they are called for short), and what intelligence and enforcement mechanisms prevail. The suspicion exists, whether justified or not, that these two countries are not as conscientious as others in implementing controls. Hanns-Dieter Jacobsen notes this suspicion especially in the case of East-West trade through Berlin, and Gordon Smith points out that the military agency in Japan is conspicuous in the control process by its absence. Much needs to be done to enhance official and public confidence that these countries, as well as Britain and France, take controls seriously.

The United States has been leading a more vigorous effort in COCOM to standardize procedures and enforcement. It should do so in closer consultation with the allies, especially Britain and France. It should avoid impetuousness, yet maintain pressure. For example, when the United States unilaterally introduced the G-COM license in 1985, COCOM was already considering a French proposal to eliminate follow-up paperwork (ICs and DVs) but retain individual licenses for low-technology items. The French were particularly annoyed when the United States eliminated the license as well as the follow-up paper requirement. Similarly, COCOM partners were unhappy when the United States unilaterally relaxed controls for China and only subsequently came to COCOM to multilateralize these measures. These mistakes on the part of the United States are unnecessary and harmful. They result in part from the untidiness and weakness of the decision-making process within the United States on export control and COCOM matters (see below). But in most cases they simply reflect inconsistent attention to COCOM.

To realize a "common market for export controls," harmonization measures are critical in two areas. First, the role of defense ministries in all COCOM countries must be strengthened to ensure greater confidence in East-West controls in these countries and, second, the general licensing arrangements, which facilitate trade and technology flows in West-West relations, must be standardized.

As the chapters in this volume detail, the role of defense ministries in the United States, Britain, and France (and Canada, which is not considered in this volume) have been considerably strengthened in recent years. It would appear from what Marie-Hélène Labbé tells us about the functioning in France of the "national procedure" and the Surveillance Committee (Comité de Surveillance) that the French Ministry of Defense has some of the same responsibilities in the French export control process that DOD has in the United States. Either defense ministry can object to certain licensing decisions and ensure that these decisions will be approved only at the highest levels of government, either by the prime minister in France or the president in the United States. In the French case the authority applies only to licenses for so-called "hard-core technologies," not products. In the U.S. case the authority is broader and, as William Root points out, the president has to report to Congress if he decides to overrule a Defense recommendation. Root and others feel this requirement goes too far. But this objection would seem to hold only in the case of a president who was perceived as weak on defense. Surely President Reagan, with his strong pro-defense policies, has not had to fear congressional reactions to a decision on his part to overrule Defense. Moreover, if the president required it, Defense would remove its objection. What Root deplores correctly is a weakness in the decision-making process in the White House. DOD's authority, as the French case suggests, is not excessive or unique. Bertsch and Elliott indicate that similar authority also seems to lie with the British Ministry of Defense. Although they are not certain of its role, the highly secretive Strategic Exports Working Party (SXWP), created in July 1983, includes the representatives of the Ministries of Trade and Industry and Defense, the Joint Intelligence Committee, MI5, MI6, and Customs. It apparently has a veto over any export control decisions.

There is no evidence that the defense ministry is involved in any significant way in Germany and clear evidence that it is not in Japan. This situation represents a serious gap in COCOM. Either defense institutions have to become more directly involved in these countries, or COCOM has to be equipped with adequate military advice to service the export control review process in these countries. Admittedly, Germany and Japan face greater internal political sensitivities on these matters than other countries. Nevertheless, they are now major producers and exporters of dual-use technologies and they will not succeed in enhancing the confidence of their COCOM partners in their export control systems until they involve their defense agencies in a more integral and systematic way. U.S. pressure and, if necessary, leverage are especially important to ensure this outcome.

The payoff for more comparable decision-making processes and controls toward the East is a standardization of general licenses for the free flow of goods and technology within the West. Eventually, all controlled items, except for the most sensitive, should be available within the West on the basis of general licenses. As the United States moves in this direction, it is critical that it harmonize these arrangements with the allies. As Labbé points out in her contribution, the United States strengthened its distribution license requirements before proposing this license for general use in COCOM. As a result, the United States sought to audit distribution license users in France (and Britain). France objected to this extension of U.S. extraterritorial authority. After extensive negotiations France introduced its own distribution license and agreed to audit imports (from the United States) as well as exports (to other countries) by these licenseholders. U.S. officials were allowed to accompany French inspectors. The friction in this case might have been avoided if the United States had come to France and its other COCOM partners while it was contemplating tightening of distribution license regulations rather than doing so unilaterally and generating unnecessary conflict.

The ultimate payoff for stronger and more harmonized East-West controls in all the COCOM countries is the relinquishment of extraterritorial controls especially, but not exclusively, by the United States. A well-kept secret of some of the COCOM allies is that they too, in certain circumstances and particularly with respect to third countries, exercise re-export authority not unlike the United States. The latter does it, of course, more extensively and openly, sometimes even flaunting it. The use of extraterritorial controls, however, is simply an expression of a lack of confidence in the other countries' controls. As the controls of all COCOM members are strengthened and standardized, re-export authority becomes redundant and disposable. With the G-COM license the United States has already eliminated re-export requirements for low-technology items exported to COCOM countries. The objective is to remove such requirements from all the new general licenses that are being considered for use within the West.

The third task COCOM faces is eventually extending COCOM-like controls to important non-COCOM countries that import COCOM technology and produce or may eventually produce comparable technology of their own. This, too, is an extraordinarily sensitive task and will require firm and consistent U.S. leadership. Some progress has already been made, as Mastanduno's article suggests, but much more is needed. The United States has to take the lead in negotiating these arrangements because the allies refuse to do it as a common COCOM project, arguing that this amounts to ganging up on the affected countries. On the other hand, bilateral agreements between the United States and these countries, which enhance licensing of U.S. but not other COCOM countries' exports, do nothing more than allow other COCOM countries to take away U.S. markets. The agreements must be simultaneously multilaterialized. Here the European and Japanese governments have to act in good faith. If the United States is willing to do the dirty work for them of negotiating with and pressing third countries for greater compliance, the allies must not only refrain from taking markets from U.S. firms, they must also be willing to impose common restrictions on COCOM items to these countries when they refuse to comply with minimal COCOM requirements. As the NAS study recommends in the paragraphs excerpted at the beginning of this essay, allowing non-COCOM countries to operate as islands of unrestricted trade activity toward the East "can only be prevented by strict community control of exports to the non-complying country." In short, all COCOM members, not just the United States, must be prepared on specific, presumably infrequent occasions to exercise leverage to strengthen controls in non-COCOM countries and thereby to make possible more unrestricted flows of Western technology to these countries. The payoff for non-COCOM countries is to receive the same treatment as COCOM countries, including the use of general rather than individual licenses and the lifting of re-export requirements.

Getting Our Own House in Order

The difficulties within the alliance alone are sufficient to make the achievement of a multilateral community of common controls a challenging task. But these difficulties are likely to prove insurmountable if the United States does not improve and strengthen its own decision-making process for export controls.

The editor of this volume, and the contributions of Steven Elliott, William Long, and John McIntyre not only elucidate the decision-making process in the United States on export controls but also set this analysis in a provocative conceptual framework. Previous work on U.S. export controls has been mostly descriptive. Elliott and Long deepen this work by arguing that export control decision making in the United States reflects a model of statism or executive dominance in which the executive branch maintains the capacity to use export controls for national security and foreign policy reasons despite growing congressional and business community concerns about the economic costs of such controls. Elliott notes several important exceptions when an alternative model of pluralism seemed to prevail—e.g., the Jackson-Vanik amendment in 1974 and the export license for Caterpillar in 1981. He also makes the intriguing argument that consistent national security uses of export controls, reflecting the requirements of U.S.-Soviet relations, may also be understood in terms of structural Marxism, the long-term campaign of a capitalist United States to curb the expansion of a Marxist Soviet Union. Nevertheless, the greater part of the evidence seems to confirm their statist interpretation. McIntyre's very detailed analysis also confirms that the export control system is "curiously resistant" to congressionally mandated change.

Within the executive, however, the distinction between statism and pluralism breaks down in practice. As McIntyre's chapter makes clear, pluralism is a characteristic of policy making inside the executive branch. Hence, congressional–executive branch conflicts, which appear to reflect the pluralist model, may also exist inside the executive branch and be interpreted in statist terms. Jackson-Vanik, for example, was an interbranch conflict which subsequently emerged within both the Carter and Reagan administrations. Under Carter the National Security Council sought to use export policy for leverage in U.S.-Soviet relations (as Senator Jackson sought to do earlier in Congress), while the State Department opposed such restrictions and even encouraged cooperation with the Soviet Union, particularly in energy (as Kissinger had sought to do under Nixon).[17] After an early period of relatively unanimous views on East-West trade, similar conflicts emerged in the Reagan administration between the Commerce and Defense departments. Indeed, the protagonist in Defense, as Gary Bertsch notes in his introduction to this volume, was Richard Perle, the former aid to Senator Jackson who originally helped engineer the Jackson-Vanik amendment in Congress.

Another way to view the U.S. policy process in recent decades is to focus on the substance of policy debates rather than the process within the various arenas. Since the early 1970s consensus on export controls within the United States has broken down. As McIntyre notes, "two sharply polarized views or schools of thought" have emerged in the U.S. Congress, the executive branch (though it is hard to find old-style détentists in the Reagan administration), and within the society at large. (These schools also exist within the alliance, as my article cited in note 1 relates.) These two points of view—labeled détente and denial for the sake of simplicity—have done combat with one another across executive branch–congressional lines. Indeed, a pattern of alliances between various executive agencies and congressmen and congressional committee staff has emerged. Interbranch rather than statist versus pluralist politics may be at work.[18]

The lack of consensus on substance has complicated and increasingly confused the process. Even after three years of debate to renew the Export Administration Act in 1985, Congress and the administration are proposing once again, in early 1987, far-reaching changes in U.S. export control policy. This ongoing debate has not yet curbed the decisive influence of the executive branch on these issues, although recent legislation chips away at executive discretion, particularly in the use of foreign policy export controls. Despite its dissatisfaction, Congress seems to be unwilling to assume primary responsibility for these matters and continues to delegate to the Executive as long as it can continue to complain. (I. M. Destler finds this pattern to apply to trade policy as a whole.)[19] This may be one of the phenomena accounting for the inertia of executive authority in this area.

What is needed are not new procedural solutions as much as a new consensus on some intermediate ground between détente and denial. I have tried elsewhere to offer such an alternative, called a deterrence approach, which would restrict strategic technology trade, permit market-determined levels of non-strategic trade, and limit foreign policy uses of export controls to foreign policy crises which are severe enough that the United States would be willing to use stronger political and even military measures if economic sanctions did not suffice to stop Soviet provocation.[20] The deterrence approach offers the best chance of stabilizing U.S. export control policy, a prerequisite, as Mastanduno argues, for effective U.S. leadership in COCOM.

The key objective has to be, as the NAS study declares, a balance between U.S. economic and security interests. In my judgment this balance cannot be achieved either by a continuation of the present situation, in which the economic and political inputs in the control process are significantly weaker than the defense inputs, or by a return to the pre-1979 process, in which the defense inputs were subordinated to economic and foreign policy objectives. Commerce is no more able to give full consideration to security objectives in export control cases than Defense is able to protect economic interests. Both agencies are needed, and both need to be strong—one representing economic arguments, the other defense considerations.

Currently Commerce is too weak; Defense is not too strong. Indeed, in the last few years Defense has demonstrated clearly that it is possible, with the right kind of priorities and incentives, to put into place a highly modern, computerized, efficient screening process for export control cases that needs cause few obstacles for American business competing in Eastern markets. DOD's system today, implemented through its Defense Technology Security Administration (DTSA), is a model, not an obstacle, for the Commerce Department. Since early 1986, in fact, Commerce has been streamlining its procedures. It needs to go much further. Eventually Commerce will have to commit the resources to employ higher-quality engineers and a fully computerized system like that Defense already has, or it will continue to abdicate to a stronger Defense capability in the review process. Defense has dominated by default in recent years, not because it has a statutory veto over export control decisions (which is how some analysts interpret paragraph 10 (g) (4) of the 1985 EAA). If Commerce and its congressional and business constituents are really concerned that the economic or competitiveness aspects of export control decisions are being neglected, they will see to it that Commerce is strengthened. The more political solution, of course, is to weaken Defense. That will only ensure that both economic and defense interests are badly served in the decision process.

If Commerce is strengthened, a second requirement is for the White

House to strengthen its own role in monitoring the competition between Commerce and Defense and intervening in a timely fashion to break deadlocks. The Reagan administration, despite all its interest in tightening export controls, has acted only sporadically to regularize decision making in this area (as, one could argue, in many other areas). In early 1987 the situation may be changing. The White House reportedly overruled Defense on a decision to export computers to Iran.[21] The White House cannot escape this responsibility. It is precisely the function for which the National Security Council and its staff exist. If this institution spent more time setting broad guidelines and refereeing inter-agency disputes, it would spend less time competing with and duplicating the activities of cabinet agencies.[22]

Finally, the State Department has a critical role to play in the U.S. process which it, too, is failing to meet. It cannot decide between Commerce and Defense on national control decisions; only the White House can do that. But it does have the responsibility to represent the United States in COCOM. Hence, it must be strong enough to communicate to COCOM on a timely basis new proposals the United States is considering (e.g., new general licenses), and it must lead the U.S. delegation on list reviews as well as coordinate the U.S. government review of COCOM exception requests made by other COCOM countries.

Currently State has insufficient clout to accomplish these tasks. For a short period of time in 1983–84 it was given more authority through the creation of a senior inter-agency group on technology transfer (SIG-TT), which the under secretary of state for security assistance, science, and technology chaired. State used this position effectively to resolve bitter disputes in the fall of 1983 over U.S. policy toward COCOM. But once the COCOM list review was completed in July 1984, State allowed the SIG-TT and its role to lapse. Into this void the Defense Department moved to assume a larger diplomatic role than it should have, often voicing independent opinions at COCOM and negotiating bilateral agreements with non-COCOM countries without adequate coordination with State. Again, however, the point is not to weaken Defense, but to strengthen State. If Defense is simply barred from negotiating independently and State is not strengthened, U.S. interests will suffer even more.

Corollary Initiatives to Insulate COCOM

The rationale and strategy outlined above for achieving a multilateral community of common export controls are practical and worthy of a new consensus to guide U.S. policy. To succeed, however, this approach will have to be accompanied by a number of other initiatives to insulate COCOM from unanticipated strategic, foreign policy, and economic crises. I have discussed these elements in detail elsewhere.[23] Here I simply enumerate them:

1. Closer relations between COCOM and NATO, where none currently exists, to ensure that export controls are consistent with strategic doctrine and are supported by the rationale of Western deterrence;

2. Some mechanism—again where none currently exists—within NATO, outside NATO, or through regular, high-level meetings at COCOM to anticipate and discuss foreign policy events, specifically various potential Soviet provocations (e.g., Poland in 1981), that might lead to the need for export restrictions for foreign policy reasons, thereby avoiding the need to discuss these highly controversial issues only in the heat of a crisis and insulating COCOM to some extent from the controversy of disputes such as the gas pipeline affair;

3. Continuous monitoring and analysis of East-West trade flows in the Organization of Economic Cooperation and Development (OECD) and the International Energy Agency (IEA) in order to assess dependencies and hence vulnerabilities associated with specific imports from the East (e.g., natural gas) or specific exports to the East (e.g., agricultural exports to the Soviet Union), thereby increasing mutual confidence among the allies that these flows do not represent a source of possible manipulation by the Soviet Union.

Summing Up

The differences between the United States and its allies in the area of strategic export controls are deeply rooted in the structure of alliance roles and geopolitical circumstances. While all the allies share a broad security interest in protecting the West's qualitative lead in advanced technology, they differ, and will always differ, on precisely what should be controlled and how it should be controlled. To contain these differences the alliance needs a more appropriate long-term goal and strengthened institutions for export controls. The objective of a common market in export controls or, as the National Academy of Sciences labels it, a multilateral community of common controls, is a realistic goal to strive for, even if it is never fully achieved. It establishes two consistent directions for U.S. and allied policies over the longer term: (1) harmonization of effective controls and enforcement of those controls vis-à-vis the East; and (2) liberalization of licensing procedures within the West. These two directions offer a true balance between economic and security interests within the alliance. The United States will tend to be the stronger advocate of security aspects. It will always be, in some sense, the defense department of the alliance. The Europeans and Japan, on the other hand, will emphasize economic aspects—the commerce department of the alliance, if you will. To reconcile these relative differences a stronger bargaining process is needed. COCOM must be strengthened administratively and technically and given regular high-level political attention.

Similar steps should be taken to ensure a better balance between security and economic interests in the export control process within the United States. A stronger White House role is needed to contain and expedite bargaining between security interests represented by the Defense Department and economic interests advocated by the Department of Commerce.

In sum, export control policy needs more consistent high-level attention in both the United States and the alliance. And it needs institutional arrangements that truly balance security and economic interests, not weaken either set of interests or both.

COCOM: An Appraisal of Objectives and Needed Reforms

William A. Root

Introduction

A common thread of the foregoing chapters is recognition that the effectiveness of controls depends on multilateral cooperation. Because of the diffusion of technology in the West, the United States cannot by itself deny transfers to the East. It is also apparent that controls have been continuously controversial.

This chapter examines the chief mechanism used to further the objective of cooperation with other countries, namely, the Coordinating Committee for Multilateral Export Controls, or COCOM. It takes a fresh look at COCOM objectives and at U.S. ways of working with (and sometimes against) other Western countries. It then proposes remedies for the controversies designed to improve rather than sacrifice security.

COCOM's objective is to harmonize the national controls of its members on exports to Eastern Europe in order to further Western security. Disagreements concerning the scope of the COCOM list and the U.S. exercise of extraterritorial jurisdiction have severely handicapped COCOM throughout its entire history. The situation is getting worse rather than better. Accordingly, it is timely to take a fresh look at the justification for the controls and the manner in which they are administered.

Seldom-considered security arguments *for* exports of militarily significant items to the USSR bring into question COCOM's reason for being. A program to transfer our highest technology to the East, as apparently intended by President Reagan's proposal to share Strategic Defense Initiative (SDI) technology with the Soviet Union, would make the entire concept of strategic export controls obsolete. However, there is no politically realistic prospect that controls will be eliminated in the near future. It is therefore useful to consider how to improve their administration.

This chapter will suggest reforms to (1) repeal the so-called Defense "veto," which makes it difficult for the U.S. government to reach balanced judgments concerning security arguments for and against controls; (2) remove U.S. license requirements for exports from other COCOM countries and also for exports from non-COCOM countries to the extent that the governments of these countries impose their own restrictions on the re-export of U.S.-origin COCOM-controlled items; and (3) open up the COCOM list review process to greater public scrutiny and participation.

The principal finding and the two principal recommendations of the 1987 export control study sponsored by the National Academy of Sciences (NAS) stressed the importance of an alliance approach to export controls:

> The panel finds that national security export controls, when developed and implemented on a multilateral basis, are an appropriate policy response. . . . Accordingly, the panel recommends that the United States exercise stronger leadership in building a multilateral community of common controls . . . which will involve further strengthening of the COCOM mechanism. . . . In the domestic context the panel recommends that executive branch policy decisions on national security export controls accord greater importance than they currently do to maintaining U.S. technological strength and the economic vigor and unity of the Western alliance.[1]

President Reagan's 1987 Competitiveness Initiative directed the cabinet to provide recommendations to achieve seven objectives aimed at improving export controls. Three of these also stressed the need for an alliance approach: first, seeking agreement with our allies to make export control procedures more uniform and enforcement more rigorous; second, seeking to level the competitive playing field while strengthening multinational controls; and third, working with our allies to further liberalize high-technology trade with China.[2]

Secretary of Commerce Baldrige's follow-up statement on the export control element of competitiveness includes four reforms that mention COCOM: first, a new general license for enterprises controlled by COCOM governments; second, an intent to extend this general license and other procedures now reserved for our COCOM partners to other Free World countries that establish adequate export control programs; third, elimination of licensing requirements for low-level exports to our non-COCOM trading partners in the Free World; and fourth, development of regulations to remove or eliminate prior U.S. authorization for re-exports into COCOM countries. The other seven are indirectly related to COCOM, and the list of eleven reforms is followed by a statement that the government "should always recognize that no export control program will be successful without international cooperation. For this reason, we have been hard at work with COCOM."[3]

All this attention—and most of the analyses in parts I–III of this book—suggest that even though COCOM has been around for almost forty years, we still don't have it quite right.

COCOM's Objectives and Major Policy Changes

COCOM was established in the late 1940s and early 1950s as a means to harmonize the national controls of its members (NATO countries less Iceland plus Japan) on exports to the USSR and its Warsaw Pact allies and to the People's Republic of China. These controls were designed to further the security of NATO and Japan. The objective of harmonizing controls designed to further Western security has continued unchanged since COCOM was formed.

During COCOM's almost forty-year history there have been major changes in only three policy areas. They involve contribution to economic potential, country differentials, and no-exceptions.

Economic versus Military Potential

Items of direct military application appear on COCOM's International Munitions and Atomic Energy lists (IML and IAEL). These lists seldom engender controversy.

Controlled items not having direct military use appear on International List I (IL I). The quantitative and watch lists—IL II, III, and IV— were dropped in the 1950s and 1960s because of practical difficulties in administering them. IL I, sometimes informally referred to as the industrial list, has been intensely controversial since its inception in 1948. Yet, with one major exception it has never been revised beyond tinkering at the margins. The one exception was the drastic reduction agreed to during list reviews of 1954 and 1958. Following the Korean War armistice in 1953, the allies insisted that items of more economic than military potential, such as oil and gas equipment, be decontrolled. Since then IL I has been limited to significant "dual-use" items, i.e., those having both military and civilian uses.

Controversy has continued concerning the proper scope of IL I. However, at no time during COCOM's history has any COCOM member sought decontrol of an item with the intent that this would result in a significant contribution to Soviet military potential.

Country Differentials

A China differential disappeared in 1957; a reverse China differential was introduced in 1985. COCOM policy on controlling exports to China changed in 1957 from a separate, much more restrictive list for China than for the USSR to an undifferentiated list. In 1985 COCOM rules were revised to permit many items requiring COCOM review for a Warsaw Pact destination to be approved for China as "administrative exceptions," i.e., at the national discretion of the government of the exporting country.

COCOM policy on controlling exports to Eastern Europe, excluding the USSR, has also vacillated but within a much narrower range than the large swings of the China differential. At times Poland, Romania, Czechoslovakia, and Hungary have been favored selectively and marginally in order to encourage their deviations from the Soviet foreign policy line or their domestic reforms. At no time has any East European country been treated more restrictively than the USSR.

No-exceptions Policy

Under COCOM "exception procedures" the committee may approve individual exports, as exceptions from the embargo, if the risk of adverse effect on Western security is judged to be slight. Prior to 1980 the United States had been trying unsuccessfully for decades to stop the creeping liberalization of COCOM controls through exception case approvals at progressively higher technical levels.

In March 1980, following the Soviet invasion of Afghanistan, COCOM acquiesced in a no-exceptions policy on exports to the USSR of COCOM-embargoed items not subject to "administrative exception" or to "favorable consideration" (the committee must review "favorable consideration" cases, but a member government may not object if the terms of the "favorable consideration" note are met). This was the first time COCOM had been used to further a foreign policy, rather than a security objective. Indeed, it was the only U.S. sanction against the USSR in response to the invasion of Afghanistan that the allies supported. They had little choice: the United States could discipline them by vetoing exception cases in COCOM. They have all reserved their sovereign rights to ignore U.S. vetoes, but they realize that COCOM cannot survive much of this. Nevertheless, they might have resisted by insisting that U.S. objections to specific cases be supported by findings of the likelihood of a use adverse to Western security, in accordance with usual COCOM exception procedures.

Poland was subjected by COCOM to a similar U.S.-initiated no-exceptions policy after the 1981 imposition of martial law in that country. This was more controversial than the Soviet no-exceptions policy, and the United States lifted this Polish no-exceptions policy in 1987.

During the 1980s very few Soviet cases have been submitted to COCOM for review other than those qualifying for "favorable consideration." The principle that COCOM will not approve exceptions from the embargo for the Soviet Union has therefore been firmly established. However, there have been substantial exports to the USSR of items nominally subject to COCOM control. This was because the COCOM list applied (and still does apply) to many products (especially personal computers and microcircuits) which are so widely available around the world that COCOM countries cannot effectively control their export, either from third countries or from their own territories.

COCOM History and the Conventional Wisdom

COCOM has undergone few major changes during its four decades of existence and has never been as effective as it might be. It has constantly operated in an environment in which the United States (1) insists that COCOM members seek to control items which are so widely available that massive unlicensed exports occur; and (2) gives a higher priority to bilateral pressure and unilateral extraterritorial controls than to nurturing opportunities for the development of closer multilateral cooperation in COCOM.

Considering the nonstop controversy engendered by these U.S. practices, it is quite remarkable that COCOM has survived. Its survival is attributable to the abiding conviction of its members that, assuming the need for some controls, a multilateral approach is necessary to reduce discrimination among commercial competitors which would result from uneven application of security export controls. It is still with us largely in spite of, rather than because of, U.S. leadership.

It is widely believed that COCOM controls were maintained with little difficulty in the 1960s, weakened during the 1970s, and have been strengthened during the 1980s. There is considerable evidence to counter each of these beliefs.

The strains of over-control, delays, and U.S. extraterritorial controls which plague the system today were also very much present in the 1960s. During this period COCOM was buffeted by strong criticisms of the United States for opposing decontrol of items which other members considered obsolete and for delays in acting on exception requests even while submitting a record number itself.

The United States reneged on an agreement made in the 1960s not to impose U.S. licensing requirements on exports from COCOM member countries which could be approved at national discretion under COCOM rules. Such U.S. extraterritorial measures are inconsistent with U.S. agreements in COCOM to permit national discretion. Nevertheless, the United States did not honor, and still has not honored, that undertaking.

During the 1970s East-West trade increased dramatically. However, only a tiny fraction of Western exports to the East were on the COCOM lists. The number and value of COCOM exception cases increased; but this was almost entirely due to U.S. refusal to remove from the list in a timely fashion low-performance computers with primarily civil applications. The COCOM list was reduced only marginally by the removal of a few obsolete items. During this period the usual practice of adding items based on emerging technologies continued.

Often-cited examples of weakening during the 1970s are largely irrelevant to an evaluation of COCOM. The U.S. Congress strongly criticized Western exports to the Kama River truck plant and a U.S. export to the USSR of ball bearing production equipment. General purpose trucks are not usually considered to be militarily significant, but some Kama River trucks showed up in Afghanistan. However, the Soviets could easily have met military requirements for such trucks from other Soviet plants that were not dependent upon imports from the West. The U.S. ball bearing equipment could not have made much difference since the Swiss had already exported the same equipment and the missiles which presumably benefited from the U.S. transaction had already been deployed.

The most militarily significant Western exports to the USSR of dual-use items during the 1970s were of semiconductor manufacturing equipment. Most of this equipment was exported in circumvention of the embargo rather than as a result of a policy to relax the embargo. In spite of massive Soviet imports from the West, the USSR still lags far behind the West in this area.

Far from strengthening COCOM in the 1980s, the United States has seemed determined to do all it can to weaken it. The most damaging development has been an acceleration of U.S. unilateralism, which has had a profoundly divisive impact on alliance export control cooperation.

The imposition in 1981 and 1982 of U.S. sanctions against European firms violating U.S. controls on re-exports of equipment for a Soviet gas pipeline has been by far the most significant development affecting COCOM in the 1980s. In pursuing a program ostensibly aimed at penalizing the USSR for its support of martial law in Poland, the United States lashed out against its principal Western European allies. U.S. sanctions against European firms were removed in November 1982. However, as pointed out by Martin Hillenbrand in chapter 12, deep resentment lingers. It will take years to recover from the resultant damage to the spirit of multilateral export control cooperation on which COCOM depends for its vitality and effectiveness. This is especially regrettable in view of the flawed arguments the United States used in seeking allied sanctions (see Hillenbrand chapter) and the greater impact of market forces than of sanctions on allied imports of Soviet gas (see chapter 10 by Bruce Jentleson).

The pipeline debacle was only the worst of many instances of U.S. unilateralism that hurt COCOM. Requiring specific allied export control measures in return for opportunities to bid on SDI contracts has been less abrasive but no more productive. If SDI is worth pursuing, seeking the most qualified bidders, wherever they are located within the alliance, should not be discouraged. When an allied country agrees to a new export control measure under pressure, effective administration is unlikely and the credibility of export controls in general suffers.

For example, it is unlikely that Germany will be able to enforce the controls on intangible technology imposed following SDI-related U.S.

pressure. Why should the United States expect Germany to do what the United States itself has not done? Under long-standing U.S. regulations on intangible transfers there have been no known prosecutions or investigations of suspected violations. There have also been no known efforts by U.S. entities to obtain nominally required export licenses except by organizers of international scientific conferences reacting to Department of Defense efforts to withhold Defense-financed research from foreigners.

As if to avoid discriminating in favor of Japan, the United States went out of its way in 1987 to discourage export control cooperation with that country as well. U.S. government actions to stop Japanese acquisition of U.S. high-technology companies (e.g., Schlumberger) for fear of a loss of U.S. control of the technology are counterproductive in both broad economic terms and narrower export control terms. If proceeds from the Japanese trade surplus were not invested in the United States the effect on the U.S. dollar would be devastating. If our export control mentality cannot tolerate Japanese financial control of a high-technology company located in the United States, we should logically find the presence of such technology in a Japanese company located in Japan even more intolerable.

Efforts to develop a close export control working relationship with Japan were also dealt a severe blow by U.S. sanctions against imports from Japan occasioned by violations of a semiconductor market-sharing agreement. COCOM can work effectively only if each member is reasonably satisfied that the other members are following the rules. It is difficult under the best of circumstances to understand what is going on in Japan, and the Japan-bashing going on in the United States in the late 1980s has compounded these difficulties.

Changes in activity within COCOM in the 1980s, other than the no-exceptions policy on exports to the USSR discussed above, have been minimal. The number of items added to the list has been about the same order of magnitude as in the 1960s and 1970s. Those which have been added have either been narrowly focused or have had more ambiguities than normal. Obsolete items have been removed at about the same, too slow, rate as in the 1960s and 1970s. Massive circumvention of the embargo is accelerating as it becomes easier for the East to acquire controlled items ever more widely available in the West, such as personal computers and microcircuits.

The national enforcement resources of COCOM member governments have increased dramatically. However, one major effect of this has been to broaden recognition of the obsolete nature of the controls being enforced. Another effect has been to sow confusion concerning export policy. For example, immediately after a Canadian firm was awarded one of twelve national prizes for increasing exports it was raided by Canadian Customs looking for a control violation.[4]

The COCOM process has also been weakened in the 1980s in the personnel area. Morale (and talent) have suffered badly in the Departments of State and Commerce and in the research area of the Defense Department as a result of efforts by the policy area of Defense to monopolize the action. Moreover, the most competent veterans on the COCOM international staff, who constituted the backbone of the organization, were forced by the U.S. government to resign their status as U.S. employees because they were also being paid by COCOM, even though the supplemental pay arrangement had been developed at U.S. initiative three decades ago.

In summary, U.S. measures in COCOM and related to COCOM over the past forty years, and especially during the 1980s, have profoundly weakened the organization. They have been, in large part, the exact opposite of a reasoned course of action to strengthen a voluntary cooperative organization.

Security Justifications for and against Export Controls

COCOM policy has its parallel in stated U.S. policy "to restrict the export of goods and technology which would make a significant contribution to the military potential of any other country or combination of countries which would prove detrimental to the national security of the United States."[5]

It has been assumed that exports which would make a significant contribution to the military potential of the USSR would be detrimental to the security of the United States and to the security of its NATO allies and Japan. This assumption is seldom questioned. Even the NAS study, by far the most thorough and thoughtful in recent years, does not examine the validity of the assumption.

The NAS panel was charged to "seek strategies to regulate the international transfer of technology . . . to balance the national objectives of national security, economic vitality, scientific and technological advance, and commercial, educational, and personal freedom."[6] The implication of the charge was that "national security" factors support controls, whereas "economic vitality, scientific and technological advance, and commercial, educational, and personal freedom" factors support the absence of controls. The panel was not asked to examine whether there are also "national security" factors that support the absence of controls. "National security" is not a precisely defined expression. In the context of export controls it has come to be associated with military considerations. But even this narrow view includes strategic as well as tactical matters.

This section of the chapter examines five factors qualifying under such a narrow interpretation of "national security," which arguably support a reduction or elimination of security controls on exports from the West to the Soviet Union. They are: (1) Soviet dependency on the West; (2) Soviet technical capability to meet military objectives; (3) sharing SDI technology with the USSR; (4) hotline communications and air traffic control; and (5) infeasibility of controlling widely available items. None of these factors is an unequivocally compelling argument to eliminate controls. But some of them question the security rationale for any control; some of them are strong arguments for reducing controls; and any one of them is adequate to warrant debate. Thus, security arguments for controls are by no means self-evident.

Soviet Dependence

The NAS panel judged that "Western security depends on the maintenance of its technology lead in military systems over potential adversaries. This lead can be sustained only through a dual policy of promoting a vigorous domestic technological base and impeding the outward flow to the Warsaw Pact of technologies useful in military systems."[7]

However, they also stated that the practice of obtaining new technology from the West "may have resulted in maintaining or perhaps even widening their lag [behind the West technologically] due to dependence on generally outdated Western equipment and technology."[8] Moreover, this was followed by a statement that it is "unlikely that an influx of Western technology will enable the Soviet Union to reduce the current gap substantially—as long as the West continues its own rapid pace of innovation."[9]

But, far from drawing the logical conclusion that controls do not prevent transfers detrimental to our security, the above was qualified by the following: "it would be foolhardy for the United States and the other technologically advanced countries of the West to facilitate Soviet access to militarily critical technology."[10] No explanation was given as to why it would be foolhardy to maintain and widen the gap by which the USSR lags behind the West technologically by encouraging Soviet dependence on exported Western technology, which is inevitably less advanced than that being developed in the West but not yet available for export.

Also not discussed was the impetus of controls toward Soviet development of a less vulnerable self-sufficiency. Trade-induced dependence would make them vulnerable to a cessation of Western trade and discourage them from the more expensive course of developing an indigenous, independent capability which could break new ground and make it possible for them to get ahead of us.

There is, of course, a risk that they would both import whatever they could from the West and develop their own, more advanced indigenous capability. But there are many instances where they have opted to copy the West (e.g., the IBM 360 computer and Intel 8080 microprocessor) rather than develop their own technology. The copying approach guarantees that they will remain behind the West, whereas the utilization of the same, or perhaps even less, effort to develop an indigenous capability might have put them out in front.

Even so, the dependency argument alone is unlikely to lead to complete abandonment of controls. Controls do make it more expensive for the Soviet Union to obtain what it wants from the West and also make it less likely that it will obtain the most effective type of technical assistance, namely, one-on-one working together. Thus, in the absence of controls one would logically expect Western technology transfers to reduce Western leads.

The issue would seem to be whether such a reduced Western lead would nevertheless be in the West's interest because a closer working relationship with the Soviets would increase their vulnerability to a subsequent cessation of Western inputs and discourage the development of a more costly but more independent and potentially more advanced Soviet indigenous capability. Such sophisticated reasoning would be difficult to apply to a specific case. But it would be reasonable for the dependency argument to be given weight when considering whether to decontrol "borderline" technologies. "Borderline" is meant as a description of those goods or technologies which are not clearly so widely available that they cannot be controlled but either have almost reached that point and could only be effectively controlled through immense effort and cost, or might increase our security if they were transferred, such as hotline communications or air traffic control.

Soviet capabilities

The NAS report also states: "Despite systemic difficulties, Soviet technical capabilities have successfully supported the military objectives of the USSR. . . . the Soviets have demonstrated an effective technical capability to meet their military objectives, which has been achieved by prioritizing the allocation of resources and key people to military R&D projects and to programs devoted to the acquisition of foreign technology and its incorporation into military systems."[11] The conclusion one would logically draw from this is that four decades of controls have had no effect because the USSR has been able, through indigenous capabilities plus imports (despite controls) to meet all its military needs. Yet the report neither draws such a conclusion nor explains why it should not be drawn.

As in the case of dependency, it is unlikely that controls will be completely abandoned because of a judgment that all Soviet military needs are being met anyway, either through indigenous means or through unpreventable circumvention of the controls. However, also as in the case of dependency, the Soviet capability argument should reasonably be given weight when considering whether to decontrol "borderline" items.

Sharing SDI Technology

The NAS report makes no mention of President Reagan's offer to share Strategic Defense Initiative technology with the Soviet Union, even though it would make little sense to continue to control lower-level technology while actively transferring our most advanced technology.

The case for sharing SDI technology has not been spelled out in detail. One argument might be that the USSR would then be better able to assist the United States and other countries in containing the effects of an accidental nuclear explosion or of an irrational nuclear attack by someone not under Soviet control. Based on experience to date, an accident or irrational act is more likely than a government-authorized nuclear attack.

SDI technology is not, and cannot be, purely defensive. Therefore one should consider the logic for our current unqualified policy of not sharing offensive nuclear strategic technology. Most knee-jerk reactions would be to assume that it would be irresponsible to transfer offensive capabilities to the USSR. However, this assumption is not self-evident. If our technology in their hands would permit them to destroy us ten times over rather than only two or three times, would that make us less secure? If our technology in their hands would permit them to target more accurately and thereby to use smaller bombs, that would arguably make us marginally more secure; although this would be a grim objective.

Thoughts such as those in the preceding paragraph, while over-simplified, are among those which have led to consideration of a Mutual Assured Protection (MAP), or Mutual Assured Survival (MAS), strategy (and SDI) as a substitute for a strategy of Mutual Assured Deterrence or Mutual Assured Destruction (MAD). Although the United States has not abandoned the deterrence strategy, it has clearly embraced survival as a goal.

If it makes sense to share SDI technology with the Soviets eventually, why not now? Sharing during early development stages could accelerate breakthroughs. If protection or survival proves feasible, the "mutual" in the designation of the strategy implies that both sides would possess the requisite technology. If the whole project came to very little, it is conceivable that the "very little" in the hands of the Soviets might be enough to avoid or contain an event, whether originating in the USSR or elsewhere, which would otherwise be catastrophic for us as well as for them. Even if SDI came to absolutely nothing in technical terms, the process of Americans and Soviets working together in an area of strategic technology would reduce the risk that one side or the other would push the button because of a miscalculation.

A judgment that it was in our interest to share strategic technology with the USSR now would assume not only the absence of logic for not sharing strategic technology under MAD, and the presence of logic for sharing strategic technology now under MAP or MAS, but also a judgment that the need to develop MAP or MAS should take precedence over concerns regarding conventional weapons technologies. Conventional weapons would be largely irrelevant in an all-out war between states who felt obliged to use their ultimate, nuclear weapons. Accordingly, it would seem unreasonable to give conventional weapons considerations a priority where such considerations might conflict with a preferred strategy to deal with the nuclear threat.

The implications of the proposal to share SDI technology with the USSR are far-reaching. These implications should be thoroughly and dispassionately debated. So far they have received almost no public attention.

Hotline Communications and Air Traffic Control

Specific areas where transfers might further our security rather than be detrimental to it include hotline communications and air traffic control (ATC). Transfers to the Soviet Union in these areas should not be undertaken lightly. Technologies that would make a hotline more secure would also improve the reliability of military command and control, and civilian ATC technologies are critical for air defense.

On the other hand, the survival of human civilization might depend on Soviet ability to communicate both internally and internationally after a nuclear accident. We have a long way to go to bring communications between the United States and the Soviet Union up to a performance level adequate to cope with a nuclear crisis. It takes about eight minutes to transmit one page of information over the facsimile equipment specified in the September 15, 1987, U.S.-USSR Nuclear Risk Reduction Centers Agreement. Better Soviet ATC capabilities might prevent future incidents such as the one involving KAL 007, or worse. Moreover, there must be military advantages to the West of Soviet military use of communications and ATC equipment with specifications known to the West.

Competition a few years ago between Sperry and Datasaab of Sweden to provide ATC systems for Moscow and Kiev is instructive. Sperry had difficulty obtaining a U.S. export license. Datasaab also needed a U.S. license because of U.S.-origin parts. Datasaab eventually obtained the U.S. license on condition that primary radar digitizers not be supplied. These digitizers were in fact supplied and Ericsson, the successor company to Datasaab, was fined. Efforts to exclude the digitizers, or to make them inoperable through controls on subsequent servicing were doomed to failure because the Swedish system could not operate without them and by that time Soviet civilian air traffic control was dependent on a functioning Swedish system. In other words, the original license condition to exclude them was simply not viable. Air defense concerns could have been more effectively met by encouragement of the Sperry system, which was not dependent on such digitizers. Alternatively, perhaps air defense concerns should have been overridden and the digitizers approved for the deal because they help to determine the altitude as well as the range of aircraft, and such information is sometimes critical for ATC in which we have an interest.

Feasibility of Controls

Commodities available from only a few suppliers or information known to only a few people can be controlled. However, commodities available in mass markets or information which is widely disseminated cannot be controlled, no matter how advanced or how militarily significant. The NAS report recognizes this in its recommendation to decontrol what it calls "technological commodities."[12]

Failure to recognize the impossibility of stopping transfers of widely available items has had a severe impact on the credibility of the entire export control system. In addition to futilely asserting a control on what cannot be controlled, the practice of over-control has also weakened controls on what can be controlled. It is not easy to ascertain precisely what falls in the category of too widely available to be controlled. Nor is it easy to define technically such products without inadvertently decontrolling other items of military significance which are not so widely available. The United States did not consciously set out to control widely available products; the present situation has evolved from the dynamics of COCOM list reviews.

If a dual-use product is not identified as strategic until after it has reached the marketplace there is great pressure to define the control item narrowly so as to avoid catching goods which already have substantial civil applications. This usually means that some areas of important actual or potential military applications remain uncovered. Accordingly, the United States has attempted to obtain COCOM agreement to list a product category before it reaches the market, as was done for computers and microcircuits in the 1960s. As civil applications have developed, the United States has responded to pressures for relaxation by agreeing to exclusions from the embargo in order to permit the sale of clearly non-strategic products. The process is very slow and, in a fast-moving technology, many virtually uncontrollable products remain nominally embargoed.

Often the decontrol process does not work at all if there are significant military uses and limited or no evidence of Soviet capability. But military uses and indigenous Soviet capability are irrelevant if the Soviets can easily circumvent the Western embargo and obtain all they want of a widely available item with minimal effort and delay.

Despite the above arguments, desires to avoid providing a military advantage to a potential adversary have kept broader controls in place than can be demonstrated clearly to be in our military security interest. The "better be safe than sorry" mentality has prevailed in the form of "when in doubt, control." But we would be more secure militarily without some of the present controls on dual-use items and perhaps without any of them. Public debate is especially urgently needed on the proposition that we might be more secure militarily without controls on nuclear defensive (SDI) technologies.

Reform Proposals

There are strong political inhibitions deterring the needed public debate concerning fundamental issues affecting the justification for controls. Therefore it is desirable to consider possible means to improve control administration.

At the time COCOM was established in the late 1940s, the United States had just embarked on the Marshall Plan to "save" Europe and Japan. Americans believed that the recipients of U.S. aid should be like them on such matters as open markets and anti-communism.[13] COCOM was an aberration from the U.S. free-trade philosophy. Although COCOM was definitely anti-communist, its multilateral cooperation approach did not fit in with the U.S. savior mentality.

With the immense U.S. international trade deficits of the 1980s it is painfully apparent that the United States is far less able to dictate COCOM control policies than it was in earlier decades. And even in the 1950s the United States was unable to have its way consistently in COCOM, as evidenced by the successful insistence of other member governments to reduce the list drastically in 1954 and 1958 and to abandon the China differential in 1957. But the U.S. government has not yet learned this lesson. The result is a control framework which is largely irrelevant to actual exports of listed items.

The principal U.S. government practices which must change in order to develop more realistic controls are the Defense "veto," extra-territorial controls, and secretiveness.

Defense "Veto"

The Export Administration Act authorizes the secretary of commerce to administer export controls in consultation with the secretary of defense. In specified instances Commerce may not overrule a Defense recommendation and even the president must inform the Congress if he does so:

> Whenever the President exercises his authority under this sub-section to modify or overrule a recommendation made by the Secretary of Defense [concerning disapproval of license applications for export to any country to which exports are controlled for national security purposes] or exercises his authority to modify or overrule any recommendation made by the Secretary of Defense . . . with respect to the list of goods and technologies controlled for national security purposes, the President shall promptly transmit to the Congress a statement indicating his decision, together with the recommendation of the Secretary of Defense.[14]

There have been instances where inter-agency disputes have gone to the president and he has decided against the Defense position. However, the president eventually backed down because Defense would not revise its recommendation based on factors brought out in the broader review and the president did not wish to notify the Congress that he had overruled Defense on a security matter. Defense working-

*

level staff realize that, if they hang tough, they can overrule the president.

From 1983 to 1985 controversy over the Defense "veto" delayed renewal of the Export Administration Act by two years. However, the question debated at that time was whether this procedure should apply to exports to Western as well as to Eastern destinations. Questions as to whether it should apply to exports to the East and to control list issues were not considered.

The NAS report refers to the disproportionate Defense influence on export control questions[15] and recommends stronger roles for the NSC and the Departments of Commerce and State to redress the balance.[16] That study does not address legislative issues such as the Defense veto.

A dominant Defense role makes sense in determining which technologies have significant military applications. However, a dominant Defense role does not make sense when considering whether to decontrol an item because of the effect of wide availability on the feasibility of control. The Departments of Commerce and State have more expertise on market availability than does the Department of Defense.

The Defense veto has had an especially adverse effect on the spirit of cooperation needed to sustain COCOM. It does not apply legally to the development of U.S. positions for COCOM deliberations. However, the environment in which Defense can overrule the president on closely related matters has often led to Defense-initiated U.S. action, or inaction, which pays scant heed to constructive views of other COCOM member or non-COCOM cooperating governments. The Defense "veto" should be repealed.

Extraterritorial Controls

The United States is the only country which asserts an authority to license exports from other countries. No other country recognizes the legal authority of the United States to impose such controls. For decades the United States has pressed its allies to impose parallel controls in COCOM and has pressed non-COCOM countries to cooperate with COCOM controls. Yet even when other countries do as requested, the United States has, in most respects, continued to impose its unilateral extraterritorial controls.

This has been particularly annoying to other COCOM member countries since, under pressure from the United States, they have agreed to control strategic exports themselves, on the basis of a COCOM list which cannot be liberalized unless the United States concurs.

In response to criticism from other countries of such U.S. extraterritorial measures, three U.S. extraterritorial controls have been relaxed: (1) Treasury recognizes allied commitments in COCOM by waiving the U.S. license requirement for a subsidiary in a COCOM country exporting a COCOM-listed item to a COCOM-proscribed destination; (2) Commerce recognizes COCOM procedures by waiving the U.S. license requirement for a transaction approved in COCOM and licensed by another COCOM member government; and (3) Commerce recognizes the low significance of items approvable at national discretion under COCOM rules by waiving the U.S. license requirement for the export or re-export of such items to most other Western countries.

But there has been as yet no action to remove U.S. validated license requirements in six other instances: (1) re-export from any country to a COCOM-proscribed destination of a COCOM-listed item approvable at national discretion; (2) export from any country to a COCOM-proscribed destination of a foreign-made, COCOM-listed product based on U.S. technology; (3) export by a U.S. subsidiary in a non-COCOM country of a COCOM-listed product to a COCOM-proscribed destination; (4) re-export from any country to any non-proscribed destination of a COCOM-listed item not approvable at national discretion; (5) re-export to any country from any country of an item controlled unilaterally by the United States (with a few exceptions); and (6) export by a U.S. subsidiary in any country of any item to North Korea, Cuba, Vietnam, or Kampuchea. Every one of these six continuing U.S. extraterritorial controls has caused major friction with other friendly governments.

The United States and Canada do not require validated licenses for exports or re-exports to each other of most items. But the United States waives such requirements for re-exports *from* Canada only if the commodity may be exported to the new destination under a general license. This is despite the Canadian undertaking to support U.S. export licensing policy by requiring a Canadian validated license for the export from Canada of any U.S.-origin item to any destination. This Canadian requirement puts U.S. exporters at a clear disadvantage, without any compensating gain from the elimination of U.S. re-export licenses.

The United States has maintained that U.S.-origin status continues even for items processed abroad or transferred within the importing country. However, the governments of most other countries do not recognize the U.S.-origin status of a commodity once it is in their territory, and even Canada considers that U.S.-origin status is lost if there is only a modest processing outside the United States. Firms in other countries sometimes try to honor U.S. conditions against re-export even if their governments do not. However, such cooperation is usually lost after processing (unless performed by a U.S. subsidiary) and is almost invariably lost even for unprocessed goods if they are retransferred within the importing country before being re-exported. Whether or not U.S. extraterritorial restrictions are effective, other cooperating countries regard the intrusive U.S. assertion of such controls as evidence of U.S. mistrust of their good intentions.

U.S. re-export license requirements contribute very little to controls. Once an item has left the country, the foreign importer, who is normally not subject to U.S. jurisdiction, is not inhibited by U.S. re-export controls unless he has signed an assurance not to divert. Such a consignee statement is not dependent on the license requirement. Indeed, U.S.-origin, COCOM-listed technical data may now be exported to other Western destinations without a validated license provided the U.S. exporter has obtained from the importer written assurance against diversion. The hundreds of thousands of license applications which COCOM member countries process for export to each other detract from the time available to process more significant transfers. Furthermore, by continuing to impose its controls even when the importing country accepts responsibility, the United States deprives itself of a logical means to encourage the expansion of cooperative arrangements.

The United States should remove validated license requirements for all exports from other COCOM member countries and for those exports from other cooperating countries which are subject to an import certificate whereby the government of the cooperating country accepts control responsibility.

Secretiveness

Governments are familiar with military applications of technologies, but less familiar with other technical matters that must be factored into COCOM negotiations. The requisite technical expertise to draw up rational COCOM embargo definitions is in the private sector. Other COCOM member governments recognize this. For example, U.K. efforts to involve industry in the COCOM process are described in Bertsch and Elliott's earlier chapter.

U.S. legislation requires negotiations to obtain COCOM agreement to publish the International List.[17] These negotiations were held successfully and COCOM has agreed that member governments may publish the list with "certain" editorial amendments. The British government has done so, editing out only language which is not relevant to an understanding of the coverage of the embargo. However, even the British publication was issued many months after completion of the 1982–84 review, omitted some notes and understandings (such as de minimus and servicing limits), and has not been revised to reflect agreements reached in the past two and a half years.

At present the U.S. government often requests that even technical advisory committees, which were established to provide a means for industry to advise the government, go into executive session when considering proposals to revise the list.

The NAS study recommends providing more information to the public about COCOM exceptions.[18] This would have to be done with care because of the need to protect commercially confidential information. The list itself, and proposals to change the list, contain no commercial or noncommercial confidential information.

The place to begin improving the COCOM list is to let those in the private sector with the capability to develop constructive recommendations know what it is. There is no substantive reason to deny public access to proposals to revise the list (although not necessarily the sources of the proposals). There is also no substantive reason to deny public access to U.S. government meetings at which these proposals are being reviewed from a technical point of view. Sensitive intelligence information can be factored into the process in closed meetings.

Accordingly, the United States government should publish and invite public comment on the substance of the COCOM list, the schedule of list reviews, and the substance of all proposals under consideration to revise the list. Public access should also be permitted at meetings considering list revision held by government-industry technical advisory committees, inter-agency technical task groups, and the U.S. delegation at COCOM.

Conclusion

Over the past forty years U.S. unilateralism has repeatedly strained the multilateral cooperation needed for effective security export controls. COCOM's survival is a testament to its resilience, but its effectiveness has suffered. Given its tempestuous history, it is reasonable to take a fresh look at its objectives.

Several potential security advantages of transferring Western high technology to the East deserve more attention than they have received. These include resultant Soviet dependency on the West, the importance to the West of high-quality Soviet hotline communications and civilian air traffic control, and the adverse impact of over-control on the credibility of the entire control structure. President Reagan's proposal to share SDI technology with the USSR could logically lead to a complete dismantling of controls.

It is unlikely that a radical change in export control policy will occur in the near term. In the meantime there is an urgent need to improve the administration of the control system so as to reinvigorate multilateral cooperative spirits. The most important U.S. steps in this direction would be repeal of the Defense "veto," removal of U.S. extraterritorial controls on exports from cooperating countries, and opening up the COCOM process to greater participation from the private sector.

Appendix
Glossary of Technical Terms
and Acronyms

Administrative exception note (AEN). A note attached to certain COCOM International List categories describing commodities that can be approved for sale to COCOM-proscribed destinations solely at national discretion.

Automatic licensing procedure. As mandated by the Export Administration Amendments Act of 1985, a requirement that individual validated license applications for most exports to COCOM countries must be approved automatically by the Commerce Department's Export Administration fifteen working days after filing unless the applicant is notified that more time (not to exceed fifteen additional working days) is required. At the end of the fifteen- or thirty-working-day period, the export is deemed to be licensed, even if no document of communication to that effect has been sent or received.

CEU. Certified end-user license.

CMEA or COMECON *(Council for Mutual Economic Assistance).* A regional group organized in 1949 by the Soviet Union to integrate the economies of Eastern Europe and to provide for national specializations.

COCOM *(Coordinating Committee for Multilateral Export Controls).* A Paris-based, informal organization formed in 1948–49 to coordinate Western efforts to control strategic exports to certain (mainly communist) countries. It consists of Belgium, Canada, Denmark, France, the Federal Republic of Germany, Greece, Italy, Japan, Luxembourg, the Netherlands, Norway, Portugal, Spain, Turkey, the United Kingdom, and the United States.

Commodity. Any article, material, or supply except technical data.

Commodity Control List (CCL), or U.S. Control List. The list of commodities under the export control jurisdiction of the Commerce Department's Export Administration.

Community of Common Controls. A proposed cooperative arrangement for trade in controlled commodities among Free World nations that share an expressed willingness to adhere to common or equivalent national security export controls.

Under such an arrangement licenses would be required (from the cooperating nation shipping a controlled commodity) only for the export of controlled commodities to nations not a party to the arrangement.

Consignee. The recipient of a shipment of commodities or technical data subject to national security export controls.

Continuous review. The process within COCOM by which one-fourth of the entries on the International List are reviewed each year on an ongoing basis and particular entries may be reviewed within any one-year period at the request of a member nation. Changes to list entries are published annually by member nations.

Country groups. Seven groups of foreign countries established by the Commerce Department for export control purposes. Canada is not included in any country group and is referred to by name in the Export Administration Regulations.

Critical technology. Technologies that would make a significant contribution to the military potential of any country and that may prove detrimental to U.S. national security. (Also referred to as "militarily critical technology"; see Militarily Critical Technologies List.)

Détente. A relaxation of previously tense relations among nations. Especially refers to the period of relaxed relations between the U.S. and USSR in the 1970s, when military competition was restrained and cooperation increased.

Distribution license. A special two-year license, without dollar value or quantity limits, authorizing the export of eligible commodities to approved consignees in specified countries. Distribution license consignees must be foreign distributors or users of the licensed commodity in Free World countries.

Diversion. Shipment of militarily significant dual-use products and technology to unapproved end users, either directly, through the export of controlled products without a license (i.e., smuggling) or indirectly, through transshipment using a complex chain of increasingly untraceable re-exports.

Dual-use. Technology or products that have both military and commercial applications.

EAA. See Export Administration Act.

EAAA. Export Administration Amendments Act of 1985.

EAR. Export Administration Regulations.

Embargo. A legal prohibition on commerce used as an economic weapon or sign of disapproval.

End use. The purpose or application for which controlled commodities or technical data will be used by the consignee.

End-user check. An investigation by officials of the Department of Commerce or Department of State to confirm that a consignee is reputable and is engaged in the business claimed in statements to licensing authorities.

End-use statement. A formal declaration by a consignee of the specific purpose or application for which controlled commodities or technical data will be used.

Espionage. Covert efforts to obtain illicitly—by theft, bribery, or blackmail—protected information or technology that is classified or of relevance to military systems.

Exception request. An application by a COCOM member, in support of an application by a domestic firm, seeking the approval of all member nations to permit the export of a commodity subject to COCOM controls to a proscribed destination.

Export Administration Act (EAA). The principal statutory instrument regulating the export of goods and technology from the United States. Exports are controlled for reasons of national security, foreign policy, and domestic short supply.

Export-Import Bank (Eximbank). U.S. financial institution designed to encourage foreign purchase of U.S. goods and technology through advances of credit to foreign purchasers.

Extraterritoriality. The assertion by the U.S. government that its export control regulations govern trade in U.S.-controlled commodities and technical data of U.S. origin outside the territorial boundaries of the United States. A source of much conflict within the Western alliance.

Farewell. The French intelligence community code name for a high-level Soviet official who provided France with extensive information on the scope, organization, and successes of covert Soviet technology acquisition activities in the West.

Favorable consideration. A category of items on the COCOM International List that by agreement among the members will be considered favorably for export to proscribed destinations, on a case-by-case basis, provided the proposed transactions meet certain conditions specified in accompanying notes.

Foreign availability. A state existing when a non-COCOM-origin item of comparable quality is available to adversaries in quantities sufficient to satisfy their military needs. Foreign availability may apply to items that COCOM-proscribed nations manufacture domestically or buy freely from uncontrolled sources.

Free World. In the context of export controls, nations not subject to the COCOM strategic trade embargo.

GATT. General Agreement on Tariffs and Trade.

G-CEU. General license, certified end user. See General license.

G-COM. General license, certain shipments to COCOM countries.

G-DEST. General license, shipments of commodities to destinations not requiring a validated license.

General embargo. Restrictions maintained through COCOM to prevent exports of certain munitions, nuclear, and dual-use items to proscribed destinations. Exceptions to the embargo are granted only for specific transactions on a case-by-case basis and must be approved unanimously in COCOM.

G-FW. General license for low-technology shipments to all Free World destinations.

General license. One of the two basic types of license (the other being a validated license) provided for by the Export Administration Regulations. A general license is an export license established by the U.S. Department of Commerce for which no application is required and for which no document is granted or issued. General licenses are available for use by all persons or organizations except those listed in and prohibited by the provisions of the Export Administration Regulations, supplement no. 1 to part 388; the licenses permit exports within the above provisions as prescribed in the regulations. These general licenses are not applicable to exports under the licensing jurisdiction of agencies other than the Department of Commerce.

Import certificate/delivery verification (IC/DV) procedure. A procedure sometimes used by the United States, other COCOM countries, Austria, and Hong Kong to monitor the movement of exports of militarily strategic commodities. When the IC/DV procedure is required by an exporting country for a specific transaction, an importer certifies to the government of the importing country that he will be importing specific commodities and will not re-export them except in accordance with the export control regulations of that country (i.e., the importing country). The government of the importing country in turn certifies to the exporting country that such representations have been made prior to the transaction. After the commodities have been shipped the importer's government certifies that the controlled items have been received by the designated consignee.

Individual validated license (IVL). Written approval by the Department of Commerce granting permission, which is valid for two years, for the export of a specified quantity of products or technical data to a single recipient. Individual validated licenses also are required, under certain circumstances, as authorization for re-export of U.S.-origin commodities to new destinations abroad.

International List I or Industrial List. The COCOM list of dual-use commodities and technical data that are subject to validated licensing requirements when proposed for export from COCOM countries to other nations.

Keystone equipment. Sophisticated devices essential to the successful operation or completion of manufacturing processes (e.g., process-control equipment and specialized machine tools).

Know-how. Knowledge and support relating to the design, manufacture, and other technical information necessary to achieve a significant development, production, or use (e.g., services, processes, procedures, specifications, design data and criteria, and testing techniques).

Letter of assurance. A written statement from the foreign recipient of restricted technical data certifying that the data will not be made available to proscribed nations.

Militarily Critical Technologies List (MCTL). A document originally mandated by Congress listing technologies that the Department of Defense considers to have current or future utility in military systems. It describes arrays of design and manufacturing know-how; keystone manufacturing, inspection, and test equipment; and goods accompanied by sophisticated operation, application, and maintenance know-how. Military justification for each entry is included in the classified version of the list.

Most favored nation (MFN). Term for countries whose exports can enter the United States at the lowest prevailing tariff rate. In practice, virtually all countries except some communist countries enjoy MFN status.

National discretion. A level of COCOM control under which some items on the International List, as indicated in administrative exception notes, may be licensed for sale to proscribed nations by one member country without the approval of the others.

National interest exception. A determination by the U.S. secretary of commerce, in accordance with section 12 (c) of the Export Administration Act of 1979, permitting the confidential disclosure of information obtained by the Commerce Department for consideration of or concerning export license applications.

National security export controls. Procedures designed to regulate the transfer of technology from one country to another in such a way as to protect militarily important technologies from acquisition by potential adversaries.

NSC. National Security Council.

PRC. People's Republic of China.

Proscribed countries. In terms of national security export controls: Albania, Bulgaria, Cuba, Czechoslovakia, Estonia, the German Democratic Republic, Hungary, Kampuchea, Laos, Latvia, Lithuania, the Mongolian People's Republic, North Korea, the People's Republic of China, Poland, Romania, the USSR, and Vietnam.

Re-export. The exportation of commodities or technical data from one foreign destination to another at any time after initial export from the country of origin.

Reverse engineering. Reproduction of a unique product based solely on examination and analysis of a sample of the product.

SDI. Strategic Defense Initiative.

Security and Technology Experts' Meeting (STEM). Group meeting informally outside COCOM to examine the military implications of various dual-use technologies.

Shipper's export declaration (SED). Any declaration required under regulations of the Department of Commerce and other U.S. government departments or agencies in connection with exports.

Strategic goods and technologies. Items designed especially or used principally for development, production, or utilization of arms, ammunition, or military systems; items incorporating unique technological know-how, the acquisition of which might give significant direct assistance to the development and production of arms, ammunition, or military systems; and items in which proscribed nations have a deficiency that hinders this development and production that they are not likely to overcome within a reasonable period.

Sunset provision. A clause mandating the periodic review and automatic termination of a COCOM export restriction unless its continued inclusion on the International List has been rejustified and agreed upon.

Table of Denial Orders (TDO). A list included in the Export Administration Regulations of specific individuals or organizations that have been denied export privileges, in whole or in part. Orders are published in full in the *Federal Register*.

Technical data. Information of any kind that can be used or adapted for use in the design, production, manufacture, utilization, or reconstruction of articles or materials. The data may take a tangible form, such as a model, prototype, blueprint, or operating manual (the tangible form may be stored on recording media); or they may take an intangible form such as technical know-how. Software is considered technical data.

Technological commodity. Mass-produced items that are marketed, distributed, and/or warehoused in large quantities for use by distributors and customers around the world. Most items that can be purchased from retail outlets on a cash-and-carry basis are also technological commodities. Examples of technological commodities currently subject to national security export controls are some personal computers and related peripheral devices, floppy discs, and microchips.

Technology transfer. The acquisition by one country from another of products, technology, or know-how that directly or indirectly enables a qualitative or quantitative upgrading of deployed military systems or the development of effective countermeasures to military systems deployed by others.

Third countries. Free World nations that are not members of COCOM.

Transshipment. The transfer, by a series of separately documented shipments, of controlled products through one or more countries en route to a final destination that may be a proscribed country. Initially, the final destination—and in later transactions the country of origin—are concealed to avoid export or re-export prohibitions.

Turnkey plant. A complete plant or production process where one has only to "turn the key" to make it fully operational.

Unilateral. Actions relating to national security export controls that are taken by only one nation.

U.S. Control List. See Commodity Control List.

U.S. Munitions List. A list of defense articles and services that was developed by the Department of Defense and is now maintained by the State Department with the advice of DOD. The International Traffic in Arms Regulations pertain only to items on the list and to directly related technical data, the export and re-export of which must be approved in advance by the State Department.

Validated license. One of the two basic types of license (the other being a general license) provided for by the Export Administration Regulations. A validated license is written approval issued by the governments of various nations granting limited permission to export controlled commodities or technical data, either on a single- or a multiple-transaction basis. In the case of the United States, validated licenses are also required, under certain circumstances, for re-export of U.S.-origin commodities to new destinations abroad.

Source: Adapted from National Academy of Sciences, *Balancing the National Interest: U.S. National Security Export Controls and Global Economic Competition* (Washington, D.C.: National Academy Press, 1987), pp. 278–84.

Notes

Chapter 1

1. For purposes of this study the Executive—the president, the appointed heads of the relevant executive agencies, and the bureaucracy—are contrasted with the role of Congress, interest groups, and individuals. For a similar approach to analyzing U.S. foreign economic policy see Graham Allison and Peter Szanton, *Remaking Foreign Policy: The Organizational Connection* (New York: Basic Books, 1976), pp. 64, 65; and Stephen Krasner, *Defending the National Interest* (Princeton, N.J.: Princeton University Press, 1978), pp. 11–12.

2. Although directed primarily at prohibiting the transfer of particular goods and technology from the West to the Eastern bloc, the export control system attempts to accomplish this end by licensing upward of 50 percent of all U.S. exports. Also, because the system is concerned not only with the direct transfer of proscribed items to U.S. adversaries, but also with the diversion of goods and technology through America's allies and neutrals, the system falls heavily on U.S. trade with allied and neutral countries, as well as trade with real or potential adversaries. By one estimate U.S. national security export controls currently cost U.S. exporters over $9 billion in lost sales and the U.S. economy 188,000 jobs. See generally, National Academy of Sciences, *Balancing the National Interest: U.S. National Security Export Controls and Global Economic Competition* (Washington, D.C.: National Academy Press, 1987).

3. Gary K. Bertsch, "American Politics and Trade with the USSR," in Bruce Parrott, ed., *Trade, Technology, and Soviet-American Relations* (Bloomington: Indiana University Press, 1985), pp. 244–45.

4. Ibid., p. 277.

5. Ibid.

6. See Joan Edelman Spero, *The Politics of International Economic Relations*, 2d ed. (New York: St. Martins Press, 1981), pp. 74–75. See also Raymond A. Bauer, Ithiel de Sola Pool, and Louis Anthony Dexter, *American Business and Public Policy* (Chicago: Aldine-Atherton, 1972); E. E. Schattschneider, *Politics, Pressures, and the Tariff*, (Englewood Cliffs, N.J.: Prentice-Hall, 1935); Stephen D. Krasner, "United States Commercial and Monetary Policy: Unravelling the Paradox of External Strength and Internal Weakness," in Peter J. Katzenstein, ed., *Between Power and Plenty* (Madison: University of Wisconsin Press, 1978), p. 87; and Krasner, *Defending the National Interest*, p. 343.

7. Most notable in this regard are works by Benjamin J. Cohen and Robert Pastor. Benjamin J. Cohen, ed., *American Foreign Economic Policy* (New York: Harper and Row, 1968), pp. 20, 21; and Robert Pastor, "The 'Cry-and-Sigh' Syndrome: Congress and Trade Policy," in Alan Schick, ed., *Making Economic Policy in Congress* (Washington, D.C.: American Enterprise Institute, 1983), pp. 160, 164, 188.

8. See, for example, Holbert N. Carroll, *The House of Representatives and Foreign Affairs* (Pittsburgh: University of Pittsburgh Press, 1958), pp. 4–8; Robert A. Dahl, *Congress and Foreign Policy* (New York: Norton, 1950), p. 58; James A. Robinson, *Congress and Foreign Policy-making* (Homewood, Ill.: Dorsey Press, 1962), p. v.

9. See Dahl, *Congress and Foreign Policy*, p. 58.

10. James G. March and Johan P. Olsen, "The New Institutionalism: Organizational Factors in Political Life," *American Political Science Review* 78 (September 1984): 742.

11. Lowi noted the limitations that attend case studies of institutional dynamics: "At the end of an empirical study, neither approach [pluralist or elitist] affords a means for cumulating the data and findings in coherent and logical abstractions with other findings; they merely provide the basis for repeating the assumptions of the beginning." Lowi concludes: "It seems to me that the reason for lack of interesting and non-obvious generalizations from cases and other specific empirical studies is clearly that the broad-gauge theories of politics are not related, perhaps not relatable, to observable cases." Theodore J. Lowi, "American Business, Public Policy, Case Studies, and Political Theory," *World Politics* 16 (July 1964): 686–87.

12. *Export Administration Act of 1979*, Pub. L. 96-72, 93 Stat. 503, 1979, later the *Export Administration Amendments Act of 1985*, Pub. L. 99-64.

13. Theda Skocpol has named these two characteristics "state autonomy" and "state capacity." By autonomy Skocpol means the ability of central state actors to formulate and pursue goals that are not merely reflections of the demands or interests of social groups, classes, or society. State capacity, in turn, refers to the ability of states "to implement official goals, especially over the actual or potential opposition of powerful social groups or in the face of recalcitrant socioeconomic circumstances." Theda Skocpol, "Bringing the State Back In: Current Research," in Peter B. Evans, Dietrich Rueschemeyer, and Theda Skocpol, eds., *Bringing the State Back In* (Cambridge: Cambridge University Press, 1985).

14. The author's forthcoming book provides a more in-depth study of the political and institutional aspects of U.S. export control policy.

15. Even U.S. export industries—the group with the most to lose from export controls —publicly supported strict export control legislation. See, for example, *Hearings on the Extension of Export Controls before the Senate Committee on Banking and Currency*, 81st Cong., 1st sess., 1949, pp. 70, 170, 186; and *Hearings on the Export Control Act of 1949 before the House Banking and Currency Committee*, 81st Cong., 1st sess., 1949, p. 171.

16. As one example of inter-branch harmony, during the four years immediately preceding passage of the 1949 Export Control Act six House committees considered the subject of export control. Only three of those committees, two of them study committees, explored the basic foreign policy implications of export control policy, and none raised serious doubts as to the need to control trade to the Eastern bloc. After the outbreak of war in Korea, the need for and approval of U.S. export controls was so apparent and widely shared in Congress that the House of Representatives devoted only two minutes to approving a two-year extension of the act. See *Congressional Record*, 81st Cong., 1st sess., February 17, 1949, 95, pt. 1:1368, 1370, 1379; and Carroll, *The House of Representatives*, pp. 59–64.

17. Krasner, *Defending the National Interest*, p. 12.

18. Senate Committee on Banking and Currency, *Export Expansion and Regulation*, 91st Cong., 1st sess., 1969.

19. Ibid.

20. There were, of course, differences of opinion within Congress on the need to reform U.S. export control policy. The minority Senate position did not perceive the need for the new legislation. Furthermore, the bill initially passed by the House contained only modest liberalizations.

21. The United States coordinates national security export controls with the NATO allies, less Iceland, plus Japan, through an informal multilateral group known as the Coordinating Committee, or COCOM. At the time of the 1969 act the United States controlled a much larger number of commodities than its COCOM allies.

22. The Nixon administration proposed an amendment that would have extended the expiration date of the Export Control Act until June 1973. S. 813, H.R. 4293, 91st Cong., 1st sess., 1969. During hearings on proposed amendments Acting Assistant Secretary of State Joseph A. Greenwald told the Senate committee, "[T]his isn't either the time or the circumstances to make what would be a major change." Senate Committee on Banking and Currency, Subcommittee on International Finance, *Export Expansion and Regulation*, Hearings, 91st Cong., 1st sess., 1969, p. 273.

23. See Raymond L. Garthoff, *Détente and Confrontation: American-Soviet Relations from Nixon to Reagan* (Washington, D.C.: Brookings Institution, 1985), pp. 90–91.

24. See Senate Committee on Banking and Currency, *Export Expansion and Regulation*, 91st Cong., 1st sess., 1969, p. 270 [hereinafter Senate Hearings], (statement of Joseph A. Greenwald, acting assistant secretary for economic affairs, Department of State); House Committee on Banking and Currency, *Hearings before the Sub-*

committee on International Trade to Extend and Amend the Export Act of 1949, 91st Cong., 1st sess., 1969, p. 118 [hereinafter House Hearings], (statement of G. Warren Nutter, assistant secretary, international security affairs, Department of Defense; and Ibid., p. 123 (statement of Kenneth N. Davis, assistant secretary for domestic and international business, Department of Commerce).

25. See Senate Hearings, pp. 274–75.
26. See House Hearings, pp. 119, 122.
27. Ibid., p. 128.
28. Ibid., pp. 116, 119, 121.
29. Under the 1969 act the president remained free to elect the purposes for which export controls were to apply and could avoid export restraints entirely by declaring that a control was implemented for foreign policy purposes, as opposed to national security reasons.
30. For example, the 1969 act required the president, before implementing national security controls, to determine that the commodities or data regulated were not readily available to such controlled nation or nations from other sources, *unless* the president determined that an export restriction was "necessary in the interest of national security" and reported his reasons to Congress. Export Administration Act of 1969, sec. 4(a)(2)(6).
31. James L. Sundquist, "Congress and the President: Enemies or Partners?" in Henry Owens and Charles L. Schultze, eds., *Setting National Priorities: The Next Ten Years* (Washington, D.C.: Brookings Institution, 1976), pp. 583–618.
32. The 1972 U.S.-Soviet Trade Agreement failed when Congress, led by Senator Jackson, linked the granting of most favored nation (MFN) status for the USSR to the improvement of human rights in the Soviet Union and in particular to the freedom of Jews and other minority groups to emigrate. Congress eventually passed what became known as the Jackson-Vanik amendment over the opposition of the Nixon administration, led by Secretary of State Kissinger. Its passage forced the Soviet Union to notify the U.S. government, by letter dated January 10, 1975, that it could not accept a trade agreement which included this amendment.

The MFN episode represents a qualification to the general characterization of executive-congressional relations with regard to U.S. export control policy. It appears to present a situation in which the Executive more enthusiastically sought expanded East-West trade and Congress pursued a more restrictive trade policy for ideological, i.e., human rights, reasons. Viewed another way, however, this episode is consistent with my general point that the Executive possesses a greater interest in national security as the goal to be served by trade, and that Congress is more responsive to domestic interest group pressures. In this instance, during the period of détente the Executive perceived American security interests as best served by limited rapprochement with the Soviet Union facilitated by expanded non-strategic trade. Congress, led by a senatorial minority that traditionally had been skeptical of East-West trade, and under the pressure of domestic human rights and religious groups, proved to be more responsive to these interest groups than the Executive.

33. Graham T. Allison, "Overview of Findings and Recommendations from Defense and Arms Control Cases," in appendixes of *Commission on the Organization of the Government for the Conduct of Foreign Policy* (Washington, D.C.: Government Printing Office, 1975), 4:21.

34. Not until mid-1973 did the Commerce Department significantly reduce the number of unilaterally controlled commodities listed on the Commodity Control List.

35. Congress explicitly strengthened its call for improved foreign availability assessment in the 1972 and 1977 amendments to the 1969 act. See *Export Administration Act of 1969 as Amended by Equal Export Opportunity Act of 1972*, Pub. L. 92-412, 86 Stat. 644, sec. 4(b)(2)(B), 1972; *Export Administration Amendments of 1977*, 95th Cong., 1st sess., 1977, p. 9.

36. An exhaustive analysis of export control administration by the General Accounting Office concluded: "[S]imply put, no single person was in charge of managing the foreign availability analysis. The task groups [of various executive agencies] dealt with the intelligence agencies on differing bases and there was some apparent breakdown in the use of the information that was available." Comptroller General, *Export Controls: Need to Clarify and Simplify Administration, Report to the Congress by the Comptroller General of the United States*, March 1, 1979, p. 29.

37. See 50 *Federal Register* 10503, March 15, 1985.

38. See Comptroller General, *Administration of U.S. Export Licensing Should Be Consolidated to Be More Responsive to Industry*, Report to the Congress by the Comptroller General of the United States, October 31, 1978.

39. House of Representatives, *International Economic Policy Act of 1972*, H. Rept. 1260, 92d Cong., 2d sess., 1972, p. 4.

40. *Equal Export Opportunity Act*, Pub. L. 92-412, 86 Stat. 644, sec. 103, 1972.

41. Ibid., sec. 105. As a result of this legislation, the secretary of commerce established the following seven TACs: Semiconductors; Semiconductor Manufacturing and Test Equipment; Numerically Controlled Machine Tools; Telecommunications Equipment; Computer Systems; Computer Peripherals, Components, and Related Test Equipment; and Electronic Instrumentation.

    Congress attempted to strengthen the TACs in 1974. See *Export Administration Act of 1974*, Pub. L. 93-500, 88 Stat. 1552, 1974.

42. See House Committee on International Relations, *Extension of the Export Administration Act of 1969*, 95th Cong., 1st sess., 1977, p. 601.

43. Comptroller General, *Administration of U.S. Export Licensing Should Be Consolidated to Be More Responsive to Industry*.

44. Senate, S. Rept. 890, 92d Cong., 2d sess., 1972, p. 3.

45. John R. McIntyre and Richard T. Cupitt, "East-West Strategic Trade Control: Crumbling Consensus?" *Survey: A Journal of East and West Studies* 25, no. 2 (Spring 1980): 81–108.

46. Comptroller General, *Export Controls: Need to Clarify Policy and Simplify Administration, Report to the Congress by the Comptroller General*, p. iii.

47. Gary K. Bertsch, "Western Strategic Trade Controls: Goals, Policies, Politics, and the Future," (paper presented at the Conference on East-West Economic Relations

in a Changing World Economy, Toronto, Canada, June 13–15, 1984). See also Robert E. Klitgaard, *National Security and Export Controls* (Santa Monica, Calif.: Rand, 1974), p. 15.

48. COCOM has no enforcement powers per se. It does have a subcommittee which develops coordinated procedures to deter violations and which exchanges information on national enforcement.

49. EDAC is chaired by the assistant secretary of state for economic and business affairs. This inter-agency committee consists of representatives from the State, Defense, and Commerce departments and from the Nuclear Regulatory Commission and the Central Intelligence Agency.

50. See House Committee on International Relations, *Extension of the Export Administration Act of 1969*, p. 310.

51. See *Report of the President's Task Force to Improve Export Administration Licensing Procedures* (draft), September 22, 1976, p. 112.

52. See House Committee on International Relations, *Extension and Revision of the Export Administration Act of 1969*, Hearings, 95th Cong., 1st sess., 1977, pp. 518–20 [hereinafter "House Hearings 1977"].

53. Office of Technology Assessment, *Technology and East-West Trade*, 1979, p. 139.

54. See for example, the results of a Hewlett-Packard study discussed at House Hearings 1977, pp. 505–18. Furthermore, license processing did not improve after passage of 1979 act. House Committee on Foreign Affairs, 98th Cong., 1st sess., March 1, 1983.

55. See Comptroller General, *The Government's Role in East-West Trade Problems and Issues*, Summary Statement of Report to the Congress by the Comptroller General of the United States, February 4, 1976, pp. 42, 43.

56. *Export Administration Act of 1969*, Pub. L. 91-184, 83 Stat. 841, sec. 3(1), 1969.

57. House Committee on Foreign Affairs, *Extension and Revision of the Export Administration Act of 1969*, 96th Cong., 1st sess., 1979, p. 259 [hereinafter "House Hearings 1979"], (statement of Mr. J. Kenneth Fasick, International Division, General Accounting Office).

58. House of Representatives, H.R. 2539, 96th Cong., 1st sess., 1979, sec. 6(b).

59. Ibid.

60. House Hearings 1979, p. 632.

61. See Senate, S. Rept. 169, 96th Cong., 1st sess., 1979, p. 8; House Hearings 1979, p. 132 (testimony of William A. Root, director, Office of East-West Trade, Department of State).

62. House Hearings 1979, p. 685.

63. Ibid., p. 687.

64. *The Export Administration Act of 1979*, Pub. L. 96-72, 93 Stat. 503, sec. 6(e), 1979.

65. Senate, S. Rept. 169, 96th Cong., 1st sess., 1979, p. 8.

66. Ibid.

67. Ibid., p. 9.

68. Ibid.

69. See Steven Elliott, "The Distribution of Power and the U.S. Politics of East-West Energy Trade Controls," in this volume.

70. It is noteworthy that phase one of the pipeline controls received little public or congressional support domestically. Before implementation of the second phase of controls, Representatives Paul Findley (R-Illinois) and Don Bonker (D-Washington) introduced legislation to terminate them. See "House Bill Would End Foreign Policy Curbs on Oil and Gas Equipment to the Soviet Union," *International Trade Reporter's U.S. Export Weekly* 412 (June 15, 1982): 404. (The bill was later revised to cover both phases of the pipeline controls.)

Congressional dissatisfaction grew with the passage of the second phase of pipeline controls. After six months of controls an increasing number of congressmen questioned their efficacy and noted the lack of allied support. Senator Charles Percy (R-Illinois), chairman of the Senate Foreign Relations Committee, stated that the embargo has had "no effect whatsoever on the Soviet Union." PBS, "MacNeil-Lehrer Report," June 21, 1982. Representative Robert Michel (R-Illinois) added, "We are aiming at the Soviet Union but we keep hitting the American worker . . . and we cannot persuade our allies to follow our lead." *Facts on File World News Digest*, June 25, 1982, p. 459.

71. In the face of extreme opposition from Congress, the business community, and a unified coalition of the NATO allies, and under the urging of his secretary of state, President Reagan reluctantly lifted the pipeline controls at the end of 1982.

The pipeline controls illustrate both the breadth and the limits on executive autonomy and discretion. On one hand, the Executive independently undertook this export control policy despite the strenuous opposition of the U.S. business community and America's allies, and pursued the policy without the encouragement of the American public and Congress to the point where the controls threatened permanent injury to the NATO alliance and may have exceeded the accepted jurisdictional bases of authority under international law. At this point the Executive retreated from the more extreme aspects of the controls, yielding ultimately to combined domestic, international, and legal constraints.

72. Effective March 20, 1984, and expanded September 28, 1984, Iran was made subject to a variety of foreign policy export controls; and effective April 3, 1984, foreign policy controls were imposed on the export to Iraq and Iran of designated chemicals that can be used in chemical warfare. The Reagan administration has also included Syria within these controls.

73. See U.S. Department of Commerce, Office of Export Administration, *Foreign Policy Report to Congress*, December 31, 1980.

74. "Banking Committee Members Hit Foreign Policy Controls Report," *International Trade Reporter's U.S. Export Weekly* 401 (March 30, 1982): 763, 765.

75. See, for example, the conclusory report sent by the Reagan administration to Congress in 1985—a report virtually identical to the one submitted by the Carter administration in 1980. U.S. Department of Commerce, Office of Export Administration, *Foreign Policy Report to Congress*, January 18, 1985.

76. Malcolm Baldrige, secretary of commerce, to the Honorable George Bush, presi-

dent of the Senate, June 23, 1982, reprinted in *Export Administration Annual Report for the Fiscal Year 1982*, p. 162.

77. Ibid., p. 169.

78. Ultimately the licensing review dispute between the Defense and Commerce departments was settled through an ancillary agreement; a memorandum of understanding between the two agencies provided for Defense Department review of individual licenses for West-West trade of selective countries and commodities.

79. See, *Washington Tariff & Trade Letter* 6 (March 17, 1986): 1.

80. Moreover, the Nicaraguan embargo decision was a clear demonstration of executive independence from Congress, domestic interest groups, and U.S. allies. The presidential embargo on Nicaragua carried out under IEEPA followed closely the congressional rejection of President Reagan's proposal for $14 million in military aid for Nicaraguan rebels. The president's actions provoked allied opposition announced during the ongoing economic summit in Bonn, strong opposition from other Central American nations, concern in the American business community —particularly from U.S. agricultural exporters—and, at best, a mixed reaction in Congress. The Executive, in announcing the Nicaraguan embargo, again ignored the Act's requirement that it consult with Congress.

Chapter 2

The author would like to thank the following people for their useful comments on earlier drafts: Christopher Allen, Arnold Fleischmann, Henry Nau, and William Root. Special thanks to Gary Bertsch and Lyn Randall for their help and encouragement.

1. Stephen D. Krasner, *Defending the National Interest: Raw Materials Investments and U.S. Foreign Policy* (Princeton, N.J.: Princeton University Press, 1978).

2. John Kurt Jacobsen and Claus Hofhansel, "Safeguards and Profits: Civilian Nuclear Exports, Neo-Marxism, and the Statist Approach," *International Studies Quarterly* 28, no. 2 (1984): 195–218.

3. David A. Lake, "The State and American Trade Policy in the Pre-hegemonic Era," (unpublished manuscript, 1985).

4. See William J. Long, "The Executive, Congress, and Interest Groups in U.S. Export Control Policy: The National Organization of Power," in this volume, n. 11.

5. Autonomy is defined in terms of the ability of the state to translate its own preferences into authoritative actions. See Eric A. Nordlinger, *On the Autonomy of the Democratic State* (Cambridge, Mass.: Harvard University Press, 1981), pp. 8, 19–20. Also see Skocpol's distinction between "state autonomy" and "state capacity." Theda Skocpol, "Bringing the State Back In: Current Research," in Peter B. Evans, Dietrich Rueschemeyer, and Theda Skocpol, eds., *Bringing the State Back In* (Cambridge: Cambridge University Press, 1985), p. 9.

6. Stephen D. Krasner, "Approaches to the State: Alternative Conceptions and Historical Dynamics," *Comparative Politics* 16, no. 2 (1984): 225.

7. Nordlinger, *On the Autonomy of the Democratic State*, p. 1.
8. Ibid., p. 7.
9. Ibid., p. 11.
10. Krasner, *Defending the National Interest*, p. 10. Nordlinger would dispute the inclusion of "institutions" in Krasner's definition because he believes that "the state must refer to individuals rather than to some other kinds of phenomena, such as 'institutional arrangements' or the legal-normative order." While institutional powers may be used in pursuing state preferences, "only individuals have preferences and engage in actions that make for their realization," in *On the Autonomy of the Democratic State*, p. 9.
11. Krasner, *Defending the National Interest*, p. 11.
12. Pluralists such as Bentley and Truman rejected the possibility of a truly national interest. See Arthur F. Bentley, *The Process of Government* (San Antonio, Tex.: Principia Press, 1949); and David Truman, *The Governmental Process* (New York: Alfred A. Knopf, 1951).
13. Krasner, *Defending the National Interest*, p. 28.
14. Ralph Miliband, *The State in Capitalist Society: The Analysis of the Western System of Power* (London: Quartet Books, 1973), p. 131.
15. Karl Kautsky, *The Social Revolution* (Chicago: C. H. Carr, 1902), p. 30.
16. Of course, it is not denied that policies which benefit the capitalist class or system may also benefit non-capitalist classes in society. The point is that the state will not pursue policies that are antithetical, for instrumental Marxists, to the capitalist class or, for structural Marxists, to the capitalist system.
17. Krasner, *Defending the National Interest*, p. 28.
18. For an overview of East-West trade in this period (from a pluralist perspective) see Gary K. Bertsch, "American Politics and Trade with the USSR," in Bruce Parrott, ed., *Trade, Technology, and Soviet-American Relations* (Bloomington: Indiana University Press, 1985), pp. 243–82.
19. *Export Administration Act of 1969*, Pub. L. 91-184, 83 Stat. 841, 1969.
20. Bruce W. Jentleson, "Pipeline Politics: The Complex Economy of East-West Trade," (manuscript), chap. 5, p. 10; published as *Pipeline Politics: The Complex Political Economy of East-West Energy Trade* (Ithaca, N.Y.: Cornell University Press, 1986). I used the earlier and fuller manuscript for research purposes.
21. "Moscow: Basic Principles of Relations: Text of the 'Basic Principles of Relations between the United States of America and the Union of Soviet Socialist Republics.' May 29, 1972," *Weekly Compilation of Presidential Documents* 8, no. 23 (1972): 944.
22. *Equal Export Opportunity Act of 1972*, Pub. L. 92-412, 86 Stat. 644, 1972.
23. Connie M. Friesen, *The Political Economy of East-West Trade* (New York: Praeger, 1976), p. 23.
24. Ibid., p. 24; and Joan Edelman Spero, *The Politics of International Economic Relations*, 2d ed. (New York: St. Martin's Press, 1981), p. 316.
25. This is not, of course, to say that the Nixon administration was unconcerned with the vote-catching potential of détente—far from it.

26. Peter G. Peterson, *U.S.-Soviet Commercial Relations in a New Era* (Washington, D.C.: Government Printing Office, 1972), pp. 3–4.

27. Henry A. Kissinger, *American Foreign Policy*, 3d ed. (New York: W. W. Norton, 1977), pp. 158–59. Of course Kissinger also recognized the possibility of using trade to further specific political objectives.

28. Senate Committee on Foreign Relations, Subcommittee on Multinational Corporations, *Multinational Corporations and U.S. Foreign Policy*, pt. 10, Hearings, 93rd Cong., 2d sess., 1974, p. 109.

29. Spero, *Politics of International Economic Relations*, p. 300.

30. See ibid.

31. Interestingly, as chairman of the Senate Foreign Relations Committee on Multinational Corporations and U.S. Foreign Policy, Senator Church was concerned about the influence of multinationals on public policy; he was also highly skeptical of the projected returns from the North Star and Yakutsk schemes. See Bruce W. Jentleson, "From Consensus to Conflict: The Domestic Political Economy of East-West Energy Trade Policy," *International Organization* 38, no. 4 (1984): 649.

32. Central Intelligence Agency, *The International Energy Situation, Outlook to 1985* (April 1977).

33. Central Intelligence Agency, *Prospects for Soviet Oil Production, A Supplemental Analysis* (July 1977).

34. R. Caron Cooper, "Opportunities for Oil Equipment Sales to the Soviet Union," *PlanEcon Report* 3, no. 7 (February 20, 1987): 6.

35. Jack Brougher, "1979–82: The United States Uses Trade to Penalize Soviet Aggression and Seeks to Reorder Western Policy," in U.S. Congress, Joint Economic Committee, *Soviet Economy in the 1980's: Problems and Prospects*, pt. 2, Joint Committee Print, 97th Cong., 2d sess., 1982, p. 448.

36. Samuel P. Huntington, "Trade, Technology and Leverage: Economic Diplomacy," *Foreign Policy* 32 (1978): 79.

37. Jimmy Carter, statement, "United States Export Policy," *Weekly Compilation of Presidential Documents* 14, no. 39 (1978): 1631–33.

38. Brougher, "United States Uses Trade to Penalize Soviet Aggression," p. 446.

39. Wilton E. Scott and Jack H. Ray, "The Role of Natural Gas in East-West Trade Relations," in Willard C. Matthias, ed., *Common Sense in U.S.-Soviet Trade* (Washington, D.C.: American Committee on East-West Accord), p. 52.

40. *Congressional Quarterly Weekly Report* 37, no. 40 (1979): 2218.

41. Export Administration Act of 1979, Pub. L. 96-72, 93 Stat. 503, 1979, sec. 6; also see Long, "The Executive, Congress, and Interest Groups," in this volume.

42. Jimmy Carter, address to the nation, "Soviet Invasion of Afghanistan," *Weekly Compilation of Presidential Documents* 16, no. 2 (1980): 26.

43. Brougher, "United States Uses Trade to Penalize Soviet Aggression," p. 428.

44. Ibid., pp. 431, 446.

45. Quoted in Jentleson, "Pipeline Politics," chap. 6, p. 14.

46. Brougher, "United States Uses Trade to Penalize Soviet Aggression," pp. 437, 452.

47. Jentleson, "From Consensus to Conflict," p. 652. Interestingly, from the instrumen-

tal Marxist perspective, the president was a former GE employee.

48. *International Trade Reporter's U.S. Export Weekly* no. 419 (1982): 673.

49. Quoted in Jentleson, "From Consensus to Conflict," p. 654.

50. *International Trade Reporter's U.S. Export Weekly* no. 420 (1982): 699.

51. Ibid. 19, no. 20 (1983), p. 745.

52. Bertsch, "American Politics and Trade with the USSR," p. 271.

53. *International Trade Reporter's U.S. Export Weekly* 2, no. 29 (1985): 920.

54. Ibid.

55. Testimony of John P. Hardt, Congressional Research Service, to Committee on Energy and Commerce, Subcommittee on Commerce, Transportation and Tourism, June 25, 1986, mimeo., p. 6.

56. *International Trade Reporter's U.S. Export Weekly* 4, no. 3 (1987): 64.

57. I opt for a narrow conception of the state which is internally cohesive rather than Lake's "disaggregated state" with its internal variations in autonomy. (Lake, "The State and American Trade Policy.") I am thereby better able to differentiate between statism and bureaucratic politics à la Allison and Halperin. See Graham T. Allison, *Essence of Decision* (Boston: Little, Brown, 1971); and Morton H. Halperin, *Bureaucratic Politics and Foreign Policy* (Washington, D.C.: Brookings Institution, 1974).

58. Seymour Hersh stresses the importance of the NSC in the Nixon-Kissinger administration. Rather than being a "clearing house for competing interests in the bureaucracy," or "an anonymous funnel," the NSC became a tool "to seize control, to tell the bureaucrats what to research and when to report." According to Hersh, the NSC was crucial to Kissinger's goal of centralizing executive institutional power within the White House. See Seymour M. Hersh, *The Price of Power: Kissinger in the White House* (New York: Summit, 1983), pp. 25ff.

59. It is recognized, of course, that the secretaries of defense and state do not always concur with the White House. In this event their roles as department heads, as opposed to White House appointees, may be said to be in the ascendant.

60. See Bertsch, "American Politics and Trade with the USSR," p. 266.

61. Peterson, *U.S.-Soviet Commercial Relations*, p. 3.

62. See Long, "The Executive, Congress, and Interest Groups."

63. Jentleson, "Pipeline Politics," chap. 5, p. 19. Emphasis added.

64. Steven Elliott, "Extraterritoriality and the Western Alliance," (paper presented at the Annual Meeting of the International Studies Association/South, Columbia, South Carolina, 1985), p. 11.

65. See Paula Stern, *Water's Edge: Domestic Politics and the Making of American Foreign Policy* (Westport, Conn.: Greenwood Press, 1979).

66. See, for example, Bertsch, "American Politics and Trade with the USSR."

67. Ibid., pp. 255–56.

68. "Light-switch diplomacy" was George Shultz's derogatory term for the Carter administration's use of trade to reward or punish Soviet behavior.

69. It is also recognized that U.S.-Soviet agricultural trade might have provided a more rigorous test of statism because the security aspects are of less importance in this

sector of East-West trade. Ideally, of course, one should apply the theoretical perspectives to a variety of sectors.

70. U.S. Department of Commerce, *1987 Annual Foreign Policy Report to the Congress*, January 1987, p. iii.

71. "Export controls lifted," *Soviet Business and Trade* 15, no. 12 (January 23, 1987): 1.

72. "US May Shortly Release Oil Technology to USSR," *Business Eastern Europe* 16, no. 2 (January 12, 1987): 9.

73. See Long, "The Executive, Congress, and Interest Groups."

74. Carter, "Soviet Invasion of Afghanistan," p. 26.

75. See David A. Baldwin, *Economic Statecraft* (Princeton, N.J.: Princeton University Press, 1985), pp. 263–66.

76. Senator Bill Armstrong (R.-Colorado), for example, criticized the Reagan administration's decision to decontrol energy equipment in 1987 as "selling the Soviets the rope to hang us." Quoted in *International Trade Reporter's U.S. Export Weekly* 4, no. 9 (1987): 294.

77. Krasner, *Defending the National Interest*, p. 32.

78. Michael J. Sodaro, "U.S.-Soviet Relations: Détente or Cold War?" in Angela E. Stent, ed., *Economic Relations with the Soviet Union: American and West German Perspectives* (Boulder, Colo.: Westview Press, 1985), p. 7.

79. Stern, *Water's Edge*, p. 203.

80. Ibid.

81. Since the Jackson-Vanik amendment is still operative, it might be argued that it represents an ongoing check on the state's autonomy. This would only be so, however, if state policy was to expand East-West trade to such levels that MFN status for Soviet exports became necessary.

82. Skocpol, "Bringing the State Back In," p. 17.

83. Krasner, *Defending the National Interest*, p. 32.

84. Ibid.

Chapter 3

1. Implementation is viewed as the bureaucratic process of interaction between the setting of goals (usually legislative) and the actions geared to achieve them. It is the "ability to forge subsequent links in the causal chain so as to obtain desired results." See Jeffrey L. Pressman and Aaron B. Wildavasky, *Implementation* (Berkeley: University of California Press, 1983), p. xv.

2. This paper does not deal with foreign policy or short-supply export controls. The 1979 Export Administration Act sharpened the distinction between foreign policy and national security controls. For a thorough review of foreign policy export controls see K. W. Abbott, "Linking Trade and Political Goals: Foreign Policy Export Controls in the 1970s and 1980s," *Minnesota Law Review* 65 (1981): 739–889.

3. Dual-use describes technology or commodities that have both commercial and military applications.

4. For a general overview of the literature on East-West trade and technology controls see U.S. Congress, Joint Economic Committee, *East-West Technology Transfer: A Congressional Dialog with the Reagan Administration* (Washington, D.C.: Government Printing Office, December 19, 1984), appendix 3, pp. 134–60. Gary K. Bertsch and John R. McIntyre, eds., *National Security and Technology Transfer* (Boulder, Colo.: Westview Press, 1983), pp. 222–45; E. Zaleski and H. Wienert, *Technology Transfer between East and West* (Paris: OECD, 1980), pp. 404–35.

5. See, for example, P. L. Ray, Jr., *Guide to Export Controls* (Chesterland, Ohio: Business Laws, 1985); John R. Liebman et al., *Export Controls in the United States* (New York: Law and Business, 1986); E. R. Berlack et al., *Coping with U.S. Export Controls 1986* (New York: Practicing Law Institute, 1986). For a literature review of economic-commercial studies, see, for example, H. Wienert and J. Slater, *East-West Technology Transfer: The Trade and Economic Aspects* (Paris: OECD, 1986); Morris Bornstein, *East-West Technology Transfer: The Transfer of Western Technology to the USSR* (Paris: OECD, 1985), chaps. 4 and 5 in particular.

6. Illustrative of this government-generated stream of research are Central Intelligence Agency, *Soviet Acquisition of Militarily Significant Western Technology: An Update* (Washington, D.C.: Central Intelligence Agency, September 1985); Office of the Under Secretary of Defense for Policy, *Assessing the Effects of Technology Transfer on U.S./Western Security: A Defense Perspective* (Washington, D.C.: Department of Defense, February 1985).

7. See J. R. McIntyre, "Controlling Dual-Use Strategic Technology in the Western Alliance: Problems and Prospects," *Crossroads*, no. 23 (May 1987); G. K. Bertsch, *East-West Strategic Trade, COCOM and the Atlantic Alliance* (Paris: Atlantic Institute for International Affairs, 1983); Stephen Woolcock, *Western Policies in East-West Trade* (London: Routledge and Kegan Paul, 1982); Phillip Hanson, *Trade and Technology in Soviet-Western Relations* (New York: Columbia University Press, 1981); John R. McIntyre and Richard Cupitt, "East-West Strategic Trade Control: Crumbling Consensus?" *Survey: A Journal of East and West Studies* 25, no. 2 (Spring 1980): 81–108; Gunnar Adler-Karlsson, *Western Economic Warfare, 1947–1969: A Case Study of Foreign Economic Policy* (Stockholm: Almqvist and Wiksell, 1968). See also A. S. Yergin, *East-West Technology Transfer: European Perspectives* (Beverly Hills, Calif.: Sage Publications, 1980).

8. For a source on the congressional oversight literature see George Holliday and John P. Hardt, *Export Controls: Issue Brief IB 75003* (Washington, D.C.: Congressional Research Service, November 19, 1985), and similar prior briefs.

9. Two doctoral dissertations have focused on this dimension: John R. McIntyre "Interagency Policy Implementation: The Case of U.S. Export Licensing of Advanced Technology" (Ph.D. diss., University of Georgia, 1981); and William J. Long, "The Role of the Executive and Executive Institutions in U.S. Export Control Policy" (Ph.D. diss., Columbia University, 1986). See also Gary K. Bertsch, "American Politics and Trade with the USSR," in Bruce Parrott, ed., *Trade, Technology, and Soviet-American Relations* (Bloomington: Indiana University Press, 1985); Gary K. Bertsch, John R. McIntyre, et al., "Decision Dynamics of Technology

Transfer to the USSR," *Technology in Society* 3 (Fall 1981): 409–22.

10. Robert E. Klitgaard, *National Security and Export Controls* (Santa Monica, Calif.: Rand, 1974), p. 6.

11. Jonathan B. Bingham and Victor C. Johnson, "A Rational Approach to Export Controls," *Foreign Affairs* 57, no. 4 (Spring 1979): 897.

12. Don Bonker, "Protecting Economic Interests," *Issues in Science and Technology* 3, no. 1 (Fall 1986): 97.

13. Carlo M. Cipolla, *Guns, Sails and Empires: Technological Innovation and the Early Phases of European Expansion, 1400–1700* (New York: Pantheon Books, 1965), p. 45.

14. Many legal scholars argue, however, that Congress alone regulates foreign commerce. See Louis Henkin, *Foreign Affairs and the Constitution* (New York: W. W. Norton, 1975), pp. 271–72. But since export control involves the president's foreign affairs and military powers, this analysis places too much emphasis on the role of Congress in this area. For example, under the International Economic Emergency Act the president has broad powers to prohibit certain economic activities. This authority, parenthetically, was used in 1976, 1983, and 1984 to extend the Export Administration Act when it lapsed for lack of congressional action. The Trading with the Enemy Act confers even greater discretionary powers on the president.

15. 50 U.S.C. App. 2401.

16. See Office of Technology Assessment, *Technology and East-West Trade* (Washington, D.C.: Government Printing Office, November 1979), pp. 111–26; Office and Technology Assessment, *Technology and East-West Trade: An Update* (Washington, D.C.: Government Printing Office, May 1973), executive summary, p. 1.

17. See *Commission on the Organization of the Government for the Conduct of Foreign Policy Report* [hereinafter Murphy Commission Report] (Washington, D.C.: Government Printing Office, June 1975), executive summary, p. 1.

18. Ibid., executive summary, p. 31.

19. Graham Allison and Peter Szanton, *Remaking Foreign Policy: The Organizational Connection* (New York: Basic Books, 1976), p. 14; I. M. Destler, *President, Bureaucrats, and Foreign Policy* (Princeton, N.J.: Princeton University Press, 1974).

20. Harold Malmgren, "Managing Foreign Economic Policy," *Foreign Policy* 6 (Spring 1972): 42, 56.

21. Stephen D. Cohen, *The Making of United States International Economic Policy*, 2d ed. (New York: Praeger, 1981), pp. 181–82.

22. H. Seidman, *Politics, Position, and Power: The Dynamics of Federal Organization* (New York: Oxford University Press, 1975), p. 152.

23. H. J. Berman and J. R. Garson, "U.S. Export Controls—Past, Present, and Future," *Columbia Law Review* 67 (May 1967): 805.

24. 50 U.S.C. App. 2024 (a), as amended.

25. Yuan-Li Wu, *Economic Warfare* (New York: Prentice-Hall, 1952).

26. Berman and Garson, "U.S. Export Controls," p. 805.

27. Klitgaard, *National Security and Export Controls*.

28. Office of Technology Assessment, *Technology and East-West Trade*, p. 112.
29. House Select Committee on Export Controls, *Investigations and Study of the Administration, Operations, and Enforcement of the Export Control Act of 1949, and Related Acts*, 87th Cong., 1st sess. (Washington, D.C.: Government Printing Office, 1961), p. 67.
30. Conversations with former Secretary of State Dean Rusk on the subject of export licensing. September, October, and November 1979.
31. Executive Order no. 12525 was signed by the president on July 12, 1985. It continues existing delegations of authorities contained in previous orders without significant changes.
32. William A. Root, "Trade Controls that Work," *Foreign Policy* 56 (Fall 1984): 80.
33. Ibid., p. 80.
34. Linda Melvern et al., *Techno-Bandits* (Boston: Houghton Mifflin, 1984), pp. 94–118.
35. *International Trade Reporter* 1, no. 13 (October 3, 1984): 366.
36. For details on the latest reorganization, see U.S. Department of Commerce International Trade Administration, Organization and Function Order no. 41-4, November 1, 1985. See also testimony of W. T. Archey, acting assistant secretary for trade administration before the House Foreign Affairs Subcommittee on International Economic Policy and Trade, October 10, 1985.
37. Department of Defense Directive 2040.2, "International Transfer of Technology, Goods, Services, and Munitions," January 16, 1984. Reproduced in Bureau of National Affairs, *International Trade Reporter* 20, no. 21 (February 28, 1984): 704–10.
38. Department of Defense Directive 5105.51, "Defense Technology Security Administration," May 10, 1985. In Department of Defense, *The Technology Security Program, A Report of the 99th Congress, Second Session* (Washington, D.C.: Department of Defense, 1986).
39. See M.S. thesis of A. J. Vogelsang on the role of Defense in technology transfer regulation, forthcoming, Georgia Institute of Technology.
40. *International Trade Reporter* 2, no. 30 (July 24, 1985): 952.
41. See Department of Defense, *The Technology Security Program*, p. 84.
42. An individual validated license (IVL) is a formal authorization issued by the Department of Commerce that permits the applicant exporter to ship a specified commodity to a named consignee in a particular country for a designated use. There are different types of validated licenses. A common one is the distribution license, which permits repeated transactions. The IVL is valid for two years from the date of issuance. IVLs can also include special conditions that the exporter must meet.
43. See Code of Federal Regulations, part 371, for details.
44. The CCL is made up of A and non-A items, which can be broken up as follows for analytical purposes:
    1. the A items include:
        a. COCOM-agreed items interpreted in the same manner throughout COCOM
        b. COCOM-agreed items interpreted more rigorously in the United States than

in other COCOM countries

c. Items coded A which, nevertheless, do not appear on the COCOM list

2. the non-A items include validated license requirements for:

a. all destinations (or all except Canada) for some security items; all nuclear non-proliferation (considered both security and foreign policy); and short supply items

b. all destinations except NATO, Japan, Australia, and New Zealand for crime control (human rights foreign policy)

c. only COCOM-proscribed destinations for some security items, e.g., the general industrial equipment and chemical baskets

d. specified destinations for specified items controlled for foreign policy purposes, such as items controlled for terrorism purposes, or truck production in the USSR

e. North Korea, Cuba, Vietnam, Kampuchea, Libya, and Nicaragua for virtually all items

45. For a detailed treatment of issues involving COCOM coverage and list review, see McIntyre and Cupitt, "East-West Trade Controls: Crumbling Consensus?" See also T. Aeppel, "The Evolution of Multilateral Export Controls: A Critical Study of the COCOM Regime," *Fletcher Forum* (Winter 1985).

46. P. Wallich, "The Dilemma of Technology Transfer," *IEEE Spectrum* (September 1982): 67.

47. Ibid., p. 67.

48. See Boyd J. McKelvain, "Determining Military Criticality," *Society* 23, no. 5 (July–August 1986): 19–21.

49. U.S. Department of Defense, Office of the Under Secretary of Defense for Research and Advanced Engineering, *An Analysis of Export Control of U.S. Technology—A DoD Perspective* (otherwise known as the Bucy Report) (Washington, D.C.: Government Printing Office, 1976).

50. Thane Gustafson, *Selling the Russians the Rope? Soviet Technology Policy and U.S. Export Controls* (Santa Monica, Calif.: Rand, April 1981), p. 4.

51. See David Buchan, "Technology Transfer to the Soviet Bloc," *Washington Quarterly* 7 (Fall 1984): 130–35.

52. National Academy of Sciences, *Balancing the National Interest: U.S. National Security Export Controls and Global Economic Competition* (Washington, D.C.: National Academy Press, 1987).

53. General Accounting Office, "Implementation of the Foreign Availability Provisions of the EAA," statement before the House Subcommittee on International Economic Policy and Trade, March 11, 1987.

54. *International Trade Reporter* 3, no. 42 (October 22, 1986): 1274–75.

55. National Academy of Sciences, pp. 116–17.

56. House Subcommittee on International Economic Policy and Trade, *Extension and Revision of the EAA of 1979*, part 1 [hereinafter House Hearings, part 1], 96th Cong., 1st sess. (Washington, D.C.: Government Printing Office, 1979), p. 293.

57. See McIntyre, "Interagency Policy Implementation," for a detailed look at how

agencies resolve differences and view their mandates.

58. See General Accounting Office, *Details of Certain Controversial Export Licensing Decisions Involving Soviet Bloc Countries*, #83-46 (Washington, D.C.: Government Printing Office, May 5, 1983), for actual case analyses illustrating the inherent problems of balancing costs and benefits in nine controversial Soviet bloc cases.

59. John V. Granger, *Technology and International Relations* (San Francisco: W. H. Freeman, 1979), p. 85.

60. McIntyre, "Interagency Policy Implementation," pp. 298–302.

61. Murphy Commission Report, 4:447.

62. See T. Carrington and R. S. Greenberger, "Bureaucratic Battle: Fight over India's Bid," *Wall Street Journal*, February 25, 1987, p. 1.

63. House Select Committee on Export Controls, *Investigations*, p. 173.

64. Statement of Congressman J. Bingham, in House Hearings, part 1, p. 545.

65. General Accounting Office, *Export Licensing: Commerce-Defense Review of Applications to Certain Free World Nations* (Washington, D.C.: Government Printing Office, 1986), p. 16.

66. As of 1985 this presidential directive meant that Defense would extend its right of review to the following countries: Austria, Finland, Hong Kong, India, Iraq, Lichtenstein, Libya, Malaysia, South Africa, Singapore, Spain, Sweden, Syria, and Switzerland. The product groups included computers, software, electronics and semiconductor manufacturing, measuring and calibrating equipment, micro- and integrated circuits, and carbon technology and related manufacturing equipment. This represents a quantum jump in the discretionary review powers vested in the Department of Defense. See General Accounting Office, ibid., p. 10.

67. McIntyre, "Interagency Policy Implementation," pp. 281–89.

68. *International Trade Reporter* 4, no. 8 (February 25, 1987): 255.

69. See Jon Zonderman, "Policing High-Tech Exports," *New York Times Magazine*, November 27, 1983, pp. 100–136; and T. W. Wu, "Export Enforcement: A National Priority," *Business America*, April 2, 1984, pp. 7–11.

70. "Corporate Export Compliance Programs," *Business America*, September 17, 1984, pp. 14–16.

71. Office of the Under Secretary of Defense for Policy, *Assessing the Effect of Technology on U.S./Western Security*.

72. National Academy of Sciences, p. 110.

73. The respondent firms included the following industries: aerospace, medical equipment, robotics, automated manufacturing, and instrumentation.

74. National Academy of Sciences, p. 116 and appendix C.

75. W. F. Finan, "Estimate of Direct Economic Costs Associated with U.S. National Security Controls," in National Academy of Sciences, appendix D.

76. *International Trade Reporter* 4, no. 6 (February 11, 1987): 179.

77. See section 10 (a) through 10 (f) of the 1985 amendments to the act, 50 U.S.C. App. 2409.

78. General Accounting Office, *Export Controls: Need to Clarify Policy and Simplify*

Administration (Washington, D.C.: Government Printing Office, March 1979), p. 64.

79. National Academy of Sciences, p. 113.
80. Ibid. This average time includes the mailing time to and from the Department of Commerce. It is, moreover, generally known that companies will not submit applications that are likely to be denied or that demand unusual amounts of time and staff resources to prepare. This further decreases average times. The National Academy of Sciences study does show some slight improvements in the process. McIntyre in 1981 found a mean processing time for a Free World license to be some thirty-five days, and the average processing time for a routine Eastern bloc application some eighty-eight days. McIntyre, "Interagency Implementation," pp. 333–36.
81. President's Commission on Industrial Competitiveness, *Global Competition: The New Reality* (Washington, D.C.: Government Printing Office, January 1985), 2:198.
82. McIntyre, "Interagency Policy Implementation," p. 34.
83. Murphy Commission Report, 4:21.
84. Cited in Melvern et al., *Techno-Bandits*, p. 256.
85. W. F. Finan and P. D. Quick, "Trading vs. National Security: Managing the Flow of Vital Technology," *New York Times*, March 28, 1987.
86. General Accounting Office, *Export Control Regulation Could Be Reduced without Affecting National Security* (Washington, D.C.: Government Printing Office, May 26, 1982).

Chapter 4

1. Reported in *Wall Street Journal*, March 5, 1981.
2. Testimony of E. D. Chapman, executive vice president, Caterpillar Tractor Co., before the Senate Foreign Relations Committee, Subcommittee on International Economic Policy, March 3, 1982, p. 2.
3. *Japan Times*, March 5, 1986, p. 7.
4. Hiroshi Oda, "Problems of Japanese-Soviet Economic Relations," *Review of Socialist Law* 11 (1985): 114.
5. From consultations with officials of Kanematsu-Gosho, Ltd.; Nissho Iwai, Corp.; and SOTOBO, March 3–4, 1986. Countertrade demands vary widely depending on the degree of competition with West European companies. Where there is strong competition for a contract, the Soviets press for more countertrade or company financing. When a piece of equipment is badly needed by the Soviets and there is little competition, Soviet officials do not demand countertrade.
6. The Foreign Exchange and Foreign Trade Control Law is available in English translation in *Japan Laws, Ordinances, and Other Regulations Concerning Foreign Exchange and Foreign Trade* (Tokyo: Chuo Chuppan Kikaku, 1986), pp. A1–A175.
7. Ibid., Cabinet Order 259, pp. A45–A47.
8. Ibid., p. A23.
9. The Export Trade Control Order is available in English translation in ibid.,

pp. C1–C163.

10. Consultation with Mr. Nishimia, commercial officer with the Japanese embassy, Washington, D.C., June 15, 1987.

11. Ibid.

12. Export Trade Control Order, Cabinet Order no. 378, December 1, 1949, as amended, p. C-61.

13. MITI Notification no. 28, January 25, 1985.

14. This was confirmed in consultation with Mr. Nishimia, June 15, 1987.

15. Cited in Robert A. Scalapino, The Foreign Policy of Modern Japan (Berkeley: University of California Press, 1977), p. 256.

16. From consultations with SOTOBO officials in Tokyo, March 4, 1986.

17. Iritani, "Policy to Prevent Outflow of U.S. High Technology," Finance (November 1983).

18. Office of Technology Assessment, "East-West Trade Policies of America's COCOM Allies: Japan," in Technology and East-West Trade (Washington, D.C.: Government Printing Office, 1979), pp. 173–202.

19. From consultations with SOTOBO officials in Tokyo, March 4, 1986.

20. Ibid.

21. Remarks by the Honorable Yoshio Okawara, ambassador to the United States, in Columbia, South Carolina, April 2, 1987.

22. Asahi Evening News, September 12, 1985, p. 3.

23. Christian Science Monitor, July 20, 1987, pp. 11, 13.

24. Christian Science Monitor, July 21, 1987, pp. 1, 36.

25. Christian Science Monitor, July 20, 1987, p. 13.

26. Ibid.

27. Ibid.

28. Christian Science Monitor, July 21, 1987, p. 36.

29. Ibid.

30. UPI (Tokyo), report of May 15, 1987.

31. Ibid.

32. Christian Science Monitor, July 2, 1987, p. 8.

33. Christian Science Monitor, July 17, 1987, p. 3.

34. Far Eastern Economic Review, July 9, 1987, p. 26.

35. Far Eastern Economic Review, August 6, 1987, p. 12.

36. Quoted in New York Times, July 29, 1987, p. 26.

37. AP (Tokyo), report of April 22, 1987.

38. Quoted in Ibid.

39. Christian Science Monitor, July 22, 1987.

40. Far Eastern Economic Review, August 6, 1987, p. 13.

41. Iritani, "Policy to Prevent Outflow."

42. See, for example, Nihon Keizai, February 8, 1984.

Chapter 5

1. See Christoph Royen, "Wirtschaftssanktionen in einer langfristigen westlichen Strategie für die Gestaltung des Verhältnisses zur Sowjetunion," in Friedemann Müller, ed., *Wirtschaftssanktionen im Ost-West-Verhältnis* (Baden-Baden: Nomos, 1983), pp. 214ff.; Hanns-D. Jacobsen, *Die Ost-West-Wirtschaftsbeziehungen als deutsch-amerikanisches Problem* (Baden-Baden: Nomos, 1986), pp. 288–95.

2. For a comprehensive overview of this early period see Gunnar Adler-Karlsson, *Western Economic Warfare 1947–1967* (Stockholm: Almqvist and Wicksell, 1968). The FRG's position during the same period has been analyzed by Michael Kreile, *Osthandel und Ostpolitik* (Baden-Baden: Nomos, 1978), pp. 36–74; Angela Stent, *From Embargo to Ostpolitik* (Cambridge: Cambridge University Press, 1981), pp. 20–92; and Claudia Wörmann, *Der Osthandel der Bundesrepublik Deutschland* (Frankfurt: Campus, 1982), pp. 12–35. For recent developments see Angela Stent, "Western Policies—The Federal Republic of Germany," in Reinhard Rode and Hanns-D. Jacobsen, eds., *Economic Warfare or Détente: An Assessment of East-West Economic Relations in the 1980s* (Boulder, Colo.: Westview Press, 1985), pp. 99–119.

3. Examples are the nonrecognition of the USSR by the United States before 1933, the containment concept of Kennan in 1947, the partial grain embargo of the Carter administration, and the boycott of the Moscow Olympics in 1980 after the Soviet invasion of Afghanistan. Most of these actions have been described in Gary C. Hufbauer and Jeffrey J. Schott, *Economic Sanctions Reconsidered: History and Current Policy* (Washington, D.C.: Institute for International Economics, 1985).

4. For a general discussion of this concept see Klaus Knorr, *The Power of Nations* (New York: Basic Books, 1975), pp. 7–8; and D. A. Baldwin, "The Power of Positive Sanctions," *World Politics* 24, no. 1 (1971): 19–36.

5. A prominent advocate of this approach has been Richard von Weizsäcker, then governing mayor of Berlin and now president of the Federal Republic of Germany: "If we succeed in developing cooperation step by step in the areas of science, technology, nutrition, pollution, transportation, energy and development policy, ultimately even arms control and the free movement of people could be possible." Richard v. Weizsäcker, "Nur Zusammenarbeit schafft Frieden," *Die Zeit*, no. 40 (August 30, 1983): 3. See also Hans-Dietrich Genscher, "Toward an Overall Strategy for Peace, Freedom, and Progress," *Foreign Affairs* 61, no. 1 (Fall 1982): 42–66.

6. The *Harmel Report* of 1967 calls for military security and cooperation with the East at the same time.

7. See Otto Wolff von Amerongen, "East-West Trade and the Two Germanys," in American Institute for Contemporary German Studies, ed., *West Germany, East Germany, and the German Question* (Washington, D.C.: American Institute for Contemporary German Studies, 1986), pp. 23–31. (Wolff von Amerongen is president of the Chamber of Commerce and Industry in West Germany.) Also see Jürgen Ruhfus, "Die politische Dimension der Wirtschaftsbeziehungen zwischen Ost und West," *Europa-Archiv* 42, no. 1 (1987): 1–10. (Ruhfus is state secretary of the West Ger-

man Foreign Office.)

8. The most recent West German export list was issued on March 10, 1987. It replaced the list of September 16, 1986.

9. This section is based on conversations with West German government officials. Also see Angela Stent Yergin, *East-West Technology Transfer: European Perspective* (Beverly Hills, Calif.: Sage Publications, 1980), pp. 28–40.

10. See Hanns-D. Jacobsen, *Security Implications of Inner-German Economic Relations* (Washington, D.C.: The Woodrow Wilson International Center for Scholars/International Security Studies Program, 1986).

11. See Office of the Military Government for Germany (U.S.), *Military Government Gazette—Germany—United States Area of Control*, September 21, 1949, pp. 20–26.

12. See "Allgemeine Genehmigung Nr. 2 (L) zur Interzonenhandels-verordnung vom 4, Juli 1980," *Beilage zum Bundesanzeiger*, no. 145 (August 8, 1980). The most recent list of goods which are under general license is the "Achte Änderung der Allgemeinen Genehmigung Nr. 2 (L) zur Interzonenhandelsverordnung," *Bundesanzeiger*, no. 135a, (July 25, 1985): anlage 1, pp. 4–21.

13. These penalties are determined by article 7 of law no. 53, which calls for "imprisonment not exceeding five years or a fine not exceeding DM 25,000, or three times the value of the property which is the subject matter of offence, or both such imprisonment or fine." See *Military Government Gazette*, September 21, 1949, p. 22.

14. This is said to be the conclusion of an unpublished CIA report, "Transfer of Strategic Technology to the Soviet Union from West Germany." See Jack Anderson, "High-tech Leaks," *Washington Post*, January 27, 1985, p. C7. The findings of this report have been rejected by the West German government. See Warren Getler, "Bonn Protests U.S. Pressure on East Bloc Trade," *International Herald Tribune*, June 25, 1986, pp. 1, 4.

15. These issues have been extensively discussed in Jacobsen, *Die Ost-West-Wirtschaftsbeziehungen als deutsch-amerikanisches Problem*. Also see Claudia Wörmann, *Osthandel als Problem der Atlantischen Allianz* (Bonn: Europa Union Verlag, 1986).

16. See Kreile, *Osthandel und Ostpolitik*, p. 58; Wörmann, *Der Osthandel der Bundesrepublik Deutschland*, p. 38; and Stent, *From Embargo to Ostpolitik*, pp. 93–126.

17. See Thomas A. Wolf, *U.S. East-West Trade Policy* (Toronto: Heath, 1973), p. 82.

18. For more on credits see Klaus Schröder, "Credit," in Rode and Jacobsen, eds., *Economic Warfare or Détente*, pp. 36–49; and Beverly Crawford, "Western Control of East-West Trade Finance," in this volume.

19. See Otto Graf Lambsdorff, "A Family Dispute to Settle Patiently," *International Herald Tribune*, July 31, 1982, p. 4; and Claude Cheysson, "The Pipeline Viewed from France," *International Herald Tribune*, June 18 and 19, 1982, p. 4.

20. The intra-German relationship itself is another example of the possibilities to employ such a strategy. In 1974, for instance, the FRG tied the granting of a high

ceiling for the interest-free "swing" credit line to a demand that the obligatory currency exchanges required of Western visitors to the GDR should be reduced. The GDR gave in and lowered the rates markedly. In 1982, however, when the GDR again raised the obligatory exchange rates unilaterally, a similar tying of the swing and obligatory exchange rates was no longer accepted by the GDR. In response the FRG used its "stick," lowering the credit ceiling. In the summer of 1985 a new agreement was negotiated and again the FRG was implicitly linking the granting of such credit subsidies to some kind of positive political response by the GDR. The FRG agreed to raise the ceiling of the swing to DM 850 million, whereas the GDR agreed to curb the access to West Berlin for immigrants from East Asian countries, who had become a factor of considerable concern for West German authorities. A second example of such positive linkage policies has been the willingness of the West German government to grant state guarantees for two large loans to the GDR in the summers of 1983 and 1984 in exchange for increased emigration and travel possibilities for East Germans to West Germany.

21. See "Transcript of Reagan Speech on the Soviet Union," *New York Times*, November 14, 1982, p. 7.

22. Angela Stent, *Technology Transfer to the Soviet Union: A Challenge for the Cohesiveness of the Western Alliance* (Bonn: Europa Union Verlag, 1983), p. 47.

23. U.S. Department of Commerce, *An Assessment of U.S. Competitiveness in High Technology Industries* (Washington, D.C.: Government Printing Office, 1983), p. 4.

24. See Michael Y. Yoshino and Glenn R. Fong, "The Very High Speed Integrated Circuit Program: Lessons for Industrial Policy," in Bruce R. Scott and George C. Lodge, eds., *U.S. Competitiveness in the World Economy* (Boston: Harvard Business School Press, 1985), pp. 176–84. Also, the Strategic Defense Initiative (SDI) can have a major impact on the international competitiveness of U.S. high-tech industries. See Hanns-D. Jacobsen, "High Technology in U.S. Foreign Trade Relations," *Aussenpolitik—German Foreign Affairs Review* 36, no. 4 (1985): 404–17.

25. A prominent example is Stuart Macdonald, "Controlling the Flow of High-Technology Information from the United States to the Soviet Union: A Labour of Sisyphus?" *Minerva* 24, no. 1 (Spring 1986): 39–73. This report was to be published by the OECD in Paris but the United States reportedly refused to accept the manuscript.

26. See Werner Hein, *Beschränkung des internationalen Technologie-transfers durch die USA: Studie im Auftrag des Bundesministeriums für Forschung und Technologie* (unpublished manuscript, 1984).

27. See Commission of the European Communities, *Analyse von Beschränkungen des Zugangs zu aussergemeinschaftlichen Informationsquellen—Abschlussbericht.* (Dr. Schulte-Hillen and B. v. Wietersheim, unpublished manuscript, 1986).

28. See Stuart Auerbach, "U.S. Eases Restrictions on Exports," *Washington Post*, February 10, 1987. These changes include removing restrictions on sales to government agencies in allied countries; easing controls on exports to other noncommunist countries, as well as on products widely available from other countries; and revising restrictions on sales of components and spare parts for U.S.-made

technology.

29. The publication of the National Academy of Sciences's study *Balancing the National Interest: U.S. National Security Export Controls and Global Economic Competition* (Washington, D.C.: National Academy Press, 1987) has been widely reported in West Germany.

30. See speech of State Secretary von Würzen from the Department of Economics on "Technologietransfer," before the Committee on Foreign Economic Relations of the European Parliament in West Berlin, November 20, 1986.

Chapter 6

This chapter is based largely on a series of interviews with government officials, corporate lawyers, and scholars involved in various aspects of French export control policy. The views expressed are those of the author and not those of any French agency. The author gratefully acknowledges the assistance of Steven Elliott in writing this chapter.

1. Renata Fritsch-Bournazel, "France," in Reinhard Rode and Hanns-D. Jacobsen, eds., *Economic Warfare or Détente* (Boulder, Colo.: Westview Press, 1985), p. 129.

2. Gérard Wild, "Les dépendances de la France dans ses relations économiques avec l'Europe de l'Est," *Courrier des Pays de l'Est* (October 1981): 3–11.

3. "Des échanges sous surveillance," *La Vie Française*, February 21–27, 1983.

4. Even the invasion of Afghanistan did not change the position of Pisar as a close adviser of President Giscard d'Estaing. See Jérôme Dumoulin, "Les Kremlinologues du Président," *L'Express*, May 24–30, 1980.

5. Valéry Giscard d'Estaing, "Foreword," to Samuel Pisar, *Coexistence and Commerce: Guidelines for Transactions between East and West* (Paris: Dunod, 1972).

6. Raymond Barre, interview in *Politique Internationale*, no. 27 (Spring 1985): 17.

7. David Buchan, *Incidences stratégiques du Commerce Est-Ouest* (Paris: Bosquet, 1985), p. 68.

8. Claude Lachaux, *Le Commerce Est-Ouest* (Paris: PUF, Que Sais-je? 1984), p. 78. In October 1987 the French government announced that Ratier-Forest had sold some machine tools to the USSR in the mid-1970s that were slightly beyond COCOM limits. The U.S. DOD claimed that these sales were partly responsible for the Toshiba violations. However, a U.S. official later said that the U.S. government was "reassured" that these exports "didn't contribute to enhancing the Soviet submarine program. See *Wall Street Journal*, October 21, 22, and 23, 1987.

9. John R. McIntyre and Richard T. Cupitt, "Multilateral Strategic Trade Controls within the Western Alliance," in Gary K. Bertsch and John R. McIntyre, eds., *National Security and Technology Transfer* (Boulder, Colo.: Westview, 1983), p. 154.

10. RAMSES 1981 Rapport annuel de l'IFRI sous la direction d'A. Bressand, p. 25.

11. Jean-François Poncet in *Le Monde*, January 8, 1980.

12. *Le Monde*, January 24–25, 1982; and *Le Point*, February 1, 1982, pp. 30–35.

13. *Le Nouveau Journal*, January 29, 1982. Barre was the only conservative leader to support the pipeline agreement.

14. *Le Monde*, January 30, 1982.

15. *Le Monde*, January 27, 1982.

16. *Le Monde*, July 23, 1982.

17. In France, "legislation" is text that has been approved by Parliament and has become "law." "Regulations" are texts issued by an administrative authority (the president, the prime minister, or ministers). Laws are always promulgated and published; regulations are not always published.

18. "Avis aux importateurs et aux exportateurs relatif aux produits et technologies soumis au contrôle de la destination finale," *Journal Officiel de la République Française*, Lois et Décrets, annexe au no. 282, December 5, 1985.

19. Christian Lamoureux and Claude Lachaux, "Le Contrôle des Exportations en France," in Claude Lachaux, Denis Lacorne, and Christian Lamoureux, eds., *De l'Arme Economique* (Paris: Collection les 7 Epées, 1987), p. 380.

20. Arrêté du 13 janvier 1986, arts. 80-1–80-3.

21. Ibid. Art. 80-4 deals with verification of the nature of the delivered goods, lists of responsible company individuals overseeing export controls, internal audit procedures to identify clients likely not to respect final destination control, training programs for people dealing with orders, and file maintenance.

22. Annexe au no. 282, *Journal Officiel de la République Française*, December 5, 1985, arts. 2–6, pp. 3–5.

23. Coincidentally, the SEC within France's Ministry of Industry appears to perform a similar function to the SEC within the U.K. Department of Trade and Industry. SERICS's U.K. equivalent would be the Electronics Application Division. See Gary Bertsch and Steven Elliott, "Controlling East-West Trade in Britain," in this volume.

24. See ibid.

25. Christian Lamoureux, "France et COCOM," *Le Figaro*, May 5, 1986.

26. See Marie-Christine Poncin, "La République Populaire de Chine et le Contrôle de la destination finale: de nouvelles opportunités pour les exportateurs français," *MOCI*, no. 713, May 26, 1986.

27. See Bertsch and Elliott, "Controlling East-West Trade in Britain."

28. Denis Lacorne, "The Management of Multilateral Embargoes: A European Perspective," (paper presented at the Annual Meeting of the American Political Science Association, Washington, D.C., August 28–31, 1986), p. 27.

29. Of course skeptics might also point out that INFOCOM could be used by the French authorities to make them wary of taking "doubtful" but important cases to COCOM.

30. See Bertsch and Elliott, "Controlling East-West Trade in Britain."

31. Philippe Deslandes, "La réglementation française des contrôles à l'exportation à des fins de sécurité," in Bernard Chantebout and Bertrand Warusfel, eds., *Le contrôle des exportations de haute technologie vers les pays de l'Est* (Paris: Masson, 1987), p. 45.

32. Françoise Haegel, "Le COCOM et les restrictions aux exportations de haute technologie vers les pays de l'Est," *Courrier des Pays de L'Est* (December 1985): 59.

33. P. Kristoffel, "Des exportations sous controle," *Le Figaro*, April 9, 1987.

34. Cited by Bertrand Warusfel, "Le contrôle des exportations stratégiques," *Revue de*

la Défense Nationale (February 1985): 112.

35. *Newsweek*, November 11, 1985, p. 23.
36. *International Herald Tribune*, February 6, 1985.
37. *International Herald Tribune*, October 12–13, 1985.
38. "France Looks for Loopholes in Pact on High-Tech Sales," *Financial Times*, August 10, 1984.
39. "Un document secret: les bons comptes de l'espionnage scientifique et technique," *Le Monde*, March 30, 1985; and "Soviet Data Show Arms Makers Rely on High Tech Spies," *International Herald Tribune*, April 1, 1985. For more details see Thierry Wolton, *Le KGB en France*, (Paris: Grasset, 1986).
40. *Newsweek*, November 11, 1985, p. 21.
41. *Le Figaro*, October 3, 1985.

Chapter 7

The authors wish to acknowledge the support of the University of Lancaster in the United Kingdom, the University of Georgia, a NATO Research Fellowship, and the Fulbright Program in facilitating the research upon which this chapter is based. Among other things, the chapter draws upon a series of interviews conducted and documents collected in Britain in 1980–81, 1984–85, and 1986. Finally, the authors would like to thank all those British officials, businessmen, and scholars whose support and cooperation facilitated this research.

1. See Michael Clarke, "Domestic Sources of British Policy towards the Soviet Union," (paper presented to the Conference on Domestic Sources of Western Policy toward the Soviet Union, Versailles, February 26–March 1, 1987), p. 4.
2. By the early eighteenth century Britain purchased over two-thirds of Russia's annual hemp exports and over half its flax. Along with timber these imports were so vital to British shipbuilding that it became an "accepted principle of British commercial policy" that maritime power and hence "national greatness and even independence" depended on this Anglo-Russian trade. M. S. Anderson, *Britain's Discovery of Russia, 1553–1815* (London: Macmillan, 1958), pp. 5, 125.
3. For the history of early Anglo-Russian relations see ibid., and Edward Crankshaw, *Russia and Britain* (London: Collins, n.d.).
4. George Kennan, *Russia and the West under Lenin and Stalin* (Boston: Little, Brown, 1961), pp. 225, 228.
5. See M. V. Glenny, "The Anglo-Soviet Trade Agreement, March 1921," *Journal of Contemporary History* 5, no. 2 (1970): 63–82. For Anglo-Soviet trade agreements more generally see K. M. Starr, "The Framework of Anglo-Soviet Commercial Relations: The British View," in K. Grzybowski, ed., *East-West Trade* (Durham, N.C.: Duke University School of Law, 1972), pp. 448–64.
6. "Trade Agreement between the United Kingdom and the USSR, March 16, 1921," p. 129. See Starr, "Anglo-Soviet Commercial Relations," p. 450.
7. Gabriel Gorodetsky, *The Precarious Truce* (Cambridge: Cambridge University Press, 1977), p. 11.

8. For more on COCOM see Michael Mastanduno, "The Management of Alliance Export Control Policy: American Leadership and the Politics of COCOM," in this volume.

9. *Mutual Defense Assistance Control Act of 1951*, chap. 575, 75 Stat. 644. This act stipulated that no American military, economic, or financial assistance would be supplied to any nation unless it controlled exports in line with U.S. policy.

10. Now Department of Trade and Industry (DTI).

11. "Long-Term Trade Agreement between the United Kingdom and the USSR, June 3, 1969," art. 1(2). See Starr, "Anglo-Soviet Commercial Relations," p. 454.

12. See Stephen Woolcock, "Great Britain," in Reinhard Rode and Hanns-D. Jacobsen, eds., *Economic Warfare or Détente: An Assessment of East-West Economic Relations in the 1980s* (Boulder, Colo.: Westview Press, 1985), p. 143.

13. The National Union of Seamen, for example, was critical of Soviet and Polish ships carrying cargo at dumping rates and therefore opposed subsidies to British construction of ships to be sold to Poland.

14. *The Times* (London), August 3, 1982.

15. Ibid., September 2, 1982.

16. Great Britain, S.I., 1985, no. 849. The COCOM lists of goods controlled for strategic reasons are not legally binding in the member states; they are only given legal effect through national legislation or executive order in each state. There have been several amendments to the 1985 order to reflect changes in the COCOM list made since the 1984 review.

17. U.K. unilateral controls include those on nuclear energy materials and equipment, which goes beyond its obligations under the COCOM agreements. They also include paramilitary items, aluminum and maraging steel alloys, and some dangerous chemicals. (The latter were added as a reaction to reports of Iraq's use of chemical agents against Iran.) It should be noted, however, that Britain's national controls are far less extensive than those of the United States.

18. Applications for all other destinations and for items on the Munitions and Atomic Energy Lists are dealt with by the DTI's Export Licensing Branch.

19. It is relatively unusual to have such "in-house" experts.

20. There is supposed to be little variance in the way in which different member states exercise national discretion. The perception of many British exporters, however, is that their government follows the American hard line much more closely than other COCOM members when exercising national discretion.

21. Interview, London, December 19, 1986.

22. Ibid.

23. The FCO is, of course, more involved in the multilateral licensing process because the British COCOM delegation is from the FCO.

24. The DESS is comparable to the U.S. Department of Defense's Defense Technology Security Administration (DTSA).

25. An exception to the preservation of public consensus came in a disagreement over whether or not to sell telecommunications equipment to Bulgaria. See Guy de Jonquieres and David Buchan, "Ministers split over Bulgaria phones deal," *Finan-*

cial *Times*, March 24, 1984.

26. "Britain Introduces Controls on Information Transfer," *Financial Times East European Markets*, July 22, 1983, p. 3. (SXWP has also been referred to as the Security Exports Working Party.) Also see Linda Melvern and Mark Hosenball, "US warns Britain to stamp on high tech smugglers," *Sunday Times*, June 19, 1983, p. 3. The British government heeded this warning by creating a special Customs-DTI team to stem illegal exports to the Soviet bloc; see David Buchan, "UK acts to plug technology leak," *Financial Times*, November 1, 1983, p. 42.

27. James Fallon, "British deny COCOM rift with US," *American Metal Market/Metalworking News*, August 8, 1983, p. 7.

28. COCOM has up to twelve weeks to reach a decision on export license applications for the Soviet Union and Eastern Europe, and eight weeks for the People's Republic of China (PRC). In practice, however, COCOM members can and do "stop the clock" to request additional information about the item, so exporters can often expect delays of six months or more.

29. This will only happen in the case of a small proportion of the total number of applications initially refused; the DTI will not waste its and the company's time on an application which has no hope of getting a COCOM exception.

30. These include Plessey, ICL, the Electronics Engineering Association (EEA), the Machine Tools Trade Association (MTTA), the Telecommunications Engineering Manufacturers Association (TEMA), the U.K.-U.S.S.R. Joint Working Group, and the 48 Group of British Traders with China.

31. Robert McCrindle (Conservative) quoted in "'Cut China Curbs' Call," *Daily Telegraph*, June 13, 1985, p. 8.

32. Great Britain, Public Records Office, *F/O 371/106007 M3424/120*, Confidential; R. S. Crawford, "Security Export Controls on Trade with the Soviet Bloc," November 16, 1953, p. 1.

33. For example, then Secretary of State for Trade and Industry Norman Tebbit stated: "like the Americans, we fundamentally believe in the need for proper controls on West/East sales of high technology equipment and know-how, so that both the West's strategic and security concerns are met and our vital technological advantage is maintained." *British Business*, October 28, 1983.

34. See "Strategic Trade: Better Read than Dead," *Economist*, August 6, 1983; and "Britain Introduces Controls on Information Transfer," *Financial Times East European Markets*, July 22, 1983, pp. 2–3.

35. Great Britain, Parliament, *Hansard's Parliamentary Debates*, 6th ser., vol. 80, 1985, cc. 117w, 565w. Serving military officers also attend when appropriate.

36. The United States is even more unusual in that its technical support in the 1980s seems to consist solely of Pentagon research staff whose major purpose, according to many COCOM members, is to provide the U.S. delegate with pro-control ammunition to shoot down exception requests and decontrol proposals under consideration.

37. Interview, London, September 1984.

38. David Marsh and David Buchan, "West Agrees on Computer Export Curbs," *Finan-*

cial Times, July 16, 1984, p. 1. The American official's statement presumably referred to the satisfaction of the governments concerned, because industry on both sides of the Atlantic was definitely not satisfied. Indeed, U.S. industry campaigned for changes long after the 1984 list review was completed.

39. David Buchan, "Export Curbs Apply to UK Telecom Gear," *Financial Times*, July 17, 1984, p. 1. Concern was expressed about British industry's dependence on U.S. technology during the 1981–82 pipeline crisis and efforts were supposedly made to reduce this dependence.

40. Linda Melvern, David Hebditch, and Nick Anning, *Techno-Bandits: How the Soviets Are Stealing America's High-Tech Future* (Boston: Houghton Mifflin, 1984), p. 135.

41. Linda Melvern and Mark Hosenball, "US Warns Britain to Stamp on High Tech Smugglers," *Sunday Times*, June 19, 1983, p. 3.

42. See, for example, U.S. Congress, Office of Technology Assessment, *Technology and East-West Trade: An Update*, Washington, D.C. (May 1983), p. 64. Cited in Melvern et al., *Techno-Bandits*, p. 131

43. The EETC and SBTC act as trade advisory groups to the British Overseas Trade Board and consist of businessmen and government officials. They thus facilitate communication between industry and the government through formal and informal channels.

44. Interview, London, December 19, 1986. Also see n. 30.

45. The minister for trade, Paul Channon, made this quite clear: "When considering the commercial implications of the strategic embargo my department has attached priority to consulting trade associations." Great Britain, Parliament, *Hansard's Parliamentary Debates*, 6th ser., vol. 72, 1985, c. 578w.

46. In a written reply to Parliament Channon said: "During the early stages of policy formulation it is sometimes necessary to consult on a confidential basis. I hope that it will be possible to consult more widely before too long." Ibid.

47. "Time to Stop the Latest US Sitcom," *Computer News*, February 21, 1985, p. 6.

48. Great Britain, Parliament, Third Report from the Trade and Industry Committee, Session 1984–85 (*Trade with China*) HC 509-II, paras. 209–15.

49. This is partly because renewal of the Export of Goods (Control) Order does not require parliamentary approval.

50. Because the SXWP is staffed by rather high-level government officials, and apparently meets infrequently, it is likely to reserve its attention for only the most problematic cases.

51. Interview, London, March 1983.

52. Expounding at length on these differences would take us far beyond our purpose here.

53. According to William Wallace, "It is part of the style of Whitehall that differences are muted and as far as possible concealed from the public eye, and that interdepartmental disputes are subject to the acceptance of an overriding common interest." *The Foreign Policy Process in Britain* (London: Royal Institute of International Affairs, 1975), p. 9.

54. "Official Handicap for UK High-tech Exports," *Financial Times East European Markets*, December 10, 1984, p. 1.

55. David Buchan, "UK Relaxes Rules for Sales of Technology to E. Europe," *Financial Times*, June 14, 1985.

56. Great Britain, Parliament, Second Report from the Foreign Affairs Committee, Session 1985–86 (*UK-Soviet Relations*), HC 28-II, p. 5.

57. Ibid.

58. Ibid., Q 695.

59. "Official Handicap for UK High-tech Exports," *Financial Times East European Markets*, December 10, 1984, p. 2.

60. "Security Export Control," *British Business*, supplement, June 14, 1985, p. ii.

61. Peter Montagnon, "Saving Face over Spot Checks on High-technology Imports," *Financial Times*, February 23, 1987.

62. For a highly critical account of American efforts to control British East-West technology transfer see Kevin Cahill, *Trade Wars: The High-Technology Scandal of the 1980s* (London: W. H. Allen, 1986).

Chapter 8

1. The standard work on the early years of COCOM is Gunnar Adler-Karlsson, *Western Economic Warfare, 1947–1967* (Stockholm: Almqvist and Wiksell, 1968).

2. The logic of a strategic embargo and its alternative, economic warfare, are examined in Michael Mastanduno, "Strategies of Economic Containment: United States Trade Relations with the Soviet Union," *World Politics* 37 (July 1985): 503–31.

3. NSC-68 is reprinted in *Foreign Relations of the United States, 1950*, 1: 234–92.

4. For information on the link between the Korean War and Western economic warfare see Michael Mastanduno, "External Weakness, Internal Strength: American Foreign Economic Policy and the Emergence of Alliance East-West Trade Strategy, 1947–1954," *International Organization* 42 (Winter 1988): 121–50. The argument put forth is at odds with the conventional interpretation, which emphasizes U.S. coercive power. See Adler-Karlsson, *Western Economic Warfare*.

5. A major alliance conflict over East-West trade policy—the 1962 pipeline crisis—did not involve COCOM in any significant sense. On the conflict see Bruce W. Jentleson, *Pipeline Politics: The Complex Political Economy of East-West Energy Trade* (Ithaca, N.Y.: Cornell University Press, 1986), chap. 4.

6. At the inception of COCOM in 1949 a Consultative Group (CG) was formed, composed of high-level policy officials from member states, that was expected to meet infrequently to resolve policy disputes and set broad guidelines for the export control regime. During the 1960s the CG was quietly disbanded (as a result of the unwillingness of the French chairman to convene), leaving the Coordinating Committee to carry out the routine, technical work of the embargo.

7. See the data presented in John R. McIntyre and Richard T. Cupitt, "Multilateral Strategic Trade Controls within the Western Alliance," in Gary K. Bertsch and John R. McIntyre, eds., *National Security and Technology Transfer* (Boulder, Colo.:

Westview Press, 1983), pp. 140–58.

8. Whereas COCOM controls involved 50 percent of traded goods during the early 1950s, by the early 1960s that figure was estimated at 10 percent. Statement of Douglas Dillon in Senate Committee on Foreign Relations, *East-West Trade*, Hearings, 88th Cong., 2d sess., March 13, 16, 23, and April 8–9, 1964, p. 220.

9. The examples are drawn from "Military Aspects of Export Control of Technology" and "Strategic Importance of Western Technology to the Soviet Bloc," (background papers prepared for the Miller Committee, March 1965), reprinted in the *Declassified Documents Quarterly* (1977), item 311A.

10. See Roger Carrick, *East-West Technology Transfer in Perspective* (Berkeley, Calif.: Institute of International Studies, 1978).

11. See William A. Root, "Trade Controls that Work," *Foreign Policy* 56 (Fall 1984): 61–80.

12. Adler-Karlsson, *Western Economic Warfare*, p. 94.

13. General Accounting Office, *Export Controls: Need to Clarify Policy and Simplify Administration* (Washington, D.C.: Government Printing Office, March 1, 1979), p. 9.

14. See John P. Hardt and Kate S. Tomlinson, "The Potential Role of Western Policy toward Eastern Europe in East-West Trade," in Abraham S. Becker, ed., *Economic Relations with the U.S.S.R.* (Lexington, Mass.: Lexington Books, 1983), pp. 105–25; and Gary Bertsch et al., "East-West Technology Transfer and Export Controls," *Osteuropa Wirtschaft* 26 (June 1981): 116–36.

15. The recent National Academy of Sciences report cites the need for such a comprehensive assessment to be made. See *Balancing the National Interest: U.S. National Security Export Controls and Global Economic Competition* (Washington, D.C.: National Academy Press, 1987), chap. 2.

16. See Central Intelligence Agency, "Soviet Acquisition of Western Technology," April 1982 and September 1985.

17. *Balancing the National Interest*, chap. 2.

18. A version of this approach is discussed in Hardt and Tomlinson, "The Potential Role of Western Policy."

19. The two approaches actually complement each other, and a comprehensive assessment of COCOM's effectiveness would require utilizing both.

20. See Carrick, *East-West Technology Transfer*. See also the contribution by William A. Root in this volume.

21. On the Toshiba diversion see the *New York Times*, June 12, 1987, p. A1. On the willingness of the Japanese government to respond by significantly bolstering national export controls see the *New York Times*, July 17, 1987, p. A1.

22. John Odell, *United States International Monetary Policy: Markets, Power, and Ideas as Sources of Change* (Princeton, N.J.: Princeton University Press, 1982).

23. Statement of Dean Rusk in House Committee on International Relations, Subcommittee on International Economic Policy and Trade, *Extension and Revision of the Export Administration Act of 1969*, Hearings, 96th Cong., 1st sess., February 15–May 9, 1979, p. 47.

24. The literature is vast. See, for example, Robert Keohane, *After Hegemony* (Princeton, N.J.: Princeton University Press, 1984); and Stephen Krasner, ed., *International Regimes* (Ithaca, N.Y.: Cornell University Press, 1982).

25. See the contribution by Bruce Jentleson in this volume.

26. See Henry Kissinger, *White House Years* (Boston: Little, Brown, 1979), pp. 150–55, 840, 1141, 1146–47.

27. See Jentleson, *Pipeline Politics;* and Gary K. Bertsch, "United States–Soviet Trade: The Question of Leverage," in Bertsch and McIntyre, eds., *National Security and Technology Transfer.*

28. See the statement of Assistant Commerce Secretary Stanley Marcuss in Senate Committee on Banking, Housing, and Urban Affairs, Subcommittee on International Finance, *Trade and Technology,* part 2: *East-West Trade and Technology Transfer,* Hearings, 96th Cong., 1st sess., November 28, 1979, pp. 59–70; and statement of Under Secretary of Defense William Perry in Senate Committee on Governmental Affairs, Permanent Subcommittee on Investigations, *Transfer of Technology to the Soviet Bloc,* Hearings, 96th Cong., 2d sess., February 20, 1980, pp. 52–53.

29. Thane Gufstafson, *Selling the Russians the Rope? Soviet Technology Policy and United States Export Controls* (Santa Monica: Rand, 1981), pp. 10–14; also see the statement of Edwin Speaker, Defense Intelligence Agency, in House Committee on International Relations, Subcommittee on International Trade and Commerce, *Export Licensing of Advanced Technology: A Review,* part 2, Hearings, 94th Cong., 2d sess., April 12, 1976, p. 18.

30. General Accounting Office, *Details of Certain Controversial Export Licensing Decisions Involving Soviet Bloc Countries* (Washington, D.C.: Government Printing Office, May 5, 1983).

31. The argument is made most forcefully in the Bucy Report. See Defense Science Board Task Force, *An Analysis of Export Control of United States Technology: A DOD Perspective* (Washington, D.C.: Office of the Director of Defense Research and Engineering, 1976).

32. Statement of Jack Vorona, Defense Intelligence Agency, in Senate Committee on Governmental Affairs, Permanent Subcommittee on Investigations, *Transfer of United States High Technology to the Soviet Union and Soviet Bloc Nations,* Hearings, 97th Cong., 2d sess., May 4–6, 11–12, 1982, p. 118.

33. Office of Technology Assessment, *Technology and East-West Trade* (Washington, D.C.: Government Printing Office, 1979), p. 167.

34. William Root points out, for example, that end-use determinations were mostly used for low-level equipment but seldom for know-how. Personal correspondence with the author, April 15, 1987.

35. This view was expressed by a European official long associated with COCOM. Interview, Bundesministerium für Wirtschaft, Bonn, July 8, 1982.

36. For example, in 1977 Japan applied to COCOM to sell three advanced computers to China after, according to Japanese government officials, the United States submitted a similar request. *Japan Times,* February 6, 1977.

37. OTA, *Technology and East-West Trade,* p. 169.

38. In 1977, for example, of thirty-one exception requests vetoes, thirty came at the hands of the United States. See "Special Report on Multilateral Export Controls," in House Committee on International Relations, Subcommittee on International Economic Policy and Trade, *Export Administration Act: Agenda for Reform*, Hearings, 95th Cong., 2d sess., October 4, 1978, p. 57.

39. On at least one occasion the United States denied an exception request for an item previously approved for an American exporter. See Angela Stent Yergin, *East-West Technology Transfer: European Perspectives* (Beverly Hills, Calif.: Sage Publications, 1980), p. 48.

40. GAO, *Export Controls: Need to Clarify Policy*, pp. 10–11.

41. Ibid., p. 14. The Commerce Department eventually waived its re-export license requirement for items reviewed in COCOM. Personal correspondence with William Root, April 15, 1987.

42. Statement of Edward Loeffler, in *Export Licensing: COCOM List Review Proposals of the United States*, House Committee on International Relations, Hearings, 95th Cong., 1st sess., 1978, p. 15.

43. OTA, *Technology and East-West Trade*, p. 168.

44. See *Daily Telegraph*, January 6, 1977; the *Guardian*, January 6, 1977; *The Times* (London), January 7, 1977; *Le Monde*, January 8, 1977; and the *Guardian*, May 27, 1977.

45. Interview, Ministre des Affaires Étrangeres, Paris, June 15, 1982.

46. GAO, *Export Controls: Need to Clarify Policy*, p. 11.

47. Ibid., pp. 13–15.

48. GAO, *Details of Certain Controversial Export Licensing Cases*, pp. 7–8; and statement of J. Fred Bucy, in Senate Committee on Governmental Affairs, Permanent Subcommittee on Investigations, *Transfer of Technology to the U.S.S.R. and Eastern Europe*, part 2, Hearings, 95th Cong., 1st sess., May 25, 1977, pp. 21–22.

49. House Committee on International Relations, Subcommittee on International Economic Policy and Trade, *Export Licensing: Foreign Availability of Stretch Forming Presses*, Hearings, 95th Cong., 1st sess., November 4, 1977.

50. *Tokyo Shimbun*, November 11, 1978; translated by the U.S. embassy, Tokyo, and printed in *Daily Summary of the Japanese Press*, November 17, 1978, pp. 11–14.

51. *Daily Summary of the Japanese Press*, November 17, 1978, pp. 11, 13.

52. GAO, *Export Controls: Need to Clarify Policy*, chap. 5.

53. Ibid., p. 52.

54. General Accounting Office, *The Government's Role In East-West Trade: Problems and Issues* (Washington, D.C.: Government Printing Office, February 4, 1976), p. 30.

55. Statement of Fred Asselin, minority investigator, in *Transfer of Technology to the Soviet Union and Soviet Bloc Nations*, p. 82.

56. GAO, *The Government's Role in East-West Trade*, p. 44.

57. GAO, *Export Controls: Need to Clarify Policy*, p. 58.

58. CIA, "Soviet Acquisition of Western Technology"; and Permanent Subcommittee on Investigations, *Transfer of Technology*.

59. Interview, British Ministry of Defense, London, June 2, 1982; and Bundeminis-terium für Wirtshaft, Bonn, July 7, 1982. See also Root, *Trade Controls that Work*; and the statement of James Buckley, in *Transfer of Technology*, p. 160.

60. See "United States Seeks Pledges from COCOM," *Financial Times*, April 28, 1983; and "COCOM Feuds over Trade to East," *Wall Street Journal*, July 17, 1984.

61. *Aviation Week and Space Technology*, September 12, 1983, p. 17; *New York Times*, July 17, 1984, p. D1; *Business Week*, September 21, 1983, p. 22; and Caspar Weinberger, *The Technology Transfer Program*, report to the 98th Cong., 2d sess. (United States Department of Defense, February 1984), pp. 11–12.

62. For analysis of the compromise see *Financial Times*, July 16, 1984, p. 1; *Wall Street Journal*, July 17, 1984, p. 35; *New York Times*, July 17, 1984, p. D7; and *Aviation Week and Space Technology*, July 23, 1984, p. 21.

63. *Japan Economic Journal*, December 25, 1984, p. 1. The Soviets placed similar pressure on West Germany.

64. *Financial Times*, July 16, 1984, p. 1, and March 24, July 17, and August 4, 1984, p. 1.

65. *Financial Times*, October 24, 1984, p. 1, and December 18, 1984, p. 1.

66. Department of Defense, *The Technology Transfer Control Program*, p. 24.

67. *Financial Times*, November 1, 1983, p. 42.

68. *Japan Economic Journal*, April 19, 1983, p. 2.

69. *New York Times*, April 2, 1985, p. A2. See the discussion of French policy by Labbé in this volume.

70. *Wall Street Journal*, July 24, 1984, p. 1; and interview, Bundesministerium der Verteidigung, Bonn, July 13, 1982.

71. For examples of enforcement success see "US, UK Halt Furnace Sale to Soviets," *American Metal Market*, April 15, 1985, p. 1; David Buchan, "The Spies Who Steal Computers," *Financial Times*, May 17, 1986; and "Washington Counters Soviet Pilfering of its High-tech Know-how," *Christian Science Monitor*, May 18, 1984. On the enduring difficulties of preventing illegal transfers see "US, Despite Technology Curbs, Sees No Big Cut in Flow to Soviet," *New York Times*, January 1, 1985.

72. On the Czech complaint see *Financial Times*, November 23, 1984, p. 7; on Swe-den see *FBIS* (Western Europe), November 8, 1984, p. G5; on the German-Soviet meetings see *Washington Post*, January 23, 1985; and *FBIS* (Western Europe), January 23, 1985, pp. J1–J2.

73. On the overall U.S. effort to gain the compliance of non-COCOM suppliers see *Wall Street Journal*, January 15, 1987, p. 1.

74. See, for example, "Bonn Protests United States Pressure on East Bloc Trade," *International Herald Tribune*, June 25, 1985; and the interim report of the Sub-committee on Advanced Technology and Technology Transfer, North Atlantic Assembly (Brussels, October 1985), pp. 6–7.

75. The attitude was conveyed repeatedly to the author in interviews with govern-ment officials during the summer of 1985 in Paris, London, and Bonn.

76. Interview, Bonn, July 8, 1982.

77. Interview, Paris, June 15, 1982.
78. An excellent review is Madelyn C. Ross, "Export Controls: Where China Fits In," *China Business Review* (May–June 1984): 58–62. See also "New Rules Ease United States Exports to China," *Aviation Week and Space Technology*, October 3, 1983, p. 23.
79. The figures are reported in "High Technology Sales to China: The COCOM Connection," *China Business Review* (January–February 1984): 7; and *Financial Times*, January 10, 1985, p. 4.
80. On the problems of the British firms Plasma and Hadland see *Financial Times*, November 2, 1984, p. 8, and January 11, 1985, p. 4; and "How United States Abuses High-tech Law," *Computing*, January 26, 1984. The complaints of U.S. firms are reported in *Wall Street Journal*, January 3, 1985, p. 14.
81. See "United States Trade Law: The Triple Threat; The Stifling of High-technology Business," *ICL Memorandum* (1984), and discussion of it in *Financial Times*, February 16, 1984, p. 1. See also "Bonn Hits at United States High-tech Curbs," *Financial Times*, August 4, 1984; "Institute Accuses United States of High-tech Protectionism," *Financial Times*, August 16, 1984; and *Financial Times*, April 5, 1984, p. 1.
82. See William Root, *Trade Controls that Work*; and "State's Unwelcome Role," *Foreign Service Journal* 22 (March 1984).
83. For discussions of ways to improve American and multilateral policy see the contributions by Henry Nau and William Root in this volume.
84. See Mastanduno, *External Weakness, Internal Strength.*

Chapter 9

Thanks for comments and suggestions to Doug Ashford, David Baldwin, Benjamin Cohen, Tim McKeown, Margaret Karnes, Henry Nau, Eric Nordlinger, and Bill Root.

1. An important exception is Paul Marer, ed., *U.S. Financing of East-West Trade* (Bloomington: Indiana University, International Development Research Center, 1975).
2. For a more detailed discussion of the conditions for stable cooperation among NATO countries in East-West trade see Beverly Crawford, "Stabilizing Factors in International Conflict Resolution," *Negotiation Journal* 3 (October 1987): 333–45.
3. This distinction is made by Robert O. Keohane in *After Hegemony: Cooperation and Discord in the World Political Economy* (Princeton, N.J.: Princeton University Press, 1984), pp. 7–10.
4. On the independent role of institutions in shaping outcomes see James G. March and Johan P. Olsen, "The New Institutionalism: Organizational Factors in Political Life," *American Political Science Review* 78 (September 1984): 734–49.
5. The most influential statement of this position is in Kenneth Waltz, *Theory of International Politics* (Reading, Mass.: Addison-Wesley, 1979).
6. See, for example, Stephen D. Krasner, *Structural Conflict* (Berkeley: University of California Press, 1985).

7. See Charles P. Kindleberger, *The World in Depression, 1929–1939* (Berkeley: University of California Press, 1974); and Robert Gilpin, *U.S. Power and the Multinational Corporation* (New York: Basic Books, 1975).

8. See Keohane, *After Hegemony*, p. 32.

9. Josef Joffe, "Dollars and Détente," in Abraham S. Becker, ed., *Economic Relations with the USSR: Issues for the Alliance* (Lexington, Mass.: Lexington Books, 1983), p. 18.

10. These categories are developed in detail in Beverly Crawford and Stefanie Lenway, "Decision Modes and International Regime Change: Western Collaboration on East-West Trade," *World Politics* 37 (April 1985): 380–84.

11. This "leadership" function of strict export controls is ignored in most critical studies of U.S. policy. For a recent example see National Academy of Sciences, *Balancing the National Interest: U.S. National Security Export Controls and Global Economic Competition* (Washington, D.C.: National Academy Press, 1987).

12. On SDI contract negotiations with European countries see Karen De Young, "Britain Joins U.S. in SDI Research," *Washington Post*, December 7, 1985, p. 1; Michael Lucas, "SDI and Europe," *World Policy Journal* 3 (Spring 1986): 219–49; and Denis Lacorne, "The Multilateral Embargo: A European Perspective," (unpublished manuscript, 1986), p. 30.

13. Eduardo Lachia, "Neutral Nations Guard American Technology to Gain Import Rights," *Wall Street Journal*, January 15, 1987, p. 1.

14. Henry Nau, in his contribution to this volume, takes issue with this argument. He argues that it is doubtful that effective bargaining within the alliance will always require the use of leverage. My argument here is not that these tactics will not be used, but rather that they do not lead to stable policy coordination.

15. Robert Gilpin, *War and Change in World Politics* (Cambridge: Cambridge University Press, 1981).

16. Robert O. Keohane and Joseph S. Nye, *Power and Interdependence* (Boston: Little, Brown, 1977).

17. See Stephen D. Krasner, ed., *International Regimes*, special issue of *International Organization* 36 (Spring 1982).

18. William Zartman argues that the commitment to agree is the most important factor explaining successful negotiated dispute settlements among states. See "Negotiating from Asymmetry: The North-South Stalemate," *Negotiation Journal: On the Process of Dispute Settlement* 1 (April 1985): 121–37.

19. Robert Axelrod, *The Evolution of Cooperation* (New York: Basic Books, 1984); and Robert Axelrod and Robert O. Keohane, "Achieving Cooperation under Anarchy: Strategies and Institutions," *World Politics* 38 (October 1986): 226–54.

20. On the role of knowledge in the creation and maintenance of international regimes see the recent work of Ernst B. Haas, in particular, "Why Collaborate? Issue-linkage and International Regimes," *World Politics* 32 (April 1980): 357–405.

21. See Robert O. Keohane, "Reciprocity in International Relations," *International Organization* 40 (Winter 1986): 1–27.

22. In 1977 the OECD Trade Committee established a separate Working Party on East-

West Trade, which generated information on the relationship between trade with the East and the health of Western economies. In the same year the OECD Ad Hoc Group on East-West Technology Transfer was formed; by 1982 the group had become permanent. It produces information for members on the relationship between East-West technology transfer and the global competitiveness of Western industry. In 1983 the International Energy Agency produced reports on Western dependence on foreign sources of natural gas with a special focus on the Soviet Union. Concern with coordinating Western East-West trade finance policies began within the Berne Union in the 1950s and negotiations moved to the OECD in the 1970s.

23. Direct buyer and supplier credits are usually granted to the importer or exporting firm for long-term loans (over five years) and by some governments for medium- and short-term loans. Credit guarantees, insurance, and interest rate support are granted for medium-term and short-term loans. They are not granted directly to the buyer or supplier, but are usually granted through an intermediary, such as a bank. Short-term support is provided through insurance or guarantees only; no funding or interest rate support is offered.

24. See Hawthorn Arey, "History of Operations and Policies of the Export-Import Bank of Washington," Senate Committee on Banking and Currency, *Study of Export-Import Bank and World Bank*, Hearings, 83d Cong., 2d sess., 1964, pp. 86–132; and Mark Feer, "Export Financing Systems," House Committee on Banking and Currency, *Hearings on a Bill to Enable the Export-Import Bank of the United States to Approve Extension of Certain Loans, Guarantees, and Insurance*, 90th Cong., 2d sess., 1968.

25. For a complete discussion of the political struggles over the creation of the Eximbank, see George N. Peek and Samuel Crowther, *Why Quit Our Own* (New York: Van Nostrand, 1936); Cordell Hull, *The Memoirs of Cordell Hull* (New York: Macmillan, 1948), 1:81–84, 296–301; Herbert Feis, *1933: Characters in Crisis* (Boston: Little, Brown, 1966), p. 312; Frederick C. Adams, *Economic Diplomacy: The Export-Import Bank and American Foreign Policy, 1934–1939* (Columbia: University of Missouri Press, 1976), pp. 106–19; Beatrice Farnsworth, *William C. Bullitt and the Soviet Union* (Bloomington: Indiana University Press, 1967), pp. 143–49; and Lloyd C. Gardner, *Architects of Illusion* (Chicago: Quadrangle, 1970), p. 18.

26. J. Chal Vinson, "War Debts and Peace Legislation: The Johnson Act of 1934," *Mid-America* 50 (July 1968): 215–16.

27. These percentages were calculated from trade figures cited in Werner Beitel and Jürgen Nötzold, "Technologietransfer und Wirtschaftliche Entwicklung: zur Conzeption der Sowjetunion in der Zeit der Neuen Oekonomischen Politik und des ersten Fuenfjahrplanes," Berlin, 1979, mimeo., pp. 129–33.

28. Harold F. Linden, "Supplemental Statement on the Berne Union," Senate Committee on Foreign Relations, *East-West Trade*, Hearings, part 1, 88th Cong., 2d sess., March 13–April 9, 1964, p. 186.

29. Nathaniel McKitterick and B. Jenkins Middleton, *The Bankers of the Rich and the*

Bankers of the Poor: The Role of Export Credit in Development Finance (Washington, D.C.: Overseas Development Council, 1972). See also George D. Holliday, "A History of the Export-Import Bank of the United States," in Marer, ed., *U.S. Financing of East-West Trade*, p. 344.

30. Between 1963 and 1970 only 3 percent of French exports were destined for CMEA countries, but those same countries received 29 percent of total French credits and guarantees. During the same period 5 percent of Italy's exports went to CMEA countries, but they received 13 percent of all export credits. CMEA countries took 3 percent of Great Britain's exports and 11 percent of its official credit support. Thomas A. Wolf, "East-West Trade Credit Policy: A Comparative Analysis," in Marer, ed., *U.S. Financing of East-West Trade*, p. 179.

31. The growth of the Eurodollar market opened new options for East European borrowers by allowing commercial banks to become involved in a major expansion of long-term lending. They did this by transforming short-term deposits into longer-term loans by offering the borrower a series of short-term advances automatically renewable at intervals, typically every six months. This became standard practice in the Euromarkets, not simply with Eastern Europe.

32. Quoted in Samuel Pisar, *Coexistence and Commerce* (New York: McGraw-Hill, 1970), p. 112.

33. Wolf, "East-West Trade Credit Policy," p. 157.

34. Pisar, *Coexistence and Commerce*, p. 110.

35. Robert W. Dean, *West German Trade with the East: The Political Dimension* (New York: Praeger, 1974), chaps. 3–5.

36. Wolf, "East-West Trade Credit Policy," p. 173.

37. See Senate Committee on Banking, Housing, and Urban Affairs, Subcommittee on International Finance, *Export-Import Bank of the United States: Hearings on Bill S. 1890*, 93d Cong., 1st sess., 1973.

38. The following discussion is based on interviews with European officials at the EC commission in Brussels, June 14 and 15, 1983.

39. W. Allen Wallis, under secretary of state for economic affairs, "East-West Economic Issues, Sanctions Policy, and the Formulation of International Economic Policy," *Hearings before the House Committee on Foreign Affairs, March 29, 1984* (Washington, D.C.: Government Printing Office, 1984), p. 7.

40. Interviews with both U.S. and European consensus officials in Brussels, June 14 and 15, 1983, revealed that the United States, with most of its official credit support in loans with long-term maturities, pressed for higher interest rates on short- and medium-term loans in order to make its own long-term loans more competitive. West Europeans, on the other hand, wished to maintain a low floor on interest rates, but to obtain agreement on shortening loan maturities. Each country pressed for its most valued trading partners to be placed in favorable categories.

41. *Wall Street Journal*, January 8, 1980, p. 3, and January 11, 1980, p. 20.

42. The disproportionate share of West German bank claims on Poland can be attributed to the trade promotion strategy of the FRG government. In early 1980 Poland

approached HERMES with a request for additional guarantees in order to obtain additional market financing. The decision to comply with that request was most certainly reached at the highest levels of government on political grounds. Economics Minister Lambsdorff announced on March 16, 1980, that the West German government had authorized HERMES to guarantee loans of DM 500 million to pay for Polish imports of West German steel, chemicals, and textiles. More lenient than usual repayment terms were provided. Again, in July, West German banks announced that they had raised a DM 1.5 billion credit package for the Polish central bank; one-third of that credit was to be guaranteed by the West German government. Clearly the West German state, through its control over institutions for trade promotion, pushed the banks into lending to Poland at limits beyond those that commercial prudence would allow. In contrast, between 1976 and 1978 U.S. banks had begun to restrict new credit to Poland, allowing claims to rise only $9 million. West European banks, on the other hand, had allowed their claims to rise to $12.9 billion. Thus, of the total Polish debt which had accumulated by 1981, U.S. banks held only $1.3 billion, while the U.S. government held $1.9 billion. See David D. Driscoll, "East European Hard Currency Debt to the West," (Washington, D.C.: Congressional Research Service, 1982, mimeo.), p. 5; and J. Andrew Spindler, *The Politics of International Credit* (Washington, D.C.: Brookings Institution, 1984), pp. 83–86.

43. Nicholas Cumming-Bruce, "Jan Woloszyn's Struggle for Poland," Euromoney (October 1980): 100–102, cited in Spindler, *The Politics of International Credit*, p. 86.

44. Driscoll, "East European Hard Currency Debt to the West," p. 5.

45. *New York Times*, February 6, 1982, p. 38.

46. Interviews, Department of State officials, Washington, D.C., May, 1985. See also John Hardt and Donna L. Gold, "Soviet Gas Pipeline: U.S. Options," (Washington, D.C.: Congressional Research Service, 1983, mimeo.), p. 4.

47. Driscoll, "East European Hard Currency Debt to the West," p. 7.

48. Karen Lissakers, "Dateline Wall Street: Faustian Finance," *Foreign Policy* 51 (Summer 1983): 27.

49. Wallis, "East-West Economic Issues, Sanctions Policy, and the Formulation of International Economic Policy," pp. 5–6, 17.

50. Interviews, Brussels, June 14 and 15, 1983.

51. In negotiating new loans, however, Poland appeared to have the upper hand. Part of a 1984 rescheduling agreement with five hundred creditor banks allowed Poland a grace period on interest payments on $200 million owed those banks. Usually banks only allow a grace period on the repayment of principal in rescheduling agreements. See editorial, *Christian Science Monitor*, December 18, 1984, p. 15.

52. *The Institutional Investor* (September 1983): 293.

53. This was a touchy situation because legally the Commodity Credit Corporation (CCC) was supposed to require a formal declaration of default before it could make good on its guarantees. Private banks, too, hesitated to take up the administration's offer because the CCC would pay only 6 percent interest on the debt, which was ten percentage points below what the banks had negotiated. Furthermore, the

offer would tie the banks' hands in future negotiations because they would have to relinquish their rights to negotiate with Poland on rescheduling outstanding debts. Only one bank, the Bank of Boston International in New York, accepted payment from the CCC. Driscoll, "East European Hard Currency Debt to the West," pp. 5–8. See also Benjamin J. Cohen, "International Debt and Linkage Strategies: Some Foreign-policy Implications for the United States," *International Organization* 39 (Autumn 1985): 699–727.

54. M. S. Mendelsohn, *Commercial Banks and the Restructuring of Cross-Border Debt* (New York: Group of Thirty, 1983), p. 4.

55. See David D. Driscoll, "Sovereign Debt: The Polish Example," (Washington, D.C.: Congressional Research Service, 1982, mimeo.), pp. 18–20; *Economist*, November 14, 1981, p. 87; and *Economist*, January 7, 1984, p. 64.

56. Frederick Kempe, "U.S. Decides to Soon Lift Polish Sanctions," *Wall Street Journal*, February 18, 1987, p. 30.

57. See Crawford and Lenway, "Decision Modes and International Regime Change," pp. 380–84.

58. OECD, "The Arrangement on Export Credits," Paris, June 7, 1982, mimeo.

59. *Financial Times*, June 7, 1982, p. 7, and June 8, 1982, p. 1.

60. The CMEA countries were moving away from official financing anyway. In the mid-1960s, 80 percent of all short- and medium-term credits extended to CMEA countries were in the form of official direct credits or backed by official credit guarantees. In 1970 50–60 percent of the debt was held or guaranteed by Western governments. By 1980 official credits and credit guarantees accounted for only 30 percent of the total gross CMEA debt of $77 billion. Based on this evidence one might argue that as the credit regime waxed, its influence waned because Eastern Europe was turning away from government and even government-supported financing. The percentages are calculated from country trade and debt figures in U.S. Congress, Joint Economic Committee, *East-West Trade: The Prospects to 1985* (Washington, D.C.: Government Printing Office, 1982), pp. 41, 94, 154, 173, 227, 264, and 300.

61. *Wall Street Journal*, May 11, 1983, p. 38.

Chapter 10

1. This article draws heavily on my book, *Pipeline Politics: The Complex Political Economy of East-West Energy Trade* (Ithaca, N.Y.: Cornell University Press, 1986).

2. The conceptualization and measurement of success in cases of economic sanctions pose both theoretical and methodological problems. See David Baldwin, *Economic Statecraft* (Princeton, N.J.: Princeton University Press, 1985); Gary Clyde Hufbauer and Jeffrey Schott, *Economic Sanctions Reconsidered* (Washington, D.C.: Institute of International Economics, 1985); and Jentleson, *Pipeline Politics*, pp. 28–34.

3. Albert O. Hirschman, *National Power of the Structure of Foreign Trade*, rev. ed. (Berkeley: University of California Press, 1980), p. 29.

4. Office of Technology Assessment, *Technology and Soviet Energy Availability*, 97th Cong., 1st sess., 1981.

5. COCOM includes all NATO nations except Iceland, plus Japan.

6. Cited in Jentleson, *Pipeline Politics*, p. 169.

7. Harold Lasswell and Abraham Kaplan, *Power and Society* (New Haven, Conn.: Yale University Press, 1950), pp. 55–56. Robert Gilpin terms prestige "the everyday currency of international relations." See his *War and Change in International Politics* (New York: Cambridge University Press, 1981), p. 31.

8. On the criteria for distinguishing strong and weak regimes, see Stephen Krasner, "Structural Causes and Regime Consequences: Regimes as Intervening Variables," *International Organization* 36 (Spring 1982): 185–206.

9. Jentleson, *Pipeline Politics*, pp. 65–67, 69.

10. David Caute, *The Great Fear* (New York: Simon and Schuster, 1978), p. 20.

11. The value of trade with Eastern Europe as a percentage of total Soviet trade increased from 42 percent in 1948 to 83 percent in 1953. The pattern was similar for the East European countries: e.g., Czechoslovakia 32 percent to 78 percent, Hungary 34 percent to 77 percent, Poland 41 percent to 70 percent. See House Joint Economic Committee, Subcommittee on Foreign Economic Policy, *A New Look at Trade Policy toward the Communist Bloc*, 87th Cong., 1st sess., 1961, p. 43.

12. Gunnar Adler-Karlsson, *Western Economic Warfare, 1947–1967* (Stockholm: Almqvist and Wiksell, 1968), p. 71.

13. Central Intelligence Agency, Office of Reports and Estimates, "The USSR Petroleum Industry," ORE 24–49, January 5, 1950, p. 6. Papers of Harry S. Truman, PSF, Harry S. Truman Presidential Library, Independence, Mo.

14. Jentleson, *Pipeline Politics*, pp. 76–81.

15. The Soviets imported an additional 100,000 tons of wide-diameter pipe from Sweden. Research Memorandum, RES-13, "Western Efforts to Prevent Large-diameter Linepipe Exports to the Soviet Bloc," Bureau of Intelligence and Research (Thomas L. Hughes) to the Secretary of State, April 3, 1963, NSF, box 223, File: NATO Pipe Embargo, John F. Kennedy Presidential Library, Boston, Mass.; and National Petroleum Council, *Import of Oil Exports from the Soviet Bloc* (Washington, D.C.: National Petroleum Council, 1962), 2:214, 216.

16. Telegram, Secretary of State Rusk to American embassies in Western Europe, Sweden, and Japan, December 18, 1962, NSF, box 223, File: NATO Pipe Embargo, Kennedy Presidential Library.

17. Cited in Angela E. Stent, *From Embargo to Ostpolitik: The Political Economy of West German–Soviet Relations, 1955–1980* (New York: Cambridge University Press, 1981), p. 107.

18. Jentleson, *Pipeline Politics*, pp. 107–13.

19. The Shultz characterization was in a guest column in *Business Week*, May 28, 1979, pp. 24–26. On the Carter policy as seen by one of its principal architects, see Samuel P. Huntington, "Trade Technology and Leverage: Economic Diplomacy," *Foreign Policy* 32 (Fall 1978): 63–80.

20. Jack Brougher, "1979–1982: The United States Uses Trade to Penalize Soviet Aggression and Seeks to Reorder Western Policy," in U.S. Congress, Joint Economic Committee, *Soviet Economy in the 1980s: Problems and Prospects*, Joint Committee Print, 97th Cong., 2d sess., 1982, pp. 446–49.

21. Central Intelligence Agency, "Prospects for Soviet Oil Production," ER 77-10270, April 1977. Among the critics of the CIA study see Marshall I. Goldman, *The Enigma of Soviet Petroleum: Half-full or Half-empty?* (London: George Allen and Unwin, 1980); David Wilson, *Soviet Oil and Gas to 1990* (London: Economist Intelligence Unit, 1980); and Senate Select Committee on Intelligence, *The Soviet Oil Situation: An Evaluation of CIA Analyses of Soviet Oil Production*, staff report, 95th Cong., 2d sess., 1978. The CIA itself toned down its predictions in "Prospects for Soviet Oil Production: A Supplemental Analysis," ER 77-10425, issued in July 1977.

22. Brougher, "1979–82: U.S. Uses Trade to Penalize Soviet Aggression," p. 445.

23. Three months later official policy shifted again to give oil and gas equipment exports a presumption of approval while maintaining the presumption of denial for oil and gas technology. The latter was intended to keep the Dresser drill bit plant from being completed, but adequate technology already had been transferred to allow the Soviets to complete the plant. (My thanks to Bill Root for clarification of this point.) As to oil and gas equipment exports, the formal presumption of approval made little difference. Exports sunk to $49.8 million, the lowest level since 1972; Brougher, "1979–82: U.S. Uses Trade to Penalize Soviet Aggression," p. 445.

24. Department of Defense, *Annual Report to the Congress of the Secretary of Defense, FY 1983* (Washington, D.C.: Government Printing Office, 1982), see 1:22–23; sec. II, pp. 26–32.

25. Jonathan Stern, "U.S. Controls and the Soviet Pipeline," *Washington Quarterly* 5 (Autumn 1982): 53.

26. Senate Committee on Banking, Housing, and Urban Affairs, *Proposed Trans-Siberian Natural Gas Pipeline*, Hearing, 97th Cong., 1st sess., November 12, 1981, pp. 115–17.

27. On December 29, 1981, President Reagan announced the following economic sanctions against the Soviet Union: extension of the existing licensing requirement for oil and gas exploration and production equipment to cover refining and transmission equipment (e.g., pipe-layers, pipeline compressor stations); suspension of all existing licenses for all high-technology exports including oil and gas equipment, and a prohibition on any new licenses; closing of the offices of the Soviet Purchasing Commission; suspension of Aeroflot flights; no renewal of exchange agreements on energy, science and technology, and maritime relations; and postponement of negotiations for a new long-term grain agreement.

28. Pieter Dankert, "Europe Together, America Apart," *Foreign Policy* 53 (Winter 1983–84): 22.

29. Ellen Frost and Angela Stent make the point that "the American concept of security is overwhelmingly military in nature, whereas that espoused by the Europe-

ans is as economic as it is military." See their "NATO's Troubles with East-West Trade," *International Security* 8 (Summer 1983): 180.

30. *New York Times*, September 1, 1982, p. A22.

31. *New York Times*, October 5, 1982, p. A1.

32. *New York Times*, November 14, 1982, p. A1.

33. International Energy Agency, "Energy Requirements and Security," May 1983; Jentleson, *Pipeline Politics*, pp. 199–203.

34. *Forbes*, April 11, 1983, p. 170.

35. Compare International Energy Agency, *World Energy Outlook* (Paris, 1982), p. 380, with International Energy Agency, *Natural Gas Prospects* (Paris, 1986), p. 59.

36. International Energy Agency, *Energy Policies and Programmes of IEA Countries: 1984 Review* (Paris, 1985), p. 346.

37. *Wall Street Journal*, December 3, 1986, p. 34, and December 2, 1986, p. 40.

38. *Financial Times*, September 28, 1982, p. 38; *Journal of Commerce*, January 25, 1982, p. 5A; Ghislaine Cestre, "Algeria's Unhappy Gamble: The Crude 0.1/Natural Gas Pricing Link," *Geopolitics of Energy* (January 1984): 5; and Jonathan P. Stern, *International Gas Trade in Europe* (London: Heinemann, 1984), pp. 74, 88, 97.

39. *The Times* (London), May 16, 1983, p. 8; *Financial Times*, March 18, 1983, p. 3; *New York Times*, March 7, 1984, pp. D1, D17.

40. The most useful sources for tracking such contracts are the *Country Profile: USSR* series published quarterly by the Economist Intelligence Unit (EIU), and *Interflo*, a monthly compilation of abstracts from a wide range of newspapers, trade journals, public documents, and other publications dealing with East-West trade.

41. According to Wharton Econometrics data, Soviet gas turbine imports shrunk to zero in 1985; Wharton Econometric Forecasting Associates, Centrally Planned Economies Service: Analysis of Current Issues, "Soviet Natural Gas Exports and Imports of Pipeline Materials and Equipment," June 19, 1986. See also Thane Gustafson, "The Soviet Response to the American Embargo of 1981–82: The Case of Compressors for the Export Gas Pipeline," in Gordon B. Smith, ed., *The Politics of East-West Trade* (Boulder, Colo.: Westview Press, 1984), pp. 129–42.

42. Goldman, *The Enigma of Soviet Petroleum*, pp. 64–65.

43. Jonathan P. Stern, *Soviet Oil and Gas Exports to the West* (Hants, England: Gower Publishing, 1987), pp. 92, 93, 123.

44. Jochen Bethkenhagen, "Soviet Energy: Oil Exports Stabilize Thanks to Increased Natural Gas Production," *Economic Bulletin* 22 (September 1985): 11, German Institute for Economic Research (DIW).

45. Economist Intelligence Unit, *Country Profile: USSR, 1986–87* 3:16.

46. Stern, *Soviet Oil and Gas Exports*, p. 123. The 1986 estimate is by Jan Vanous, who expresses its significance as meaning that by July 1986 it took almost five times as much Soviet oil to purchase a given piece of West German machinery than in early 1985; "The Soviet Trade Crisis: Choose Tractors or Tanks," *Washington Post*, August 17, 1986, p. C1.

47. Josef Joffe, "Europe and America: The Politics of Resentment," *Foreign Affairs* 61 (America and the World) (1982): 569–90.

48. Bruce W. Jentleson, "The Political Basis for Trade in U.S.-Soviet Relations," *Millennium: Journal of International Studies* 15 (Spring 1986): 22–47; and "East-West Trade and Superpower Relations," in Walter Goldstein, ed., *Clash in the North: Polar Summitry and NATO's Northern Flank* (London: Pergamon-Brassey, 1988), pp. 45–70.

49. See, for example, the recent study by Harvard University's Energy and Environmental Policy Center, *Natural Gas in Western Europe: Structure, Strategies, and Politics* (Cambridge, Mass.: 1987).

50. *Journal of Commerce*, October 15, 1986, p. 9A; *Financial Times*, December 3, 1986, p. 5.

51. *Dun's Business Month* (November 1982): 73.

52. The Troll development plan is based on an oil price of $28 per barrel, something which clearly still is an uncertainty. Even then there remains what the *Wall Street Journal* called the "daunting technical difficulties and high production costs of working in more than a thousand feet of water"; August 12, 1986, p. 30.

53. Robert J. Lieber, "International Energy Policy and the Reagan Administration: Avoiding the Next Oil Shock?" in Kenneth A. Oye, Robert J. Lieber, and Donald Rothchild, eds., *Eagle Resurgent? The Reagan Era in American Foreign Policy* (Boston: Little, Brown, 1987), pp. 167–89.

54. Jentleson, *Pipeline Politics*, pp. 138–39.

55. In May 1987 Soviet oil production reached 12.72 million barrels per day (b/d)—a world record. The average for the first five months of 1987 was 12.47 million b/d. This was above the official target of 12.34 million b/d, and a substantial improvement on the 11.94 million b/d for the same period in 1985. However, long-term forecasts remain problematic. The average yield of oil wells, already less than 100 b/d, is expected to fall to 72–75 b/d by 1991. To compensate the Oil Ministry has increased the number of new fields it hopes to bring into production during 1986–90 to 222. *Oil and Gas Journal*, July 6, 1987, p. 24.

56. As an example of the multitude of factors which enter into future trade scenarios, in November 1986 France stopped buying Soviet crude oil and petroleum products to protest the deficit in their bilateral trade; *Wall Street Journal*, November 21, 1986, p. 37. This kind of factor cannot be predicted from production or other trade data but can have a major impact.

57. *Oil and Gas Journal*, December 2, 1985, pp. 48–51; *Oil and Gas Journal*, February 10, 1986, p. 34; Economist Intelligence Unit, *Country Profile: USSR, 1986–87* 3:17. Even the Chernobyl nuclear disaster may prove to be a spur. In April 1987 West Germany and the Soviet Union signed a five-year nuclear energy cooperation agreement. Reports indicated that the contracts involved for nuclear safety equipment and other exports could reach $3 billion. *Financial Times*, April 23, 1987, p. 2, and April 29, 1987, p. 4.

58. Morris Bornstein, *East-West Technology Transfer: The Transfer of Western Technology to the USSR* (Paris: OECD, 1985); Central Intelligence Agency, *Soviet Needs for Western Petroleum Technology and Equipment* (unclassified version of longer CIA study entitled "Role of Western Equipment in Soviet Oil and Gas Develop-

ment"). A further example is the study by the Fridtjof Nansen Institute of Norway on Soviet drilling operations in the Barents Sea, which concluded that "large scale Western participation is a prerequisite for major progress." Cited in *Financial Times*, October 22, 1986, p. 28.

59. One example is the energy cooperation agreement signed by Great Britain and the Soviet Union in April 1986. No specific deals were set but British Minister for Energy Peter Walker was quoted as saying that it would involve "quite a considerable flow of business and trade," in *Financial Times*, April 25, 1986, p. 6. See also the report by Wharton Econometrics that Soviet imports of oil and gas equipment and technology from the West increased in 1986 over 1985, and that further increases were expected in 1987; *Oil and Gas Journal*, May 4, 1987, p. 64.

60. Bruce Russett, "The Mysterious Case of Vanishing Hegemony; or, Is Mark Twain Really Dead?" *International Organization* 39 (Spring 1985): 207–32.

61. What follows is based on interviews with and information provided by PESA and NAM officials (January–February 1987).

Chapter 11

This paper represents the views of the author and not necessarily those of the Congressional Research Service or the U.S. Congress.

1. See John P. Hardt and Donna L. Gold, "Soviet Commercial Behavior with Western Industrial Nations," in Dan Caldwell, ed., *Soviet International Behavior and U.S. Policy Options* (Lexington, Mass.: Lexington Books, 1985).

2. John P. Hardt and Donna L. Gold, "Changes in East-West Trade: The Policy Context," paper presented at the Conference on the Future of East-West Economic Relations in a Changing World Economy, Canadian Institute on International Affairs (Westview Press, 1988); and Angela Stent, *From Embargo to Ostpolitik: The Political Economy of West German–Soviet Relations, 1955–1980* (New York: Cambridge University Press, 1981).

3. John P. Hardt and George D. Holliday, *U.S.-Soviet Commercial Relations: The Interplay of Economics, Technology Transfer, and Diplomacy* (Washington, D.C.: Government Printing Office, June 1973).

4. John P. Hardt, George D. Holliday, and Young C. Kim, *Western Investment in Communist Economies, A Selected Survey on Economic Interdependence* (Washington, D.C.: Government Printing Office, August 1974).

5. John P. Hardt, "United States–Soviet Trade Policy," in *Issues in East-West Commercial Relations* (Washington, D.C.: Government Printing Office, 1979), pp. 267–86; and John P. Hardt, "East-West Economic Relations: Alternative Scenarios for the Atlantic Alliance," *Berichte des Bundesinstituts für Ostwissenschaftliche und Internationale Studien*, no. 39-193 (December 1983).

6. See John P. Hardt and Kate Tomlinson, *An Assessment of the Afghanistan Sanctions: Implications for Trade and Diplomacy in the 1980s* (Washington, D.C.: Government Printing Office, April 1981.)

7. "The President's Competitiveness Initiative," White House press release, January 27, 1987, p. 8, pt. 31. Statement by Secretary of Commerce Malcolm Baldrige, February 9, 1987, in *U.S. Department of Commerce News.* Testimony of Paul Freedenberg to House Foreign Affairs Committee, March 11, 1987.

8. See John P. Hardt, "Agricultural Trade: USA and USSR," in Christopher T. Saunders, ed., *East-West Trade and Finance in the World Economy: A New Look for the 1980s* (London: Macmillan, 1985).

9. National Academy of Sciences, *Balancing the National Interest: U.S. National Security Export Controls and Global Competition* (Washington, D.C.: National Academy of Sciences Press, 1987).

10. Testimony by Paul Freedenberg, assistant secretary of commerce for trade administration, before the House Foreign Affairs Subcommittee on International Economic Policy and Trade, March 11, 1987, mimeo.

11. John P. Hardt, "Long-Term Agreement (LTA), Some Considerations for Agricultural Trade," in Gordon B. Smith, ed., *The Politics of East-West Trade* (Boulder, Colo.: Westview Press, 1984), pp. 143–58.

12. Ivan D. Ivanov, *The Soviet Union in a Changing Global Economic Setting: The Prospects for Trade-Oriented Growth,* UNCTAD/ST/TSC/4, April 25, 1986.

13. Yevgeni Primakov, "New Philosophy of Foreign Policy," *Pravda,* July 11, 1987.

14. *Export Administration Act of 1979,* Pub. L. 96-72, September 29, 1979, as amended by Pub. L. 97-145, December 29, 1981, and Pub. L. 99-64, July 12, 1985.

15. See John P. Hardt and Donna Gold, in Senate Committee on Foreign Relations, *The Premises of East-West Commercial Relations,* workshop sponsored by the Committee on Foreign Relations (Washington, D.C.: Government Printing Office, December 1982), pp. 83–111. Also see the chapters by Mastanduno and Root in this volume.

16. See John P. Hardt, "Gorbachev's Domestic Economic Strategy and East-West Commercial Connections: An Interpretative Essay," in Charles M. Perry and Robert L. Pfaltzgraff, Jr., eds., *Selling the Rope to Hang Capitalism? The Debate on West-East Trade and Technology Transfer* (Elmsford, N.Y.: Pergamon Brassey, 1987). See also Lionel Olmer, "National Security Export Controls in the Reagan Administration," in Perry and Pfaltzgraff, *Selling the Rope.*

17. Raymond F. Mikesell, "Negotiating at Bretton Woods, 1944," in Raymond Dennett and Joseph E. Johnson, eds., *Negotiating with the Russians* (New York: World Press Foundation, 1947).

18. Interview with Mikhail Pankin, chief of the International Economic Organization, USSR Ministry of Foreign Trade, in *London Morning Star,* October 3, 1986, p. 7.

19. John H. Jackson, *World Trade and the Law of GATT* (New York: Bobbs Merrill, 1969), pp. 780–85.

20. John P. Hardt and Jean F. Boone, "United States–Soviet Exchanges: Perspectives and Prospects," House Committee on Foreign Affairs, Subcommittee on Europe and the Middle East, Hearings (Washington, D.C.: Government Printing Office, July 1986).

21. See the Proceedings of the CRS Symposium on *U.S. Export Control Policy and*

Competitiveness, compiled by John P. Hardt and Jean F. Boone, April 30, 1987 (787-388S).

22. See John P. Hardt, *United States–Soviet Economic and Technological Interaction*, Occasional Paper, Atlantic Council of the United States (Fall 1987).

23. John P. Hardt, "Economic Strategy of Gorbachev: Change and Uncertainty," in Murray Feshbach, ed., *National Security Issues of the USSR*, (Dordrecht, Netherlands: Martinus Nijhoff Publishers, 1987), pp. 175–88.

24. Henry R. Nau, "Trade and Deterrence," *National Interest* (Spring 1987): 48–60.

25. See the Proceedings of the CRS Symposium on *U.S. Trade: Policy Issues Confronting the 100th Congress*, compiled by William Cooper. March 30, 1987 (87-267E).

26. U.S. Congress, Joint Economic Committee, *East-West Trade: Prospects to 1985* (Washington, D.C.: Government Printing Office, 1982); U.S. Congress, Joint Economic Committee, *East-West Commercial Policy: A Congressional Dialogue with the Reagan Administration* (Washington, D.C.: Government Printing Office, 1982).

27. Shevardnadze memorandum on "International Security of States: An Important Condition for Improvement of International Relations," submitted to the United Nations secretary, January 27, 1986.

28. Statement by V. A. Zvezdin, USSR representative, in the General Debate in the Second Committee at the 41st session of the U.N. General Assembly, October 6, 1986.

29. See John P. Hardt and Ronda Bresnick, "Brezhnev's European Economic Policy," in George Ginsburg and Alvin Z. Rubenstein, eds., *Soviet Foreign Policy toward Western Europe* (New York: Praeger, 1978), pp. 205–6; John P. Hardt and Kate S. Tomlinson, "Soviet Economic Policies in Western Europe," in Herbert J. Ellison, ed., *Soviet Policy toward Western Europe* (Seattle: University of Washington Press, 1983), pp. 159–208; revised for Erik P. Hoffmann and Robbin F. Laird, eds., *Soviet Foreign Policy in a Changing World* (Hawthorne, N.Y.: Aldine Press, 1985).

30. See John P. Hardt, "The German Question Revisited: The Future of Inter-German Economic and Political Relations," in Angela E. Stent, ed., *Economic Relations with the Soviet Union: American and West German Perspectives* (Boulder, Colo.: Westview Press, 1985); and Axel Lebann, "Financing German Trade with the East," *Ausen politik* [Eng. ed.] 33, no. 2 (1982): 123–37.

31. See John P. Hardt, "Soviet Energy Policy in Eastern Europe," in Sarah Terry, ed., *Soviet Policy in Eastern Europe* (New Haven, Conn.: Yale University Press, 1984).

Chapter 12

1. See Hanns-D. Jacobsen, chapter 5 in this volume.

2. I draw here on my own observations from many continuing contacts with European officials and businessmen both as consultant and during my years as director general of the Atlantic Institute for International Affairs in Paris.

3. "Protocol Relating to German Internal Trade and Connected Problems," *Treaty Establishing the European Economic Community and Connected Documents* (Brussels: Publishing Services of the European Community, n.d.), p. 243.

4. See Martin J. Hillenbrand, *Germany in an Era of Transition* (Paris: Atlantic Institute for International Affairs, 1983), pp. 57–58.

5. Complete text of the chancellor's speech provided by German Information Center, New York.

6. *Aviation Week and Space Technology*, March 17, 1986, pp. 66–68. See also National Academy of Sciences, *Balancing the National Interest: U.S. National Security Export Controls and Global Economic Competition* (Washington, D.C.: National Academy Press, 1987), pp. 147, 195.

7. *New York Times*, December 30 and December 31, 1981.

8. *Balancing the National Interest*, p. 191.

9. *New York Times*, October 5, 1973. The author was the American ambassador to the Federal Republic of Germany in 1973 and 1976 and recalls well the damage done to our reputation as a reliable supplier of nuclear fuel by withholding deliveries to our allies. See also *Business Week*, December 1, 1973; Gaddis Smith, *Morality, Reason, and Power: American Diplomacy in the Carter Years* (New York: Hill and Wang, 1986), pp. 59–61; Michael Brenner, "Carter's Nonproliferation Strategy: Fuel Assurances and Energy Security," *Orbis* 22, no. 2 (Summer 1978): 333–56; and Michael Brenner, "Proliferation Watch: Carter's Bungled Promise," *Foreign Policy* 36 (Fall 1979): 89–101.

10. Felix Rohatyn, "The Economy on the Brink," *New York Review of Books*, June 11, 1987, p. 3.

11. This was a perceptive point made first by a political scientist, David Calleo, long before most economists began to appreciate it. See, for example, his *The Imperious Economy* (Cambridge, Mass.: Harvard University Press, 1982).

12. See Hanns W. Maull, *Natural Gas and Economic Security* (Paris: Atlantic Institute for International Affairs, 1981), for a well-informed discussion of the whole subject.

13. See Bruce W. Jentleson, *Pipeline Politics: The Complex Political Economy of East-West Energy Trade* (Ithaca, N.Y.: Cornell University Press, 1986), pp. 183ff., for a good description of the whole natural gas pipeline dispute.

14. This is a generalization based on personal observation from within the government, but see also I. M. Destler, *Making Foreign Economic Policy* (Washington, D.C.: Brookings Institution, 1980), and I. M. Destler and Leslie H. Gelb, *Our Own Worst Enemy: The Unmaking of American Foreign Policy* (New York: Simon and Schuster, 1984).

15. I reported on this to Washington while I was minister and deputy chief of mission in Bonn. The idea, of course, never got off the ground and received no publicity.

16. *New York Times*, June 7, 1987.

17. *Balancing the National Interest*, p. 269.

18. See Crawford, "Western Control of East-West Finance," chapter 9 in this volume.

19. See Thomas H. Naylor, "Changing the Economic Mechanism in the Soviet Union," *Planning Review* 14, no. 1 (January 1986): 30–33, 46.

20. See Nau, "Export Controls and Free Trade," chapter 13 in this volume.

21. *Balancing the National Interest*, pp. 203ff. William Root takes a somewhat different view in a personal letter to the author. He writes, "There is a growing availabil-

ity of COCOM listed items from third countries. For the most part, this is of embargoed products which are so widely available in retail outlets around the world that neither COCOM nor non-COCOM countries can, in fact, control them. Such items should be removed from the COCOM list. To the extent that third country production of COCOM-listed items does not fall in that "widely available" category, it is largely carried on as off-shore production by firms headquartered in COCOM countries, especially the United States. There are quiet ways to work with such firms to prevent diversions through their off-shore producers, such as understandings that any export from such a producer would be construed as an export from the United States because of U.S.-origin parts or technology."

22. Lewis Regenstein, "Lenin was Right: Capitalist Nations Sell Soviets the Rope that Can Hang the West," *Atlanta Constitution*, May 9, 1987. The author is billed as a former intelligence officer with the U.S. Central Intelligence Agency.

Chapter 13

The author gratefully acknowledges the support of the Smith Richardson Foundation and the Woodrow Wilson International Center for Scholars of the Smithsonian Institution, where he was a fellow when he wrote this chapter.

1. Henry R. Nau, "Trade and Deterrence," *National Interest* 7 (Spring 1987): 48–61.
2. *Balancing the National Interest: U.S. National Security Export Controls and Global Economic Competition*, Panel on the Impact of National Security Controls on International Technology Transfer, Committee on Science, Engineering, and Public Policy, National Academy of Sciences, National Academy of Engineering, and Institute of Medicine (Washington, D.C.: National Academy Press, 1987).
3. Ibid., p. 47.
4. *FY 1987 DOD Program for Research and Development*, statement by the under secretary of defense, research, and engineering to the 99th Cong., 2d sess., 1986.
5. "The High Tech Race: Who's Ahead?" *Fortune*, October 13, 1986, pp. 26–44.
6. *Balancing the National Interest*, p. 48.
7. Michael Mandelbaum, *The Nuclear Future* (Ithaca, N.Y.: Cornell University Press, 1983).
8. Henry R. Nau, *Technology Transfer and U.S. Foreign Policy* (New York: Praeger, 1976); and Phillip Hanson, *Trade Technology in Soviet Western Relations* (New York: Columbia University Press, 1981).
9. *Soviet Acquisition of Militarily Significant Western Technology: An Update*, September 1985 (no publisher is cited but it is widely known to be the Central Intelligence Agency).
10. *Balancing the National Interest*, p. 41.
11. Henry S. Rowen, "Living with a Sick Bear," *National Interest* 2 (Winter 1985-86): 14–27; Jerry F. Hough, "Gorbachev's Strategy," *Foreign Affairs* 64 (Fall 1985): 35–56.
12. *New York Times*, June 3, 1986.

13. On these licenses see statement by Secretary of Commerce Malcolm Baldrige, Office of the Secretary, *U.S. Department of Commerce News*, February 9, 1987; and interview with Paul Freedenberg, assistant secretary of commerce for trade administration, *Washington International Business Report*, March 30, 1987.

14. See North Atlantic Assembly, Scientific and Technical Committee, Subcommittee on Advanced Technology and Technology Transfer, *Interim Report*, November 1984, AB 222, STC/AT(84)5.

15. David Hobbs, "Technology Transfer: Can Sharing and Protection be Harmonized," (paper presented at Conference on High Technology, Western Security and Economic Growth: An Agenda for the Future, Palais d'Egmond, Brussels, February 6–8, 1986).

16. Another study is a recent paper contained in the working papers of the National Academy's study. See William A. Root, Solveig B. Spielmann, and Felice A. Kaden, "A Study of Foreign Export Control Systems," in working paper, *Balancing the National Interest* (Washington, D.C.: National Academy Press, 1987), pp. 207–48.

17. Samuel P. Huntington, "Trade, Technology, and Leverage: Economic Diplomacy," *Foreign Affairs* 32 (Fall 1979): 63–80.

18. Robert A. Pastor, *Congress and the Politics of U.S. Foreign Economic Policy, 1929–1976* (Berkeley: University of California Press, 1980).

19. I. M. Destler, *American Trade Politics: System under Stress* (New York: Twentieth Century Fund, 1986).

20. See Nau, "Trade and Deterrence."

21. *Wall Street Journal*, March 13, 1987.

22. See Samuel P. Huntington, ed., "National Security Decision Making in the White House and its Organization," *World Affairs* 146, no. 2 (Fall 1983), including my comment essay in this special issue.

23. See Nau, "Trade and Deterrence."

Chapter 14

1. *Balancing the National Interest: U.S. National Security Export Controls and Global Competition*, Panel on the Impact of National Security Controls on International Technology Transfer, Committee on Science, Engineering, and Public Policy, National Academy of Sciences, National Academy of Engineering, and Institute of Medicine (Washington, D.C.: National Academy Press, 1987).

2. "The President's Competitiveness Initiative," White House press release, January 27, 1987, p. 8, pt. 31.

3. Statement by Secretary of Commerce Malcolm Baldrige, February 9, 1987, *U.S. Department of Commerce News*.

4. Interview with officials of Canadian Exporters' Association, Ottawa, March 24, 1987.

5. Section 3(2)(A) of the Export Administration Act of 1979, Pub. L. 96-72, September 29, 1979, as amended by Pub. L. 97-145, December 29, 1981, and Pub. L.

99-64, July 12, 1985.

6. *Balancing the National Interest*, appendix A, p. 81.
7. Ibid., pp. 151–52.
8. Ibid., p. 49.
9. Ibid., p. 49.
10. Ibid., p. 49.
11. Ibid., pp. 154–55.
12. Ibid., p. 170.
13. Robert J. Samuelson, "Marshall's Mixed Legacy," *Washington Post*, June 17, 1987.
14. Export Administration Act, sec. 10(g)(4).
15. *Balancing the National Interest*, pp. 93–96.
16. Ibid., pp. 173–74.
17. Export Administration Act, sec. 5(i)(1).
18. *Balancing the National Interest*, p. 143.

Index

Contributors

Gary K. Bertsch is Professor of Political Science and Co-director of the Center for East-West Trade Policy at the University of Georgia. He is a specialist on U.S. and Western trade policy toward the Soviet Union and other communist states. His publications include: *East-West Strategic Trade, COCOM, and the Atlantic Alliance*, and *National Security and Technology Transfer: The Strategic Dimensions of East-West Trade*.

Beverly Crawford is Assistant Professor in the Graduate School of Public and International Affairs at the University of Pittsburgh. She is the author of a forthcoming book, *Beyond Power and Profit: International Regimes and East-West Trade*, as well as numerous articles and chapters on East-West trade.

Steven J. Elliott is a graduate of the University of Lancaster in the United Kingdom. He is currently finishing a dissertation on business-government relations in U.S. export control policy and is a Research Associate at the Center for East-West Trade Policy at the University of Georgia.

John P. Hardt is Associate Director for Research Coordination and Senior Specialist in Soviet Economics at the Congressional Research Service, and Adjunct Professor in Economics at George Washington and Georgetown Universities in Washington, D.C. He frequently accompanies congressional trade delegations to Eastern Europe and the People's Republic of China, and has edited and contributed to many volumes on communist economies for the U.S. Congress.

Martin J. Hillenbrand is Dean Rusk Professor of International Relations, Director of the Center for Global Policy Studies, and Co-director of the Center for East-West Trade Policy at the University of Georgia. He is a former State Department official (1939–76), whose appointments included Ambassador to Hungary, Assistant Secretary of State for European Affairs, and Ambassador to the Federal Republic of Germany. He is author, co-author, and editor of numerous books and articles on international politics and economics.

Hanns-Dieter Jacobsen is a Senior Research Fellow at the Stiftung Wissenschaft und Politik in Ebenhauser, and a faculty member of the Department of Political Science at the Freie Universität Berlin. He has published extensively on East-West economic relations and is the author of *Ost-West Wirtschaftsbeziehungen als Deutsch-Amerikanisches Problem* and co-editor of *Economic Warfare or Détente* (with Reinhard Rode).

Bruce W. Jentleson is Assistant Professor of Political Science at the University of California, Davis. His dissertation on East-West energy trade won the American Political Science Association's Harold D. Lasswell Award in 1985. He is the author of *Pipeline Politics: The Complex Political Economy of East-West Energy Trade*, as well as numerous articles on East-West trade. He is currently an International Affairs Fellow of the Council on Foreign Relations.

Marie-Hélène Labbé is a graduate of the Institute for Political Science and is currently a researcher at the National Foundation for Political Science in Paris. She is the author of "L'embargo cerealier de 1980 ou les limites de l'arme verte," *Politique Étrangere* (December 1986); "L'embargo cerealier americain: une arme boomerang?" in Lachaux, Lacorne, and Lamoureaux, eds., *De L'Arme Economique*; and "La politique américaine de contrôle des exportations de technologie vers l'Est," in Chantebout and Warusfel, eds., *Le Contrôle des Exportations de haute technologie vers les pays de l'Est*.

William J. Long is Assistant Professor of International Relations at the American University and a former international trade attorney with Paul, Weiss, Rifkind, Wharton & Garrison. He is the author of a forthcoming book on the domestic politics of U.S. export controls and a prescriptive essay, with Lionel H. Olmer, on the need for fundamental reform of the current export control system.

John R. McIntyre is Associate Professor of International Relations and Management, and Director of the International Business in Technology Program at the Georgia Institute of Technology. His publications include *Uncertainty in Business-Government Relations: The Dynamics of International Trade Policy; National Security and Technology Transfer: The Strategic Dimensions of East-West Trade; and The Political Economy of International Technology Transfer*.

Michael Mastanduno is Assistant Professor of Government at Dartmouth College. His dissertation on the Western coordination of export control policy won the American Political Science Association's Helen Dwight Reid Prize in 1986. His articles on East-West trade have appeared in *World Politics* and *International Organization*. He is currently completing a book on the relationship between American export control policy and COCOM.

Henry R. Nau is Professor of Political Science and International Affairs and Associate Dean of the School of International Affairs at George Washington University. He is a former Special Assistant to the Under Secretary of State for Economic Affairs

(1975–77), and a former senior staff member of the National Security Council responsible for international economic issues (1981–83). His publications include *Technology Transfer and U.S. Foreign Policy* and *National Politics and International Technology*.

William Root is currently a self-employed consultant on export controls. He is a former State Department official (1950–83), and was responsible for coordinating the U.S. position on COCOM issues within the Office of East-West Trade. He also had experience within the State Department managing U.S.-USSR scientific and technical cooperation programs. He is the author of numerous articles on export controls, including "Trade Controls that Work," *Foreign Policy* (Fall 1984).

Dean Rusk is Samuel H. Sibley Professor of International Law at the University of Georgia. He served as Secretary of State during the Kennedy and Johnson administrations, 1961–69.

Gordon B. Smith is Professor of Government and International Studies at the University of South Carolina. He is the author of numerous articles on East-West trade, editor of *The Politics of East-West Trade*, and co-editor of *Law and Soviet Economic Development*.

Library of Congress Cataloging-in-Publication Data

Controlling East-West trade and technology transfer: power, politics,
and policies / edited by Gary K. Bertsch.
p.   cm.
Bibliography: p.
Includes index.
ISBN 0-8223-0829-0   ISBN 0-8223-0843-6 (pbk.)
1. East-West trade (1945–   ) 2. Technology transfer—Communist
countries. 3. Export controls—United States. 4. Export controls—Europe.
I. Bertsch, Gary K.
IN PROCESS (ONLINE)   88-4101 CIP